S0-BRS-457

CRITICAL ACCLAIM FOR LEN DEIGHTON'S WORLD WAR II EPIC *BLOOD, TEARS, AND FOLLY*

"Stirring, well-researched and packed with revealing military and technological information, *Blood, Tears, and Folly* is Deighton's heartfelt tribute to those brave Allied men and women who found themselves 'drowning in the Atlantic, crews in stricken planes, tank men bleeding into the desert sand.'"

—*San Francisco Chronicle*

"A description and criticism of the conduct of both world wars. Its anger is brilliantly controlled, and it provides a marshalling of facts with great care, building up a picture of incompetence and waste, yet never losing touch with the fighting men and women, the victims and the brave ones."

—Martin Gilbert, *The Sunday Times* (London)

"Len Deighton, that engaging critic of how World War II was won and lost, has given us another of his brilliant exercises in hindsight that are the historian's privilege, the general's despair and the reader's delight."

—*Chicago Sun-Times*

"Deighton . . . meticulously chronicles the early years of the war on six fronts . . . scrutinizes the German navy's attempt to disrupt Allied shipping [and] drives home the effectiveness of German Blitzkrieg tactics. He examines the different kinds of aircraft both sides used. And he takes a fascinating look at the Japanese military mentality."

—*Cleveland Plain Dealer*

"Well-researched and balanced history of World War II. Deighton, writing with great clarity, offers a balanced view, debunking many popular myths. Deighton . . . has delved into nonfiction before but never more effectively. Anyone wishing a comprehensive and absorbing look at this century's major conflict need look no further."

—*Booklist*

"Deighton's opinions are explained reasonably, and his writing is both easily understood and thoroughly researched."

—*Library Journal*

PRAISE FOR *FIGHTER*

"The best, most dispassionate story of the battle I have read."

—*The New York Times*

"Must surely rank as the most honest attempt yet to tell how the Battle of Britain really was."

—*The Observer*

PRAISE FOR *BLITZKRIEG*

"Has a freshness that makes it welcome. Deighton has keenly wanted to find out and explain the matter for himself, and has then retained the flavour of discovery for his audience. It is an attractive technique with a genuine ring."

—*Times Educational Supplement*

Books by Len Deighton:

NONFICTION
Fighter: The True Story of the Battle of Britain
Blitzkrieg: From the Rise of Hitler to the Fall of Dunkirk
Airshipwreck
ABC of French Food
Basic French Cookery Course
The Battle of Britain (with Max Hastings)

FICTION
Faith
Violent Ward
The Ipcress File
Horse Under Water
Funeral in Berlin
Billion-Dollar Brain
An Expensive Place to Die
Only When I Larf
Bomber
Declarations of War
Close-Up
Spy Story
Yesterday's Spy
Twinkle, Twinkle, Little Spy
SS-GB
XPD
Goodbye Mickey Mouse
MAMista
City of Gold

THE SAMSON STORIES
Berlin Game
Mexico Set
London Match
Game, Set and Match (presentation set)
Winter
Spy Hook
Spy Line
Spy Sinker

LEN DEIGHTON

BLOOD, TEARS, AND FOLLY

Volume I
An Objective View of World War II

With maps and drawings by
Denis Bishop

HarperPaperbacks
A Division of HarperCollinsPublishers

HarperPaperbacks
A Division of HarperCollins*Publishers*
10 East 53rd Street, New York, N.Y. 10022

If you purchased this book without a cover, you should be aware
that this book is stolen property. It was reported as "unsold and
destroyed" to the publisher and neither the author nor the
publisher has received any payment for this "stripped book."

Copyright © 1993 by Pluriform Publishing Company B.V.
Maps and drawings copyright © 1993 by Denis Bishop
All rights reserved. No part of this book may be used or
reproduced in any manner whatsoever without written
permission of the publisher, except in the case of brief
quotations embodied in critical articles and reviews.
For information address HarperCollins*Publishers,*
10 East 53rd Street, New York, N.Y. 10022.

A trade paperback edition of *Blood, Tears, and Folly* was
published in 1994 by HarperPerennial, a division of
HarperCollins*Publishers*

ISBN 0-06-101067-7

HarperCollins®, 📖®, and HarperPaperbacks™
are trademarks of HarperCollins*Publishers* Inc.

First HarperPaperbacks printing: September 1996

Printed in the United States of America

Visit HarperPaperbacks on the World Wide Web at
http://www.harpercollins.com/paperbacks

10 9 8 7 6 5 4 3 2 1

CONTENTS

Part Three: The Mediterranean War

ILLUSTRATIONS

FIGURES

MAPS

TABLES

Permission to reproduce the photographs is acknowledged to the following sources: Bilderdienst Süddeutscher Verlag, Munich (nos. 2, 3 and 6), E.C.P. Armées,

France (no. 5), Hulton Deutsch Collection (no. 1), Robert Hunt Library (no. 8), Imperial War Museum, London (nos. 8, 9, and 10), and Ullstein Bilderdienst, Berlin (nos. 4 and 7). The maps and drawings are by Denis Bishop.

To your children, and ours

ACKNOWLEDGEMENTS

I have taken the time, picked the brains and raided the archives of a great number of people while writing this book—so many that I would need another book to give them all proper credit. It is more appropriate to ask forgiveness of all those generous helpers in museums, archives, bookshops, air shows, trains, planes and cafés who have provided me with ideas, books, photocopies and references galore and now don't have their names mentioned.

This book, like *Fighter* and *Blitzkrieg* before it, would never have seen publication without the late A. J. P. Taylor, who told me that an amateur historian is an historian nevertheless.

But first and foremost I must thank Tony Colwell at Jonathan Cape, my publisher, who has contributed an immense amount of good advice and has nursed the book along for over a decade, as he nursed *Fighter* and *Blitzkrieg* and many of my novels. Steve Cox, my editor, has made contributions far beyond editing and research. Thanks too to David Godwin at Jonathan Cape, and to Kate Fitch, who double-checked so many facts when I was far away, and my warm appreciation to my friends at HarperCollins New York—George Craig, Bill Shinker and Buz Wyeth—who have been extremely patient and supportive over many years.

Thanks too to Jonathan Clowes, my agent, Anton Felton and Brie Burkeman, ace co-ordinator, and to John Ellis, who was kind enough to read the typescript.

The mistakes I made all on my own.

Death and sorrow will be the companions of our journey; hardship our garment; constancy and valour our only shield.

Winston Churchill,
addressing the House of Commons,
8 October 1940

INTRODUCTION

It is a national characteristic beloved of the British to see themselves as a small cultured island race of peaceful intentions, only roused when faced with bullies, and with a God-given mission to disarm cheats. Rather than subjugating and exploiting poorer people overseas, they prefer the image of emancipating them. English school history books invite us to rally with Henry V to defeat the overwhelming French army at Agincourt, or to join Drake in a leisurely game of bowls before he boards his ship to rout the mighty Armada and thwart its malevolent Roman Catholic king. The British also cherish their heroes when they are losers. The charge of the Light Brigade is seen as an honourable sacrifice rather than a crushing defeat for brave soldiers at the hands of their incompetent commanders. Disdaining technology, Captain Scott arrived second at the South Pole and perished miserably. Such legendary exploits were ingrained in the collective British mind when in 1939, indigent and unprepared, the country went to war and soon was hailing the chaotic Dunkirk evacuation as a triumph.

Delusions are usually rooted in history and all the harder to get rid of when they are institutionalized and seldom subjected to review. But delusions from the past do not beset the British mind alone. The Germans, the Russians, the Japanese and the Americans all have their myths and try to live up to them, often with tragic consequences. Yet Japan and Germany, with educational systems superior to most others in the world, and a generally high regard for science and engineering design, lost the war. Defeat always brings a cold shock of reality, and here was defeat with cold and hunger and a well clothed and well fed occupying army as a daily reminder that you must do better. The conquerors sat down and wrote their memoirs and bathed in the warm and rosy glow that only self-satisfaction provides.

Half-finished wartime projects, such as the United Nations, fluid and unsatisfactory frontiers and enforced allegiances suddenly froze as the war ended with the explosion of two atomic bombs. The everpresent threat of widespread nuclear destruction sent the great powers into a sort of hibernation that we called the Cold War. The division of the world into two camps was decided more by the building of walls, secret police and prison camps than by ideology. Expensively educated men and women betrayed their countrymen and, in the name of freedom, gave Stalin an atomic bomb and any other secrets they could lay their hands on. Only after the ice cracked half a century later could the world resume its difficult history.

But not everyone was in hibernation. With the former leaders of Germany, Italy, and Japan disposed of as criminals, more criminal leaders came to power in countries far and wide. The Cold War that seemed to hold Europe's violence in suspense actually exported it to places out of Western sight. The existence of Stalin's prison camps was denied by those who needed Lenin and Marx as heroes. The massacre of Communists in Indonesia raised fewer headlines than Pol Pot's year zero in Cambodia, but they were out on the periphery. Newspapers and television did little to counteract the artful management of news at which crooks and tyrants have become adept. Orthodontics and the hair-dryer have become vital to the achievement of political power.

The postwar world saw real threats to the democratic Western ideals for which so many had died. Is the European Community—so rigorously opposed to letting newsmen or public see its working and decision-making—about to become that faceless bureaucratic machine that Hitler started to build? Is the Pacific already Japan's co-prosperity sphere?

Hasn't the Muslim world already taken control of a major part of the world's oil resources, and with the untold and unceasing wealth it brings created something we haven't seen since the Middle Ages—a confident union of State and Religion?

Britain's long tradition of greatly over-estimating its own strength and skills leads it to under-estimate foreign powers. Our Victorian heyday still dominates our national imagination and our island geography has often enabled us to avoid the consequences of grave miscalculations by our leaders. Such good fortune cannot continue indefinitely, and perhaps a more realistic look at recent history can point a way to the future that is not just 'muddling through'.

In Germany in 1923 runaway inflation produced the chaos in which the Nazis flourished. Today the United States is very close to the position where even the total revenue from income tax will not pay the *interest* on its National Debt.[1] While the Japanese enjoy one of the world's highest saving rates, Americans are notoriously reluctant to put money into the bank. Furthermore Japan, with a population less than half that of the USA, employs 70,000 more scientists and engineers, uses seven times more industrial robots, and spends over 50 per cent more per capita on non-military research and development.[2]

Hans Schmitt, who grew up in Nazi Germany, returned to his homeland as an officer of the American army and became professor of history at the University of Virginia, wrote in his memoirs: 'Germany had taught me that an uncritical view of the national past generated an equally subservient acceptance of the present.'[3] It is difficult to understand what happened in the Second World War without taking into account the assumptions and ambitions of its protagonists, and the background from which they emerge. So in each part of this book I shall take the narrative far enough back in time to deal with some of the misconceptions that cloud both our preferred version of the war, and our present-day view of a world that always seems to misunderstand us.

One good reason for looking again at the Second World

War is to remind ourselves how badly the world's leaders performed and how bravely they were supported by their suffering populations. Half a century has passed, and the time has come to sweep away the myths and reveal the no less inspiring gleam of that complex and frightening time in which evil was in the ascendant, goodness diffident, and the British—impetuous, foolish and brave beyond measure—the world's only hope.

Part One

THE BATTLE OF
THE ATLANTIC

1 BRITANNIA RULES THE WAVES

For the bread that you eat and the biscuits you nibble,
The sweets that you suck and the joints that you carve,
They are brought to you daily by all us Big Steamers
And if any one hinders our coming you'll starve!

RUDYARD KIPLING, 'BIG STEAMERS'

It is not in human nature to enshrine a poor view of our own performance, to court unnecessary trouble or to wish for poverty. Myths are therefore created to bolster our confidence and well-being in a hostile world. They also conceal impending danger. Having temporized in the face of the aggressions of the European dictators, Britain went to war in 1939 without recognizing its declining status and pretending that, with the Empire still intact, the price of freedom would not be bankruptcy.

In 1939 the British saw themselves as a seafaring nation and a great maritime power, but the two do not always go hand in hand. In order to understand the Royal Navy's difficult role in the Atlantic in the Second World War, it is necessary to return to the past and separate reality from a tangled skein of myth. Later in the book similar brief excursions will give historical perspective on the performance of the army and the air force, both in Britain and in the other main wartime powers.

After the Renaissance it was Portuguese and Spanish sailors who led the great explorations over the far horizons, while the English concentrated upon defending the coastline that had insulated them from the rest of Europe for centuries. By the middle of the sixteenth century Spain and Portugal had established outposts in America, Asia and Africa, and their ships carried warriors, administrators and freight around the globe in 2,000-ton ships made in India from teak and in Cuba from Brazilian hardwoods. But when England's shores were threatened, small and less mighty vessels made from English oak and imported timber, sailed by skillful, intrepid and often lawless Englishmen, came out to fight. Using fireships, and helped by storms and by the hunger and sickness on the Spanish vessels, Francis Drake and his men decimated the mighty Armada.

Such dazzling victories have prevented a proper appreciation of the maritime achievements of our rivals. While English privateers were receiving royal commendations for preying upon the Spanish galleons from the New World, the Dutch and the Portuguese were fighting on the high seas for rule of the places from which the gold, spices and other riches came.

The Dutch were an authentic seafaring race. They had always dominated the North Sea herring fishing, right on England's doorstep, and traded in the Baltic. Their merchant ships carried cargoes for the whole world. By the early 1600s one estimate said that of Europe's 25,000 seagoing ships at least 14,000 were Dutch. The English sailor Sir Walter Raleigh noted that a Dutch ship of 200 tons could carry freight more cheaply than an English ship 'by reason he hath but nine or ten mariners and we nearer thirty'.

In 1688 the Dutch King William of Orange was invited to take the English throne. Dutch power at sea was subordinated to English admirals. At this time England had 100 ships of the line, the Dutch 66 and France 120. England's maritime struggles with the Netherlands ended, and France—England's greatest rival and potential enemy—was outnumbered at sea. The French were not a seafaring race, they were a land power. Their overseas colonies and trade were not vital to France's existence. Neither were exports vital to England, where until the 1780s the economy depended almost entirely upon agriculture, with exports bringing only about 10 per cent of national income.

The Dutch king's ascent to the English throne was the

sort of luck that foreigners saw as cunning. It came at exactly the right moment for England. From this time onwards the French seldom deployed more than half of the Royal Navy's first-line strength. Soon the industrial revolution was producing wealth enough for Britain to do whatever it pleased. But that wealth depended upon the sea lanes, and the Royal Navy had to change from a strategy of harassing and plundering to escorting and protecting merchant shipping. It was not easy to adapt to the shepherd's role. The Royal Navy was by tradition wolflike; its speciality had always been making sudden raids upon the unprepared. 'It could be fairly said', wrote the naval historian Jacques Mordal, 'that with the exception of Trafalgar, the greatest successes of the British navy were against ships at their moorings'.[1] Damme, Sluys, La Hougue, the Nile, Copenhagen, Navarino and Vigo Bay were all such encounters. So were the actions against the French navy in 1940.

It was Napoleon's defeat at Waterloo that gave the Royal Navy mastery of the seas. France, Holland and Spain, weakened by years of war, conceded primacy to the Royal Navy. Britain became the first world power in history as the machines of the industrial revolution processed raw materials from distant parts of the world and sent them back as manufactured goods. Machinery and cheap cotton goods were the source of great profits; so were shipping, banking, insurance, investment and all the commercial services that followed Britain's naval dominance. The British invested abroad while Britain's own industrial base became old, underfinanced, neglected and badly managed, so that by the mid-nineteenth century the quality of more and more British exports was overtaken by her rivals. Manufacturing shrank, and well before the end of the century service industries became Britain's most important source of income. The progeny of the invincible iron masters dwindled into investment bankers and insurance men.

To cement the nineteenth century's Pax Britannica Britain handed to France and the Netherlands possessions in the Caribbean, removed protective tariffs and preached a policy of free trade, even in the face of prohibitive tariffs against British goods and produce. The Royal Navy fought pirates and slave traders, and most of the world's great powers were content to allow Britain to become the international policeman, especially in a century in which restless civil populations repeatedly threatened revolution against the existing order at home.

The British fleet showed the flag to the peoples of the Empire in five continents and was a symbol of peace and stability. Well-behaved children of the middle classes and workers too were regularly dressed in sailor costumes like those the British ratings wore.[2] But appearances were deceptive. The Royal Navy was unprepared for battle against a modern enemy.

As the nineteenth century ended the importance of the Royal Navy was diminishing. Population growth, and efficient railway networks, meant that armies were becoming more important than navies. The new-found strength that industrialization, much of it financed by Britain, had given to other nations ended their willingness to let Britain play policeman. Although in 1883 more than half of the world's battleships belonged to the Royal Navy, by 1897 only two of every five were British[3] and countries such as Argentina, Chile, Japan and the United States had navies which challenged the Royal Navy's local strength.

Since the time of Nelson the cost of the Royal Navy had increased to a point where it tested Britain's resources. Nelson's ships were cheap to build and simple to repair. Needing no fuel, sailing ships had virtually unlimited range, and by buying food locally cruises could be extended for months and even years. But the coming of steam engines, screw propellers and turbines, together with the improving technology of guns, meant supplying overseas bases with coal, ammunition and all the tools and spares needed for emergencies. Full repairs and maintenance could only be done in well equipped shipyards. A more pressing problem was the steeply increasing cost of the more complex armoured warships. In 1895 the battleship HMS *Majestic* cost a million pounds sterling but HMS *King George* in 1910 cost almost double that.

The time had come for Britain's world role, its methods and its ships, to be totally revised. An alliance with Japan, and the recognition that cultural ties made war with the USA unthinkable, released ships from the Pacific stations. An alliance with France released ships from the Mediterranean so that the Royal Navy could concentrate virtually its entire sea-power in home waters facing the Germans. Germany had been identified as the most potent threat, and anxiety produced a climate in which talk of war was in the air.

THE GERMAN NAVY

Germany dominated Europe. Prussia, where in 1870 nearly 45 per cent of the population was under twenty years of age, dominated Germany. Otto von Bismarck (nominally chancellor but virtually dictator) had remained good friends with Russia while winning for his sovereign quick military victories over Denmark and Austria-Hungary. Then to the surprise of all the world he inflicted a terrible defeat upon France. Reparations—money the French had to pay for losing the war of 1870—made Germany rich, universal conscription made her armies large, and Krupp's incomparable guns made them mighty. After the victory over the French, the German king became an emperor and, to ensure France's total humiliation, he was crowned in the Hall of Mirrors in Versailles. Bismarck now had everything he wanted. He looked for stability and was ready to concede the seas to Britain.

But in 1888 a vain and excitable young emperor inherited the German throne. Wilhelm II of Hohenzollern had very different ideas. 'There is only one master in the country, and I am he'. He sacked Bismarck, favoured friendship with Austria-Hungary instead of Russia, gave artillery and encouragement to the Boers who were fighting the British army in southern Africa (a conflict that has been called Britain's Vietnam), spoke of a sinister-sounding *Weltpolitik* and, in an atmosphere of vociferous anti-British feeling, began to build his *Kaiserliche Marine*.

Despite Britain's small population[4] and declining economic performance, the strategic use of sea-power had given the British the most extensive empire the world had ever seen. Yet although a large proportion of the world lived under the union flag, Britain had nothing like the wealth and military power to hold on to the vast areas coloured red on the maps. Tiny garrisons and a few administrators convinced millions of natives to abide by the rules of a faraway monarch. The army's strategic value was in guarding the naval bases where the Royal Navy's world-ranging ships were victualled, coaled or oiled. Luckily for Britain, its military power was not seriously challenged for many years. Only when the Boers in South Africa erupted was Britain's tenuous grip on its territories clearly demonstrated.

The German army on the other hand had shown its might and skills again and again, and having seen their army march into Paris in 1870 the German navy itched to test itself against the British. With almost unlimited funds at his disposal Rear-Admiral Alfred Tirpitz was to build for the Kaiser the sort of fleet that would be needed to challenge the Royal Navy. In anticipation of this moment, German naval officers more and more frequently held up their glasses and toasted 'Der Tag!'—the day of reckoning.

Admiral Tirpitz claimed to be unaware that his preparations were aimed at war with Britain. 'Politics are your affair', he told the Foreign Ministry, 'I build ships'.[5] And as if to prove his point he sent his daughters to study at the Cheltenham Ladies' College in England.

The British were alarmed by the prospect of an enlarged German navy. Still more worrying for them was the rise in German trade, which went from £365 million in 1894 to £610 million in 1904, with a consequent increase in German merchant ship tonnage of 234 per cent. In fact Britain's foreign markets were suffering more from American exporters than from German ones but—still smarting from Germany's pro-Boer stance—the British resented the Germans, while Anglo-American relations on personal and diplomatic levels remained very good.

In December 1904 Britain's new first sea lord, Admiral Fisher, started planning his new all-big-gun battleships. Although naval architects in Italy, America and Japan had all predicted the coming of a super-warship, this one was so revolutionary in design that it gave its name to a new category of battleship.

FIGURE 1:
HMS *Dreadnought*

The big hull had spent only one hundred days on the stocks when King Edward VII launched HMS *Dreadnought* on a chilly February day in 1906. He wore the full dress uniform of an admiral of the fleet, which Britain's monarchs favoured for such ceremonials, when he swung the bottle of Australian wine against her hull. The bottle bounced and failed to break and he needed a second attempt before the wine flowed, and the great warship went creaking and groaning down the slipway into the water.

She was completed in record time: one year and a day. The use of the rotary turbine, instead of big upright pistons, made her profile more compact and thus better armoured. According to one admiral the bowels of previous battleships were uncomfortable:

> When steaming at full speed in a man of war fitted with reciprocating engines, the engine room was always a glorified snipe marsh; water lay on the floor plates and was splashed about everywhere; the officers often were clad in oilskins to avoid being wetted to the skin. The water was necessary to keep the bearings cool. Further the noise was deafening; so much so that telephones were useless and even voice pipes of doubtful value . . . In the *Dreadnought,* when steaming at full speed, it was only possible to tell that the engines were working, and not stopped, by looking at certain gauges. The whole engine room was as clean and dry as if the ship was lying at anchor, and not the faintest hum could be heard.[6]

Gunnery was also changed. Ships armed with many short-range guns—exemplified by the 100-gun *Victory*—were no match for ships which could fire salvos of very heavy shells at long range. The big gun had proved itself. For the Americans sinking the Spanish ships at Santiago and Manila Bay, for the Japanese destroying the Russian fleet at Tsushima, the big gun had proved the decisive weapon. 'Dreadnoughts'—as all the new type of capital ships were now to be called—would have speed enough to force or decline a naval action. Furthermore the long-range gun would offset the threat of the torpedo; a sophisticated weapon that, wielded by dashing little vessels, threatened the future of the expensive warships.

The introduction of the Dreadnought design was a denial of Britain's decline. It signalled that Britain had started to build its navy afresh, and that its sea-power could be equalled only by those who kept pace with the building programme. Almost overnight Admiral Tirpitz found his

15-battleship fleet completely outclassed. The Kaiser responded at once. SMS *Nassau*, the first of Germany's Dreadnoughts, was ready for action by March 1908. On paper the German ships seemed inferior in design to the Dreadnoughts of the Royal Navy—for instance *Nassau* employed reciprocating engines and had 11-inch guns compared with HMS *Dreadnought*'s 12-inch ones. But the *Nassau*'s guns had a high muzzle-velocity, which gave a flat trajectory for better aim and penetration. The ship's interior was very cramped, but top-quality steel was used as armour. Her small 'honeycomb-cell' watertight compartments made her extremely difficult to sink; a feature of most German warships.

The big new German ships provided the Berlin planners with an additional problem. The 61-mile-long Kiel Canal was essential to German naval strategy, for it eliminated a long and hazardous journey around Denmark, and the need for a separate Baltic Fleet to face the threat of Russian seapower. But the Kiel locks had been built for smaller warships; there was no way that the Germans could squeeze a ship the size of a *Dreadnought* through the Canal.

CHURCHILL—FIRST LORD OF THE ADMIRALTY

In 1911, when the 36-year-old Winston Churchill was appointed first lord of the Admiralty (the minister responsible for the Royal Navy), he was appalled to find his Whitehall offices deserted, and ordered that there be always officers on duty. On the wall behind his desk he put a case, with folding doors which opened to reveal a map on which the positions of the German fleet were constantly updated. Churchill started each day with a study of that map.

Churchill revolutionized the navy. His principal adviser was the controversial Sir John Arbuthnot Fisher, who predicted with astounding accuracy that war against Germany would begin on 21 October 1914 (when widening of the Kiel

Canal for the new German battleships was due to be completed). The Royal Navy did not welcome Churchill's ideas. When he wanted to create a naval war staff, they told him they did not want a special class of officer professing to be more brainy than the rest. One naval historian summed up the attitude of the admirals: 'cleverness was middle class or Bohemian, and engines were for the lower orders'.[7]

Churchill forced his reforms upon the navy. He created the Royal Naval Air Service. Even more importantly, he changed the navy's filthy coal-burning ships, with their time-consuming bunkering procedures, to the quick convenience of oil-burning vessels with 40 per cent more fuel endurance. As industry in Britain was built upon coal but had no access to oil, this entailed creating an oil company—British Petroleum—and extensive storage facilities for the imported oil. He ordered five 25-knot oil-burning battleships—*Queen Elizabeth, Warspite, Barham, Valiant* and *Malaya*—and equipped them with the world's first 15-inch guns. Normally a prototype for such a gun would have been built and tested, but rather than waste a year or more, Churchill put the guns straight into production so that the ships could be ready as soon as possible.

Britain's need for naval alliances had dragged her into making an agreement with France that should war come Britain would send an army to help defend her. This was a dramatic change in Britain's centuries-old policy of staying out of mainland Europe. Cautious voices pointed out that no matter what such an expeditionary force might achieve in France, Britain remained vulnerable to foreign fleets. It was a small offshore island dependent upon imported food, seaborne trade and now oil from faraway countries instead of home-produced coal. The extensive British Empire was still largely controlled by bureaucrats in London. Defeated at sea, Britain would be severed from its Empire, impoverished and starved into submission.

THE FIRST WORLD WAR

To what extent Emperor Kaiser Wilhelm was set upon war with England in 1914 is still difficult to assess. If there was one man who, by every sort of lie, deceit and stupidity, deliberately pushed the world into this tragic war, that man was Count Leopold 'Poldi' Berchtold, Austrian foreign minister. But the German Kaiser stood firmly behind him and showed no reluctance to start fighting.

Bringing recollections of Fisher's warning, elements of the Royal Navy were at Kiel, celebrating the opening of the newly widened canal, when news came of the assassination at Sarajevo. A few weeks later Europe was at war. It was also significant that Britain's widely distributed warships were told 'Commence hostilities against Germany' by means of the new device of wireless.

Germany had 13 Dreadnoughts (with ten more being built); Britain had 24 (with 13 more under construction, five of which were of the new improved *Queen Elizabeth* class). However this superiority has to be seen against Britain's worldwide commitments and Germany's more limited ones.

Britain's Admiral Fisher had gloated that the Germans would never be able to match the Royal Navy because of the untold millions it would cost to widen the Kiel Canal and deepen all the German harbours and approaches. The Germans had willingly completed this mammoth task. The British on the other hand had refused to build new docks and so could not build a ship with a beam greater than 90 feet. Sir Eustace Tennyson-d'Eyncourt (Britain's director of naval construction) was later to say that with wider beam, 'designs on the same length and draught could have embodied more fighting qualities, such as armour, armament, greater stability in case of damage, and improved underwater protection'.

The Germans built docks to suit the ships, rather than ships to fit the docks. With greater beam, the German ships also had thicker armour. Furthermore the German decision to build a short-range navy meant that less space was required for fuel and crews. More watertight compartments could be provided, which made German warships difficult to sink. This could not be said of ships of the Royal Navy.

The Royal Navy's planners would not listen to the specialists and experts and continuously rejected innovations for the big ships. While British optical instrument companies were building precise range-finders (with up to 30 feet between lenses) for foreign customers, the Admiralty was content with 9 feet separation. When Parsons, the company founded by the inventor and manufacturer of turbine engines, suggested changing over to the small-tube boilers that worked so well in German ships, the Admiralty turned them down. The triple gun-turrets that had proved excellent on Russian and Italian ships were resisted until the 1920s.

The German navy welcomed innovation. After a serious fire in the *Seydlitz* during the Dogger Bank engagement of 1915 they designed anti-flash doors so that flash from a shell hitting a turret could not ignite the magazine. On Royal Navy ships cordite charges in the lift between magazine and turret were left exposed, as was the cordite handling room at the bottom of the lift, and the magazine remained open during action. This weakness was aggravated by the way that British warships were vulnerable to 'plunging fire' that brought shells down upon the decks and turrets. Typically turrets would have 9-inch-thick side armour and 3-inch-thick tops. This deficiency would continue to plague the Royal Navy in the Second World War.

Churchill's gamble with his 15-inch guns paid off, but the smaller German guns had the advantage of high muzzle-velocity. The Royal Navy knew that its armour-piercing shells broke up on oblique impact with armour but had not solved this problem by the time the First World War began. Only eight Royal Navy ships had director firing (as against gunners choosing and aiming at their own targets), while it was standard in the German navy. The superior light-transmission of German optics gave them better range-finders, and German mines and torpedoes were more sophisticated and more reliable. The Royal Navy neglected these weapons, regarding them as a last resort for inferior navies. It was a view open to drastic revision when HMS *Audacious,* a new *Dreadnought,* sank after collision with a single German mine soon after hostilities began.

As warfare became more dependent upon technology German superiority in chemistry, metallurgy and engineering became more apparent. The German educational system was ahead of Britain. In 1863 England and Wales had 11,000 pupils in secondary education: Prussia with a smaller population had 63,000. And Prussia provided not only *Gymnasien* for the study of 'humanities' but *Realschulen* to provide equally good secondary education in science and 'modern studies'.[8] The French scholar and historian Joseph Ernest Renan provided an epilogue to the Franco-Prussian War by saying it was a victory of the German schoolmaster. The education of both officers and ratings, coupled to the strong German predilection for detailed planning and testing, produced a formidable navy. Its signalling techniques and night-fighting equipment were superior to those of the British and this superiority was to continue throughout the war. Churchill warned in 1914 that it would be highly dangerous to consider that British ships were superior or even equal as fighting machines to those of Germany.

For many years the American Rear-Admiral A. T. Mahan's book *The Influence of Sea Power upon History* had specified the way in which all sea wars must be fought: by big ships battling to contest sea lanes. But the British would not play this game. Surprising many theorists, the Royal Navy of 1914 refused battle and instead set up a blockade of German ports. The geographical position of the British Isles, and a plentiful supply of ships, persuaded the Admiralty to create barriers across the open water by means of mines and patrols. The Germans responded by a less ambitious blockade of Britain. German warships prowled the sea routes to sink the merchant ships bringing supplies to the British Isles.

Given this strategy, German engineering and the development of the torpedo, it was inevitable that the German navy became interested in submarines. Although they were the last of the major powers to adopt that weapon, the Germans had watched with interest the designs and experiments of other nations. The first German-built submarines were supplied to overseas customers. The *Forel*, built and tested at Kiel, was supplied to Russia and went by railway to Vladivostok.

The Germans rejected ideas about using submarines for coastal defence, or as escorts for their fleet. They wanted an offensive weapon. This meant longer-range, more seaworthy vessels. Because they considered the petrol engines used by the Royal Navy as too hazardous, their early U-boats used a kerosene (liquid paraffin) engine, but it was the development of the diesel engine that made the submarine a practical proposition. The first production diesel was made in the M.A.N. factory in Augsburg in 1897, and a much improved version was tested in a U-boat in Krupp's Germania Works in Kiel in 1913. At that time the U-boat was still a primitive device. During the First World War the submarine tracked, attacked and escaped on the surface, its low silhouette making it difficult to spot. It could only hide briefly below the surface but (in a world without asdic, sonar or radar) hiding was enough. The British had more or less ignored the dangers of commerce raiding by submarines because the Hague Convention denied any warship the right to sink an unescorted merchant ship without first sending over a boarding party to decide if its cargo was contraband.

Whatever the rights and wrongs of commerce raiding, any last doubts about the value of torpedo-equipped submarines vanished in 1914, less than two months after the outbreak of war, when Germany's *U-9,* commanded by a 32-year-old on his first tour of duty, hit HMS *Aboukir* with a torpedo and she sank before the lifeboats could be lowered. HMS *Cressy* lowered her boats to pick up men in the water, but while so doing was hit by a second torpedo. A third torpedo hit HMS *Hogue,* which also sank immediately. More than 1,600 sailors died. About three weeks later the same rather primitive type of submarine sank the cruiser HMS *Hawke*.

The development of wireless was changing naval warfare, as it was changing everything else. The admirals seized upon it, for it gave the men behind desks the means of controlling the units at sea. Intelligence officers saw that enemy ships transmitting wireless signals could be located by direction-finding apparatus. Better still, such radio traffic could be intercepted, the codes broken, and messages read.

Intercepted wireless signals played a part in the battle of Jutland in 1916, when Britain's Grand Fleet and the German High Seas fleet clashed in the only modern battleship action fought in European waters. Lack of flash doors caused HMS *Queen Mary* to disappear in an explosion, HMS *Indefatigable* blew up and sank leaving only two survivors, and HMS *Lion* was only saved because a mortally wounded turret commander ordered the closing of the magazine doors. The loss of the Royal Navy's three battle cruisers and three armoured cruisers could all be ascribed to their inadequate upper protection.

There were many ways to evaluate the battle of Jutland, and both sides celebrated a victory with all the medals and congratulatory exchanges that victory brings for the higher ranks. In tonnage and human lives lost the British suffered far more than the Germans, but the Royal Navy was more resilient. The British were seafarers by tradition, and regular long-service sailors who fought the battle accepted its horrors in a way that conscripted German sailors did not. Britain's Grand Fleet took its sinkings philosophically. Within a few hours of returning to Scapa Flow and Rosyth, the fleet reported itself ready to steam at four hours' notice.

There can be no doubt however that Britain's technological shortcomings were startingly evident at Jutland. Once the envy of all the world, Britain's steel output had now sunk to third place after the United States and Germany, and German steels were of higher quality. Anyone studying the battle had to conclude that German ships were better designed and better made, that German guns were more accurate and German shells penetrated British armour while many of the Royal Navy's hits caused little damage.

Radio had also played a part in the battle. Helped by codebooks the Russians salvaged from a sunk German cruiser, the men in Room 40 at the Admiralty ended the war able to read all three German naval codes. After the war the work in Room 40 was kept completely secret so that even the official history made only passing mention of it.

By the end of 1916, despite patrols by planes, dirigibles and thousands of ships, U-boats had sunk 1,360 ships. The German U-boat service, which grew to 100 submarines, had lost only four of them to enemy action. The Admiralty stubbornly refused to inaugurate a convoy system, and produced rather bogus figures to 'prove' that convoys would block up the ports and harbours. Convoys might never have been started but for the French government insisting that their cross-Channel colliers sail in convoy. The result was dramatic but the Admiralty remained unconvinced. Perhaps the Admiralty officials thought that escorting dirty old merchant ships was not a fitting task for gallant young naval officers. Whatever their reasons, it took an ultimatum from the prime minister to make them change their minds. (Although later the admirals petulantly said they were about to do it anyway.) When convoys began in May 1917, only ships that could do better than 7 knots, and could not attain 12 knots, were allowed to join them. Losses fell about 90 per cent. The British had come close to losing the war, and before the effect of the convoy system became evident the nerve of the first sea lord, Admiral Jellicoe, broke. On 20 June he told a high-level conference that, owing to the U-boats, Great Britain would not be able to continue the war into 1918. He proved wrong and, thanks to the convoys, the crisis abated.

German U-boats continued sinking passenger ships even after negotiations for peace began on 3 October 1918. The following day *Hiramo Maru* was sunk off the Irish coast, killing 292 out of the 320 aboard. The following week the Irish mail boat *Leinster* was torpedoed without warning and torpedoed again while it was sinking: 527 drowned. 'Brutes they were, and brutes they remain', said Britain's foreign secretary. President Wilson warned that America wouldn't consider an armistice so long as Germany continued its 'illegal and inhuman practices'. The U-boat's Parthian shots had not helped to create a climate suited to negotiations for a lasting peace.

By the time the First World War ended, about 200 U-boats had been sunk, but the submarine menace had been countered only by means of escorted convoys and the use of about 5,000 ships, hundreds of miles of steel nets and a million depth charges, mines, bombs and shells. Yet for those who wanted to find it, the most important lesson of the 1914–18 war in the Atlantic lay in the statistics. In the whole conflict only five ships were sunk by submarines when both surface escort and air patrol was provided, and this despite the fact that no airborne anti-submarine weapon had been developed.

2 DAYS OF WINE AND ROSES

The man who with undaunted toils
Sails unknown seas to unknown soils
With various wonders feasts his sight:
What stranger wonders does he write!

JOHN GAY, 'THE ELEPHANT AND THE BOOKSELLER'

By the end of the First World War Britain was exhausted, financially bankrupt and in debt to the USA. The Empire, having made a selfless and spontaneous commitment to the war, no longer wanted to be ruled by men of Whitehall. British leaders, both civilian and military, had proved inept in conducting a war which, had the United States not entered it, Germany might well have won.

In 1922, Britain formally acknowledged her declining power. Since Nelson's day Britain's declared policy was to have a navy as strong as any two navies that could possibly be used against her. Even into the 1890s Britain was spending twice as much on her fleet as any other nation. With the Washington treaty of 1922 such days were gone. The politicians agreed that the navies of Britain, USA and Japan should be in the ratio of 5:5:3. Britain also accepted limitations upon the specifications of its battleships, and promised not to develop Hong Kong as a naval base and to withdraw altogether from Wei-hai-wei, China. In conforming to the treaty, the Royal Navy scrapped 657 ships including 26 battleships and battle-cruisers. One history of the British Empire comments: 'So ended Britain's absolute command of the seas, the mainstay and in some sense the raison d'être of her Empire'.[1]

After the First World War, the surrendered German fleet

sailed to Scapa Flow, between Orkney and the Scottish mainland. There, in a gesture of defiance, they scuttled all their ships. This provided Germany with a chance to start again with hand-picked personnel and modern well designed ships, while the victorious nations were patching up their old ships to save money.

The treaty of Versailles stipulated that Germany's navy must be kept very small but in June 1935, acting without reference to friends or enemies, the British government signed an Anglo-German naval agreement permiting Hitler to build a substantial navy, up to 35 per cent as strong as the Royal Navy, and include battleships, virtually unlimited submarines and eventually cruisers and aircraft-carriers.[2]

This notable concession to Hitler's belligerence encouraged him to ever more reckless moves and deeply offended Britain's closest ally France. It went against all Britain's international undertakings and, in grossly breaching the peace treaty, nullified it. The first lord of the Admiralty said: 'the naval staff were satisfied and had been anxious to bring about an agreement'. Stabilization of Anglo-German naval competition would release RN ships to distant waters. Perhaps the British politicians—and the men in the Admiralty who advised them—believed that showing good will towards the Nazis would bring lasting peace. One suspects that it revealed some calculation in the minds of Britain's leaders that a more powerful Fascist Germany would keep Communist Russia contained.

Significantly perhaps, the Reichsmarine was renamed Kriegsmarine and the Germans began building immediately. Germany's four biggest battleships, *Scharnhorst, Gneisenau, Bismarck* and *Tirpitz,* which were later to give the Royal Navy so many sleepless nights, were laid down as an immediate result of this treaty. The following year Germany agreed—in the London Submarine Protocol of 3 September 1936—that it would adhere strictly to the international prize law, which provided for the safety of merchant ship passengers and crews in time of war.

In 1937 came a supplement to the 1935 treaty. A German

naval historian, Edward P. von der Porten, has described it as 'a German attempt to convince the British of sincerity'. The Germans affirmed that they would build no battleships bigger than 35,000 tons. The *Bismarck* and *Tirpitz*, then in production, were 41,700 and 42,900 tons respectively. The extra tonnage, explained U-boat C-in-C Karl Dönitz after the war, was for 'added defensive features'. In fact the extra size was due to Hitler specifying 15-inch guns instead of the previous 11-inch ones.

While German shipyards were producing these impressive warships Britain's shipbuilding industry was antiquated and inefficient. It had suffered from the strikes and slumps that other British industry knew well. Yet while Britain's merchant navy, although still large, was in decline, no such decline befell the bureaucrats of Whitehall. In 1914, with 62 capital ships in commission, the Admiralty employed 2,000 officials. By 1928—with only 20 capital ships in commission, and the Royal Navy officers and men reduced from 146,000 to 100,000—there were 3,569 Admiralty employees. Although the Washington naval treaty prevented any increase in Britain's naval forces, there were by 1935 no less than 8,118 Admiralty staff on the payroll.[3]

Germany had ended the war without ships or shipbuilding facilities but the creation of a strong navy and a merchant fleet had been decided upon long before Hitler came to power. In the summer of 1929 these plans bore fruit as the ocean liner *Bremen* snatched the Atlantic Blue Ribbon from the elderly British liner *Mauretania*. The following year *Bremen*'s sister ship *Europa* took the record. Both German liners displaced about 50,000 tons, with top speeds of about 27 knots. These products of German shipyards were given energetic publicity by the Nazi propaganda machine. Germany had staked its claim to the Atlantic sea routes and intended to remain there.

EQUIPPING FOR WAR

On Sunday 3 September 1939 Britain declared war on Germany. Although there were no treaty obligations between Britain and the Dominions, Australia and New Zealand also declared war at once. The Canadians declared war on Germany after Britain (but were later to declare war on Japan before Britain). South Africa followed after some fierce parliamentary debate, and the Viceroy took a similar decision for India seemingly without reference to anyone. Virtually the whole of the Empire and Commonwealth, from Ascension Island to the Falklands, joined the mother country. A newly independent Ireland remained neutral and was represented in Berlin throughout the war by an ambassador accredited in the name of King George.

In the course of time, 5 million fighting troops were raised from these overseas countries, with India contributing the largest volunteer army that history had ever recorded.[4] But warships were in scarce supply. The navy was still regarded as the factor which both bound the countries of the Empire and protected their sea routes. So, for Britain's Royal Navy, the war was a global one right from the first hour of hostilities.

Britain went to war with a Royal Navy that was highly skilled and totally professional, although its officers and men were poorly educated when compared with men of the other industrialized nations. Most of its 109,000 sailors had joined as boys aged sixteen, and most of its 10,000 officers as thirteen-year-old cadets. Steeped in tradition, its ratings wearing curious old uniforms which could not be put on without help, the navy provided a tot of rum each day for every man, and the fleet retained corporal punishment long after the other services had abolished it.

When wartime's compulsory military service first sent civilians to sea, they regarded this narrow-minded, time-

warped community with awe. They took it over, and changed
it for ever. Soon the regular sailors with their distinctive
rank badges were outnumbered by HO (Hostilities Only)
ratings and RNVR (Volunteer Reserve) officers with 'wavy-
navy' rings on their cuffs. By the middle of 1944 the wartime
navy totalled 863,500 personnel of whom 73,500 were
WRNS (Women's Royal Naval Service). The sailors who
fought and won the Atlantic battle were in the main civilians.

When war started the Admiralty was calm and confident.
With fifteen battleships, of which thirteen had been built
before 1918 (and ten of these were designed before 1914),
and six aircraft carriers of which only HMS *Ark Royal* was
not converted from other ships' hulls, it knew exactly what
sort of war it was going to fight. Unfortunately Germany's
naval staff, the Seekriegsleitung (SKL), had a different rule
book.

A less parsimonious British government or a more realistic Royal Navy might have expected the Germans to break
their agreements, but the interwar years had been noted for
self-delusion, and the admirals did not readily learn lessons.
The Royal Navy seemed indifferent to the threat of air attack. Its multiple pom-pom anti-aircraft guns had proved
completely ineffective, but only when war was imminent
were Swedish Bofors and Swiss Oerlikon guns put into production.

A closed eye had been turned to the potential of the
submarine. With lofty disdain, most Royal Navy officers regarded the submarine service as a refuge for officers of low
ability. Submarines participating in fleet exercises were always ordered to withdraw during the hours of darkness.
Anyone who suggested that in a future war the enemy might
not be willing to withdraw during the hours of darkness was
told that the miracle apparatus asdic could counter submarines.

Asdic (later named sonar) was a crude device first introduced at the end of the First World War, although never
used operationally in that war. Mounted under a ship's hull,

it emitted sound waves and picked up their reflections to detect submarines. Always demonstrated in perfect weather by well rehearsed crews, it enabled a confident Admiralty to declare the U-boat to be a weapon of the past. By 1937 the Naval Staff said that 'the submarine would never again be able to present us with the problem we were faced with in 1917'. Even if the Admiralty's assessment of asdic had been right, there were only 220 warships equipped with it, while the British merchant service had 3,000 oceangoing ships and 1,000 large coasters to be protected.

The range of the asdic was a mile at best. It could not pierce the layers of differing temperature and salinity that are commonly found in large bodies of water. Nor could it be used by a ship steaming at more than 20 knots, or in rough weather. It was useless in locating a surfaced submarine and did not reveal the depth of a submerged one. All of these shortcomings could benefit a skilful U-boat commander, and it might have been remembered that by the end of the First World War attacks by surfaced U-boats had become the favoured tactic.

Admirals everywhere prefer big ships. The United States navy lined them up in Pearl Harbor and, even in the middle of the war, German admirals were still telling each other that the battleship was the most important naval weapon and pressing for a programme to build more and more of them. So the British navy, like the United States navy, began the war with plenty of expensive battleships for which there was little or no need and a grave shortage of small escort vessels.

Canada wanted to make a contribution to the war without having its soldiers decimated at the commands of British generals on some new 'western front'. It elected to concentrate on ships, which could be kept under its own control. The Canadian navy started a construction programme exclusively devoted to escort vessels—corvettes and frigates—to protect the Atlantic traffic. The corvettes were slow and seaworthy, although the way in which they rolled and wallowed from wave top to wave top made crewing them one of the war's most queasy assignments. Nevertheless by May 1942 Canada had 300 ships—a magnificent achievement.

THE U-BOAT

Since the First World War, submarine design had improved only marginally, and then chiefly in greater hull strength. This enabled them to dive far deeper, and provided escape for many U-boats under attack. (Due largely to inter-departmental squabbles, it took some time before British depth charges were designed for deep water use.) Although more efficient electric batteries enabled submarines to stay submerged longer, they still spent almost all their time on the surface, submerging only to escape attacks from the air or avoid very rough seas.

A submarine of this period consisted of a cylindrical pressure hull like a gigantic steel sewer pipe. To this pipe, a stern and bow were welded and the whole vessel was clad in external casing to give it some 'sea-keeping capability', although submarines could never be manoeuvred like ships with regular hulls. A casing deck and a conning tower—what the Germans called an 'attack centre'—was added to the structure. Directly below the conning tower was the 'control room' where the captain manned the periscope. The tower was given outer cladding to provide some weather protection to men standing there, as well as some measure of streamlining when the boat went underwater. An electric motor room and an engine room with supercharged diesels of about 3,000 bhp were positioned well aft for the sake of sea-keeping and to cut diving time. The great bulk of a submarine was below the water-line, and visitors going below are always surprised to discover how big they are, compared with the portion visible above water. For instance, the long-range Type IXC U-boat that displaced 1,178 tons submerged would still displace 1,051 tons when on the surface.

There were two basic types of German U-boat used operationally in the Atlantic campaign, the big long-range Type IX and the smaller Type VII, which was the standard German U-boat of the Second World War.[5] The VII typically had a displacement of 626 tons, a crew of four officers and forty-four ratings (enlisted men), and carried about fourteen 21-inch torpedoes. Four tubes faced forward and one aft. All the tubes were kept loaded and when they had been fired, the awkward business of reloading had to be done. On the surface the diesel engines gave a range of 7,900 nautical miles at 10 knots. If they pushed the speed up to 12 knots it would reduce their range to 6,500 nautical miles. In an emergency the diesels could give 17 knots for short periods. With a fully trained crew a Type VII dived in thirty seconds and when submerged used electric motors. The rechargeable batteries could go for about 80 nautical miles at 4 knots. Maximum speed underwater was reckoned to be 7.5 knots, depending upon gun platforms which obstructed the water flow. Most reference books give manufacturer's specification speeds which are faster than this.

The whole purpose of the submarines was to fire torpedoes. These big G7—seven metres long—devices were no less complicated than the submarine itself, and in some respects exactly like them. They were treated with extraordinary care. Each torpedo arrived complete with a certificate to show that its delicate mechanisms had been tested by firing over a range. It had been transported in a specially designed railway wagon to avoid risk of it being jolted or shaken. One by one, with infinite concern, the 'eels' were loaded into the U-boat, which was usually moored inside a massive concrete pen. From then onwards, all through the voyage, each and every eel would be hung up in slings every few days, so that the specialists could check its battery charge, pistols, propellers, bearings, hydroplanes, rudders, lubrication points and guidance system.

To make an attack it was necessary to estimate the bearing and track of the target. Usually the submarine was surfaced, and the captain used the UZO (*U-Boot-Zieloptik*) which was attached to its steel mounting on the conning

FIGURE 2:
German submarine U-boat, type VIIC

tower. This large binocular device had excellent light-
transmission capability, even in semi-darkness, and from it
the bearing, range and angle of the target vessel was sent
down to the *Vorhaltrechner*. This calculator sent the target
details to the torpedo launch device, *Schuss-Empfänger,* and
right into the torpedoes, continuing to adjust the settings
automatically as the U-boat moved its relative position. By
means of these instruments the U-boat did not have to be
heading for its target at the moment of launching its torpedo. The torpedo's gyro mechanism would correct its heading after exiting the tube. Thus a 'fan' of shots, each on a
slightly different bearing, could be fired without turning the
boat. This device was coveted by British submarine skippers
who aimed their torpedoes by heading their submarines towards the target.

By using 'wakeless' electric G7e torpedoes—and suppressing the water swell—a submarine could fire without be-
traying its position. Smaller targets were sunk by means of
the deck gun, which was usually an 8.8-cm artillery piece. To

fire it in anything but calm water without going overboard demanded the agility of an acrobat. Hitting anything other than a large target was very difficult. When war began there was also a single 2-cm Flak gun (short for *Flugabwehrkanone,* anti-aircraft gun) but this proved of little use against aircraft and bigger and better ones were fitted as the war continued.

Life aboard a submarine was rigorous. The hull's interior was the size and shape of a passenger train but the 'train' was crammed with machinery into which the men were artfully fitted. There was no privacy whatsoever for anyone. Even the captain had no more than a curtained desk, past which everyone pushed to get to their stations. This is how an official German navy war correspondent saw it:

My bunk is in the petty officers' quarters, the U-room, the most uncomfortable on board: it has the most through traffic. Anyone who wants to get to the galley, or to the diesels or the E-motors has to come through here. At every change of watch the men from the engine room squeeze through from astern, and the new watch comes through from the control room. That means six men each time. And the stewards have to work their way past with their full dishes and pots. In fact, the whole place is nothing more than a narrow corridor with four bunks on the right and four on the left. In the middle of the passage, screwed to the floor, there's a table with folding leaves. The space on both sides is so narrow that at mealtimes the men have to sit on the lower bunks with their heads bent. There is far too little space for stools. And there is mess and confusion whenever someone has to get from the engines to the control room or vice versa during a meal.[6]

There were no bathing facilities, and only one lavatory which could not be used when the submarine dived. When under attack the lavatory might well be out of action for 24 hours. No one shaved and most didn't change even one article of clothing for the entire voyage. The stink of human bodies was mixed with those of oil and fuel. There was also the pervading smell of mould, for in the damp air everything, from bread to log books, went mouldy. The men—mostly young, for only young men could endure the hardships and the stress—were apt to douse themselves in eau de cologne to exchange one smell for another.

The Commander is astride the periscope saddle in the narrow space between the periscope shaft and the tower wall, his face pressed against the rubber shell, his thighs spread wide to grip the huge shaft. His feet are on the pedals that enable him to spin the great column and his saddle through 360 degrees without making a sound; his right hand rests on the lever that raises and lowers it. The periscope motor hums. He's lowering it a little, keeping its head as close to the surface of the water as he possibly can.

The Chief is standing immobile behind the two men of the bridge watch who are now operating the hydroplanes. His eyes are glued to the Papenberg and its slowly rising and falling column of water. Each change in it means that the boat is doing the same.

Not a word from anyone. The humming of the periscope motor sounds as if it's coming through a fine filter; the motor starts, stops, starts again, and the humming resumes. The Commander ups periscope for fractions of a second and immediately lets it sink below the surface again. The destroyer must be very close.[7]

Most of the time was spent on the surface. In the Atlantic this meant endless rolling and pitching. Boats on the surface needed lookouts who got very cold and wet. In the northern waters lookouts grew accustomed to icy water breaking over them with such force that they required a leather harness to secure them to the bridge brackets. Reminders about wearing such restraints sometimes included the names of U-boat men who had recently been washed overboard. The men on watch wore protective clothing of leather, or sometimes of rubber, under their oilskins, with towels around their necks. Even so they usually became soaked to the skin in anything but calm weather. Almost every submariner complained of rheumatic pains. Below decks the crew were permitted to wear any clothing they wished. 'Lucky' sweaters, knitted by loved ones, were popular, so were British army khaki battle-dress jackets, thousands of which had come from captured dumps in France. Some captains would distribute a measure of schnapps at times of great joy or great suffering; other boats were completely dry.

The men of the preceding watch come down the ladder stiffly. They are soaking wet. The navigator has turned up his collar and drawn his sou'wester down over his face. The faces of the others are whipped red by spray. All of them hang their binoculars over hooks and undress as silently as the new watch dressed, peeling themselves awkwardly and heavily out of their rubber jackets. Then they help one another off with their rubber pants. The youngest member of the watch loads himself with the whole mass of wet oil-skin trousers, jackets, and sou'westers, and carries it aft. The spaces between the two electric motors and on both sides of the stern torpedo tube are the best for drying. The men who have come off duty gulp down a mouthful of hot coffee, polish their binoculars, and stow them away.[8]

When in May 1941 a young British officer led a boarding party to search a U-boat captured at sea, he was impressed by its fine construction, the fittings and the way in which the ward room had varnished woodwork and numbered cupboards with keys to fit them. He remarked upon the magnificent galley and the cleanliness of the boat throughout. During his search he found other evidence of the high living standards the Germans enjoyed; cameras and even a movie camera were among the crews' personal effects. He said the sextants were of far better quality than the Admiralty issue and the binoculars the best he'd ever seen. He kept a pair for himself.[9]

In the war at sea, as well as on land and in the air, radio brought changes in tactics. Better longer-range radios enabled the submarines to be sent to find victims in distant waters or concentrated against a choice target. Admiral Karl Dönitz was the German navy's single-minded submarine expert. He thought primarily, if not solely, in terms of war against Britain. He had long since decided that a future submarine war would be an all-weather one, and that (with asdic unable to detect small surface targets) he would coordinate night attacks by surfaced submarines. This line of thinking was published in his prewar book. It was to prove one of the most effective tactics of the war.

The Royal Navy liked to believe that U-boats could be countered by means of 'hunting groups' of warships. Such warfare had the name, colour, speed and drama that suited the navy's image of itself. But this idea had been tried and found useless in the First World War. Experience proved that in the vastness of the seas the submarine could remain undetected without difficulty. It was one of these hunting groups—an aircraft carrier with a destroyer escort—which was attacked at night by *U-29* just two weeks after the declaration of war. The carrier HMS *Courageous* sank with heavy loss of life.

The way in which *Courageous* was exposed to danger was proof that the Admiralty truly believed that asdic and depth charges provided adequate protection against the U-boat. But now there were second thoughts about 'hunting groups' which had depleted the number of escorts available for the merchant convoys. The way to kill U-boats was to guard the merchantmen. Then the submarines would have to come and find you.

3 EXCHANGES OF SECRETS

We shall not cease from exploration
And the end of all our exploring
Will be to arrive where we started
And know the place for the first time.

T. S. ELIOT, *LITTLE GIDDING*

After the war Churchill admitted that the U-boat suc-cesses had been the only thing that frightened him, and it has been widely assumed that Hitler went to war under-standing the submarine's potential value. The truth is that the German navy was completely unprepared for war. At its outbreak, Germany had built 56 U-boats,[1] of which some were short-range Type IIs seldom used beyond the North Sea. The building programme was providing two or three submarines a month (in some months only one), and it was taking about a year to build and test each boat. After the war Admiral Dönitz said: 'A realistic policy would have given Germany a thousand U-boats at the beginning'. We can but agree and shudder.

One of the war's most eminent naval historians, S. E. Morison, said Hitler was *landsinnig* (land-minded) and be-lieved, like Napoleon, that possession of the European 'heartland' would bring England to heel. Winston Churchill, like President Roosevelt, knew that Britain's survival de-pended upon sea-lanes, for without supply by sea there could be no continuation of the war.

DÖNITZ AND RAEDER: THE GERMAN COMMANDERS

Hitler had only one sailor among his high commanders, the 63-year-old Grand Admiral Erich Raeder, who was commander in chief (Oberbefehlshaber) of the navy. He was old-fashioned and aloof, as photos of him in his frock-coat, sword and high stiff collar confirm. Although Raeder looked like a prim and proper officer of the Kaiserliche Marine, his speech in 1939 declared his full support for 'the clear and relentless fight against Bolshevism and International Jewry whose nation-destroying deeds we have fully experienced.' At the Nuremberg trial he was found guilty of having issued orders to kill prisoners. His memoirs, published a decade after the war ended, reiterated his belief in Hitler.

The man conducting the submarine battles, Karl Dönitz, was a quite different personality. The son of an engineer working for Zeiss in Berlin, he had never had staff college training. As a U-boat commander in the First World War, he had survived a sinking to become a prisoner of war. Despite other jobs in signals, and command of a cruiser, his primary interest was with undersea warfare. The rebuilding of Germany's submarine fleet gave him status. He was a dedicated Nazi and his speeches usually included lavish praise for Hitler: 'Heaven has sent us the leadership of the Führer'. Anything but aloof, he delighted in mixing socially with his officers, who referred to him as 'the lion'. Luncheons and dinners with him were remembered for their 'tone of light-hearted banter and camaraderie'. Dönitz was 47 years old at the start of the war. Morison (the author of the official US navy histories) was moved to describe him as 'one of the most able, daring and versatile flag officers on either side of the entire war'. Eventually, in January 1943, Dönitz was to become C-in-C of the navy, succeeding Raeder, and in the final days of the war it was Dönitz whom Hitler chose to take his place as Führer of the collapsing Third Reich.

Widespread misunderstandings persist as to Dönitz's role in the war at sea. The submarine arm was not controlled by him; it was run from Berlin by the Seekriegsleitung, which was both a staff and an organ of command. In May 1940 Dönitz was not even among the thirty most senior naval officers. He was not consulted on such matters as crew training, submarine design, or construction schedules, nor on technical matters about weaponry such as mines and torpedoes. His chief, Admiral Raeder, emphasized this to him in a memo dated November 1940: 'The Commander-in-Chief for U-boats is to devote his time to conducting battles at sea and he is not to occupy himself with technical matters'. It is also a revealing sidelight on the cumbersome way in which dictatorships distort the chain of command that, when there came a shortage of torpedoes, Dönitz went to Raeder and asked him to persuade Hitler to order increased production.

In the opening weeks of the war the opposing navies were discovering each other's weaknesses as well as their own. Dismayed at first by the severe limitations of asdic, the Royal Navy found that skilled and experienced operators could overcome some of its faults. The German navy, like other navies, was discovering that under active service conditions the torpedo was a temperamental piece of machinery.

All torpedoes normally have two pistols which can be selected quickly and easily immediately before use. A hit with the cruder contact pistol will usually result in a hole in the ship's hull, which can often be sealed off and the ship saved. A magnetic pistol is activated by the magnetism in a ship's metal hull and explodes the charge *under* the ship, which is likely to break its back. The German magnetic pistols gave so much trouble that crews switched to contact pistols and found that they were faulty too. The trigger prongs were too short: a torpedo sometimes hit a ship and was deflected without the prongs being touched. The torpedoes of the submarine fleets were also affected by a design problem in the detonators. Constant pressure variations inside the U-boats affected the torpedoes' depth-keeping mechanisms.

Although the official explanation for some of the failures was that magnetic triggers could be affected by changes in the earth's magnetic field, due to latitude or to iron ore or volcanic rock in the sea bed, to me it seems extremely likely that the degaussing of British ships—to protect them against magnetic mines—protected them against magnetic pistols too. Whatever the causes, these troubles continued all through the war, and the faults were not finally diagnosed until after hostilities were over.[2]

Understandably Dönitz complained bitterly to the Torpedo Directorate. He said pointedly that he remembered the same trouble in 1914 but in the first war the Torpedo Inspectorate knew how primitive mechanisms worked! The torpedo experts—their experimental firing ranges frozen in the first winter of war—responded to most criticism by blaming the U-boat crews. Postwar research suggested a failure rate of almost 30 per cent overall. On one war cruise the *U-32* fired 50 per cent duds. An inquiry showed that the contact pistols had only been tested twice before the war, and had failed both times. It became clear that torpedo failures had been experienced and reported since December 1936 but nothing had been done about them. When the war made it impossible to ignore the faults any longer, Raeder demanded action. A rear-admiral was court-martialled and found guilty, a vice-admiral dismissed. The scandal shook the navy and affected the morale of the U-boat service, as well as provided a glimpse of the sort of bureaucratic bungling that was a well established feature of Hitler's Third Reich, when Nazi loyalty tended to outrank competence.

UNRESTRICTED SUBMARINE
WARFARE

Article 22 of the 1930 London naval treaty, which Germany
signed, held that merchant vessels might not be sunk until
the passengers, crew and ships papers were in a place of
safety, adding that the ship's boats were not regarded as a
place of safety unless land or another vessel was nearby in
safe sea and weather conditions. Anyone who hoped that the
Germans might observe their treaty obligations had only
twelve hours to wait after the declaration of war. The *U-30*,
commanded by Kapitänleutnant Fritz-Julius Lemp, sighted
the unescorted passenger ship *Athenia* while it was 200 miles
off the coast of Donegal. It had left Liverpool at 4 o'clock on
the afternoon before war began. Its passenger accommodation was fully booked and included 316 Americans heading
home before war engulfed them.

Lemp saw the 16-year-old liner at 7.30 pm. It was getting
dark and he made little or no attempt to distinguish whether
she was a passenger ship or an auxiliary cruiser which would
have been a legitimate target. He fired a salvo of torpedoes,
one of which wrecked the bulkhead between the boiler
rooms. In the words of one ship's passenger:

> I was standing on the upper deck when suddenly there
> was a terrific explosion. I reckon I must be a very lucky
> woman because when I recovered from the shock I saw
> several men lying dead on the deck.[3]

The passengers in the tourist and third class dining rooms
were trapped when the explosion wrecked the stairways.
Athenia listed and settled down. About half an hour later
Lemp's submarine surfaced and fired at his victim with the
deck gun. Now it must have been clear that she was a passenger liner, the torpedoing of which was explicitly forbid-

den by the prize laws of the Hague Convention. Without making contact, or offering directions or assistance of any kind, Lemp submerged and went away.

The *Athenia* sank: 112 people died, including many women and children. The German Admiralty instantly denied the sinking and ordered Lemp to remove the page from his boat's war diary and substitute false entries.[4] Those officers and men of the German navy who knew the truth were sworn to secrecy and the Reich propaganda ministry issued a statement that a bomb had been placed aboard the *Athenia* on the instructions of Winston Churchill.

The *Athenia* sinking came just as President Roosevelt asked Congress to pass Neutrality Act amendments, allowing Britain and France to buy war material. Seeing that the unlawful sinking of *Athenia* would persuade Congress to say yes, the German propaganda machine employed its formidable resources. An American survivor was persuaded to say that the ship was carrying coastal defence guns, destined for Canada. The allegation that Churchill put a bomb aboard the liner, in order to drag America into his war, was repeated time and time again in radio broadcasts, newspaper items and in letters mailed to prominent Americans. The German navy in Berlin issued a series of warnings about Churchill's bombs on other American ships. This bombardment of lies scored many hits. A Gallup poll revealed that 40 per cent of Americans believed the Germans. The Senate voting reflected a similar feeling when Roosevelt's amendments passed by 63 votes to 31. The House of Representatives also voted in favour of the French and British, by a majority of 61.

By Christmas 1939 Berlin's orders decreed that all ships except fully lit ones identified as Italian, Japanese, Russian, Spanish or Portuguese (United States shipping was excluded from the 'war zone' by American neutrality laws) must be sunk without warning. U-boat captains were told to falsify their logs and describe unlit target ships as warships or auxiliary cruisers.

Just in case there was any misunderstanding, Dönitz's

Standing Order No. 154 told his commanders: 'Rescue no one and take no one aboard. Do not concern yourselves with the ship's boats. Weather conditions and the proximity of land are of no account'.

However there was another more heroic aspect of the U-boat war. On 14 October 1939 there came a dashing action that was planned and briefed by Dönitz himself. Kapitänleutnant Günther Prien, commander of the *U-47*, is said by one historian to have been to Scapa Flow and studied the Royal Navy anchorage as a tourist before war began. Whether this is true or not, Prien showed amazing skill as he threaded his boat through the defences and into the British main fleet anchorage there. Two of his torpedoes hit HMS *Royal Oak*. There were explosions and the battleship turned over. Kirk Sound, through which Prien navigated, was 170 metres wide and only seven metres deep. It was such a notable achievement that even after an Admiralty inquiry had identified fragments of the German torpedoes, many people in Britain insisted that the sinking was due to sabotage. Another, completely unfounded, story told of a German spy who shone lights to guide the U-boat through Kirk Sound. In fact the sinking of the *Royal Oak* was one more indication of the Royal Navy's failure to prepare for war.

Britain's loss was an ancient battleship, but at this time unrestricted U-boat warfare was being criticized, and the German propaganda ministry saw its opportunity. The *U-47* crew were heroes and gained headlines across the world. In Berlin they were congratulated by Adolf Hitler. Prien was awarded the Knight's Cross[5] and Dönitz was promoted to admiral and appointed BdU, Befehlshaber der Unterseeboote (C-in-C of U-boats). The whole German U-boat arm rightly rejoiced in this proof that the Royal Navy were unable to protect their battleships even in their fleet anchorage.

Benefiting from their First World War experience, the British started convoys as soon as war began. It paid off: between September 1939 and the following May, 229 ships were sunk by U-boats but only twelve of these were sailing in convoy. The organization of the convoys was managed, despite the difficulties of making the civilian ships' captains do things the Royal Navy way, and there were fast and slow convoys to accommodate ships of varying performance. The layman usually supposes that it was the protection given by escort vessels that made it safer to go in convoy, but this was not so. Churchill provided the true reason:

> The size of the sea is so vast that the difference between the size of a convoy and the size of a single ship shrinks in comparison almost to insignificance. There was in fact very nearly as good a chance of a convoy of forty ships in close order slipping unperceived between the patrolling U-boats as there was for a single ship; and each time this happened, forty ships escaped instead of one.[6]

The basic Dönitz tactic was to have surfaced submarines patrol across known shipping routes until one of the lookouts spotted a convoy. The radio monitoring service in Germany, with its ability to read the secret British merchant ship code, helped Dönitz to position his 'rake' of boats. The first submarine to sight a convoy sent high-frequency radio signals to a master control room ashore, and made medium-frequency signals to nearby submarines to bring them to the convoy.

At night on the surface the U-boats engaged the merchant ships independently, and often at point-blank range. Before daylight came, they ran ahead to concentrate for another attack on the following night, the submarine's surface speed being faster than its speed underwater.

THE *ADMIRAL GRAF SPEE* ACTION

Submarines were not the only threat to Britain's sea lanes. *Admiral Graf Spee* and *Deutschland* had put to sea a few days before war began. Construction of these cruisers had been started before Hitler came to power, when the peace treaty restricted Germany to ships of less than 10,000 tons. Perhaps in reaction to the way in which the Royal Navy had lost three cruisers at Jutland by single well placed shots, these Panzer-schiffe ('armour ships') were given thick armour and big guns. Newspaper writers called them 'pocket battleships' but they were designed to prey upon merchant shipping. Their innovations included electrically welded hulls. Welding requires metal to be heated to an even temperature; for that reason the welding of thick steels is vastly more difficult than welding light aircraft alloys. The new ships had very shallow draught, and their honeycombed hulls reduced the danger from torpedoes. Heavy top-side armour protected them from air attack and their 11-inch guns had a range of 20 miles. They were powered by diesel engines—which until that time had only been used as auxiliary engines in such vessels—and could steam at 26 knots, an unimpressive speed for a cruiser but suitable for a raider. Each warship had a tanker at its disposal.

The *Deutschland* was assigned to raid the routes of the North Atlantic. She sank two merchant ships and captured a third (the *City of Flint* sailing under a US flag) and then returned to Germany, skilfully using the long November nights to elude the Royal Navy blockade. Her two-month voyage had destroyed 7,000 tons of small shipping; it was a disappointing debut for the 'pocket battleship'. Soon she was renamed *Lützow* because Hitler feared the propaganda effect of a mishap to a ship named *Deutschland*.

Admiral Graf Spee was sent to the sea lanes of the South Atlantic and the Indian Ocean. By 7 December 1939, in a voyage that included the South African coast and South America, she had sunk nine merchant ships. The captain, Hans Langsdorff, a handsome fifty-year-old, had strict ideas about the rules of war. His targets were sunk without loss of life, his prisoners were all treated well and German morale was high. His only setback was a cracked engine block in the battleship's spotter plane and no spare to replace it.

When *Graf Spee* sank the *Trevanion* in the South Atlantic

FIGURE 3:
HMS Ajax

on 2 October 1939, the men in the Admiralty had looked at their charts and guessed that the raider would head for the shipping lanes of South America. They stationed HMS *Ajax* off the River Plate, the New Zealand warship *Achilles* off Rio de Janeiro, and HMS *Exeter* off Port Stanley in the Falklands. But the next signal was an RRR—'raider sighted'—from the tanker *Africa Shell* off the East African coast. Had *Graf Spee*'s captain immediately sent a signal to inform Berlin of his success things might have ended quite differently for him; there would have been no way of guessing whether he was bound for the Indian Ocean or back into the South Atlantic. But Langsdorff waited ten hours, and when his signal was transmitted, three British Direction Finding Stations took a bearing on the signal. These bearings were sent to London on priority channels but even the Hydrographic Section at the Admiralty had no charts large enough to plot them.

Fortunately Merlin Minshall, a young officer of the Volunteer Reserve, had bought a globe four feet in diameter. It was, he calculated, 'equivalent to a flat chart nearly twelve feet from top to bottom . . . Within seconds I had placed three thin loops of rubber round my newly acquired globe. Their intersection clearly showed that the *Graf Spee* was heading not north up into the Indian Ocean but south back into the Atlantic'.[7] It was 4 o'clock in the morning. Rear Admiral 'Tom Thumb' Phillips, the vice-chief of naval staff, arrived dressed in a scruffy kimono to see the globe which

FIGURE 4:
HMS Exeter

was too big to be moved. 'Good idea using the globe', he said. (Admiral Dönitz had come to the same idea as Lieutenant Minshall and was using a similar globe in his situation room.)

More sinkings confirmed this route. *Graf Spee* was in the southern hemisphere and the 13 December 1939 was an idyllic calm summer's day. Visibility was perfect and at 0614 hours *Graf Spee*'s spotters saw the heavy cruiser HMS *Exeter* (8-inch guns) and turned towards her. The *Graf Spee* had six 11-inch guns and Langsdorff assumed that the two vessels with *Exeter* were destroyers escorting a merchant shipping convoy of the sort that *Graf Spee* was seeking as prey, but without the use of his spotting aircraft he was unable to confirm this.

In fact Langsdorff was heading towards one of the many 'hunting groups' that were looking for him. *Exeter* had seen *Graf Spee*'s smoke and had turned towards it. And the destroyers Langsdorff had spotted were actually light cruisers: HMS *Ajax* and the New Zealand navy's *Achilles* (each with eight 6-inch guns). He was probably misled by the fact that both ships were of unusual profile, having single funnels serving boilers sited together so as to economize on weight.

These three ships provide three different answers to the question that had plagued the world's navies for half a century: what should a cruiser be? Should it be a light vessel, fast at 32 knots with small 6-inch guns like the *Ajax* and *Achilles;* should it be of medium weight like the *Exeter,* with 8-inch guns; or should it be a heavy ship with massive

11-inch guns that make it so formidable that it is called a pocket-battleship but unable to exceed 26 knots? No wonder the camouflage experts had painted a huge white wave curling from the *Graf Spee*'s bow. It would never make such a wave in real life—and now it could not speed away.

Ajax—the group's flagship—catapulted a Seafox aircraft into the air. The difficulties of launching and recovery made this the only time such a warship used aircraft in a surface action.[8] On most Royal Navy ships, space designed for aircraft, catapults and hangars was soon to be occupied by radar and AA guns. With the reconnaissance plane in the air searching for her, *Graf Spee* turned away and made smoke. The encounter presented tactical problems for both sides. The *Graf Spee*'s guns far outranged her adversaries, but with enemy ships to both port and starboard the German captain hesitated before choosing his target.

Eventually *Graf Spee* opened fire at maximum range. At first one turret was firing to port and the other to starboard but then all six big guns were concentrated on the *Exeter,* whose 8-inch guns were the most dangerous threat. While the British force had no radar, the German Seetakt radar provided hits on *Exeter*'s turret and then on her main steering. Had it not been for the fact that some of the German shells failed to explode, she would have been sunk. After an unsuccessful riposte with torpedoes, the badly damaged *Exeter* withdrew, listing to starboard and taking in water forward. There were serious fires below decks and a near miss had put enough water through the shell holes in her side to short-circuit the electricity to her last remaining turret. Telephones and radio links were also lost. There was a real chance that *Exeter* would sink.[9]

Langsdorff might have closed and finished off the stricken vessel had the two 6-inch-gun ships not dashed in close and forced the *Graf Spee* to switch her attention to them, moving fast enough to avoid mortal hits by the big German guns, which could not change elevation and bearing fast enough.

After one and a half hours, during which the British warships got close enough to use even secondary armament, all four ships had suffered damage. Having taken hits from two 11-inch shells, the *Ajax* lost two of her four turrets, while the hoist failed in a third turret. The main top mast was chopped off by one of *Graf Spee*'s last salvoes. Three of her guns were still operating but she had used up 80 per cent of her ammunition. *Achilles* had suffered the least damage but she had no radio gunnery control in operation. *Graf Spee* had been hit many times but all her armament was still in operation.

The action was broken off by the British commander, who put up a smokescreen. There is no doubt that Langsdorff would have done better to have pressed home his attack on the battered trio but he did not, and afterwards it was said he had suffered flesh wounds and been knocked unconscious during the encounter. This might have been enough to affect his decision to head for a neutral port.

According to one account the *Exeter* had suffered more than one hundred serious hits. Five of her six big guns were out of action and there was so much smoke and flame that the Germans expected her to blow up and sink at any moment. With 61 dead, and many wounded, she made for the Falkland Islands while the two light cruisers trailed *Graf Spee* to the neutral South American port of Montevideo in Uruguay.

Had the Germans gained access to the sort of port facilities that the British had provided for themselves at strategic spots throughout the world, *Graf Spee* could have been replenished with ammunition and her minor battle damage— which might have proved dangerous in heavy seas—quickly repaired. But Germany was unable to provide for such needs in distant seas. With a more audacious captain the *Graf Spee* might have turned north and braved the northern seas in winter despite the battle damage and her 36 dead and 59 wounded. It was not to be.

When the *Graf Spee* docked in Montevideo, many local people, many of them expatriates, warmly welcomed the Germans but diplomats began arguing fiercely about the rights of belligerent warships in neutral ports. The Uruguayan government gave Langsdorff permission to remain in port for no more than 72 hours, the minimum permitted by international law. It was not enough time for repairs to be effected. Langsdorff tried, and failed, to charter a plane from which to see any Royal Navy ships that might be waiting for him.

To deter Langsdorff from fighting his way past them, the British were keen to give the impression that a large naval force was waiting for *Graf Spee*. A deception plan included the BBC radio bulletins and the British naval attaché who, knowing that the phones were tapped, called the ambassador in Buenos Aires and told him the Admiralty wanted 2,000 tons of fuel oil to be made available for two capital ships that evening at the Argentine naval base of Mar del Plata. It was enough to get the story circulated. There can be little doubt that Langsdorff believed that a sizeable naval force was ready to pounce on him.

On the evening of 17 December the *Graf Spee* moved out of harbour watched by the world's Press and newsreel cameras. At sunset the great ship came to a standstill and, to the astonishment of most of the spectators, blew up. Torpedo heads had been suspended above open ammunition hatches which led to the main magazines. Petrol was ignited to burn through the ropes. The explosion in the forward part of the ship went as planned but seawater came in and doused the aft fires. *Graf Spee* lurched forward and settled fo'c'sle down. Langsdorff shot himself. The German crew were interned but many of them escaped and got back to Germany to fight again.

Those ship designers who said the German pocket battleships were misconceived had been proved right. A commerce raider did not need 11-inch guns to sink merchant ships. With smaller guns the specifications would have been lighter and considerably faster. Raiders which fight and run away live to fight another day.

Still today little is said of the contribution that German gun-laying radar made to this or any other sea battle. Frequently throughout the war, German naval gunners seemed

to enjoy 'lucky shots' for which we might read accurate gun-
laying. In London the Admiralty was sufficiently impressed
by *Graf Spee*'s performance to offer the government of Uruguay £14,000 for the *Graf Spee*'s smoking hulk, whose decks
remained above water. British radar experts rowed out and
boarded her to examine, sketch and dismantle the Seetakt
radar. HMS *Exeter* and *Ajax* were eventually fitted with British Type 79, an air defence radar that could be used for gun-
laying and gave a performance not unlike the German
Seetakt.

While Raeder, the German naval chief, said the *Graf
Spee* should have run rather than fight, Hitler found the loss
of his battleship intolerable, but neither man was deterred
by the sinking. During the winter of 1940–41 the *Scheer,* the
Gneisenau and the *Hipper* left their ports to raid Atlantic
shipping. The men in the Admiralty had cause to worry, for
the German naval Enigma code[10] remained unbroken and
the spectre of the German surface raider was given new
substance by the trouble that *Graf Spee* had given them.
Precious warships—including battleships, cruisers and carriers—were to spend the next few years chasing phantom German commerce raiders 'seen' by nervous merchant seamen
on distant horizons.

THE CHANGING MAP OF EUROPE

At the start of the war the only fully updated operational
maps in Whitehall were to be found in the Admiralty's Upper War Room. This 300-year-old library had been made
into a map room which was manned round the clock. The
maps were coloured in pastel shades (because Churchill said
primary colours gave him headaches) and pins showed the
position of every British and Allied warship and convoy as
well as the position of every German vessel reported by intelligence. The U-boat war, complete with a day-by-day ac-

count of shipping sunk and the import figures, was the room's most important concern.

The map room became a regular treat for guests after Churchill's Tuesday evening dinner parties. He was first lord of the Admiralty[11] at this time, slept nearby, and would appear suddenly in his multicoloured dressing-gown inquiring about the latest news. Last thing at night and first in the morning he was briefed. When in May 1940 he became prime minister he no longer had this map room close at hand but the same officers provided a similar early morning briefing to him throughout the war.

In September 1939 Germany went to war with only minimal need for ocean trading. Agriculture, which the Nazis had encouraged, supplied enough food; and German mines enough coal and iron-ore. When and if some special top-grade ores were needed by the armaments industry Sweden was very close and willing to sell. Other imports came from Switzerland and Italy. Rubber and oil were the most vital necessities but German scientists were already able to provide adequate synthetic versions of both, and the Romanian oilfields were on the doorstep. Furthermore Germany had a new friend and trading partner—the USSR—which had oil to spare. Poland had been invaded by both countries, split down the middle and shared between them. Direct cross-border trade began. The Germans could now reach the whole of Asia without worrying about the Royal Navy's blockade.

All this was evident from a map, but there was little sign that many members of the British government looked at a map. In March 1940 Prime Minister Chamberlain was calling blockade 'the main weapon'. Britain's Ministry of Economic Warfare said, and believed, that the German economy was on the point of breakdown. On 27 May 1940 Britain's chiefs of staff predicted that Germany's economic collapse would take place by the end of 1941. By September 1940— with Hitler controlling Europe from Norway to the Spanish border, and the Battle of Britain still undecided—the chiefs of staff had not changed their mind. The prevailing opinion was that Germany's inevitable collapse would now be speeded by the rebellious people of the occupied countries. The role of the British army in 1942, they cheerfully predicted, would merely be to keep order in that chaotic Europe left by the German disintegration! We must not be too hard on those wishful thinkers: such fantasies kept Britain and her Dominions fighting in a situation that more realistic minds would have pronounced hopeless.

The division of Poland, between Germany and the Soviet Union, and the trade between them was not the only bad news that the admirals had to swallow in that 1940 summer. The Admiralty had always assumed that in the event of war it would enjoy port facilities in Ireland. From fuelling bases at Queenstown (Cobh) and Berehaven and the naval base at Lough Swilly on the west coast, anti-submarine flotillas would have ranged far out into the Atlantic. Without them every escort vessel would add 400 miles to its patrol. The use of the bases in wartime had been confirmed in a conversation between the Irish patriot Michael Collins, Admiral Beatty and Winston Churchill as long ago as 1922, when Churchill, as colonial and dominions secretary, was concerned with the Irish Settlement.

The story behind this change has still to be told to everyone's satisfaction. In April 1938 the Chamberlain government renounced the right to use the ports which it had been granted under the 1922 Irish treaty. Churchill was appalled and said that it would be hard to imagine a more feckless act at such a time. In the House of Commons he spoke against what he called a 'gratuitous surrender' and a 'lamentable and amazing episode'. He found himself unsupported. Virtually the whole Conservative party, and the Labour (Socialist) and Liberal opposition, sided with Chamberlain. But when war came, the Irish Republic remained neutral and Churchill's warnings proved exactly true. Ireland's government resisted Britain's requests to use the ports, although some of the material brought in the convoys was destined for neutral Ireland.

The convoys, channelled into the narrow waters around

Ireland, provided rich pickings near home for bold U-boat captains. The Admiralty was still coming to terms with these difficulties when, in the summer of 1940, an even worse change came to the operational maps. The Germans conquered Denmark, so providing a gate to the Baltic, and Norway, with its bases and access to the North Atlantic. The only alleviation of this gloom was that the Norwegian merchant fleet—one of the world's largest—sailed to England to evade the Germans. This enormous addition to the shipping tonnage was to become the margin by which Britain survived in the dark days to come.

When in the summer of 1940 France was conquered by the Germans its fleet did not sail to British ports to continue the fight. In the Atlantic and Mediterranean the Royal Navy took on the whole load the French navy had shared. France's Atlantic coast also provided magnificent submarine bases, well away from RAF bomber airfields. From these ports the U-boats could sail directly into the world's oceans.

When Admiralty radio interceptions and bearings indicated that U-boats were using French ports the Foreign Office insisted that it was impossible; the French would not permit it. Lt Minshall RNVR, the same young officer who had provided the globe for the Admiralty, volunteered to investigate. One of the Royal Navy's submarines took him to the French coast, where he spotted and commandeered a French boat which he sailed into the mouth of the Gironde. He stayed there for six days, noting the U-boat movements and enough details to convince even the men of the Foreign Office that the ports were being used.[12] He got back to England in the sailing boat and was awarded a 'mention in dispatches'.[13]

Britain's armed forces had gone to war expecting to fight in the way they had fought in 1914. The British Expeditionary Force would go to France and hold a small section of the Western Front while the Royal Navy—aided by the French fleet—protected the sea routes and waited to re-fight the battle of Jutland. Now everything was changed. Britain was isolated and the Germans held most of Europe, including the Channel coast just twenty-one miles away. With Italy fighting alongside Hitler the Mediterranean sea routes were fiercely contested and Britain's army in Egypt was under constant threat. By the summer of 1940 no one could continue to believe that this war would much resemble the previous conflict.

CRACKING THE NAVAL CODES: ENIGMA

In 1920 the organization known in the First World War as I.D. 25, and usually referred to as Room 40, changed its name to the Government Code and Cypher School (GC&CS). This name served to hide its true purpose, which was to protect British official communications and intercept foreign ones. It was a part of the Secret Intelligence Service, and in 1925 it was moved from a building behind Charing Cross railway station to the SIS headquarters at 54 Broadway, London, near St James's Park underground station, a site conveniently close to the Foreign Office. A few days before the outbreak of war its name was again changed—to Government Communications Headquarters—and it moved to an endearingly ugly but conveniently secluded Tudor-Gothic Victorian house at Bletchley Park, about fifty miles north of London. Its principal task was to read German radio messages encoded on Enigma machines.

The Enigma started its career as a commercial enciphering machine, a sort of typewriter that scrambled text using notched wheels or rotors. The message could be unscrambled by a recipient using an identical Enigma with its rotors adjusted to the same settings, known only to the sender and the receiver. When the Germans bought some Enigma machines they adapted them to make them more difficult to counter. The improved machine had plugs, varying the circuits, which the operators changed every twenty-four hours according to a dated instruction book of 'keys'.

This gave an astronomical number of alternatives for each letter.

The story of the breaking of the Enigma can be said to

FIGURE 5:
German Enigma coding machine

start in October 1931, at the Grand Hotel, Verviers, a town in Belgium not far from the German border. Hans-Thilo Schmidt, a highly placed official in the German Defence Ministry, made contact with Rodolphe Lemoine, an agent of the Deuxième Bureau, the French military intelligence service. Lemoine, a widely travelled linguist, had been born in Berlin, the son of a jeweller. A naturalized French citizen, he had taken his French wife's name and, despite being a successful businessman, he went to work as a secret agent. Lemoine got along well with his fellow Berliner. Schmidt's father was a professor and his mother a baroness, but this highly intelligent and well educated veteran of the First World War found it difficult to manage on the salary he earned as a clerk distributing cipher material. He offered to sell the operator's instruction manual for the Enigma machine and some other notes and manuals. He also offered to continue to supply information about the updating of the machine and its codes as well as details of the workings of the German High Command (where Schmidt's elder brother was now a lieutenant-colonel and chief of staff of the signal corps). At one time Rudolf had been the head of the cipher section—Chiffrierstelle—where Hans-Thilo now worked, and it had been Rudolf's decision to purchase the Enigma machines that his brother was offering to compromise.

It was Lemoine's stated belief that every man had his price, and at their first meeting he offered Hans-Thilo Schmidt payments equal to three times what he was getting in salary. The Service de Renseignement in Paris approved the deal and gave Schmidt the codename HE, which spoken in French eventually gave way to the German word *Asche*, ash. Although the material from Hans-Thilo enabled the French to read a few messages, the complex wiring inside the machine made it a daunting challenge. Paris, deciding that cracking such a machine was beyond their resources, offered to share the task with the British, but the Secret Intelligence Service in London was not interested. The French decided to give everything they had collected to the Poles.

The successes of French and British linguistic cryptanalysts, working on methods perfected during the First World War, persuaded their masters to ignore the problems of mathematical cryptanalysis. This was why the Enigma machine defeated them. The Poles had superior mathematicians, more men familiar with the German language, and the will to succeed at a task no one else believed possible.

By 1933 the Poles had rigged up a reproduction of the Enigma. They kept the French informed about their progress and the French faithfully passed to Warsaw the new codes and whatever mechanical changes to the machine

Hans-Thilo could discover. However over a period of five years few of these messages got to the codebreakers. The Polish high command wanted its men to crack the German codes without outside help, and it doled out the material from Hans-Thilo only in small amounts when the codecrackers were stuck.

The Germans improved their coding machines while the Poles improved their codecracking ones, constructing what they called a bombe, a computer consisting of six linked Enigma machines. In September 1938 the fears of the Polish intelligence chiefs came true. Hans-Thilo was transferred to Göring's Forschungsamt and the supply of codes ended. But by now the codecrackers had learned to manage without his help.[14]

On 24 July 1939, with war only a week away, the Poles invited the French and the British to Warsaw to show them in great detail the work they were doing breaking the German codes. They showed them the bombe, a method of using overlaid perforated sheets, and calculations about wiring. Mathematical talent was at the heart of the Polish work. Some of the most notable breakthroughs had been made by Marian Rejewski, a young mathematician who has been described as one of the greatest cryptanalysts of all time.[15]

As a going-away present both French and British representatives were given a 'replica' Enigma machine. Although as the Germans got nearer to war they changed the codes, and added an extra rotor to their Enigmas to make the machine codes more complex, this gift was beyond price. Gustave Bertrand, a senior French intelligence officer, described how he brought the machine to the chief of Britain's Secret Intelligence Service.

On 16 August 1939 I was on my way to London accompanied by Uncle Tom—the diplomatic courier of the British Embassy in Paris—who was carrying a diplomatic bag with the Enigma machine. At Victoria Station Colonel Menzies, head of the [S] IS wearing the rosette of the Legion of Honour in the buttonhole of his dinner-jacket (he was going to a soirée) was waiting for us: triumphal welcome! Which occasioned him to say one day [that the French intelligence service] had done him a 'considerable service on the eve of the war'.[16]

Considering how little accurate information his SIS was able to supply about even peacetime Nazi Germany, the ill-judged rejection of the French offer of the Enigma secrets and a total lack of any preparations for war, Colonel Menzies did not exaggerate.

Poland was invaded, but keeping ahead of the Germans the Polish codecrackers moved to France. Then France fell too. The French team escaped the German invaders, set up shop near Uzès in the unoccupied sector of France, and continued their work, sending their solutions to London (enciphered in Enigma!). Many Polish and French cryptologists ended up as captives of the Germans, but all managed to convince their interrogators that Enigma was beyond their abilities. The Germans believed them; such is the power of self-deception.

In 1943 some Polish members of the original team reached England after harrowing experiences. According to one notable historian of the Enigma story: 'The Poles reaped the customary reward of the innovator whose efforts have benefited others: exclusion. The British kept Rejewski and the others from any work on Enigma, assigning them instead to a signals company of the Polish forces in exile, where they solved low-level ciphers. It was not one of Britain's finest hours'.[17]

Bletchley Park was sited halfway between Oxford and Cambridge universities, and with more and more big wooden huts built in the grounds, GC&CS were able to recruit and accommodate academics including the junior dean and mathematical tutor of Sidney Sussex College who arrived on the first day of war. Hurrying back from an International Chess Olympiad in Buenos Aires came Britain's chess team. More such men and women followed.

No one in the world had ever attempted to break

machine-enciphered messages on a regular basis with all the urgency that war brings to such a task. The resulting intelligence—eventually to be called Ultra—came solely from radio transmissions in Morse code. No teleprinter message or telephone conversation was included, and since most of the vital messages were sent by those means, the greater proportion of secret enemy communications were never intercepted. Sometimes a radio message in Enigma was answered by telephone or teleprinter, or vice versa, so that only one side of a dialogue was available. Radio reception was often subject to interference, and errors were commonly included, making the job even more perplexing.

The British took up where the Poles left off. The first breakthroughs came from analysis of the uncoded message prefixes that told the recipient the key settings for the Enigma machine. Analysing the electrical wiring in rotors and plug boards, mathematicians and 'probability specialists' soon 'reduced the odds against us by a factor of 200 trillion'.[18] However there was still about a million to one against the men trying to conquer the Enigma messages. Wheel order and ring settings, the two most vital secrets, were sometimes guessed at by 'sheet stacking', a technique the Poles had pioneered. Holes—one per letter—punched in large sheets of paper allowed light through to reveal the pattern of the day's key.

The repetitive phrases used in much of the traffic also helped: especially the formal way in which people and organizations were addressed in full. Often the codebreakers were waiting for the Germans to describe something that had already happened, such as a bombing attack or a weather report. Sometimes the same message was sent in a low-grade code—already cracked—and in Enigma too. In that case the two messages could be compared.

From time to time a rotor or two was retrieved from the pocket of a rescued U-boat crewman. By summer 1941 much-improved bombes came into use at Bletchley Park. These were 10-feet-high electro-mechanical machines like calculators. Using rotors like those inside the Enigma machines, the bombe searched rapidly through, not every possibility but the limited number chosen by the operator. The clickety-clickety sound came to a sudden stop when the bombe found a letter substitute for which the operator was looking. This would provide a setting that could be tried on a British encoding machine that had been adapted to perform like an Enigma. The printer started and produced a long strip of text. If it was 'a good stop' it might mean a batch of messages could be broken.[19]

If it was a navy message it would then go to the Royal Navy section in one of the huts, where a dozen or more men juggled with the German military jargon to make an intelligible message in English. This done, English and German versions might be sent by teleprinter to the Submarine Tracking Room in the OIC Operational Intelligence Centre in the Admiralty's Citadel near Trafalgar Square in London.

The 'key', the settings of the rotors and the plugs, changed daily, or sometimes every two days. It was the most difficult problem, but even after the settings were discovered, the deciphered messages still had to be translated and made intelligible. Many messages were long, and included codenames and complicated service references that would be baffling to any civilian. There were technical aspects of stores, requisitions, meteorology, aviation or maritime matters. There were newly minted technical words and acronyms. A great deal of the intercepted material was banal and of little or no possible use as intelligence. And of course everything was in German. For some messages a result in two or three days was too late, and this was usually the case with the constantly moving war at sea.

The military wisely gave way to the boffins in the matter of getting useful results quickly. The first stage was a job for mathematicians; the second stage for men who spoke German. One of the Bletchley Park team remarked:

The rise to prominence of the translators—their pivotal position was already an accomplished fact by the winter of 1940–41—inaugurated a revolution which gave primacy to the end over the beginning.[20]

A navy, army or air expert assessed and annotated the translation to underline its significance. He would add, for instance, references to a unit, a place or person mentioned, bringing into use the big card-reference system that each service maintained. The next stage was the drafting of a signal to the field commander who could make use of the intelligence. The syntax of the message was changed, or 'sanitized', so that if the Germans encountered it they would not be able to identify the original message and guess how it had been obtained.

The British army monitors at Chatham, on the Thames estuary, and later other stations too, listened to all German short-wave radio traffic. According to the weather, reflections from the upper atmosphere would sometimes enable transmissions from U-boat to U-boat in the farthest reaches of the Atlantic to be heard.

The Enigma coding machine was a remarkable invention. The most surprising aspect of the story is that the experts agree that a few simple changes to the original design could have made it foolproof in use, and its output totally invulnerable. Messages were usually broken because of German carelessness and lax procedures. The Luftwaffe provided most opportunities; the navy was far more careful, so the German navy's Enigma codes were not broken on anything like a regular basis. A founder member of the Bletchley Park team commented: 'At any time during the war, enforcement of a few minor security measures could have defeated us completely'.[21]

In any case it wasn't necessary to understand what a message said to benefit from knowing where your enemy was. High Frequency Direction Finding (HF/DF or what the Royal Navy called 'Huff Duff') could estimate the position of U-boats (or enemy surface ships) by getting a compass bearing on the transmissions. BP staff also made valuable assessments of German preparations and operations by studying the volume, character and point of origin of signals traffic.

Oscilloscope patterns (which depict voltage or current fluctuations on a cathode ray tube) were also photographed and filed to provide a 'fingerprint' that could positively identify a radio transmitter, and this in effect was enough to identify a ship or U-boat. Such fingerprinting was another of Lt Merlin Minshall's ideas. It was in this way that the *Bismarck* was positively identified.[22]

Britain's Secret Intelligence Service retained control of their GC&CS, and so deciphered material went to their Broadway HQ for distribution to whoever 'C'—Colonel Stewart Menzies, the organization's chief—thought deserving. The Royal Navy did not trust SIS with this task, and right from the beginning the navy kept its facilities at Bletchley Park entirely separate from those of the army and the RAF. The admirals had not been satisfied with SIS since November 1939 when Menzies, an army man, was appointed to be 'C'. The navy said that previous SIS chiefs—Captain Smith-Cumming and Admiral Sinclair—had established a tradition that 'C' would always be a job for a sailor.

So all naval material was handled independently and went to the OIC (Operational Intelligence Centre) in Whitehall. In early 1941 the OIC moved to the Citadel (a lumpy brown granite building between Admiralty Arch and Horse Guards; it is still there, mercifully hidden under ivy).

The navy's system worked reasonably well. By the end of July 1941—due largely to the capture of some Enigma machine rotors and dated settings in February, March and May—there was regular interception of Enigma signals. These were being added to all the other signals intelligence, collectively known as SIGINT, which included data from diplomats, foreign newspapers and secret agents, as well as from interrogating, bugging and planting stool-pigeons among captured U-boat crewmen. It was all analysed and put together, and with these sources the Admiralty's Submarine Tracking Room tried to predict the intention of the U-boat captains.

Radio transmissions from U-boats were few and far between. Getting one solitary fix on a U-boat simply put a coloured pin into a big plotting table. From that there was no telling which way the submarine was heading. Was it outward-bound, with a full complement of torpedoes, or was it limping home with engine troubles? Or was it part of a 'rake' of other U-boats across the expected route of a convoy? The Submarine Tracking Room—using all its resources—tried to answer such questions, often guessing right and telling transatlantic convoys to change route and avoid the places where the U-boat packs were waiting. This rerouting of convoys was to become the most effective counter to the U-boats, and—since signals avoided all references to German movements—it was unlikely to reveal British successes with Enigma.

By 1941 the German armed forces had thousands of Enigma machines in use. One of the disadvantages to such machines was that they could be lost or stolen, and so could the keys, the settings for rotors and plug boards. Ever since the remarkable luck of finding some Enigma settings in the patrol boat *VP2623*, captured off Norway long before in April 1940, the codebreakers had been crying out for more.

On 23 February 1941 during a commando raid on the Lofoten Islands, northern Norway, the destroyer HMS *Somali* fought off a suicidal attack by a tiny German trawler, *Krebs*, which was left holed and beached. The *Somali*'s signals officer volunteered to search the little ship. From it he got some spare rotors and the Enigma 'keys' for the month of February. It was a splendid haul, more important to the war than the destruction of ships and factories and oil that had been the purpose of the commando raid.

It wasn't the rotors found on *Krebs* that pleased the men at BP—they already had them. The keys however were very valuable; with them current messages could be read without any delay. Even outdated keys were useful, enabling older messages to be examined. Such keys were always printed in water-soluble ink, and a dousing in seawater was enough to render them illegible. Ian Fleming, later to gain fame as the creator of James Bond, was at this time in naval intelligence and he came up with a hare-brained scheme to get some more of these keys. A captured airworthy German plane would be crash-landed in the sea and (it was hoped) found by a German ship. The rescued airmen would thereupon seize control of the ship and grab its codes. It says a lot about the desperate need for settings that this idea was taken seriously and a captured Heinkel made ready. Fortunately one of the boffins came up with a more practical adventure. The bounty of the February intercepts revealed that German weather-ships out in the Atlantic used Enigma. It also disclosed their movements. Why not capture one of those? The weather-ships were on station for months, so they might have longer lists of keys.

The destroyer *Somali* was used also in this engagement, which depended upon closing on the little weather-ships as quickly as possible in the hope that not everything would be tossed overboard. In the case of the weather-ship *München* the seizure and boarding went according to plan, and among the bundles of paperwork seized there were German Enigma keys for June. This would not enable the Bletchley Park men to read the whole of German naval traffic, for the navy had many different keys. But now the important 'home waters' radio traffic would be available. A second weather-ship, the *Lauenberg*, was intercepted on 28 June, just as the next month's settings were due to come into use. Now traffic up to the end of July could be read.

By this time there had been another dramatic success in the story of Enigma. It was early morning on Friday 9 May 1941 and the outward bound convoy OB 318 was seven days out of Liverpool. There was reason for the British sailors to feel that the most hazardous part of the voyage was done; no U-boat had made a kill this far west. But trailing the convoy came *U-110*, one of the big long-range Type IX submarines. It was commanded by Kapitänleutnant Lemp, the man who sank the passenger liner *Athenia* in the first hours of the war. He now wore the Knight's Cross—or 'tin tie'—at his collar. With him to the *U-110* he had brought his cousin, who was regarded as a Jonah by the crew, after having two previous boats sunk under him.

In daylight, submerged, Lemp fired three torpedoes. Two merchant ships were hit. One ship's stern tipped up so steeply that crates on her deck rolled into the ocean like 'a child pouring toys out of a box'.[23] One of the convoy's escorts spotted the racing white wake of his periscope, sped towards it and dropped a pattern of depth charges. But Lemp escaped and without delay came back up to periscope depth just in time to see the destroyer coming at him. The second scatter of depth charges was close. The underwater explosions stopped the electric motors, started leaks in the oil bunkers and sent the U-boat plunging downwards. Lemp ordered the tanks blown. This not only stopped the descent but brought *U-110* back up to the surface with a boiling of water that got the immediate attention of the deck crews of all three destroyers. Flustered, Lemp failed to have the pressure valve released, so that when the hatch opened a great cloud of dust came pouring out of the submarine. So did the crew, who jumped into the sea with their captain.

The captain of HMS *Bulldog* was shouting for a boarding party almost as soon as the mortally damaged *U-110* surfaced. Ignoring the probability that the Germans had set explosives before abandoning ship, a 20-year-old sublieutenant, rowed out by five sailors, clambered aboard the slippery hull of the wallowing boat and went down into the dark interior followed by his men. They formed a human chain to pass back the codebooks, charts and, having unscrewed it from its mounting, the Enigma machine itself. With great thoroughness and an iron nerve the sublieutenant scoured through everything on the U-boat from charts to 'art studies'. He searched through discarded clothes to find anything of value to intelligence from the contents of wallets to recreational reading matter. It took three or four hours to get everything valuable aboard *Bulldog*.

From the water Lemp watched the British go aboard his command. Realizing that his detonators had failed and knowing that he was responsible for the destruction of the Enigma machine and all the secret material, he seems to have deliberately allowed himself to drown. (Ex-U-boat men—and at least one account[24]—say that Lemp swam back to the U-boat to sink her and was shot by the British boarding party as he climbed on to the deck, but I find no evidence to support this allegation.)

HMS *Bulldog*'s captain tried to tow the U-boat back to port but failed. He showed masterly restraint and impeccable good sense in keeping his extraordinary success secret, so that no news of it could leak back to German intelligence, but he little knew what a tremendous coup he had brought off. The men from BP had never had such a wonderful collection of data: a new machine, spare rotors and a list of the prescribed rotor settings for the length of the U-boat's cruise—three months—and a mountain of helpful material that enabled them to read most Enigma machine messages in the code Hydra for the rest of the war. It also helped with the big warship code Neptun and the Mediterranean codes Sud and Medusa.

The ups and downs of the Enigma struggle meant that messages were sometimes read almost immediately and at other times there were long delays. Most messages were never read. The naval Enigma was the most difficult to crack and many successes came from captured current German keys. Without such helpful clues the German naval secrets could seldom be tapped. And yet it was only because Bletchley Park had been set up with its Enigma machines and bombes that the captured keys could be used.

But Enigma was only one part of the Atlantic battle. Nothing was more decisive than the rate at which merchantmen and escorts could be constructed in British and North American shipyards. The construction of U-boats was equally telling, and so were the global demands that took warships and U-boats to other parts of the world. The weather played a part, and so did the successes of the German B-Dienst, the service which intercepted British signals. The availability of Allied air cover and of long-range aircraft, and the extent of Luftwaffe reconnaissance and anti-shipping operations, influenced the monthly figures, as did the operations of German surface raiders. The rationing of food and petrol was vital to the struggle, as was the improving technology of anti-submarine weapons—such as the hedgehog depth-charge thrower—and the use of better explosive charges. Just as deadly in effect were airborne and shipborne radar and, perhaps most important of all, 'Huff Duff', which provided ever better 'fixes'.

The Germans never suspected that the British might be reading their Enigma traffic on a regular basis. The chief of the German Navy's Signals, and the head of the Naval Intelligence Service, assured Dönitz that it was not possible to crack such machine codes. After the war Dönitz still believed them. To some extent of course this was true.

By 23 June 1941 British penetration of the Hydra traffic had given the OIC (Operational Intelligence Centre, of which the Submarine Tracking Room was a part) a great deal of supplementary data, including details of all German inshore traffic and thus minelaying operations, as well as the routine messages that marked the beginning and end of a U-boat's cruise.

Enigma intercepts also revealed the positions of five tankers, two supply ships and a scouting ship positioned for the commerce-raiding cruise by *Bismarck* and *Prinz Eugen*. When plans were made to attack these auxiliary vessels, the navy decided to leave two of them—the tanker *Gedania* and the scout *Gonzenheim*—unmolested. To attack them all might prompt the Germans to guess their Enigma had been penetrated. By chance the Royal Navy happened upon those ships too, and so the whole lot was sunk. As feared, this massacre—five of the sinkings occurring over a three-day period—made the Germans investigate the possibility that Enigma was insecure. They decided that the spate of sinkings was probably a coincidence, but additional security measures were introduced just to be on the safe side.

One of the planned measures was a fourth rotor for the navy's Enigma machines. A shiny new Enigma machine had been recovered from *U-570*, which in August 1941 surfaced near Iceland and fell victim to an RAF plane. The Enigma machine had been built with an extra window, all ready for the extra rotor when it was issued. The sight of it sent a shudder through the personnel at BP, for the mathematicians calculated that it would multiply their already Herculean task by a factor of 26! They were right: 1942 brought the four-rotor machine and a year of darkness for the men peering into the German navy Enigma. Sinkings went from 600,000 tons in the second half of 1941 to 2,600,000 tons in the second half of 1942.[25]

A last word about Bletchley Park is a cautionary one. Considerable opportunities for intelligence gathering were neglected because the pre-war SIS took no interest in foreign radio transmissions other than messages. It wasn't until 1940 that there was any attempt to intercept or analyse radar or radio navigation signals. GC&CS was responsible not only for cryptography and communications intelligence but also for safeguarding British communications. Whatever its glittering, and much trumpeted, successes at the former, its role as guardian was a chronic and dismal failure.

THE SUBMARINE TRACKING ROOM

The Submarine Tracking Room used a wide range of incoming data. Anything that could possibly help was funnelled here. For the admirals perhaps the most disconcerting thing about this place, where Britain's most vital battle was being fought and from which came the operational decisions that sent orders to the warships, was that by 1941 no regular naval officer was anywhere to be seen.

The room was run by Rodger Winn, a 30-year-old lawyer with degrees from Cambridge and Harvard. He had drifted into this job as a civilian, after volunteering to interrogate enemy prisoners. Winn would never have passed a Royal Navy physical examination: childhood polio had left him a hump-backed cripple who walked with a limp. Neither would he have found favour in the peacetime navy, for he had limited respect for authority. Like many barristers he was a talented story-teller with a sharp tongue. The security of having a well paid profession waiting for him encouraged him to stand firm against authority. When a decision of Winn's was challenged by an admiral, Winn put a vast heap of reports, sightings, charts and intercepts on to the admiral's desk and politely asked him for his solution.

When Winn joined the Tracking Room staff, the emphasis was on plotting the present state of the Atlantic battle, rather than predicting the future. But such was Winn's talent for reading the minds of the U-boat men, that in January 1941 his boss was moved out of the Tracking Room and Winn was given sole command of it and made a commander in the Royal Navy Volunteer Reserve. And when in January 1942 he chose an assistant, it was another 'civilian', a bespectacled insurance broker from Lloyd's.

Most of the Tracking Room's floor space was occupied by a seven-foot-square plotting table depicting the North Atlantic. It was covered with sheets of white paper and brightly lit from above, like a billiards table. Pins showed the progress of the convoys on their two-week voyages across the ocean, while others showed the U-boats on their month-long sorties. All the evidence of U-boat activity—radio fixes, sightings, signals and sinkings—was written in pencil on to the paper table cover. The coloured pins revealed the source: red-topped pins for a fix, white for a sighting, blue for Enigma intercepts. Red lines showed the extreme limits of air cover. A cluster of pins showed where a convoy was at that moment under attack by a wolf pack.

Another large table was covered by a captured map to show the German navy grid. There was also a map showing the Huff Duff stations that took bearings on U-boat radio messages. Strings could be stretched across the map to intersect. A 'good fix' was within 40 or 50 miles, a 'very good fix' meant within 10 to 15 miles. On one notable occasion a U-boat was found within three miles of its fix in the Baltic, and sunk by a Coastal Command plane, all within 30 minutes of the U-boat's tell-tale radio transmission.[26]

The walls of the Tracking Room were covered in charts and graphs showing such things as U-boat sinkings and estimated production. There were pictures too, including a photograph of Dönitz. Winn tried to make this room as he imagined Admiral Dönitz had his operations room.

Each day at noon the information from the table was translated into a situation report. The most vital parts of the plot were used each day to update Churchill's map in the War Room. Once a week, during the night, staff renewed all the white paper sheets on the plotting table, carefully transferring all the current data to them. The Submarine Tracking Room became a favourite place to take VIPs. For extra security the plotting table used coded references so that visitors would not get an accurate or complete view of what was happening.

Around the Tracking Room there were offices for the watchkeepers. Winn's office had a glass front so that he could see the civilian watchkeepers plotting the convoys while RNVR officers (wearing mufti) plotted the enemy movements. Civilian dayworkers kept the records and card indexes. A nearby office held telex machines connected by direct line to Bletchley Park. Arriving Enigma messages were brought into the Tracking Room by a Wren (Woman's Royal Naval Service) who was called 'the secret lady'.[27] One of the tasks of the Tracking Room staff was to compile an account of each new U-boat. Such a record might start with the low-grade radio traffic sent while the new boat was working-up in the Baltic. From that time onwards every possible detail of boat and crew would be filed for reference. Names, sinkings, medals and commendations, damage and refits were all noted.

Because the Royal Navy gave most of its officers sea duties between spells at a desk, the plotting table often showed the hazards of friends who had recently worked here. One officer, Commander Boyle, was well known to the men in the Tracking Room and was married to a secretary who worked there. He was escort commander for a convoy of eleven tankers and his friends watched the plot day after day as its ships were picked off one at a time. Finally only one ship survived but Boyle was saved.[28]

By using his background material, and watching all the movements on the plotting table, Winn made decisions about re-routing convoys or even detaching precious warships if the situation required it. Each morning he phoned to the Western Approaches Command in Liverpool and spoke with RAF Coastal Command too. When Enigma material was available, it made Winn's job incomparably easier. Often he phoned directly to those other civilian boffins at Bletchley Park and asked them to keep a lookout for messages with some known component.

B-DIENST

The German navy's Observation and Cryptanalytic Service, Beobachtungs und Entzifferungs Dienst, was housed at 72 Tirpitzufer, Berlin. In the first two years of war there is no doubt that the German navy gained more advantage from the intelligence provided to them by their Beobachter-Dienst than did the Royal Navy from the Enigma work at Bletchley Park. The men of the German navy's B-Dienst (modelled after the Royal Navy's Room 40) had been listening to British fleet signals long before war began, and they broke the British convoy code (BAMS: British and Allied Merchant Ship Code) without difficulty. The Germans could read a great deal of the Royal Navy traffic too, and Dönitz planned his Atlantic operations upon the wealth of material he got from B-Dienst.

The British Admiralty had resisted the idea of having coding machines. The Typex, resembling the Enigma, had been offered to them but was turned down. One would have thought that a sample of what a potential enemy was using might have been recognized as a worthwhile investment.

Lord Louis Mountbatten, when still a Lieutenant-Commander, had drawn attention to the weakness of the whole system of Royal Navy codes and was ordered 'to mind his own business'.[29]

The Royal Navy's refusal to use ciphering machines made it easier for the Germans. Even the convoy designations gave vital information: ONS was a slow outward-bound convoy to North America (Nova Scotia); HX homeward bound from Halifax. From such tags it was possible to guess the routes, and merchantmen were listed by name with a short description of their cargo: war material, eight aircraft on deck, locomotives on deck, chemicals, machine parts. Thus Britain's most critical supply convoys were exposed to attack and continued to be so until the codes were changed in the summer of 1943.

All the same the U-boat commander's task was not an easy one. The convoys maintained radio silence most of the voyage. On a clear day, an alert lookout on a submarine conning-tower might spot a convoy's smoke (against clear sky or cloud) at 50 miles. In calm seas, and at the right depth, a submarine's hydrophones might pick up the sound of a convoy at the same distance. Yet endless chivvying by the convoy commodores discouraged smoke, and the North Atlantic's clear days, and calm days, are not numerous. Lookouts, even German lookouts, are not always alert. We can therefore think in terms of a 25-mile visibility or less.

Always we must remember the speeds at which the opposing units could travel. It has been nicely depicted by a historian who suggested that we think of the Atlantic in terms of European distances: a U-boat in Vienna is told to attack a convoy in London. On the surface he can move at the speed of a pedal cycle, submerged he will go at approximately walking pace. Then we understand why convoys sometimes escaped intact, despite the men of B-Dienst.

4 SCIENCE GOES TO SEA

> Do you really believe that the sciences would ever
> have originated and grown if the way had not been
> prepared by magicians, alchemists, astrologers and
> witches . . .
>
> FRIEDRICH WILHELM NIETZSCHE

In the opening days of the war, the German magnetic mine
gave the Royal Navy one of its first big shocks. It was a
simple weapon, but the method of its activation demonstrated some of the curiosities of the natural world. The
mines sat on the seabed and came to the surface to explode
against the hulls of ships that passed over them. Inside each
mine there was a 'dip needle' which was pushed down by the
'downwards north pole' of the ship passing over it. Such
mines were activated only by ships built in the northern
hemisphere. Ships built south of the equator had a 'downwards south pole' which pulled the contacts further apart, so
they could pass quite safely over magnetic mines.

In fact it was more complex than that: the magnetism of a
ship's hull was not simply north or south. Each ship was
different. The hulls varied according to the direction, relative
to magnetic north, in which the ship's keel had been laid
down when built. Even more surprisingly, it was discovered
that ships sailing to the southern hemisphere and back again
changed their 'magnetic signature'. Prefabricated ships were
sometimes assembled from two halves made in different
places; the halves then had different magnetic properties.
Once a ship's signature was known, it could be demagnetized
by means of a fluxmeter. When the threat of the magnetic
mine was suddenly understood, Britain's only manufacturer

of fluxmeters was asked to supply 500 on a rush order; before that only a dozen had been made since 1898.

By their nature these 'influence mines' were restricted to use in shallow water, the type TMB in 15 fathoms and the TMC no deeper than 20 fathoms. Smaller mines could be laid through the U-boat's torpedo tubes; three of them together were about the length of a torpedo. Laid by U-boats or parachuted from low-flying aircraft into harbours, estuaries and coastal sea routes, the German mines caused consternation. The battleship HMS *Nelson* and the cruiser HMS *Belfast* were seriously damaged by mines, three destroyers were sunk and so were 129 merchant ships. The Thames Estuary became so littered with German mines that there was talk of closing down the Port of London.

It seemed at first as if it was a problem easily solved, since the Royal Navy had used magnetic mines in 1917. In the interwar years Admiralty scientists had experimented with the magnetic properties of ships' hulls, but the emphasis was upon counter-measures to the magnetic torpedo. This meant a powerful magnetism that would prematurely explode a torpedo as it approached. But scientists and technicians were few in number and their work was overruled by officials at the Admiralty who thought that mines, like submarines, were weapons for inferior naval powers. Dusting off their old research, the navy tried it out. But they found that magnetic sweeps that countered British magnetic mines exploded German ones. The sweeping devices were often destroyed and sometimes mine-sweepers were badly damaged.

The night of 22/23 November 1939[1] was dark and moonless. Between 9 and 10 pm a Heinkel He 111, following the Thames Estuary, flew very low over the tip of Southend pier. It was a good landmark: probably Luftwaffe crews were briefed to use the pier as a navigating fix. A machine-gun team at the pier's far end opened fire and saw two parachutes fall from the plane. Startled by the unexpected gunfire, the Germans had dropped two mines into the shallow tidal water. Its load lightened, the Heinkel sped away.

The report that men had jumped out of the aircraft was

discounted. Before midnight, Churchill was told that there was probably going to be a chance to examine the new weapon. By 1.30 am on that same night two experts briefed by Churchill, and the first sea lord, were on their way by car to Shoeburyness, where the mines were exposed by the outgoing tide. By 4 am—with rain falling heavily—the investigating team was out on the exposed mud-flats. Using a powerful portable signal lamp, they were looking at a black aluminum cylinder, seven feet in length and about two feet in diameter. Before anything much could be done, beyond securing the mines, the incoming tide had swallowed them out of reach until the following afternoon.[2]

Next day steel-nerved technicians from HMS *Vernon* (the RN's mine school) defused the weapon. By a stroke of fortune, a mechanical device to keep the mine safe until it had settled on the seabed had jammed. It was actuated by the technicians rolling the mine over but by that time the mechanism had been rendered safe. Stripped of its detonators and priming charges the mine was taken for examination to a 'non-magnetic laboratory'. In a matter of hours the new weapon was understood: it operated on a vertical magnetic field and required about 50 milligauss to fire it. The threat remained.

When, on Saturday morning, Rear-Admiral W. F. Wake Walker told government scientist Frederick Brundett about the capture of the mine and that he would need twelve engineers by Monday morning, Brundett drove to the south coast to seek out individually men with special engineering skills and sign them up on the spot. One whom he considered essential was already being paid £2,000 a year. 'As it happened the Director of Scientific Research at the time was only getting about £1,700 a year, and I was subsequently told by the Treasury that I couldn't do it. I pointed out that I'd already done it and that he was in fact already working for us'.[3]

Some anti-mine experiments were performed by sailors who towed toy ships backwards and forwards over cables in 'canoe lake', a children's boating pool in Southsea, near to

HMS *Vernon*. Various counter-measures were devised and put into operation immediately. These included 'de-gaussing', which neutralized the vertical magnetism of a ship. The mines could be swept by floating electrical cables (through which a current pulsed) behind a de-gaussed ship. Large coils were also installed in low-flying aircraft as a quick way to neutralize minefields.

Such measures were not enough to solve the problem completely. Channels swept by aircraft were narrow and un-marked. The German aviators were bold: one minelaying seaplane landed in Harwich harbour, carefully placed its mines, and then took off again. It was the minelaying opera-tions of low-flying aircraft that led to the construction of new radar stations with apparatus designed for low-level detec-tion. When the Battle of Britain began, these stations were to play a vitally important part in detecting low-flying forma-tions that would otherwise have got in under the radar screen.

The de-gaussing that all British warships were given at this time probably saved some of them from attack by mag-netic torpedoes, notably during the Norwegian campaign. At the time these failures were considered to be due to faults in German torpedoes, and no one can be sure of what exactly happened inside the warheads.

The Germans hit upon the idea of sowing mixed minefields with both magnetic and moored mines. These re-quired tricky sweeping techniques. They reversed polarity to catch ships that had been 'over-de-gaussed'. Delayed-action fuses kept the mines inactive for a period; thus sweeping would be without result.

Then came acoustic mines, which had to be swept with noisy 'hammer boxes'. There were double fuses that would work only when two triggers were activated, such as noise and polarity. But by the summer of 1940 the magnetic mine had ceased to be a real danger.

On 7 May 1940 a new threat arose. A modified version of the BM 1000, intended as a sea mine in the Clyde, overshot and landed on the Clydeside hills near Dumbarton. These ingenious dual-purpose 'bomb mines' were fitted with Rheinmetall inertia fuses when used against land targets. Falling into water at least 24 feet deep they functioned as a magnetic mine; on soft mud or in shallow water they would self-destruct. They would also self-destruct (by means of a hydrostatic valve) when the water pressure lessened, as it would when they were lifted to the surface. It was an example of German thoroughness that, despite all the foregoing precautions, the BM 1000 also incorporated one of the most cunning booby traps ever built. A set of photo-electric cells connected to a detonator would explode the bomb if light got inside it. This was a way of killing any bomb team who got to see the workings. By amazing luck, the bomb found at Dumbarton had suffered a circuit failure.[4]

A few months later this sort of bomb-mine was extensively used during the night bombing of London. They parachuted down and caused widespread destruction without forming a crater. Londoners found it easy to recognize the results and called them 'land mines'.

The menace of the magnetic mine had been overcome by the scientists, and this was the important fact. Before the war the admirals and generals in Whitehall had showed little interest in science and technology, but success with the magnetic mine changed that attitude. According to Dr C. F. Goodeve, who was a physicist and RNVR officer: 'it was the first technical battle in which we won a decisive victory over the enemy; but more important still, it was one which brought science fully into the war in the very early days'.[5]

In Germany the Nazis had broken with the nineteenth- and early twentieth-century tradition of political encouragement and social respect for science and its practitioners, and there was little or no collaboration between the scientists and the military until the end of 1943, when German scientists were invited to help with the Battle of the Atlantic. Even then they were simply asked to identify Allied radio and radar transmissions.

But Nazi distrust of science and top-level obstruction of research did not change the way in which German industry employed men who knew how to apply science and engineering to design and production. The magnetic mine provides a good example of the excellence of German design. The only reason for the mine's failure to cripple British shipping was that Germany went to war with only 1,500 of them in stock. After the first sequence of minelaying operations, the Germans had to wait until March 1940 for more to be manufactured.[6] It was this respite that saved Britain's defences from being overwhelmed, and provided an interval during which the menace could be countered.

ADMIRAL DÖNITZ AT HIS COMMAND POST

From its creation, the German U-boat arm had its most important bases at Kiel and Wilhelmshaven, in that flat and lonely part of Germany that has long belonged to the German navy. To get to the Atlantic shipping, U-boats had to negotiate the narrow sea lane between Scotland and Norway. Worse, German coastal regions were shallow and could be mined. So, as soon as France was defeated, Admiral Dönitz moved his submarine fleet to its west coast which faced directly to the Atlantic. It was done with remarkable speed and efficiency. On his own initiative, Captain Godt, chief of staff to Dönitz, dispatched workmen from the Germania construction yards at Kiel, and selected men from the flotilla commands. A train loaded with fuel, torpedoes, supplies and paperwork departed from Wilhelmshaven on the day following the French armistice. Less than three weeks later, the *U-30*, commanded by Kapitänleutnant Lemp, was in Lorient, loading torpedoes. One account records that:

> The advance guard of the flotilla staff had moved into the French Naval Préfecture at Lorient. They had plenty of booty—uniforms, footwear, equipment—some of it bearing the names of British and American firms and the date

1918: there were piles of tropical kits, arms, ammunition, food, and a thousand and one items which the enemy had had no time to destroy . . . And now the flotilla depot was there, with everything one's heart could desire—transport, fuel, money; only the sanitary arrangements left something to be desired, but that was soon rectified.[7]

After a brief spell in Boulevard Suchet, Paris, Dönitz set up his headquarters in Kernéval, near Lorient, on 1 September 1940. His commandeered villa near the sea at Lamorplage had belonged to a sardine merchant. Sheltered by trees, it had a view towards Port Louis and the old fort at the harbour entrance. From here Dönitz could watch his U-boats as they came into the harbour and tied up at the wooden prison ship *Isère* which had once been used to transport French convicts to Devil's Island in French Guiana. Now it was the first and last mooring for each U-boat that went on an operational trip. Comrades, female naval telegraphers and other well-wishers would gather on the *Isère;* sometimes a military band played patriotic songs and marches. U-boats departing had their crews paraded on deck; those arriving would often be flying the home-made pennants that denoted the tonnage of their victims.[8]

One room in the Dönitz mansion was called 'the museum'. Here, by means of charts, diagrams and the graphs he liked so much, he could see, or show others, the progress of the submarine war measured by such things as the Allied tonnage sunk per operational U-boat day at sea. Here were the turn-round times and the changing enemy tactics and routes. The next room—his 'situation room'—had a big plotting table and walls covered with maps and charts. Pins showed the positions of the U-boats and of convoys and RN units, and even—thanks to the men of B-Dienst—the places where the British believed the U-boats to be! There were air-reconnaissance photos and, from secret agents, reports of the sailing of individual ships or convoys. On the map could be seen the way in which long-range Sunderland aircraft were being sighted further and further west. Dönitz described the room in which he spent so many hours:

> The maps were supplemented by a number of diagrams showing the differences between our local time and that in the various areas of operations, charts showing tides and currents and ice and fog conditions with special reference to the north-west Atlantic . . . A large globe more than three feet in diameter gave a realistic picture of the wide Atlantic as it really is and was of great assistance in determining distances which could be worked out only approximately on ordinary charts, which, where great distances are concerned, make no allowance for the curvature of the earth's surface.[9]

On that first day of September 1940 his charts showed that his U-boat losses to date—28—exactly equalled the number of new boats commissioned in the same period. That still left him fewer than at the start of the war because of the needs of training, repairs, trials and shakedowns. Of his 27 operational U-boats only seven or eight would be at sea on an average day, too few for Dönitz to operate the sort of 'wolf-pack' tactics he wanted, though sometimes several boats could be brought together to converge on a target.

The chart recording his successes would have shown an aircraft-carrier, a battleship, three destroyers, two submarines, five auxiliary cruisers and 440 merchant ships estimated at a total 2,330,000 tons. Dönitz used tonnage sunk per U-boat day at sea as a measure of the U-boat arm's efficiency. By this measure October 1940 was the peak of his success, with five and a half ships sunk each month per U-boat at sea. (The high figures achieved later in the war were sinkings by larger numbers of boats, and Dönitz remained acutely aware of his failure to get back to his 1940 peak.)

The French bases at Lorient, Brest, St Nazaire and La Rochelle were near deep water and difficult for the British to mine. RAF Bomber Command did not mount an all-out bombing campaign against them until it was too late. For in 1941, at Hitler's command, concrete shelters were constructed over the pens and made so thick and strong that normal RAF bombs had little effect. Virtually indestructible, these pens are still there today. The French show perverse pride in them and permit only their own citizens to look inside.

The Germans also had the benefit of skilled French technicians. Delighting their German masters, the French shipyard workers laboured even harder than their counterparts in Germany. They reduced the turn-around time that U-boats spent in port by no less than 22 per cent. 'Until this time two and a half boats had been in port for every submarine at sea and the French helped to reduce this figure to a ratio of 1.8:1'.[10]

As German armies consolidated their conquest of France and the Low Countries in the summer of 1940, the British kept many destroyers and other craft in base, ready to repel an invasion of their islands. Convoys sailed with few escorts, and for much of the crossing had to manage without protection. Out in the North Atlantic the U-boats were sinking merchant ships at a dismaying rate. U-boat commanders, with their battered hats and white roll-neck sweaters, were coming home from patrol to report the sinking of forty or fifty thousand tons of shipping. These undersea aces got the same sort of film star treatment in Germany that the Spitfire pilots (often with similarly battered hats and similar white roll-neck sweaters) were enjoying in Britain. U-boat crews were cosseted. French resort hotels were converted to rest homes for them, or they could return to Germany on the special U-boat train that went backwards and forwards with supplies, ammunition and spare parts. If they stayed near their bases, their high pay (with double pay for each day in the Atlantic operational zone) ensured their warm welcome in restaurants, nightclubs and brothels despite their reputation for boisterous behaviour.

From the bases in France U-boat men could strike at ships bringing fuel, wheat and war supplies to Britain from the United States and Canada, as well as beef from South America, while the routes of vital ore from South Africa and oil from Nigeria were almost on their doorstep. The African convoys were seeking safety further west and the transatlantic routes were going ever more northwards into icy seas. The U-boats followed them.

AIRCRAFT: THE LONELY SEA AND THE SKY

Until war started, the British had given little thought to the weapons needed if aircraft were to sink submarines. The Blackburn Kangaroo, a twin-engined biplane used against

FIGURE 6:
British shipping losses in the first year of the war—Royal Navy and merchant total 452

U-boats in the final weeks of the First World War, could carry four 250-lb bombs. The twin-engined Avro Anson, which in 1939 comprised well over half of RAF Coastal Command's aircraft, could carry only four 100-lb bombs. Although these were specially designed anti-submarine bombs their efficiency had never been properly tested. The first chance to measure Coastal Command's anti-submarine bombs came on 5 September 1939, two days into the war, when an Anson of 233 Squadron dropped two 100-lb bombs on a submarine that surfaced off the coast of Scotland. The bombs bounced off the water and exploded in mid-air, causing enough damage to bring the Anson down into St Andrews Bay. The submarine proved to be one of the Royal Navy's fleet.

A few days later, on 14 September, two Blackburn Skua dive-bombers from the aircraft-carrier HMS *Ark Royal* attacked the *U-30* which had surfaced alongside the freighter *Fanad Head* while a German boarding party searched for food (the U-boat rations had gone mouldy) prior to opening its sea valves to sink it. Again the anti-submarine bombs exploded in the air, bringing down both planes. The U-boat crew, commanded by Kapitänleutnant Lemp, rescued two of the aviators and then dived with them as prisoners. The next day another Anson was damaged by its own bombs without causing damage to the target. A year later, on 25 October 1940, three Hudson bombers from 233 Squadron subjected the *U-46* to a concentrated attack in which one 100-lb anti-submarine bomb scored a direct hit. The U-boat's pressure hull remained intact and the vessel managed to get back to port.

It is no surprise to learn that the first U-boat sinking from the air was carried out by Bomber Command using ordinary 250-lb general purpose bombs. A Bristol Blenheim on an armed reconnaissance went dangerously low to deliver a determined attack upon *U-31,* which on that day, 11 March 1940, was undergoing sea trials off Heligoland Bight. One, perhaps two bombs, hit the hull. Everyone aboard, including many dockyard workers, died though the hull was salvaged, refitted and went back into action. At last, a month later, a Fairey Swordfish flying off HMS *Warspite* did manage to score with two 100-lb anti-submarine bombs, sinking the *U-64* at anchor.

In view of the ineffectiveness of the anti-submarine bombs, the airmen decided to throw at the enemy the only other anti-submarine weapon available: the depth charge designed in the First World War. This thin metal drum, packed with explosive, had an adjustable fuse which detonated according to water pressure. A nose and tail were fitted and it was dropped with reasonable success on practice targets, although only large aircraft could carry the depth charge since it weighed 450 lb. Altogether different to the bomb, it was designed to go into the water alongside the target rather than strike it (those that hit a submarine seldom exploded), and since the explosion took place underwater it posed far less danger to the airmen. But such depth charges were not in general supply until the summer of 1941.

FIGURE 7:
Focke-wulf Fw 200C Condor

In 1939 both sides were acutely short of large long-range aircraft. The Luftwaffe had been forced to use a civil airliner, the Fw 200C Condor, a beautiful machine that in August 1938 had flown nonstop from Berlin to New York and back at an average speed of 205 mph. Pressed into use for long-range maritime reconnaissance, the Condor was not rugged enough for the rigours of military flying.

The RAF had the equally fine Short Sunderland flying

boat, a four-engined machine with a crew of anything up to 13. It came complete with kitchen and beds. Although it looked like the same manufacturer's civil flying boat, this aircraft was built to a military specification and so was much better suited to a military role than the adapted Condor. One Sunderland, forced down on to a very rough Atlantic, with winds gusting up to 100 mph, remained afloat for the nine hours that it took HMAS *Australia* to arrive and rescue its crew.

FIGURE 8:
Short Sunderland flying boat

The Sunderland had won headlines a few days after war began when two of them landed on the sea and rescued the 34-man crew of a torpedoed tramp steamer. Any flying boat—let alone one with a crowd of unscheduled passengers—is difficult to unstick from open water. It was a remarkable feat of airmanship, and seamanship too. With a range of almost 3,000 miles at 134 mph the Sunderlands would no doubt have seriously depleted the U-boat flotillas if suitable bombs or depth charges had been available in the early days of the Atlantic battle.

Since 1936 the United States navy had been using as their patrol plane a reliable two-engined flying boat which the RAF called a 'Catalina' after an island near Consolidated's San Diego plant. The RAF ordered 30 of these aircraft in 1939 and they began arriving in 1941. It was one of these flying boats that sighted the *Bismarck* on 26 May 1941. The

FIGURE 9:
Consolidated Catalina flying boat

pilot who shadowed the German battleship was actually on a
check flight with a US navy instructor aboard.[11] They were
flying out of Lough Erne in Northern Ireland, which in great
secrecy had already been allotted funds and materials for
conversion to a US naval air base. The official account of the
interception seems to have had some expletives deleted:

> I was in the second pilot's seat when the occupant of the
> seat beside me, an American, said 'What the devil's that?'
> I stared ahead and saw a dull black shape through the
> mist which curled above a very rough sea. 'Looks like a
> battleship', he said. I said: 'Better get closer. Go round its
> stern'. . . . two black puffs appeared outside the star-
> board wing tip. In a moment we were surrounded with
> black puffs. Stuff began to rattle against the hull. Some of
> it went through and a lot more made dents in it . . . The
> only casualties occurred in the galley, where one of the
> crew who was washing up the breakfast things dropped
> two china RAF plates and broke them.[12]

During the *Bismarck* surveillance a Catalina created a
Coastal Command record of 27 hours of continuous reconnaissance. The Cat was remembered by those who flew it for
its particularly good auto-pilot, which made it possible to
endure long hours at the controls of this heavy machine—
patrols regularly lasted 17 hours—and meant there could be
an extra pair of eyes watching for U-boats. Later, at the

direct instruction of President Roosevelt, these flying boats were joined by another Consolidated aircraft: the B-24J Liberator, a four-engined aircraft with extra fuel tanks fitted. Able to carry antenna, radar sets, bombs, depth charges and even searchlights, the Liberator played a vital part in narrowing that mid-Atlantic 'gap'.

Long-range flying was pioneered during the war by hastily trained young men plucked from civilian jobs. RAF Sunderlands flew a thousand miles out over the Atlantic, and did it day after day. When America entered the war Boeing B-17 Flying Fortress pilots, at the end of their US army air force training, flew their Forts to Britain. It was a Catalina delivered to Australia that made the third air crossing of the Pacific. In normal times these events would have made newspaper headlines.

Maritime patrol aircraft needed a very long range, for they had to reach the convoys far out in the ocean before work could start. Once in place, their chief value arose from the fact that U-boats had to remain below when aircraft were present, or risk being bombed. Even a slow 7-knot convoy would soon outdistance a submerged submarine, and a submerged submarine could be detected on asdic.

The start of a convoy's trouble came when one of a rake of submarines spotted smoke, began trailing it at a distance, and then transmitted signals to bring others. A U-boat forced to submerge might well lose contact with the convoy and would have to cease transmitting.[13]

An unforeseen dimension of the encounter between aircraft and submarine was the fact that land-based aircraft could not pick up survivors in the sea. This brought an unexpected outcome in August 1941 when a Lockheed Hudson bombed *U-570* in the open sea to the south of Iceland. The U-boat was one of the large long-range Type IXC vessels that were notorious for the way in which sea water came over the conning tower at above-average speeds or in rough weather. The bombs damaged *U-570* enough for seawater to get to the batteries and create deadly chlorine gas: a constant worry for all submarine crews. The U-boat crew signalled surrender with the captain's white shirt and then found a white board and waved that too. The Hudson circled with guns trained, not realizing that the U-boat could not dive again. While circling the pilot suggested that his co-pilot parachute down as a prize crew, 'but he didn't fancy it' he joked in a BBC broadcast. A Catalina arrived and the Hudson signalled: 'Look after our sub, it has shown the white flag'. Ships sent to rescue the submariners arrived just before nightfall and took the U-boat in tow until eventually it ran aground off Iceland. It was refitted and put into action by the Royal Navy as HMS *Graph*.

BOFFINS JOIN THE NAVY

During the 1930s scientists in Germany, France, the USA and Britain, working independently and in secret, discovered that a beam of very short pulses, sent and reflected from a target back to a cathode ray tube, would define that object's bearing and range. It was not advanced technology, and it certainly wasn't a British invention. Even the Russian armed forces were equipped with radar by the time war began.

The German battleship *Graf Spee* had excellent gun-laying radar and the *Scharnhorst* and *Gneisenau* both used radar to evade HMS *Naiad* in January 1941. *Naiad*'s Type 279 radar was outranged by the German radar, so that after one brief visual sighting by the British (who never made radar contact) the German ships were able to keep clear of their pursuers. In the Norwegian campaign the same two German ships had surprised HMS *Renown* by using gun-laying radar to hit her while remaining concealed in a snow squall.

The Royal Navy began to equip its ships with Type 79 radar in 1939, although at the outbreak of war only HMS *Rodney* and HMS *Sheffield* had been fitted with it. These sets were intended for the location of enemy aircraft, and were given to the big ships and to anti-aircraft cruisers such as HMS *Curlew,* HMS *Carlisle* and HMS *Caracoa.* In May 1940 two hundred Type 284 (50-centimetre) gun-laying radar sets were ordered. New urgency was given to radar development when, in the Mediterranean in 1941, ships without it were found to be at a grave tactical disadvantage. The US navy had been fitting radar to its ships since 1940, and in the August of that year, long before the United States went to war, the USN and RN began to share their technology.

At the start of hostilities, German radar was more accurate and sophisticated than that of any other nation. The first radar success of the war was on 18 December 1939 when a formation of 22 RAF Vickers Wellington bombers was detected 70 miles off the German coast. Only ten of the bombers returned.

While British designers concentrated on longer-range sets, the Germans wanted accuracy and, where possible, mobility. In the summer of 1940 a German mobile unit on the Cherbourg peninsula fixed the position of an RN destroyer near the British coast and it was sunk by a Luftwaffe attack.

Radar—or Radio Direction Finding as the British called it at that time—was cumbersome, and the use of delicate glass vacuum tubes, known as valves, made it fragile. Such apparatus was regarded as a land-based, or shipborne, anti-aircraft weapon that could also be used against ships. It was probably the British who first tried another idea. A team under Dr Edward Bowen put an early EMI television receiver into an old Handley Page Heyford bomber and was encouraged by getting a flickered reception from a transmitter. From this they went on to design a small high-frequency set to go inside an Avro Anson aircraft. By 3 September 1937 it could detect big ships at about five miles.

The vital factor in the development of British radar was a willingness to improvise. Priority was given to radar—and other scientific ideas—when radar was credited with having saved Britain from defeat in the Battle of Britain. The Nazi creed gave emphasis to rural traditions and old 'Germanic' customs; and the political leaders of the Third Reich were apt to be antagonistic to modern science, sometimes defining it as Jewish. German scientists were not automatically exempted from military service, and civilian scientists assigned to work with the armed forces did not find the welcome that their British counterparts were given. Britain invented the technique of 'operational research', which meant scientists (cheerfully nicknamed 'boffins')[14] advising the armed forces on the most effective way to use existing weapons rather than having to devise new ones.

Operational research boffins demonstrated that you could double the size of a convoy without doubling the length of its perimeter; in fact the perimeter of an 80-ship convoy was only one seventh longer than a convoy of 40 ships. Thus big convoys meant more effective use of escort vessels. Moreover average losses decreased from 2.6 per cent to 1.7 per cent when convoys comprised more than 45 ships. This was partly due to the fact that a wolf pack's activities were limited by the availability of torpedoes, reloading time, stress and fatigue, whatever the size of the convoy.

Operational research also helped decide at what depth a depth charge should be set to explode. The scientists suggested that, given enough time, a U-boat crash-diving usually turned away to escape. Such targets should be abandoned as a lost cause. Depth charges dropped from aircraft should be set to explode near the surface, ensuring the more certain kill of those U-boats attacked early enough. Such ideas brought an immediate and dramatic benefit to British anti-submarine tactics.

When war began, Coastal Command had 12 Lockheed Hudson aircraft fitted with ASV (Air to Surface Vessel) Mark I radar. Better sets—fitted in the larger Armstrong Whitley bombers and Sunderland flying boats—followed. At its best, airborne radar could pick up a U-boat at 25 miles, but these valuable aircraft, with their ineffective anti-submarine bombs, seldom sank U-boats.

The boffins were asked why out of 77 U-boat sightings

from aircraft in August and September 1941 only 13 were originated from airborne radar contact. The hastily built equipment was poorly serviced, they said, and operating it was a job assigned to anyone with time to spare. Better training gave aircrews faith in their equipment, and towards the end of 1941 airborne radar became more and more effective. Swordfish biplanes of 812 Squadron Fleet Air Arm showed what it could do by patrolling systematically by day and night against U-boats trying to get through the narrow Strait of Gibraltar in to the Mediterranean. One U-boat was sunk and five damaged so badly that they had to return to base.[15]

In addition, the Royal Navy's big ships were being fitted with its own more sophisticated gun-laying as well as air-warning radar, yet the range of British radar sets was still less than that of an alert lookout on a clear day. The urgent problem was to develop something that could be fitted into an escort vessel, such as a corvette, and detect the conning tower of a surfaced U-boat at night.

Dr S.E.A. Landale was one of the team that set up a short-wave centimetric radar on the cliffs at Swanage and traced a submarine seven miles away. He found practical difficulties when fitting his radar into a ship: 'Corvettes are very wet and in rough weather the discomforts, inconvenience and inflow of water whenever the office door was opened had to be experienced to be believed'.[16] Antenna systems had to be protected against the weather. More problems arose from the rolling and pitching and the effects of engine vibration and of gunfire. Even so, by the end of 1941 the Type 271 radar had been designed, one hundred were built and fifty ships were equipped with it. This was the first operational magnetron-powered centimetric radar in the world. In use it was a revelation: it could even locate the top of a periscope. No longer could a surfaced U-boat sail at night with impunity.

FRAGILE BUT LETHAL: U-BOATS AT WORK

But in September 1940, long before such sophisticated devices played a part in the Battle, Admiral Dönitz became agitated enough to tell his staff that 'It will not be long before the entire U-boat fleet is lost on our own doorstep'. His distress was due to two factors which still today have scarcely been recognized, says one of the most reliable historians of the U-boat war, J.P.M. Showell. Dönitz was distressed about the number of boats lost to British submarines and mines while crossing the Bay of Biscay. The dangers of the Bay had led U-boat crews to call it Totenallee, or death row.

Leaving aside the efficacy of the mines and submarines, the fears that Dönitz showed were to have an immediate and immense effect upon the U-boat war, for he told his crews to send a radio signal as soon as they had traversed the Bay safely. This signal was transmitted when the U-boat passed the 10 degrees west line (later this was changed to 15 degrees west). The crews looked forward to this stage of the journey, for their daily rate of pay increased. The Admiralty's Submarine Tracking Room personnel also liked it for, using HF/DF, an exact longitude could now be added to an approximate latitude for every U-boat going on patrol. With this 'fix' pinned in to the map it was usually possible to guess which of the convoy routes the U-boat was heading for.

Operating with less than 30 U-boats, Dönitz was fretting for a chance to experiment with his 'wolf pack' tactics. His theories about surface engagements were confirmed. Nearly three-quarters of all successful torpedo attacks were made at night from surfaced U-boats which could not be detected by asdic apparatus. At this stage of the war there were vast areas of ocean where Allied aircraft were never seen, allowing U-boats to function more like torpedo boats than submarines.

Even without the men of B-Dienst the U-boat men could roughly estimate a probable convoy route. Dönitz would assign some his available U-boats to line up across it and wait on the surface, watching for a smudge of smoke on the horizon. When a convoy was sighted, the other U-boats would be called in. Some would be too far away, others would fail to find the rendezvous, but a force would assemble. After dark, without submerging, the U-boats sailed right through the columns of ships. Even on a dark night the sky is faintly visible, and from a conning tower it was usually possible to see the outlines of ships high above. On the other hand U-boats were small, and even in daylight the low silhouette of a conning tower was not easy to spot in the grey Atlantic water.

In October 1940 the experts at B-Dienst provided a map reference for the 35-ship convoy SC 7, a slow convoy out of Sydney, Nova Scotia, made up of five columns of four ships and, in the centre, three columns of five ships.[17] The columns were half a mile apart, each ship 600 yards from the one ahead. This typical broad-fronted rectangle was less likely to straggle and, since U-boats preferred to attack from the flank, it provided a smaller target than a long rectangle.

Thus convoy SC 7 covered an area of about five square miles and was protected by two sloops and a corvette. A gale came and the convoy straggled. Four Great Lakes steamers, not intended for Atlantic rollers, fell back and were lost (U-boats sank three of them). In looking for U-boats, one sloop lost contact and never found the convoy again. U-boats converged. Here was Günther Prien, who had crept into Scapa Flow to sink *Royal Oak*. Here was Joachim Schepke, adding up his score of sunken tonnage. Here was 'Silent Otto' Kretschmer, promptly sinking four ships and finishing the last one off with his 8.8-cm deck gun. The sinkings went on and on until 17 ships were lost and the convoy's passing was marked by survivors in open boats and drowned men floating amid the oil and wreckage. It was October, and in the northerly latitudes the convoys were forced to take the wind was bitterly cold, the seas heavy and the days short. Thirty minutes immersed in the North Atlantic was enough to kill most men. Survivors in an open boat had little chance of reaching land, or of sighting another ship.

The assembled U-boats, feasted and happy, were just in time to encounter the HX 79 (a fast convoy out of Halifax). That night 14 more ships went down. But the slaughter was not finished, for the U-boats found yet another convoy, HX 79A, and on that same night sank seven of them.

Before October was ended, there came another blow to Britain's maritime fortunes. A Focke Wulf Fw 200C Condor, far out over the ocean on a long route from Bordeaux to a base in Stavanger in Norway, spotted the Canadian-Pacific liner *Empress of Britain* about 70 miles from Donegal Bay in the north of Ireland. She was carrying servicemen and their families home to Liverpool. Captain Bernhard Jope of I/KG 40 group was at the controls of his four-engined plane and this was his first sortie. Bombs dropped from very low level set the liner afire and it was finished off by a U-boat's torpedoes. Jope received the Knight's Cross. After the war he became a Lufthansa captain.

The loss of the *Empress of Britain* was not an isolated incident. Aircraft played an important part in the battles of the sea lanes, and by war's end no less than 13 per cent of Allied shipping losses were attributed to air attack. (The U-boat arm accounted for 69 per cent of shipping losses; surface raiders and mines for 7 per cent; navigational hazards and reasons unknown for 4 per cent.)

The bombing of the convoys prompted Churchill to increase the air patrols around northern Ireland but they remained inadequate. A more desperate measure was to shoot a Hawker Hurricane fighter plane from a small platform fitted to a tanker's deck. After combat the pilot was instructed to ditch his plane into the sea near the convoy and be rescued. It was a grim prospect. The first catapult-equipped ship sailed for New York in May 1941 but was the victim of a U-boat. The first kill by such a 'Hurricat' was not until August. Few German planes fell victim to the new device. The MSFU (Merchant Ship Fighter Unit) was a deterrent rather than a weapon, and as the word spread that convoys could produce this spiteful jack-in-the-box, the long-range Condors grew more wary.

Of course not every convoy was attacked from the air or by U-boat. A German historian thinks about nine out of every ten convoys escaped. But there were not many sailors who spent six months at sea without seeing flashes and flames in the night, and a dawn that exposed spaces in their ranks. Only a few sailors took off their shoes—let alone any other articles of clothing—when they went to sleep.

THE BATTLE AT ITS PEAK

After a slow start in 1941 the U-boat building programme began to bear fruit. By the end of the year Dönitz had 247 boats to command. His losses were going up slowly: 9 in 1939; 26 in 1940; 38 in 1941. His building rate was 64, 54, 202.

In the opening months of 1941 the long-range German reconnaissance aircraft showed their teeth. In January aircraft sank 20 ships, while U-boats sank 21. In February the U-boats sank 39 ships while aircraft added 27 and surface raiders brought the total to over one hundred (and over 400,000 tons for the first time since October 1940). More than half the ships lost during this period were stragglers, alone and defenceless.

Dönitz calculated that sinkings (including those by the Luftwaffe) must reach 750,000 tons before Britain could be forced to surrender. The British set the red-line at 600,000 tons. On the charts at his headquarters at Kernéval, the rate of Allied sinkings for early 1941 was shown as 400,000 tons per month. In fact his captains—awarded medals on the basis of tonnage sunk—were giving him outrageous estimates of the size of their victims.[18] But the losses were grave nevertheless, especially when augmented by the depredations of aircraft and surface raiders (see Table 1).

TABLE 1
Allied shipping losses May–Nov. 1941
(total gross register tonnage)

	Claimed	Actually sunk
May	421,440	367,498
June	441,173	328,219
July	227,699	105,320
August	168,734	83,427
September	399,775	207,638
October	601,569	370,345
November	85,811	68,549

In the early part of 1941 RAF Coastal Command was put under the operational control of the navy, and a reconnais-sance squadron was sent to be based in Iceland. British air activity, as little as it was, persuaded Dönitz that he too must have air cover for his submarines. He had the experienced bomber group I/KG 40 put at his disposal. After January 1941 Condor aircraft regularly ranged far out into the Atlantic between Bordeaux and Stavanger in Norway. As time went on, Allied ships had enough anti-aircraft weapons to deter bombing attacks. It then became the task of these four-engined planes to scout specific convoy routes, provide Atlantic weather reports and cooperate with the U-boats.

In fact there were too few Condors to make much difference, and despite using radio beacons, few Luftwaffe navigators could pinpoint a position exactly enough to bring a U-boat within sighting distance of a convoy. To add to the confusion, the Luftwaffe map grids did not tally with the navy's charts. At this time, anyone standing at the bar in a U-boat mess could get an easy laugh from any joke about 'air support'. The unseen value of aircraft in the Atlantic battle was the morale boost they gave to their own side and the disturbing sight they made for any enemy seaman.

At first the convoys outward-bound from Britain had been given RN escorts on only the first stage of their journey, about 15 degrees west longitude. Then the escorts stayed as far as 25 degrees west and then—by July 1941—convoys were given continuous escort. Relays of escorts operated from Britain, from Iceland and from Newfoundland. But warships were scarce, so that even by the end of 1941 the average convoy had no more than two escort ships.

The escort ships were not immune to torpedoes either. I make no apologies for the extra length of this excerpt from one of the most graphic accounts the Atlantic battle provided:

> The sky suddenly turned to flame and the ship gave a violent shudder . . . Looking ahead, I could see something floating and turning over in the water like a giant metallic whale. As I looked it rolled over further still and I could make out our pennant numbers painted on it. I was dumbfounded. It seemed beyond reason. I ran to the after-side of the bridge and looked over. The ship ended just aft of the engine room—everything abaft that had gone. What I had seen ahead of us had really been the ship's own stern. There were small fires all over the upper deck. The First Lieutenant was down there organizing the fire parties. He saw me and called, 'Will you abandon ship, sir?' 'Not bloody likely, Number One . . . We'll not get out till we have to'.

But a ship with its stern blown away does not stay afloat for long:

> The deck began to take on an angle—suddenly—so suddenly. She was almost on her side. I was slithering, grasping all kinds of unlikely things. My world had turned through ninety degrees . . . I jumped for the galley funnel which was now parallel with the water and about two

feet clear, and flat-footed it to the end. I paused at the end of my small funnel to look at the faces. They were laughing as if this were part of some gigantic fun fair. The men called to me.

'Come on, sir. The water's lovely'.

'I'm waiting for the Skylark', I shouted back. But the galley funnel dipped and I was swimming too— madly . . . We swam like hell. I turned once more, but now there were very, very few bobbing heads behind me. I swam on. The destroyer of my old group was passing through us. I could see her men at action stations. They were attacking. They were attacking the wreck of the *Warwick!* I screamed at them in my frenzy. Wherever else the U-boat might have been it could not have been there. The depth charges sailed up in the air. Funny how they wobbled from side to side, I'd never noticed that before. When, I wondered, would they explode? It was like being punched in the chest, not as bad as I had expected. I swam on. Things were a bit hazy. I was not as interested in going places as I had been. I could only see waves and more waves, and I wished they would stop coming. I did not really care any more. Then I felt hands grasp my shoulders and a voice say, 'Christ, it's the skipper. Give me a hand to get the bastard in', and I was dragged into a Carley-float which was more than crowded to capacity.[19]

To make the most of their pitifully few escorts, the RN had started 'Escort Groups', which usually meant in effect nothing more than RN captains getting together—under one of their number named as escort group commander—to exchange ideas about anti-submarine tactics.

It was the 5th Escort Group which in March 1941 was in the same area as the German navy's three most famous U-boat captains: Günther Prien, Joachim Schepke, the celebrated and colourful captain of *U-100,* and Otto Kretschmer of *U-99.* At their collars these men wore the Ritterkreuz, to which the insignia of the oak leaves had been added to celebrate 200,000 tons of ships sunk. Kretschmer and Schepke were both determined to be the first to sink 300,000 tons of Allied shipping. Kretschmer had left his base at Lorient credited with 282,000 tons (although, as we have seen, such German figures were usually very much inflated).

It was Prien in *U-47* who sighted the outward-bound convoy OB 293 and summoned his colleagues: Kretschmer, Matz in *U-70* and Hans Eckermann in *UA*.[20] Although a primitive seaborne radar set played its part, this encounter marked little change in the methods or technology of either side. But there was a change in the men: the Germans, solidly professional, were at the zenith of over-confidence, while the Royal Navy's landlubbers and weekend yachtsmen had discovered a new determination.

Kretschmer started the sinkings. Firing while surfaced, he hit a tanker which burst into flame and a Norwegian whaling ship *Terje Viken* which remained afloat. Using the same tactics in *U-70,* Matz hit a British freighter and the *Mijdrecht*, a tanker, which with true Dutch resilience steered at him and rammed as *U-70* dived. The *UA* was detected and dived, its course followed by asdic. Depth charges damaged it enough to make the German set course for home.

Matz in *U-70* had submerged. He now came under coordinated attacks from two corvettes. Wallowing and unstable he went to 650 feet: far deeper than the submarine was designed to endure. The damage sustained from the Dutchman which rammed him, together with the depth-charging, started leaks and made the U-boat impossible to control. Despite the crew's efforts the *U-70* surfaced and was fired upon. The crew surrendered as the stricken boat reared, bow in the air, and slid under, taking 20 of the crew with it.

Even the stubborn Kretschmer dived deep and sat 'in the cellar'. He watched the rivets pop and the lights flicker as the explosions came and went. Carefully he withdrew, with half his torpedoes still unused. The convoy sailed on, having lost two ships and had two damaged.

Prien followed the convoy and tried again at dusk, his approach covered in fitful rainstorms. But in a clear patch he was spotted by a lookout on HMS *Wolverine* and his crash dive failed to save him from the depth charges that damaged his propeller shafts. Instead of turning for home, he surfaced after dark for another attack, perhaps not realizing how clearly the damaged propellers could be heard on the asdic. This time *Wolverine,* which had tenaciously waited in the vicinity, made no mistake. As the U-boat crash-dived, an accurately placed depth charge caused the submarine to explode under water, making a strange and awful orange glow. 'The hero of Scapa Flow has made his last patrol', said the obituary notice personally dictated by Admiral Dönitz when, after 76 days had passed, they finally told the German public of their hero's death. Even then stories about him having survived circulated for months afterwards.

A few days later on 15 March 1941, south of Iceland, Fritz-Julius Lemp, now promoted to Korvettenkapitän, signalled the approach of a convoy. It was an attractive target but the escort was formidable. The escort commander was Captain Macintyre RN, who was to become the war's most successful U-boat hunter. He was in an old First World War destroyer, HMS *Walker.* There were four other old destroyers with him, and two corvettes. The homeward convoy HX 112 consisted of almost 50 ships, in ten columns half a mile apart. They were heavily laden tankers and freighters, and even in this unusually calm sea they could make no more than 10 knots (11.5 mph).

Lemp's sighting signal was intercepted by direction-finding stations in Britain. Such plots could only be approximate, but Captain Macintyre was warned that U-boats were probably converging on HX 112. Without waiting for other U-boats, Lemp's *U-110* surfaced and used darkness to infiltrate the convoy. Two torpedoes from his bow tubes missed, but one from his stern hit *Erodona,* a tanker carrying petrol, and the sea around it became a lake of flames.

The next day other U-boats arrived. The uncertainties of U-boat operations are illustrated by the way in which *U-74* never found the rendezvous and *U-37,* having surfaced in fog, was run down by a tanker and had to return to base for repairs. But Schepke (*U-100*) and Kretschmer (*U-99*) provided enough trouble for the resourceful Captain Macintyre. Having spotted Schepke's boat, the escorts started a systematic search which kept it submerged and allowed the convoy to steam away. At this stage of the war the escorts had not discovered that U-boats impudently infiltrated the convoys to fire at point-blank range. The search for the attackers always took place outside the convoy area. So the chase after Schepke was Kretschmer's opportunity to penetrate the columns of the virtually unprotected convoy, and at 2200 hours there was a loud boom which marked the beginning of an hour during which Kretschmer hit six ships. Five of them sank. The hunt for Schepke's *U-100* was abandoned as the escorts closed upon their charges.

Schepke's *U-100*, damaged by the continuous attacks, soon caught up with the convoy. Although a surfaced submarine was immune to asdic, it was vulnerable to detection by radar, and despite the darkness he'd been detected a mile away by a primitive Type 271 radar set aboard the escort HMS *Vanoc*. A surfaced submarine, if spotted, did not have much time in which to dive to safety. This was Schepke's predicament as *Vanoc* was suddenly seen accelerating to full speed. As she sped past HMS *Walker,* the escort commander ordered a signal made to caution her about speeding. He received the reply 'have rammed and sunk U-boat'. By that time the shriek of the destroyer's bow tearing through the steel U-boat came echoing through the night air. Schepke and the duty watch standing on the tower were all crushed and lost. Someone below gave the order to crash-dive but depth charges ripped the hull open and *U-100* sank with all but seven of its crew.

While *Vanoc* was repairing its damage, and picking up German survivors, HMS *Walker*'s asdic showed another U-boat nearby, and then the set broke down. This brief encounter was with Kretschmer's *U-99*. It was surfaced and heading home under cover of darkness. Kretschmer was below. On the conning tower there was the usual complement of four men: an officer, a petty officer and two ratings. Each man was assigned a quarter of the horizon to watch through his Zeiss 7×50 binoculars. Lighter, smaller and more water-proof than RN binoculars, such glasses were coveted by every Allied sailor who saw them. The officer occasionally swept the entire horizon: it was the routine. Suddenly they came upon the warships that had sunk Schepke's boat. One of them was searching for survivors. One of the German lookouts on *U-99* saw the moonlight reflecting off a gun turret: it was a destroyer about 100 yards away. Had they done nothing they would probably have escaped—standing orders said submarines sighting the enemy at night must stay surfaced—but the submariners were tired. Thinking he'd been seen, and contrary to orders, the officer on watch dived the *U-99*, and it was then that *Walker*'s asdic operator saw it briefly before his screen went blank.

The *Walker*'s depth charge attack had to rely upon skill, instinct and practice. Those first explosions brought Kretschmer's damaged boat to the surface. Both destroyers opened fire. 'With an understandable enthusiasm', rescued merchant seamen taken on board the *Walker* piled up so much ammunition around the guns as to cause confusion.

Kretschmer was forced back to the surface. All torpedoes expended and his boat crippled, he realized that his career was at an end, but his tonnage claims were foremost in his mind. He ordered his radio operator to send a message claiming 50,000 tons of shipping and telling Dönitz that he was a prisoner of war. When Kretschmer saw *Walker* lowering a boat he took it to be an attempt to capture his submarine. He sent his engineer officer to flood the aft ballast tanks so that the U-boat would sink stern-first. It reared up suddenly and steeply, and slid back into the ocean, leaving the crew swimming. When he climbed aboard the ship that rescued him Kretschmer still had his binoculars round his neck and wore the white-topped hat that had become a captain's prerogative in the U-boat service. All but three of the U-boat's crew were saved, but the engineer officer was one of those lost. Captain Macintyre, the escort commander, used Kretschmer's Zeiss binoculars for the rest of the war.

Kretschmer, a prisoner aboard HMS *Walker,* remarked to

George Osborne, her chief engineer, upon the coincidence that both ship and submarine had a horseshoe badge but one was the wrong way up. It was explained to him that in Britain a horseshoe pointing down is considered bad luck. An eyewitness said 'it brought a rueful laugh from our prisoner'.

A destroyer was a cramped place, even without shipwrecked seamen and enemy prisoners aboard, and there was evidence of bad feeling. But the master and chief officer of *J.B. White*, a sunken merchant ship, and Otto Kretschmer an unrepentant Nazi, were persuaded by the chief engineer to join him in a game of contract bridge. Osborne said it was the only decent game he managed to get in the entire war.

Germany had lost her three U-boat aces and the Propaganda Ministry discovered that stardom for fighting men is a two-edged weapon. The loss of three 'experts' made Dönitz suspect that the British must have some new secret weapon. But then he changed his mind and decided it was just bad luck.

Dönitz had been right with his first guess. HMS *Vanoc* had used a primitive radar set, and in this same month, March 1941, a far more sophisticated 10-centimetre set was being tested at sea. It was the cavity magnetron which made such advanced radar possible and put the British work far ahead of the Germans. But in the summer of 1941 the range at which radar gave the first indication of an enemy's presence was not always better than an alert observer could provide on a clear day. In May 1941 the pursuit of the *Bismarck* provided a better example of the contribution radar played in the naval encounters of that period.

5 WAR ON THE CATHODE TUBE

> When snatched from all effectual aid,
> We perished, each alone:
> But I beneath a rougher sea,
> And whelmed in deeper gulfs than he.
>
> WILLIAM COWPER, 'THE CASTAWAY'

The battleship *Bismarck* had been launched by the grand-daughter of Germany's great nineteenth-century German chancellor in February 1939. Commissioned in August 1940, it was the most modern and powerful battleship afloat, with eight 15-inch guns in four turrets controlled by the world's best gun-laying radar.

Admiral Raeder's original plan called for *Bismarck* and the heavy cruiser *Prinz Eugen* to sail from the Baltic, while the battleships *Scharnhorst* and *Gneisenau* would sally into the Atlantic from Brest in France. In mid-ocean this powerful force would rendezvous to form a fighting fleet powerful enough to sink convoys, and defeat any escort force they might encounter.[1] This operational plan was code-named Rheinübung, Rhine Exercise, and Raeder saw it as a way of providing a big victory of the sort that 'battleship admirals' still cherished, while continuing the battle of the sea lanes that was obviously the key to victory. He knew that Hitler would invade Russia soon, and Rheinübung had to be staged before the army's needs on the Eastern Front took precedence over everything the navy wanted.

Rheinübung was put under the command of Admiral Günther Lütjens, a bony-faced man with close-cropped hair and a permanent frown. The operation was thwarted when it was found impossible to have the *Scharnhorst*'s high-pressure turbine engines ready in time. Such engines were a notable and chronic failing in German marine engineering. Then, when *Gneisenau* was hit by a desperately brave attack by a Coastal Command torpedo aircraft in Brest Roads, Raeder decided stubbornly to go ahead using only *Bismarck* and *Prinz Eugen*. This plan too was delayed when *Prinz Eugen* was damaged by a British magnetic mine in the Baltic, thus losing the advantage of a month's dark winter nights which would have made it much easier to slip past the Royal Navy.

In May 1941, Hitler was persuaded to make the trip to Gotenhafen (the now renamed Polish port of Gdynia) to inspect his new battleship and address the crew. That evening he dined with his senior officers aboard the *Tirpitz*. Hitler had doubts about the proposed expedition, but Admiral Lütjens reminded him of 'Operation Berlin'. In the first three months of the year Lütjens had taken *Scharnhorst* and *Gneisenau* into the Atlantic, causing the British great anxiety as well as sinking 115,600 tons of shipping. He told Hitler that *Bismarck* was unsinkable. 'Mein Führer, there is virtually nothing that can go wrong with a ship like this. The only danger that I can see is torpedo-aircraft coming at us from aircraft-carriers'. This prophetic caution was due to *Bismarck*'s conservative design: its underwater protection had not kept pace with what was now considered essential for British and American ships.

For anyone who believes that the British reading of Enigma traffic provided a constant insight into German intentions, it has to be said that Bletchley Park provided nothing to suggest the *Bismarck* was about to put to sea. And none of the transmissions from *Bismarck* at sea were decrypted until after she was sunk. At that time naval Enigmas were taking anything from three to seven days to crack.

The first tip concerning *Bismarck*'s movements was provided by Britain's naval attaché in Stockholm after a cruiser of neutral Sweden spotted 'two large warships' with escorts and air cover steaming through an area cleared of German shipping. Subsequently RAF Spitfires equipped for high-speed photo-reconnaissance scoured likely anchorages and found two German warships in Grimstad Fjord. Photographs revealed the *Bismarck* with an unidentified cruiser. It was alarming news and there were urgent requests for more information. Bad weather grounded RAF aircraft but a particularly daring Fleet Air Arm crew, flying a Martin Maryland that had been used for target-towing and had no navigational instruments or cameras, found an opening in the cloud above Grimstad Fjord at twilight without seeing the big ships. Just to make sure, they flew over Bergen and into a storm of German Flak. Their radio message said: 'Battleship and cruiser have left'.

Anxiously the men in the Admiralty looked at their maps: six homeward and six outward convoys were on the move, including a troop convoy to the Middle East with 20,000 men. Now earlier Luftwaffe Enigma signals, showing Fw 200C Condors on long-range reconnaissance surveying the extent of the pack-ice in the Denmark Strait, began to make sense. RN warships—most of them with radar—were immediately dispatched to patrol the waters round Iceland and in particular the Denmark Strait where, even in May, pack-ice and RN minefields made navigation so restricted that if *Bismarck* went that way it was almost sure to be sighted.

At 1922 hours on 23 May, a lookout on HMS *Suffolk* spotted *Bismarck* and *Prinz Eugen* emerging from a snow-squall at a distance of 11 miles, before the *Suffolk*'s radar made contact. As soon as *Suffolk*'s operator had *Bismarck* on the screen of his Type 284 gun-laying radar she slipped back into the gathering darkness.

The two German ships had obviously seen *Suffolk* on their radar, so they were prepared when a second RN cruiser, HMS *Norfolk,* came close enough for its lookout to sight them (again before making radar contact).[2] *Bismarck* opened fire on her. Unhit, *Norfolk* promptly fell back. The *Bismarck*'s radio room intercepted *Norfolk*'s sighting report and was able to decode the message without difficulty or delay. They kept listening.

FIGURE 10:
The German battleship *Bismarck*

For ten hours the two RN cruisers shadowed their prey until powerful naval forces could be brought up from Scapa Flow in the Orkneys. HMS *Hood* and HMS *Prince of Wales*, with destroyer escorts, were ordered to sea from Iceland.

It was a strange twist of fortune that chose HMS *Hood* for this task force, for she was exactly comparable to *Bismarck* in main armament (eight 15-inch guns), secondary armament, speed, thickness of belt and turret armour. In the 1930s *Hood* had been the pride of the Royal Navy, the fastest, most powerful and arguably most beautiful ship afloat. She had spent so much time showing the flag that there never seemed to be an opportunity for the total overhaul and refurbishing that was so badly needed. Nineteen years older than *Bismarck*, the *Hood*'s 15-inch guns remained unchanged in design since those of 1914, while the big guns of the *Bismarck* provided excellent examples of the way in which gun technology had improved.

Hood was old, but with her was the brand-new *Prince of Wales,* which still had civilian contractors aboard, working on the gun-turret machinery of its ten 14-inch guns. This was a calibre new to the RN. Two of its three turrets had been fitted only four weeks earlier, and one gun was still not in use. The *Prince of Wales* had five of the best radar sets then available, but the warships were ordered to maintain radio and radar silence so that they would not be detected.

It was not easy to keep radar contact with an enemy warship which had excellent radar, eight 15-inch guns and a top speed of over 30 knots: as soon as you were close enough to see your prey on the radar screen, it had not only been watching you for a long time but was all ready to blow you to pieces. In addition the Germans were deciphering and reading all the radio traffic of their pursuers. It was hardly surprising that the two RN cruisers lost contact with both *Bismarck* and *Prinz Eugen.*

As day was breaking at 0530 hours on Saturday 24 May 1941 *Bismarck* was sighted at 17 miles distance, again by a lookout, not by radar. On German radar the RN ships were clearly visible, and Admiral Lütjens must have been pleased to notice that their angle of approach made it possible for the British to use only forward armament, while the Germans could fire broadsides from all their big guns. This dangerous British tactic can only be explained by the commander of the British force wanting to close quickly on the Germans because British deck armour was thin and vulnerable to plunging fire. Close range would ensure that German fire would hit only side armour.

Although *Hood*'s Type 284 radar was no use for ranges beyond 22,000 yards *Hood* opened fire at 26,500 yards. It aimed at the less dangerous *Prinz Eugen,* which had been mistaken for *Bismarck.* Then all the other big ships started firing. The *Prince of Wales*'s first salvo fell 1,000 yards beyond *Bismarck.*

The *Bismarck*'s first salvo was fired at the *Hood,* which

was in the lead. Its improved Seetakt 90-cm radar provided the correct range but the shells fell ahead of *Hood* and she steamed into the spray they made. The second salvo from *Prinz Eugen* scored a direct hit on *Hood*. A shell burst on the upper deck, igniting anti-aircraft ammunition stored there in ready-use lockers. The midship section of *Hood* was soon enveloped in flames and giving off dense smoke. *Bismarck*'s third salvo was the high-trajectory fire to which British battleships were so vulnerable. Still today experts disagree on whether an armour-piercing shell penetrated the *Hood*'s thin deck armour to explode in an aft magazine or whether this 42,100-ton battleship was blown in two as a result of fires spreading to a magazine from the earlier hit. The explosion was horrendous. After separated bows and stern had risen high from the water, *Hood* disappeared leaving only a smoky haze over the disturbed water. An officer on a destroyer which went to pick up *Hood*'s survivors wrote:

> But where were the boats, the rafts, the floats? . . . And the men, where were the men? . . . far over to starboard we saw three men—two of them swimming, one on a raft. But on the chilling waters around them was no other sign of life.[3]

Of the crew of 1,419 men, only one midshipman and two ratings survived. The midshipman's survival was especially miraculous. He was in a spotting top, 140 feet above the water. He told his rescuers that 'he didn't know what the hell was happening, save that the compartment was filled mysteriously with water'.

Korvettenkapitän Jaspers, *Prinz Eugen*'s gunnery officer, who was watching the *Hood* said: 'The aft magazine blew up, shooting into the air a molten mass the colour of red lead, which then fell back lazily into the sea—it was one of the rear gun turrets . . . And in the midst of this raging inferno, a yellow tongue of flame shot out just once more: the forward turrets of *Hood* had fired one last salvo'.

Now the *Prince of Wales* became the target for both German ships. The compass platform was hit by a 15-inch shell. It didn't explode but fragments of the binnacle killed or wounded everyone there but the captain and the yeoman of signals. The difficulty of making shells that would penetrate thick steel and then explode was demonstrated now as six more German shells struck home, all of them detonating only partially or not at all. Undeterred, *Prince of Wales* continued on course until it had closed to 14,600 yards. Six salvoes were loosed at *Bismarck* before one of the shells found its mark, flooding the forecastle, rupturing one of the fuel tanks and disconnecting tanks forward of it, so that 1,000 tons of fuel were cut off. Two other shells had hit *Bismarck*: one damaged a dynamo, the other was a dud that glanced off the deck causing only slight damage.

Either ship might have gone on and destroyed its opponent but both had had enough. *Prince of Wales* was badly damaged as well as having trouble with the gun turrets. She turned away under a smoke screen.

In London, as in Berlin, the news that the action had been broken off was not welcomed. Churchill saw the prospect of a rampaging *Bismarck* as a direct challenge to Britain's traditional role, and feared that it would be 'trumpeted round the world to our great detriment and discomfort'. The disengagement was a 'bitter disappointment and grief to me'. Hitler felt the same way and said that *Bismarck* should have immediately dealt with the *Prince of Wales* too, and not run away.

Out in the cold grey ocean, *Prince of Wales* and *Norfolk* were joined by the carrier *Victorious*. So grave was the emergency that the carrier had been detached from escorting Troop Convoy WS 8B to the Middle East. These warships trailed the two Germans using the *Suffolk*'s radar to keep in contact, but again the operators found it difficult to keep radar contact at extreme range. That night the pursuers decided to use the carrier's aircraft in an attempt to slow the *Bismarck*.

With the equipment available at that time, carrier take-offs and landings at night were sometimes permitted in perfect weather. Now the carrier was pitching and rolling in a rising gale and rainstorms from low scudding clouds made visibility zero. The air crews were fresh from training school; some had never made a carrier take-off or landing before. (The desperate shortage of navy pilots had sent these aircrews to *Victorious* to be instructed while the carrier was on convoy duty.) It was 2200 hours (Double Summer Time), and light was changing and deceptive. Dutifully *Victorious* flew off a striking force of Swordfish torpedo-carrying biplanes and Fulmar fighters.

One of the Swordfish was equipped with an ASV MkII radar and its operator 'saw' a ship through cloud. But when the plane descended it was identified as a US coast guard cutter on Atlantic weather patrol. Now that the planes were below the cloud, they spotted *Bismarck* about six miles away, but the element of surprise was lost. It was through heavy gunfire—*Bismarck* had 84 anti-aircraft guns—that they made the slow, low, straight and steady approach that is required for torpedo dropping.

Despite the way in which the aircraft came in from different angles, *Bismarck* was able to swerve violently and avoid seven torpedoes. The eighth one hit the starboard side, near the bridge. This hit shifted one of the heavy side-belt armour plates but its backing of thick teak wood absorbed much of the armour's displacement. The *Bismarck* reported to Naval Group Command West that the torpedo had done no more than 'scratched the paintwork'. It had achieved more than that, but its immediate effect upon *Bismarck*'s performance was negligible.

To find a carrier at night over the ocean is a daunting task, and the *Victorious*'s homing beacon was not working. Upon hearing the planes returning the carrier's captain ordered searchlights on to help them, but they were swiftly doused on the repeated order of the vice-admiral. Despite the admiral's exaggerated caution, and with the help of the flight leader's ASV radar, the 'Stringbags' found their home ship again and landed in the dark. Not all the Fulmar aircraft were so lucky. It was midnight. The crews had had an eventful Saturday night out and a memorable introduction to carrier flying.

Bismarck was not slowed. When the Swordfish aircraft attacked, it had already parted company with *Prinz Eugen.* Now it turned southwest on a direct route for the Bay of Biscay and the French ports. The *Suffolk,* unready for such a move, lost both German ships on the radar, and when daylight came, more flights from the *Victorious* failed to discover any sign of the enemy. Low on fuel, the force—*Prince of Wales, Victorious* and *Suffolk*—turned west, still failed to find *Bismarck,* and soon headed for various ports to refuel.

There was no rejoicing aboard *Bismarck.* It was Sunday 25 May 1941 and the 52nd birthday of Admiral Lütjens. He addressed the ship's company, delivering a melancholy message of doing and dying. Gerhard Junack, one of the *Bismarck's* engineer officers said: 'The admiral wished with these words to rid the crew of their over-exuberance and bring them into a more realistic frame of mind; but in fact he overdid it, and there was a feeling of depression among the crew which spread through all ranks from the highest to the lowest . . . The crew began to brood and neglected their duties'.

Examples of this neglect now played a vital part in the battle. Because *Bismarck's* electronics specialists were still picking up radar impulses from *Suffolk* they didn't guess that *Suffolk's* radar could not 'see' *Bismarck's* pulses. *Bismarck's* decrypt specialists were neglectful too. They were intercepting *Suffolk's* regular radio transmissions, and failed to notice that the shadower was no longer sending position reports. And so it was that Admiral Lütjens didn't know that he had given the slip to his pursuers. He betrayed his position by sending a very long signal to the German Naval Command Group West (Paris). They replied telling him that the British cruisers had lost contact with him six and a half hours before.

Lütjens' long message gave the Royal Navy a chance to fix *Bismarck's* position on the map, but owing to confusion and misunderstandings at the Admiralty—compounded by

the fact that the flagship navigator used the wrong charts—
the big ship was not found. In the ensuing muddle, signals
from other ships were intercepted and plotted and declared
to be *Bismarck*. The German navy's radio traffic looked
identical as regards letter-grouping, spacing, serial numbers
and so on. At 1320 on 25 May, when the search was at its
most frantic, a signal from a U-boat was intercepted. The
Admiralty intelligence officers decided that this was from
the *Bismarck* pretending to be a U-boat, and using the
U-boat radio signals and transmitting frequency.

The bungling began to be sorted out when these transmissions were compared with oscilloscope photos of the radio wave of *Bismarck*'s transmitter (taken when it passed
Denmark on the outward leg). By that time *Bismarck*'s approximate position had been estimated by someone in signals intelligence who noticed the flurry of German naval
signals was no longer coming from Wilhelmshaven; it was
coming from Paris. This suggested that *Bismarck* could probably be found somewhere along the line from its last known
position to one of the French ports.

Still it was only guesswork; the *Bismarck* might have escaped but for a curious misfortune. The only Enigma signals
that the British could read regularly and quickly were those
of the Luftwaffe.

In Athens in connection with the Crete invasion, the
Luftwaffe's chief of staff, Hans Jeschonnek, worried about
his youngest son who was in the crew of the *Bismarck*. Anxiously he called his staff in Berlin to ask what was happening
to the ship. His staff in the Berlin Air Ministry found out
and transmitted a radio signal (using Luftwaffe Enigma),
telling him that his son's ship was heading for the west coast
of France. It was a parent's anxiety that provided London
with the information that settled the fate of the *Bismarck*.

An RAF flying boat crew of 209 Squadron, Lough Erne,
Northern Ireland, and the flyers on the aircraft-carrier *Ark
Royal* were briefed on the supposition that *Bismarck* was
somewhere on a line drawn from there to Brest. It seems
that no one at the Admiralty was aware that the only French

port with a dry dock large enough to hold the *Bismarck* was St Nazaire.

It was 31 hours later, on 26 May, that a Catalina flying boat using ASV Mk II radar found *Bismarck*. About 45 minutes later a Swordfish from the aircraft-carrier *Ark Royal* flew to the spot and confirmed the sighting. HMS *Sheffield*, equipped with an old Type 79 radar designed for air-warning, used it to make contact with the *Bismarck*, and trailed along waiting for *Ark Royal* and the battleship *Renown*.

With the end of the flight deck pitching 60 feet, and a wind over the deck recorder wavering between 45 and 55 knots, the deck crews readied the aircraft aboard *Ark Royal*. No one there had ever tried to fly-off planes in this sort of weather but there was no alternative. One Swordfish pilot gives us this account:

Ranging the Swordfish that morning called for the strength of Hercules and the patience of Job. Time and time again, as the flight deck tilted at fantastic angles, a plane would slide bodily towards the catwalks, dragging with it forty to fifty ratings who were struggling to man-handle it aft. But somehow by 8.30 am ten planes were ranged and ready to fly off on a broad fronted search to locate *Bismarck*. At 8.35 am the carrier reduced speed and swung into the wind. [Deck officer] Traill choosing his moment carefully, dropped his flag, and aboard both *Ark Royal* and *Renown* ship's companies held their breath as the leading plane gathered way. Would she make it?

As the flight deck tilted down, the take-off degenerated into a frantic, slithering glissade. It looked for one terrible moment as though the aircraft were plunging straight into the maw of an approaching wave. But Traill had timed his signal well. At the last second the deck swung up and the plane was flung off through the spume of a sixty-foot wave as it cascaded over the carrier's bow. And the almost unbelievable thing was this. The miracle was repeated not once, but nine times, until the whole of the searching force was airborne.[4]

The weather was foul, but the Swordfish made good radar contact from above cloud using ASV Mk II radar and launched a low-level attack that failed completely. The torpedoes were set to activate their magnetic pistols but most of them exploded as they hit the water; others dived and disappeared. This was just as well, for the ship they attacked was HMS *Sheffield*! 'Sorry about the kippers', the attackers signalled the angry men aboard *Sheffield* as they flew back to their carrier. Three of the aircraft crashed on to the pitching deck.

The pilots of the 15-plane second strike were prudently ordered to locate HMS *Sheffield* first and then go to attack the *Bismarck*. And this strike force did not try the magnetic pistols again; its torpedoes were set to 'contact' and they would run at ten feet. It was old technology but more reliable. Three planes attacked just as *Bismarck* went into an evasive turn. One torpedo 'ripped a large hole in the stern structure beneath the steering room gear'. This probably weakened a weld aft of the transverse armoured bulkhead at Frame 10.[5] The immediate effect was damage to the starboard propellers and steering gear and a jammed rudder.

It was dark, late and overcast as the planes returned. All the Swordfish got back safely, although most of them had been damaged by gunfire and many were wrecked on landing. One plane had been hit 175 times. The aircrews claimed no strikes with the torpedoes. The failure of the airstrike was received with mixed feelings. Admiral Tovey in command had never had much faith in the torpedo planes, and the captain of nearby HMS *Rodney* personally took the microphone to tell his crew, over the ship's loudspeakers, that the planes had failed.

But the strike had not failed. The first indication of this was a surprising signal from *Sheffield* that said that *Bismarck* was doing a U-turn and reversing course. Admiral Tovey refused to believe the report and added a sarcastic remark about the *Sheffield*'s seamanship. But the men aboard *Sheffield* were right and *Bismarck* was in a desperate situation. With steering jammed, it could only go round in gigantic circles. An attempt to cut the rudder away with underwater equipment proved impossible in the heavy swell. A suggestion that explosives should be used was rejected because it would inevitably damage the finely balanced propellers.

Now, in his final hours, Admiral Lütjens signalled to Germany 'ship unmanoeuvrable' and to Hitler 'We shall fight to the end trusting in you, mein Führer'. During the night, four destroyers, one of them Polish, attacked *Bismarck* with torpedoes. The German gunnery radar demonstrated its effectiveness in the hours of darkness, and none of the torpedoes scored a hit. No progress was made in mending the ship's rudders.

Afterwards there were those who thought that the melancholy Lütjens had some sort of death wish. At the start of the voyage he had chosen to go through the Kattegat (between Sweden and Denmark) where the gigantic battleship was sure to be noticed by the Swedes, instead of through the Kiel Canal; then, against the advice of his staff, he had chosen the Denmark Strait where pack-ice and a minefield left him only a narrow and predictable course; and after that he had failed to hammer the *Prince of Wales* and escape. When safe at last, he sent a radio message that endangered him. The survivors also remembered that, before leaving Norway, Lütjens had declined the chance to have the fuel tanks topped up.

On *Bismarck*'s long last night afloat it was decided to catapult the three undamaged Arado Ar 196 aircraft and fly them to France with the ship's log and other valuables. Men were invited to send mail home, and many last letters were written. Lütjens asked Berlin if his gunnery officer could be awarded the Knight's Cross for his successful sinking of HMS *Hood* and the ceremony took place at 4 am. When daylight came, and the first Arado plane was loaded with mail, it was discovered that none of the planes could be launched because the catapult had been damaged beyond

The pursuit and sinking of the *Bismarck*

DENMARK STRAIT

MINEFIELDS

ICELAND

HVALFJORD

PACK ICE LIMIT (MAY)

HOOD SUNK 0600

CONVOY HX 24TH.

VICTORIOUS CS2

KGV 25TH.

AIRSTRIKE FROM VICTORIOUS 0001/25TH.

BISMARCK ESCAPES

24TH. RODNEY

CONVOY WS8 B 4TH.DF
24TH.

BISMARCK 26TH.

BISMARCK SIGHTED BY CATALINA 1030/26TH.

27TH.

PRINZ EUGEN (TO BREST 1 JUNE)

CONVOY WS8B 26TH.

BISMARCK SUNK 1040 27TH.

SHEFFIELD RENOWN ARK ROYAL.

U-BOAT SCREEN

NARVIK

OCCUPIED NORWAY

BISMARCK AND
PRINZ EUGEN

BISMARCK'S
DESTROYERS
TO TRONDHEIM

TRONDHEIM

GERMAN

FAEROE Is.

WOLLIN
(TANKER)

SHETLAND Is.

BERGEN

ORKNEY Is.

SCAPA FLOW

MARSTRAND

SKAGERRAK

BRITISH ISLES

HAMBURG

GDYNIA
BISMARCK AND
PRINZ EUGEN
SAILED 21 30
18 MAY

GERMAN   AND

GERMAN OCCUPIED EUROPE

BREST

LORIENT

ST NAZAIRE

U. BOAT BASES

LA ROCHELLE

BRITISH
SUBMARINE
PATROL 25/27TH

repair. That morning, at 7 o'clock, a doleful radio message from Lütjens asked for a U-boat to collect the log-book but the vessel (*U-556*) assigned to this task was submerged and didn't get the order until 10 o'clock, by which time the battleships *Rodney* and *King George V* (sister ship of *Prince of Wales*) were on the scene. One of the first shells fired by the British destroyed the admiral's bridge and killed Lütjens. Shelling *Bismarck* at point-blank range, *Rodney* fired broadsides from her nine 16-inch guns, instead of the more usual four- or five-gun salvoes. This failed to sink *Bismarck*, yet sheared so many of *Rodney*'s rivets, and damaged the foretower so badly, that the vessel had to go to the Boston navy yard for repairs.[6]

At 9.25 am, planes were launched from *Ark Royal* in order to sink *Bismarck* with torpedoes, but when they flew over their target the men in the RN battleships would not pause in their firing, making a low run-in impossible. The airmen sent a signal asking Admiral Tovey to cease fire while they attacked. The only response to this was for *King George V* to fire its anti-aircraft guns at the planes.[7] It would seem that the battleship admirals were determined that *Bismarck* would not be sunk by airmen, even naval airmen.

More ships gathered and more torpedoes were fired at *Bismarck* but she did not sink. At 10.44 a signal from the C-in-C desperately commanded: 'Any ships with torpedoes are to use them on *Bismarck*'. Finally the Germans aboard decided to finish the job themselves. They exploded charges and all became 'a blazing inferno for the bright glow of internal fires could be seen shining through numerous shell and splinter holes in her sides'. Only then did *Bismarck* die. 'As it turned keel up', said a proud German survivor who was in the water, 'we could see that its hull had not been damaged by torpedoes'. The Germans never lowered their colours. At 11.07 HMS *Dorsetshire* made the signal: 'I torpedoed *Bismarck* both sides before she sank. She had ceased firing but her colours were still flying'. The Swordfish aircraft, which had not been permitted to participate in *Bis-*

marck's end, now had to jettison their torpedoes, as it was too dangerous to land carrying them.

Despite the concentration of so many British warships, the *U-74* was determined to get to the scene in order to assist *Bismarck,* or take its log-book back to Germany. But the submarine arrived too late. *Bismarck* had sunk and the water was covered in its fuel oil, its debris and its men. The U-boat periscope was spotted by a lookout on one of the RN ships during the time it had stopped to pick up survivors. Immediately the warning was given, the British ships moved off leaving many Germans to drown. The *U-74* rescued three men, and the RN saved 107. Another German ship, *Sachsenwald,* retrieved two more of the crew. Of a complement of about 2,400 men, all the others perished.

At 1.22 pm German signallers at Naval Group Command West told *Bismarck:* 'Reuters reports *Bismarck* sunk. Report situation immediately'. But by this time *Bismarck* was resting upright on the sea bed 15,317 feet below water.

Prinz Eugen reached Brest safely on 1 June. *Bismarck*'s fate convinced the German navy—and Hitler, who needed far less convincing—that the Atlantic was fast becoming an Anglo-American lake in which submarines might survive but surface raiders could not. In future all German shipbuilding facilities were to give priority to enlarging and repairing the U-boat fleet.

The Royal Navy, ably supported by Britain's Ministry of Information, pronounced the *Bismarck* episode a triumph. Others were not so sure. Churchill thought the Royal Navy had shown a lack of offensive spirit. He persuaded the first sea lord and chief of naval staff that the admiral in HMS *Norfolk,* as well as the captain of *Prince of Wales,* should be court-martialled for failing to engage *Bismarck* during the run south. The C-in-C Home Fleet blocked this[8] and Churchill must have soon realized how damaging such proceedings would be for the British cause.

Hitler became 'melancholy beyond words' at the loss of *Bismarck.* He was furious that the naval staff had exposed the mightiest warship in the world to such dangers. He had expressed doubts from the beginning and now he was proved right. The Führer complained of 'red tape and wooden-headedness' in the navy and said that the commanders wouldn't tolerate any man with a mind of his own. From that day onwards, Admiral Raeder's ideas were treated with suspicion: eventually command of the navy would be given to Dönitz, whose ideas were more in line with Hitler's.

The 'hunting of the *Bismarck*' certainly provided lessons for those who would learn them. The battleship admirals saw it as proof of the value of the big ship, and the way in which more big ships had to hunt for them. Such people stubbornly persisted with the story that *Bismarck* had been sunk solely by gunfire and denied that the Germans might have opened the sea-cocks. They were wrong: in 1989 the wreck was inspected and the German version of her sinking confirmed.[9]

Hindsight shows that the real lesson was the importance of aircraft. A land-based Catalina had discovered the *Bismarck*; a torpedo-carrying Swordfish had crippled it and thus decided its fate. History provides no evidence that those in authority at the time were converted to this line of thought. The US navy continued to line up the big ships of its Pacific fleet in 'battleship row' Pearl Harbor until the bombers smashed them. Before the year was over the *Prince of Wales,* which had exchanged salvoes with *Bismarck,* would be sent to the bottom by Japanese aircraft. Those tempted by the 'what if?' game asked what might have happened to the two German ships had *Prinz Eugen* been an aircraft-carrier.

On 22 June 1941 Germany invaded Russia, and Churchill immediately declared Britain to be Stalin's ally. Sorely needed Hurricane fighters and other war supplies were loaded and the first North Cape convoy departed for Murmansk in northern Russia in August. These tanks and guns and aircraft were all desperately needed elsewhere, and they would certainly make little difference to the outcome of Barbarossa, the most colossal clash of armed might in the world's history. Perhaps it was a worthwhile gesture in propaganda terms, although Stalin made sure that his people heard little about it. As for the drain upon shipping that would come from sailing heavily escorted convoys so close to German bases in Norway, and mostly in cruel weather, this prospect must have filled the Royal Navy with gloom. It was a time when every ship was badly needed in the Atlantic.

AMERICA LOSES HER NEUTRALITY

America's neutrality had been defined by Congress and decreed in the Neutrality Act of 1937, but soon after Britain's war began, the Act was modified to permit belligerent powers to buy war materials if they shipped them themselves: so-called 'cash and carry'. This of course benefited Britain and

France—whose navies dominated the North Atlantic—while providing no benefit to Germany.

In July 1940—as France collapsed—Roosevelt signed an act to provide $4 billion to build for America a two-ocean navy. It was an amazing sum of money by any standards. Yet there were many Americans wondering how soon the French fleet, and the British fleet too, would be taken over by the Germans. Meanwhile, in response to an urgent request from Churchill, Roosevelt exchanged 50 old United States destroyers for 99-year leases on naval bases in Newfoundland, British Guiana, Bermuda and islands in the West Indies. British sailors were hurried to Halifax and picked up the first of these 'four-stackers' on 6 September 1940. This was essentially a political action; a signal to friends and enemies that Roosevelt, if re-elected in November, would move closer to an endangered Britain. In the latter part of the year, the US navy began to escort its own shipping on 'threatened transatlantic routes'.

Then in December 1940 something happened that would influence the outcome of the Battle of the Atlantic far more than the 99-year leases on naval bases. The American steel magnate Henry Kaiser launched the first 'Liberty Ship'. Its welded hull showed the way to unprecedented production speeds. Welded ships were subject to all sorts of troubles but welded steel—for ships and tanks—was none the less a leap forward in technology. Such welding was strenuously resisted in British yards. It was not until 1943 that the Admiralty supported it. Even then the strikes of angry riveters, confronting timid management, ensured that the speed of change was slower than need be.

By January 1941, with the presidential election won, Roosevelt authorized his military leaders to have secret talks with their British counterparts. Soon it was decided that, should America ever go to war against both Germany and Japan, the conquest of Germany would take precedence. It was not a decision easily arrived at, and for some American military commanders it remained a contentious issue for years to come.

The ever-present threat of a successful German occupation of England, which would have deprived America of a base for operations in Europe, made the 'Germany First' policy logical. Looking back now, it seems that arguments to reverse this policy were bluffs used by American military commanders to get more resources for the Pacific war, and also by American politicians as a threat that kept Churchill under control. The policy, all the same, was never seriously challenged.

In April the United States signed an agreement that gave them the right to build and maintain military installations in Greenland, and in this same month the Americans extended their 'ocean security zone' to longitude 26 degrees west, which is about halfway to England. An agreement with the Icelandic government to install and use military bases there followed in July. It was a vitally important development, for Iceland provided a vital base from which ships and aircraft could protect the Atlantic convoys. Without it there would have always been a mid-Atlantic gap in which the U-boats could operate at will.

Roosevelt and Churchill met in a warship off Newfoundland in August 1941 and pledged themselves to the common goal of destroying Nazi tyranny. It was no empty boast. In a decision no less than breathtaking, America extended $1 billion of credit to a USSR that most observers believed to be near total defeat.

Aboard *Prince of Wales,* returning home from his meeting with the president, Churchill was provided with a chance to see the merchant service at work. On the prime minister's instructions, the battleship went right through a convoy, the escorts taking the outer lanes. The convoy was making a steady 8 knots; the warships doing 22. From the signal halliards *Prince of Wales* flew 'Good luck—Churchill' in international code.

Those seventy-two ships went mad. Quickly every ship was flying the 'V' flag; some tried a dot-dot-dot-dash salute on their sirens. In the nearest ships men could be seen waving, laughing and—we guessed though we could not hear—cheering. On the bridge the Prime Minister was waving back to them, as was every man on our own decks, cheering with them, two fingers on his right hand making the famous V-sign.

Soon we were through them and well ahead, when to everyone's surprise we did an eight-point turn, and shortly after another. Mr Churchill wanted an encore.[10]

The US navy entered a shooting war in September 1941 when *U-652* was attacked by depth charges and fired two torpedoes at a nearby destroyer. Both missed. The U-boat captain had made two errors: the destroyer was the US navy's *Greer* (a First World War four-funnel profile making it look like those sent to the Royal Navy); and the depth charges had come from an RAF plane. *Greer* retaliated with a pattern of depth charges but did only minor damage to the German boat which crept away. Roosevelt was angry about the 'unprovoked attack' and said that U-boats were the rattlesnakes of the Atlantic. The press echoed his verdict, and reported that the US navy had been ordered to 'shoot on sight' in future. It was a phrase which Roosevelt himself was happy to repeat.[11]

The next month the American destroyer USS *Kearney* was damaged in a convoy battle and eleven American sailors died. At the end of October the American destroyer *Reuben James*—convoying merchant ships between the States and Iceland—was sunk by a U-boat and only 44 of its 120 men were rescued from the ocean. By this time the US navy was fully integrated into the Atlantic battle, to the extent that American orders often went out to Allied warships in the two-thirds of the Atlantic Ocean that was now 'American'.

It was in the final weeks of December 1941 that the Atlantic battle reached a new and ferocious pitch. Dönitz coordinated his U-boats and Condors with skill. The route from Gibraltar to Britain had become especially hazardous. To escort a 32-ship convoy the Royal Navy had sixteen warships, and one of them was a new sort of vessel: the escort carrier.

FIGURE 11:
The US long-range Liberator, used for convoy escort duties.

Cheap and hastily prepared, HMS *Audacity* was converted from an ex-German prize, the *Hannover*.

Commanding this escort group there was one of those rare breeds, an RN officer who had specialized in antisubmarine warfare in the prewar years. Commander F.J. 'Johnny' Walker RN had had enough differences of opinion with authority to have damaged his career. Passed over for captain he had spent the first two years of war in 'uninspiring shore appointments'. Now he was about to become the most famous and most successful group commander of the entire Atlantic campaign. His desperate battle with the U-boats lasted six days and nights. Two of the convoy were lost, and so was the escort carrier, but four U-boats were sunk and a Condor shot down. It was a setback for Dönitz and proof that cheap little aircraft-carriers could give convoys air protection far away from land. And on the morning of 22 December 1941, the sixth day of the fight, the weary sailors looked up and saw another new and welcome sight. One of the very long-range Liberators had come 800 miles to perform escort duties. It circled the convoy and dropped depth charges upon some U-boats trailing behind. Dönitz called off his submarines. Air power had begun to turn the tide of the battle.

THE SHIPS KEPT COMING

The Atlantic campaign was the longest and most arduous battle of the war, much of it fought in sub-arctic conditions, in gales and heavy seas. When considering the moral questions arising from the RAF 'terror bombing' of cities, consider too the civilians who manned the merchant ships. Casualties of the air raids upon cities usually had immediate succour; the merchant seamen, and ship's passengers too, men, women and children, were mutilated, crippled and burned. There was no warning save the crash of a torpedo tearing the hull open. Few men from the engine room got as far as the boat deck. The attacks usually came at night and, on the northerly routes the convoys favoured, it was seldom anything but very cold. Many of the merchantmen's crews were not young. Survivors, many of them bleeding or half-drowned, were abandoned to drift in open boats upon the storm-racked ocean where they went mad or perhaps died slowly and agonizingly of thirst or exposure.

Almost all Britain's oil and petroleum supplies came across the Atlantic by ship.[12] So did about half its food, including most of its meat, cheese, butter and wheat, as well as steel and timber, wool, cotton, zinc, lead and nitrates. British farmers could not have produced home-grown crops without imported fertilizers: neither could farmers in neutral Ireland have survived. 'Ships carried cargoes they were never built for, in seas they were never meant to sail', said one official publication. During the war I remember that in London scarcely a day passed without someone in my hearing mentioning our debt to the merchant service. Anyone leaving a particle of food uneaten on a plate was risking a reprimand from any waiter or passer-by who saw it. No heroes of the war—not even the fighter pilots—excelled in valour and dogged determination more than the men of the merchant service and their naval escorts. The public knew it. One merchant navy officer said:

> armed with free railway ticket issued by 'Shipwrecked Mariners Society' to my home in Colchester, Essex, I proceeded on leave. My journey across London via the Underground from Euston to Liverpool Street Station clad in a salt-stained (not to mention vomit!) uniform and still jealously clutching my orange-coloured life-jacket was more of an ordeal than the whole of the western ocean with the masses of people sheltering from the nightly blitz all wanting to crowd around me to slap my back or shake my hand.[13]

The Battle of the Atlantic continued until Germany surrendered. When that happened, U-boats were ordered to surface, hoist black flags, report position and proceed by fixed routes to designated ports and anchorages. I remember spotting them, one after another, from a Fleet Air Arm plane as they made that final journey up the Channel. It was a heartening sight.

Churchill, in a letter to Roosevelt dated 8 December 1940, declared that the decision for 1941 lay upon the seas. He went on to detail the threat to Britain's lifelines, and his concern was real. 'PM very gloomy on shipping situation', Sir Alexander Cadogan of the Foreign Office wrote after a meeting of the war cabinet in February 1941. A few days later, on 1 March, the Australian prime minister noted that Churchill called shipping losses the supreme menace of the war. To Mackenzie King, Churchill telegraphed on 24 March: 'The issue of the war will clearly depend on our being able to maintain the traffic across the Atlantic'. Churchill was so concerned that he formed a special Battle of the Atlantic Committee which discussed every aspect of shipping, escorts, imports, repairs and so on. As part of this allotment of resources, 17 squadrons from Bomber Command were assigned to Coastal Command. These heavy aircraft could range out into the ocean where the U-boats were operating so freely. Howls of protest and pain came from Chief of Air Staff Sir Charles Portal and his deputy, Air Vice-Marshal Arthur Harris, who later became known as 'Bomber' Harris.

Harris insisted that patrolling the sea lanes with bombers was a complete waste of time and effort. Citing the records of the Armstrong Whitley bombers used by 502 Squadron over a six-month period, he pointed out that on 144 sorties only six submarines had been spotted: four were attacked and one, perhaps two, sunk. Harris could not resist the observation that this meant 250 flying hours per sighting. In his note to his boss Portal, he scoffed at the Admiralty and the ineffectiveness thus proved. Portal was able to prevent any of the new long-range four-engine Halifax bombers going to Coastal Command. By July 1941 Churchill had been persuaded to switch priority back to the build-up of Bomber Command. Harris and Portal refused to admit the vital difference their planes could have made to closing the 'gap'. They would not see that success in the vital battle for the sea lanes was measured by the number of ships that arrived safely, not by U-boat sinkings.

All the Royal Navy's requests for long-range aircraft to aid in the Atlantic battle were dismissed contemptuously by the RAF. (Three things you should never take on a yacht: a wheelbarrow, an umbrella and an RN officer, advised 'Bomber' Harris in one of his less caustic remarks about the senior service.) Even in 1941, when the April total of lost shipping tonnage went to almost 700,000 and Britain's rations were reduced—'the moment when Great Britain came nearest to losing the war', said A.J.P. Taylor[14]—the RAF were vehemently resisting the transfer of any aircraft away from their ineffective bombing campaign.[15]

The battle of the Atlantic was never won in the sense that land battles were. Germany could win the war by cutting the sea traffic to Britain but Britain could not win by conquering the U-boat menace. In fact the submarine was never conquered, which is why the victors all built submarine fleets after the war. Far from being the weapon of minor naval powers, the nuclear submarine became the modern capital ship.

The German navy failed to win the Battle of the Atlantic despite the willingness that Dönitz showed to flout international treaty. In theory it should have worked. Obsessed by the desire to starve Britain, he directed his forces to sink the merchantmen and rewarded his captains according to tonnage sunk. During the entire war his U-boats sank only 34 destroyers and 37 other escort vessels. Strategically it was right and his tactics were sound, but the shipbuilders defeated this effort.[16] And Hitler's Third Reich never put its full strength behind the submarine campaign. Hitler was a soldier and he was determined upon a land victory over the Bolsheviks he detested. Unlike his predecessors, a naval victory over Britain was not something of which he dreamed. Partly for this reason the German navy did not improve their submarines and torpedoes in the fundamental ways that the army's tanks and guns were endlessly modified. Submarine technology did change of course, but the German U-boat fleet did not improve well enough or fast enough. Most of the changes were defensive. By the end of the war German submariners were neither expert nor determined.

Their opponents, on the other hand, learned quickly, and invented tactics and weapons that countered the U-boats, most of which were little different to those in service in 1939. High-frequency direction-finding sets were made small enough to go into ships, and these gave a more exact position for immediate tactical response. Radar improved and it was used more skilfully from ships and from aircraft. Land-based aircraft flew from Newfoundland, Iceland and Britain to provide better and more effective air cover. Escort carriers—their decks built upon merchant ship hulls—brought aircraft to eliminate any last 'gaps' in the ocean.

Technical developments contributed to the Allied success but (senior officers on both sides say) the German U-boat arm liked to declare that Enigma intercepts, radar or HF/DF decided the war because these allowed them an excuse for losing. For many postwar years the British over-emphasized the role that HF/DF had played. This was a way of keeping their Enigma work secret. Once the Enigma secret was out, the contribution of Bletchley Park was in turn exaggerated.

In the final year of war, the U-boat arm became worn out and demoralized. These men, more than any other Germans, were provided with evidence that Germany could never win. On every operational mission they encountered bigger and better convoys of new ships stacked high with shiny new tanks and planes. They faced tired but highly motivated and ever more expert Allied seamen who knew they were winning. The German sailors, at sea for many weeks, became concerned about what was happening to their friends and families in the cities under Allied air attack by night, and later by day too. As the Russians started their remorseless advance the U-boat men had new worries about what was happening to their families in cities overrun by the vengeful Red Army.

It was German policy to send conscripts (draftees) into the submarines. This was a mistake. The policy in most other navies was to use only tested volunteers in this specialized warfare. And while RN training improved and became more practical as time went on, the U-boat training schools in the Baltic remained out of touch with the latest anti-submarine techniques, and even the sea conditions of the Atlantic. Shortages of men caused U-boat trainees to be posted to operational duties even when instructors had doubts about their ability. Half-trained men made less expert and less resolute adversaries; they also were crippled and killed by the remorseless ocean. Some fell down companionways, others lost their fingers in machinery and still more were swept overboard and never seen again. Towards the end U-boat crews were no longer singing old songs like '*Denn wir fahren gegen Engeland*' but cynical ditties about the failings of the mechanisms they operated and about the radar that hunted them. A German historian acknowledges: 'The men knew that they were beaten and that their end was inevitable . . .'[17]

0   100   200 feet

H M S DREADNAUGHT (battleship)

H M S SHEFFIELD (cruiser)

H M S HOOD (battle-cruiser)

BISMARCK (battleship)

U BOAT VII C

SCHARNHORST (battle-cruiser)

H M S DUKE OF YORK (battleship)

'HUNT' class (escort)

H M S RODNEY (battleship)

PRINZ EUGEN (heavy cruiser)

ADMIRAL GRAF SPEE
(pocket-battleship)

LIBERTY SHIP

'FLOWER' class Corvette

U S S BOGUE (escort carrier)

FIGURE 12:
Comparative ship sizes

Yet the U-boat as a weapon was certainly not defeated. The *schnorchel* (anglicized as snorkel) enabled the diesel engines to breathe air while the submarine remained just below the surface. Postwar trials showed that 94 per cent of U-boats using the snorkel went undetected by airborne radar. The German Type XXI U-boats could go 300 miles on electric motors while remaining totally submerged. Added to this there were some remarkable target-seeking torpedoes: ones that homed on engine noise and others that turned and (programmed for the forward speed of the target) made run after run until they hit something or exhausted their propellant. But such devices were gimmicks rather than innovations.

The Allied sea lanes were kept open because in the long run there were enough ships built, and enough brave men to man them. Britain's merchant service had gone through bad interwar years but during the war seamen were formed into a 'pool' by means of the 'Essential Work Order' of May 1941. This brought permanent engagement and regular pay. Crew accommodation in many ships was squalid, dirty, unhealthy and cramped, and would have horrified any factory-inspector. Yet during the war Britain's Shipping Federation was receiving a hundred letters a day from boys (16 was the minimum recruiting age) asking for a job afloat.

When war began Britain's merchant service included 45,000 men from the Indian sub-continent (including Pakistan) and over 6,000 Chinese, as well as many Arabs. When it ended, the Official History says, 37,651 men had died as a direct result of enemy action, and the true total, including deaths indirectly due to war, was 50,525.

The U-boat war was no doubt difficult and dangerous, and the German navy lost 27,491 men out of approximately 55,000.[18] Perhaps the most important figure—and the most surprising—is that less than 50 per cent of all U-boats built got within torpedo range of a convoy. Of the 870 U-boats that left port on operational trips, 550 of them sank nothing.

The sea has always attracted men from far and wide. On the escorts there were Dutchmen, Free French, Poles, Norwegians, Americans and many Canadians. The Atlantic convoys were not the worst perils the sailors faced: those convoys to Murmansk saw ships labouring under tons of ice and attacked constantly from German bases in Norway. Convoys through the Mediterranean to Malta were equally hazardous.

Ultimately it was the vast resources of the United States of America which decided the outcome. Using the techniques of mass-production, American shipyards proved able to build a freighter in five days! Despite the war in the Pacific, the US spared carriers, escorts and aircraft to supplement British and ever-growing Canadian naval forces in the Atlantic. Soon there would be US armies to be supplied in Europe and North Africa. During a war of unprecedented supply lines and unprecedented amphibious operations, a war in which every front demanded more and more seagoing vessels, the ships kept coming.

Part Two

HITLER CONQUERS
EUROPE

6 GERMANY: UNRECOGNIZED POWER

> I have to report that M. Blériot, with his mono-
> plane, crossed the Channel from Calais this morn-
> ing. I issued to him a Quarantine Certificate,
> thereby treating it as a yacht and the aviator as
> Master and owner.
>
> THE COLLECTOR OF CUSTOMS AT DOVER,
> 25 JULY 1909[1]

To understand why an improvised and inadequate mixture of British military formations were sent to war in
1939 it is necessary to remember that her army had always
been quite different in tradition, formation and function to
any of the continental armies.

In the late sixteenth and seventeenth centuries, standing
armies were established on the Continent, not so much in
response to foreign wars as to civil strife and rebellions.
From that time onwards continental rulers made sure that
every town had its barracks and parade ground. The constant sound of bugles and drums reminded the discontented
that 'who draws a sword against a prince must throw away
the scabbard'. A centralized and severely regulated life is
still the normal one for most Europeans, who remain subject
to compulsory military service and are required to carry
identity papers that they have to produce for any authorized
inquirer.

Apart from a riot here and there Britain did not need
such control of its population. England's civil war had ended
in a consensus as the English discovered that they hated
foreigners more than they hated their own countrymen.
Once England was united with Scotland no army was needed
to guard the frontiers; keeping invaders at bay was the Royal
Navy's job. Britain had no need for a mighty army: its power

and wealth came from peace and stability, its wars took place overseas, and agile politicians ensured that England was always allied with the winning side.[2] When the continental powers were evenly balanced, England tipped the scales.[3] The army was simply a refuge for the disinherited rich and the unemployable poor.

The role of Britain's navy was to raid and harass shipping, ports and coastlines to bring the enemy to the negotiating table. Within such a policy, overseas possessions were primarily needed as bases to revictual the fleets. From these, in the course of time, merchants, soldiers and adventurers conquered vast tracts of land. They found that a small armed presence was usually enough to maintain control of even the largest overseas dominions, although much of these were hostile uninhabitable land like the northern part of Canada and the Australian interior. Weapons improved, and in a short time Britain acquired and maintained a vast empire extending far beyond any real power that it could deploy.

CITIZEN ARMIES

Compulsory military service is not a new device. Press-gangs that kidnapped able-bodied men in seaports and forced them into the slavery of naval service had been keeping the navies manned for many years before Prussia set up a system of compulsory military service in 1733. Prussian regiments, each based in a Kanton or county, kept records of local men and summoned them to military service as needed. But when Napoleon attacked, the Prussian army was mauled and humiliated by the French and the defeat was blamed upon its inefficiency. Two out of three men had been given exemption from military service, so that the Prussian army in the field consisted of mercenaries and peasants in about equal numbers.[4] Now Prussia created a system of service which exempted very few healthy men whatever their social class. They were not simply called in time of war. Each citizen

spent a year in uniform and returned to the colours throughout his life.

But compulsory military service as we know it was born,
like so many other intolerable devices of the centralized totalitarian state, out of the French Revolution. In 1793 the
war minister proposed to the National Assembly that every
healthy single Frenchman aged between 18 and 25 should be
summoned to the army. Married men of the same age would
go into the armoury workshops, and males aged from 26 to
40 would be entered on a reserve list for service in wartime.

Thus Germans and Frenchmen spent their adult lives at
the beck and call of the generals. In 1870 the two systems of
mobilization could be compared. The Germans attacked
France with an army of 1,200,000 men. In that same two
weeks of crisis France had mustered only half that number.

By 16 February 1874 Helmuth von Moltke was able to
stand up in the Reichstag and claim that the army's prodi-
gious use of civilian manpower had been 'raising the nation
for almost sixty years to physical fitness, mental alertness,
order and punctuality, loyalty and obedience, love of our
country, and manliness'.[5] It had also enabled Prussia to thoroughly thrash her neighbours, including France, into abject
submission.

It is difficult to be sure whether the prospect of military
service was as unpopular in France and Germany as it was in
Britain. But in France and Germany public opinion was disregarded by the government; Britain was different. Dating
from Anglo-Saxon times, its army consisted of small companies raised by noblemen under royal commission. Only in
dire emergencies were citizens called to serve. Although
nineteenth-century Britain was not a democracy—no European state enjoyed democracy—public opinion in Britain
was important. This importance did not depend upon the
vote. In Britain in 1901 only two-thirds of the men, and no
women, had the vote. Government was confined to a small,
carefully defined and exclusive class, and these men decided
that universal conscription was not politically acceptable.

During the nineteenth century, Britain was protected by

its coastline and its unchallenged navy. Half of the army was stationed in India, and most of the other half was winning a succession of small colonial wars in other distant possessions. Only at the century's end was Britain's power tested. In southern Africa, where the world's largest gold deposits had recently been discovered, the Boers, farmers of Dutch descent, besieged garrison towns. Closing their minds to the appalling inefficiency their army had demonstrated in the Crimean War (1854–56), the British decided to exercise their unique resources by dispatching an army to fight six thousand miles away from home. No other country could equal or counter such an expedition. The part that wealth played in such power had long been celebrated in a music hall ditty: 'We don't want to fight but by Jingo if we do, we've got the ships, we've got the men, we've got the money too'.[6]

Britain still had the money but, despite the tied markets provided by her Empire, less and less of it was coming from manufacturing and exporting goods. Financiers, rather than factory owners, were the new elite. Overseas investments in railways, mines and urban expansion were now bringing enough money into London to make up for the drop in exports, but it was another ominous sign that Britain was losing the trade wars to rivals such as Germany and America.

There were also danger signals about the workforce. The British government was reportedly shocked to find that 38 per cent of men volunteering to fight the Boers—a sampling one would expect to be in good health—were not fit enough to serve with the colours. And this despite the way in which the army's height requirement had been brought down to five feet! A subsequent official report stated that about a quarter of the inhabitants of Britain's industrial towns were undernourished because they were poor.

The Boers were fit and strong, hunters and farmers fighting in terrain they knew how to exploit. Moving rapidly on horseback, they fought on foot, using Mauser repeating rifles with deadly accuracy. Lacking discipline, organization, medals and military textbooks, they knew when to sneak away from a lost encounter. There were never more than

40,000 Boers in the field but it took a British army of unprecedented size almost three years to subdue them. Helped by the Dominions, Britain mobilized half a million men.

The controversies, scandals, triumphs and disasters of the war came at a time when rotary presses and improved typesetting machines provided cheap newspapers for a newly literate public. Winston Churchill reported the war for the *Daily Telegraph,* Edgar Wallace, a famous crime novelist, covered it for the *Daily Mail* and Rudyard Kipling worked there on an army newspaper. Arthur Conan Doyle, creator of Sherlock Holmes, was running a field hospital and Mahatma Gandhi was a stretcher-bearer.[7]

The conflict had a profound effect on European politics. The French, the Dutch and the Germans, who had colonized foreign lands with varying degrees of cruelty, objected to the British colonizing European settlers. And Britain's rivals relished the sight of her army suffering humiliating defeats at the hands of a few skilful and tenacious white farmers. When the British started to get the upper hand, their European neighbours became more critical of them and more pro-Boer. Disease-ridden prison camps caused the deaths of many thousand Boers and brought accusations of deliberate murder. The British explained that it was incompetence, but by the time the war was over, Britain's relationship with the rest of Europe was clouded by resentment.

The fighting in South Africa had provided some glimpses of how future wars might be fought. But the machine-gun, which would dominate future battlefields, played little part in the fight against the Boers. It was not a weapon unknown to the British army. Various forms of machine-gun had been used by them since 1871. It had been used in the Ashanti campaign in 1874, the Zulu War, and by General Kitchener in the Sudan. It had killed some 11,000 Dervishes at Omdurman. No wonder Hilaire Belloc's poem, 'The Modern Traveller', confidently claimed that:

> 'Whatever happens, we have got
> The Maxim Gun, and they have not'.

But machine-guns did not defeat the Boers. Some said the British sense of fair play and an antipathy to replacing heroes with machinery made them reluctant to massacre white men with automatic fire.[8] There are other reasons too. The army had given the Maxim, which weighed 40 lb, to artillery-men who put it on a carriage weighing 448 lb, with wheels almost five feet in diameter. Such a large and cumbersome weapon was not so effective against Boers who avoided frontal attacks, used ground and cover with great skill and were masters of the arts of camouflage and sniping. The role of the machine-gun went unremarked in the war, and after it the British army preferred to admire the horsemanship of the foe and concentrated its reforms upon its own horsemen. By 1914 British cavalry were the finest in the world, but there were to be no battles for them to fight.

The decisive components of future warfare were more easily seen in the savage civil war which had torn nineteenth-century America in two. Here was a country where public opinion counted for a great deal. Even in the most desperate days of the war its leaders had stopped short of universal conscription. (The Confederate army was 20 per cent conscript, the Union army 6 per cent.) A cunning combination of cash bounties for volunteers, plus the threat of conscription, had bulldozed enough men into uniform. The inescapable lesson of the civil war was that the industrial might of the North inevitably prevailed. Frequent demonstrations of military prowess by Confederate generals came to nothing because the Union had more soldiers, more miles of railroad, and more factories to produce armaments and all the other resources of war.

Neither the British nor the French seemed to learn much from the American battlefields and the terribly high casualties that were suffered there. After the stunning German victory in 1870, the defeated French generals concluded that it was the nature of the offensive that had been the true secret of Germany's lightning campaign. Assault became the new theory of warfare. France soon paid off the punitive reparations demanded by its conquerors and, inexplicably, regained its reputation as the world's most formidable land power. With Britain's navy considered indomitable, the Anglo-French alliance was not actively challenged.

As the dust of war blew away, it was starkly evident that France would not be content with the European borders that the Germans had imposed upon her. Frenchmen were determined to regain the provinces of Alsace and Lorraine, and redress their humiliating defeat. The thought of Wilhelm posturing in the great Hall of Mirrors in the Palace of Versailles, amid the German princes and the battle-torn standards, while the grand duke of Baden hailed him as emperor had ignited a lasting desire for revenge in every French heart.

A different sort of German ruler might have guided his country through this prevailing French resentment but Wilhelm was a neurotic and enigmatic personality. Despite his seven children, his closest friends were homosexuals. From them he seemed to get the warmth and affection that he needed in order to play the role of a tough and pitiless warlord. When he became ruler of a united and powerful Germany, a war to decide the hegemony of Europe was almost inevitable. Furthermore the unified Germany that came after the victory of 1870 was being transformed. In the following 25 years the national income doubled. Railroads spread across the land. Giant electrical, chemical and industrial enterprises flourished and booming cities absorbed a population which increased 50 per cent. 'German universities and technical schools were the most admired, German methods the most thorough, German philosophers dominant', said Barbara Tuchman.[9]

TECHNICAL ADVANCES

Displayed by the Americans at Britain's Great Exhibition of 1851 there were half a dozen mass-produced rifles, every part of them easily and quickly interchangeable. The advantage such precision production brought to an army will be readily understood by those British soldiers who used a hammer and file, and sometimes a hacksaw, when servicing their vehicles and equipment during the Second World War. In the German section of the Exhibition in London, Alfred Krupp displayed a cannon made from cast steel, instead of the usual iron or bronze. He found no buyers.

The nineteenth century transformed warfare, with machine-guns used in conjunction with barbed-wire. Mass-produced weapons and citizen armies were moved by railways. Two inventions were yet to bear fruit: nothing would change the nature of war more than the wireless telegraph and the internal combustion engine.

Britain's industrial revolution had been made possible by the invention of such devices as George Stephenson's steam engine, Richard Arkwright's water-frame, Edmund Cartwright's power loom, Hargreaves' spinning jenny and Samuel Crompton's mule. These inventions were brilliantly simple; the inventors were unsophisticated men. Arkwright was a barber assisted by a watchmaker, Hargreaves a carpenter, Cartwright a clergyman, Crompton a spinner and Stephenson a collier's son who didn't learn to read until he was 17 years old. But the next step in modern progress would delve into such mysteries as chemistry, microbiology, physics and precision engineering. It would require educated people working in well equipped workshops and laboratories.

Inventions were improved at a dazzling speed. A gas engine invented by Dr N. A. Otto in 1876 was developed by Gottlieb Daimler to propel a vehicle. Before the end of the century there was an automobile race covering 744 miles from Paris to Bordeaux and back. By 1903 the Wright brothers were flying their curious contraptions. Six years later Europeans suddenly understood the significance of powered flight when Louis Blériot flew across the English Channel in 31 minutes. The world had been irreversibly transformed and so had the way in which men would fight. War had entered the third dimension.

Wireless was no less important. By 1901 Guglielmo Marconi's development of work by Rudolf Hertz enabled a wireless message to be transmitted 3,000 miles. While the industrial revolution had used crude machines and unskilled labour to produce wealth, this new 'technical revolution' was far more demanding. Nations with leaders who failed to respond to the complexities of this new world ran the risk of rapid decline. In the words of one British major-general who was also an historian:

> Mind more than matter, thought more than things, and above all imagination, struggled to gain power. New substances appeared, new sources of energy were tapped and new outlooks on life took form. The world was sloughing its skin—mental, moral and physical—a process destined to transform the industrial revolution into a technical civilization. Divorced from civil progress, soldiers could not see this. They could not see that as civilization became more technical, military power must inevitably follow suit: that the next war would be as much a clash between factories and technicians as between armies and generals. With the steady advance of science warfare could not stand still.[10]

In 1890 Germany's production of iron and steel had been half that of Britain; by 1913 Germany produced twice as much as Britain and half that of the United States. Such advances were matched by progress in manufacturing. German industry—chemical and electric firms in particular—set up research institutes, and worked closely with the universities. By the end of the nineteenth century German technology had left Britain behind. By the time Hitler came to power, Germany had collected one-third of all the Nobel prizes for physics and chemistry.

Since the early nineteenth century, Prussia had given great emphasis to the technical training of the workforce. It had invented such educational refinements as graduate schools, Ph.D. degrees, seminars, research laboratories and institutes, and scholarly and scientific journals. All of these innovations were quickly adopted by American universities. France recognized the importance of education and technology and pioneered colleges for the advanced study of engineering and science. The achievements of such men as J.J. Thomson at the Cavendish laboratory did not allay the fears of the British educational establishment, which, fortified by State and Church, saw science as a dangerous first step towards Godless social reform and resolutely opposed it. Britain's 'public schools' (actually private, fee-paying and exclusive) prepared upper middle-class boys to study in the choice universities where science and engineering were virtually ignored. Association between university and industry was fiercely resisted. As the First World War began, most of Britain's population could expect no education beyond their fourteenth birthdays. Teachers were ill paid and difficult to recruit. Decisions about the nation, its industries and commercial life were made by men who had studied the Classics, Law or Philosophy. Few spoke any modern foreign language fluently.

Britain's contribution to its wars is celebrated by memorable prose and poetry rather than by military successes. The country's subsequent industrial and economic history has been blighted by the way its middle classes have continued to hold any sort of technical accomplishment in low esteem, and prefer their children to study liberal arts in outmoded buildings lacking modern facilities.

OUTBREAK OF THE FIRST WORLD WAR

The assassination that led to the outbreak of war in 1914 took place in the Balkans. The foreign minister of Austria-Hungary was determined to provoke the Serbians into a war. The Serbians, with strong ties to the Slavic nations, were confident and ready to fight. Obligations, both real and imagined, divided Europe into the Central Powers (Germany and Austria-Hungary plus Turkey) on one side and the Allies (France, Russia and Britain) on the other. Britain's commitment to join in the 1914 war was flimsy.[11] So was that of Germany. The war was fought for trade and territory, but men on both sides were moved by romantic ideas rather than practical considerations. The British saw it as a war to resist the German invasion of 'poor little' Belgium. Germans saw it as a war for German *Kultur* against barbaric enemies. In Berlin a Socialist deputy saw the Reichstag vote on war credits and wrote in his diary:

> The memory of the incredible enthusiasm of the other parties, of the government, and of the spectators, as we stood to be counted, will never leave me.[12]

When war was declared there was satisfaction everywhere. In London, Paris and Berlin the crowds cheered the announcement. German artists and intellectuals were foremost among those succumbing to war fever and thousands of students joined the army immediately. At Kiel University, Schleswig-Holstein—following an appeal by the rector—virtually the whole student body enlisted.

What did the cheering men—so many of them doomed to death by the announcements—envisage? Certainly they thought the war would be quick and decisive; in every country there was the stated belief that 'it would be all over by Christmas'.

The thinking of most of the top soldiers was no less carefree. General Ferdinand Foch, who ended the war as commander of the combined French, British and United States armies on the Western Front, thought: 'A battle won is a battle in which one will not confess oneself beaten.'[13] Such folly might have proved less tragic had it not been coupled with Foch's obsession with attacking, and his rationalization that any improvement in armaments could add strength only to the offensive. Such generalship resulted in French *poilus* charging into machine-gun fire dressed in bright red pantaloons. It was only in 1915 that the French army went over to less conspicuous attire, and even that was 'horizon blue'. In an amazing demonstration of the military mind at its most tenacious, Foch ended the war with his views more or less intact.

Because so many of the ideas, events and even the equipment of 1914 clearly foreshadows that of 1939 it is worth while taking a closer look at this 'war to end wars'. It was called 'The Great War' until 1939 brought another and even greater war. Like that second war, the first began with a 'blitzkrieg'. Germany's 'Schlieffen Plan' called for a lightning thrust through (neutral) Belgium, then a massive left wheel across northern France to capture Paris. After that all German resources would be turned upon Russia, which would need more time to mobilize its army and prepare for war.

The man called upon to implement Schlieffen's ambitious plan was Helmuth von Moltke, who said: 'I live entirely in the arts'. He proved it by painting and playing the cello and working on a German translation of Maeterlinck's *Pelléas et Mélisande*. Moltke did not capture Paris; but he got close.

According to plan and aided by a national railway service that was built to a military design, Moltke's armies rolled through Belgium, suffering only a brief delay before flattening its massive fortresses with Krupp's incomparable howitzers. But the Germans failed to capture Paris.

At first it was a war of movement but then weary regiments, slowed by mud and cold and suffering the losses of their best and most experienced soldiers, came to a standstill. Here and there the order to stand fast was best met by digging a trench in which to shelter. Soon, from the North Sea to the Alps the armies were standing in a vast line of muddy trenches garlanded with barbed-wire and traversed by machine-guns. Behind them the cavalry regiments were held in reserve. There they remained, waiting for a gap through which to gallop, until the war ended. Meanwhile the infantry gradually abandoned their fine uniforms as part of the process of adapting to living in wet ditches where artfully positioned machine-guns ensured that any man who climbed out and stood up, almost certainly died. High-ranking officers—who unfortunately never went to the trenches, climbed out and stood up—resolutely refused to recognize the fact that the machine-gun had changed warfare as much as had gunpowder itself.

Lord Kitchener, who had been responsible for the organization and transport of the British Expeditionary Force sent to France, said: 'I don't know what is to be done—this isn't war'. What he really meant was that this was not the short sharp action that so many volunteers had envisaged.

On the Eastern Front, the Germans (and to their south the soldiers of Austria-Hungary) faced the mammoth armies of Russia. Their men were stretched more thinly than in the West, and now and again attacks broke through the frontline defences. But for most of the time the Eastern Front was as static as the Western Front. There the weather was even more cruel.

THE BRITISH AND GERMAN ARMIES

Unlike other continental nations, the British had never revered army officers, nor indeed given the army much attention at all. Until 1870 the British army remained a hundred years behind the times. Officers purchased their commissions, men were enlisted for life and flogging was a regular punishment. Reforms were slow and heartily resisted. By the time war came in 1914 the small professional army was made up of poor human material. A prewar study found that British soldiers had a mental age between 10 and 13. Many were illiterate. Troops going on leave were marched to the railway station and put on the trains, because of the problems they had if doing this unaided.

Supporting the regular army there was a part-time defence force called the Territorial Army. In 1914 it had about 250,000 men instead of its establishment of 320,000. Youngsters were not given a medical: 'The men were enlisted only

FIGURE 13:
British Lee-Enfield rifle Mk 111

for Home Defence and an inquiry in time of peace as to those willing to serve abroad in event of war disclosed 20,000 ready to take this obligation. The training of the men was limited to an hour's drill at odd times, and an annual training of eight to fifteen days'.[14] The 'Terriers' carried long Lee-Enfield rifles and were armed with converted 15-pounder guns, both weapons which the regular army had discarded.

The army may have been unfit for battle but the civilians were in high spirits. When war started in the summer of 1914 great numbers of men volunteered. The nation's health was still poor but medical examinations were cursory. According to the chief recruiting officer for the London District at that time, some doctors examined over 300 men per day while between 20 and 30 per cent of the recruits were given no medical examination at all.[15]

By the middle of 1915 over 3 million British men had volunteered to fight but casualties meant 'the outflow was greater than the intake'.[16] To maintain the field army envisaged for 1916, men would have to be drafted. A Conscription Bill passed through Parliament with overwhelming majorities, and Britain's traditional opposition to citizen armies was overcome with scarcely a ripple of protest.

The drafted men were subjected to no greater scrutiny than had been given to the volunteers. It was only after three years of war that the medical boards were re-organized and improved. Then the doctors were examining about 60 men a day. A very high percentage of these were found unfit for front-line service,[17] but by this time many men unsuited to the physical and mental strains of trench warfare were fighting in France.

All through the war there were shortages of uniforms and equipment and also of instructors. The exceptionally high casualty rate suffered by junior officers might have been met by commissioning experienced NCOs, but this was not considered. The British army believed that officers must be recruited from the middle classes. The normal way to officer rank was through the Officers' Training Corps which were formed in Britain's 'public' schools. The OTC did not provide serious military training. It organized summer camps and training drills, and gave the schoolboys Certificate A, which guaranteed them officer rank.

Young patriotic clerks and manual workers responded well to being commanded by 18-year-old subalterns fresh from school. For the first time 'nicely raised young men from West Country vicarages or South Coast watering places came face to face with forty Durham miners, Yorkshire furnacemen, Clydeside riveters, and the two sides found that they could scarcely understand each other's speech'.[18] All ranks were motivated by patriotism. Their officers were fired also with the public school ethic of service, but they had never been properly trained to fight or to command. Committed to the leadership ideas of the sports field, youthful officers were unyielding in their courage, which is why they suffered disproportionate casualties. A junior officer reporting to his infantry battalion had a 50 per cent chance of being killed or seriously wounded within six months.

War poets have provided an interesting record of the good relationship between British officers and men in the front line. But whatever its virtue and valour, an army based upon improvisation was no match for German professionalism. Neither were the British high commanders.

The commander-in-chief of the British Expeditionary Force in France from December 1915 onwards was Lieutenant-General Sir Douglas Haig. 'A dour hard-working ambitious Scot with little money and few friends, who was not too particular about the methods he used to get to the top of his profession', said the historian Michael Howard. 'But he was a dedicated professional none the less'.[19] This 53-year-old autocrat distrusted all foreigners, including his French allies, thought that Roman Catholics were likely to be pacifists and detested all politicians, especially Socialists, into which category he was inclined to put anyone with new ideas. These shortcomings were grave, all the more so because Haig proved totally unequipped for the unprecedented military task he had taken upon himself.

In the higher ranks of the British army Haig made sure that important promotions came only to the prewar regulars. Even worse, promotion was decided by the traditional system of age, service and seniority. This ensured that only the grossest incompetents were ever removed, and they almost invariably got a job where they could do even more damage.

The German army was equally reluctant to allow the working class across the great divide into the exalted realm of the commissioned ranks. Officers had always enjoyed a privileged place in German society, and German schools of all kinds prepared youngsters for the military service that followed their schooling. A century of conscription had ensured that German officers, like German other-ranks, were thoroughly trained. Fit 20-year-old men served two years with the army (one year for students). Training was methodical and rigorous; some said it was sadistic. Emphasis was given to specialized skills, such as operating and maintaining engines, artillery and machine-guns. Each man also learned the job of his immediate superior so that every senior NCO was trained to fill an officer's role, should his officer become a casualty.

Until they reached the age of 40, Germans returned to the army for refresher courses that amounted to about eight weeks' training every five years. In this way reservists were taught about new weapons and tactics, and the system provided Germany with a well trained army of over 4 million men in 1914.

THE BATTLE OF THE SOMME

Engineers, like scientists of all kinds, were respected in Germany. With the German army reduced to static fighting on the Western Front, engineers built a well designed defence system behind their front line. They dug trenches along contours, taking advantage of every hill and ridge, and where possible the line was linked to shell-racked villages, where machine-gun positions and observation posts were concealed in the rubble.

On the Somme sector, chalk provided a chance to dig deep; 40 feet was not exceptional. Dug-outs were reinforced with cement and steel and had multiple exits. Many underground quarters had electric light and were ventilated by fans. The soldiers had bunkbeds and in some places there was even piped water. No wonder that on 8 August 1916 a British serving soldier's letter in *The Times* said: 'But the German dug-outs! My word, they were things of beauty, art and safety'.

When these defences were ready, the Germans pulled back to them. The British generals moved their men forward to lap against the German line. It was what the Germans wanted them to do, for here the British were constantly observed and under fire. It was this German line that Douglas Haig was to assault on 1 July 1916 in the battle of the Somme, throwing in thirteen British and five French divisions.

Whether Haig's plan was based upon his low opinion of the professional army, or his low opinion of the civilians which now largely manned it, is not clear. The battle plan was detailed and robotic. No opportunity for initiative or independent action was granted to any of the combatants.

The Somme battle opened on a hot July day when 143 battalions attacked and about 50 per cent of the men, and some 75 per cent of the officers, became casualties. Karl Blenk, a German machine-gunner, recalled:

> I could see them everywhere; there were hundreds. The officers were in front. I noticed one of them walked calmly, carrying a walking stick. When we started firing we just had to load and reload. They went down in their hundreds. You didn't have to aim, we just fired into them.[20]

The German machine-gunners had been ordered to set up their positions at the rear of their trenchline, where they would command a better view and 'In addition, owing to the feeling of safety which this position inspires, the men will work their guns with more coolness and judgement'.

With a thoroughness and dedication that the world usually ascribed to the Prussians, the British infantry had spent many hours preparing for the attack. They practised walking forward in close and exactly prescribed intervals carrying almost 70 lb of equipment.

The Germans were at this time practising carrying their machine-guns from their deep and comfortable dug-outs to position them for firing. They did this as soon as the preliminary artillery barrage lifted for the attack. It took them three minutes.[21]

By the end of the first day, the British attackers had suffered 60,000 casualties, about one-third of them fatal. It was the worst day suffered by any army during the war and the worst in the British army's history.

Haig was not deterred. His futile battle continued for six months, until the Allied casualties numbered 420,000 men.[22] Few of the soldiers engaged in the Somme fighting had been given proper infantry training. Even the British artillery-men were not adequately trained. Afterwards the high command tried to make the artillery's performance an excuse for the disaster.

Between 1914 and 1918 a distinct difference was to be seen in the German and the Anglo-French methods of fighting the war. When France's General Pétain analysed the fighting in Champagne in 1915 he concluded that surprise attacks were useless because of the great depth of defences on both sides. He said artillery bombardment was the only way of preparing for a breakthrough. Britain's General Haig was convinced. Apart from the Neuve Chapelle fighting, in the early summer of 1915, and the Cambrai raid of 1917, Haig studiously avoided surprising the Germans. He said his guiding principle was wearing down the enemy: it was to be a war of attrition. Unfortunately for everyone concerned, Haig's methods wore his own men down more thoroughly than they wore down the enemy.

7 PASSCHENDAELE AND AFTER

The past is a foreign country: they do things differently there.

L. P. HARTLEY, *THE GO-BETWEEN*

Douglas Haig was not a man to be deterred by failure, or even to learn from it. One year later the Somme battle was staged all over again in the sloppy clay of the north. Men drowned in a quagmire made worse by bombardment. Even artillery pieces were swallowed up into the morass. It was the ultimate nightmare of the war, and many soldiers who were there—such as my father—would not speak of it. Like the Somme fighting of the previous year, it lasted from July until November and secured only a tiny strip of land.

Of this gloomy drama the military historian Liddell Hart said: 'So fruitless in its results, so depressing in its direction was this 1917 offensive, that "Passchendaele" has come to be . . . a synonym for military failure—a name black-bordered in the records of the British Army'.[1]

In the last year of the war the Germans, having knocked Russia out of the war, could turn to the Western Front and stage a 'Somme Battle' of their own design. It was a massive attack, and some of the ideas employed in it were still in evidence in the blitzkrieg of the Second World War.

General Ludendorff—probably the most expert general on either side in the war—in *Notes on Offensive Battles,* published in 1918, drew attention to broad differences in the German approach. The British had based their attacks upon artillery schedules, he said. The 'creeping barrage'—which fell behind the advancing infantry as well as ahead of it—drove the British infantry forward. Men who lingered, and men immobilized by injuries, came under intense shell-fire from their own guns. In such a scheme, said Ludendorff, commanders ceased to have proper control of their men. He condemned such tactics as wasteful and ineffective. Infantry should be used more flexibly, always seeking to get round behind the enemy on the flanks, and thus roll up the enemy and widen the attack.

The Germans did not disdain surprise. It was essential to these new methods. Specially selected men—storm-troops—would lead the assault. They'd use flamethrowers, have large canvas bags crammed full of hand-grenades, and be equipped with a revolutionary development of the machine-gun—the MP 18 machine-pistol. This was a small light-weight automatic, fitted with the barrel and 32-round magazine of the Luger pistol. It sprayed fire at about 400 rounds per minute and by the end of the war the Germans had put into use 35,000 of them.[2]

The opening of the attack was prepared in great secrecy. The storm-troops moved to jumping-off positions under cover of darkness. Artillery was not brought up to the place of attack until five days before it began; heavy mortars came two days before the attack. Such secrecy should have ensured surprise, but General Haig's intelligence section described with considerable accuracy the attack that was about to come. Haig made no changes whatever to his dispositions and even confirmed high-level changes of command that came into effect just hours before the attack started.[3] He decreed that the British tanks were spread out to be employed as static strong-points, in other words not tanks at all.

The Kaiser's Battle, as the Germans named it, started on 21 March 1918 and was aided by fog and by Haig's dispositions in depth. With much of his force too far forward, the unexpected penetration of the front caused a large section of his line to give way. By the 5 April he had lost 1,000 square miles of ground and 160,000 men (killed, wounded and taken prisoner) and many thought Haig's army was on the verge of collapse.

And then, in May, 42 German divisions struck the French armies with such force that Foch issued preliminary orders to prepare for a final stand before Paris. In London the cabinet panicked and even discussed the time it would take to pull the British army out of France. This too was a harbinger of the blitzkrieg of 1940, the evacuation from Dunkirk, and the bitterness that followed it.

But the worst did not happen and the fighting stabilized. Haig put the British forces under the French commander Foch, and the German advance slowed. This time it was the British machine-guns that did the killing. One man remembered: 'When I think of all those brave German infantry, walking calmly and with poise, into our murderous machine-gun fire, now, and as then, we had nothing but admiration for them. Unqualified courage! Poor devils'.[4]

Ludendorff had restored mobility to the fighting, but tanks, which might have transformed the chances of success, were in short supply. On the first day he used four German A7 V tanks—clumsy 33-ton machines with 18 men inside— and five captured British Mark IVs. The British Official History says the British line was broken wherever the tanks appeared.[5]

Even Ludendorff could not change the fact that, with machine-guns on the battlefield, attacks were costly. The greater resources of the Allies, with America now included, paid off as the Germans became exhausted by their successes. Front-line German troops were demoralized to find so much food and equipment piled up in the Allied rear areas. The Allied generals soon recovered their valour. They were drafting plans for ever more mighty battles to be fought in 1919 and 1920, when suddenly the Germans asked for an armistice.

There were a thousand explanations for the German collapse. The men and material from the United States, the strangulating effects of the naval blockade upon Germany's food supply, the naval mutineers roaming through the streets of Kiel, the surrender of their Turkish allies, the break-up of Austria-Hungary, and so on. Even today the real reason for the German collapse is not clear and simple. Many Germans believed that they had been tricked. As they saw it, US President Wilson proposed a peace in which Germany kept her colonies and armies intact. Once fighting ceased the Germany army disengaged and could not be sent back to start fighting again. The Allies then dictated terms and divided Germany's colonies between them. Whatever the reasons, the war came to an end, leaving the historians to continue hostilities by other means.

Throughout the war, troops from Canada, Australia and New Zealand proved to be particularly effective fighting soldiers, and Haig used them, like storm-troops, for most of the toughest attacks. The bloody fiasco at Passchendaele proved too much for the prime ministers of New Zealand and Canada, who had watched General Haig feeding their countrymen into his meat grinder. At a meeting of the imperial war cabinet on 13 June 1918, the New Zealand prime minister, William Massey, complained that his men had been sent against barbed-wire and shot down like rabbits. The Canadian prime minister, Sir Robert Borden, became so enraged that he was said to have grabbed the British prime minister—Lloyd George—by his coat lapels and shaken him vigorously.

Government and bureaucracy conspired to conceal the incompetence of the British commanders. Even three-quarters of a century later, vital documents and statistics of the First World War are still withheld from public scrutiny, and many papers are said to have been lost in the air raids of 1940. 'Scholars have for long been dissatisfied with the patchy nature of the First World War records in the Public Record Office which were clearly ruthlessly "weeded" before being made available to the public', said the historian Michael Howard.[6]

The official histories were apt to provide a constructive account of the war. Cyril Falls, who took the chair of Military History at Oxford University, said: 'Our army was the best disciplined and the least effective in the war, though one can't say so in the Official History'.[7] Haig knew what to say, and it was his account of the war that went into the history books. He rewrote his diary to suit his public image, and the British government instructed the official historian to follow his falsified account. Then the original records were burned, which prevented other historians from discovering the truth. So it remained until Denis Winter pieced together a different account of Haig's flawed generalship by using the papers stored in overseas archives.[8]

The public is not so easily fooled. They had seen so many sons go off to war armed with that sense of duty and dedication that is the currency of the young. Wives, sisters and daughters too had scoured the ever-lengthening casualty lists fluttering in the wind outside the town halls. Nearly a million British soldiers never returned home; of these over 700,000 were from Great Britain. About 2.5 million men were wounded. Even if one includes the men serving in the lines of communication, those on home defence in Britain, and British army garrison troops in India and the Far East, it still means that of ten men joining the army, two were destined to be killed and five injured; only three would survive the war intact. Intact? These figures take no account of the psychological effects of the fighting and the long-term damage done by the various types of war gases. Pensions for the widows and the disabled were minuscule, and the cruelly contrived demands of postwar medical boards persuaded some veterans to give up their pensions rather than annoy their employers by frequent absences.[9]

The First World War marked the death of many human values, and if Christianity was not numbered among the fatalities it certainly suffered injuries from which it has not yet recovered. Another faith shattered on the battlefield was the faith that the Empire had in the Motherland. Haig had ordered too many Australians, New Zealanders and Canadians to certain death for their countrymen ever again to trust their regiments to the direct command of Whitehall. The Australian Official History quotes one officer saying his friends were 'murdered' through 'the incompetence, callousness and personal vanity of those in high authority'. Of the Somme another Australian officer is quoted as saying 'a raving lunatic could never imagine the horror of the last thirteen days'.

Mammon too was among the wounded. In July 1917 Britain's chancellor of the exchequer had admitted to the Americans that Britain's financial resources were virtually at an end. The United States began lending the British $180 million per month. By war's end Britain's national debt had risen from £650 millions in 1914 to £7,435 millions (of which £1,365 millions was owed to the USA). This provided an unbearable postwar burden for the taxpayer, and in 1931 Britain defaulted on its debt. Congress responded with the Johnson Act of 1934: Britain's purchases would now have to be paid for in cash.[10]

PAYMENTS IN FULL

The British liked to ascribe Germany's remarkable fighting record to its robotic, merciless war machine, but it was the British soldiers who had been unceasingly ordered into futile and costly offensives. And, while 345 British soldiers faced firing squads during the war, only 48 German soldiers were executed.[11] Prince Rupprecht of Bavaria wrote in his diary in 21 December 1917 that while he knew of only one death sentence in his army, the British had executed at least 67 men between October 1916 and August 1917.

This disparity was partly due to the reckless way in which the British army had recruited men without consideration of their mental and physical stamina. It was also accounted for by the fact that the British army retained no less than 25 offences for which the penalty was death. Some of these, such as 'imperilling the success of His Majesty's forces', gave the courts wide powers. General Haig, who confirmed every sentence, believed that the firing squads were essential to maintaining discipline, and repeatedly demanded that Australian soldiers be made to face them. But the Australian government resisted Haig's pleas, in the confident knowledge that their infantrymen were widely acknowledged to be the best anywhere on the Western Front.[12]

All information about military executions was concealed from the British public. The government would not even tell the House of Commons how many soldiers were being shot, because publishing such figures was 'contrary to the public interest'. No one, not even next of kin, was permitted to know anything of the court-martial proceedings, and British soldiers had no right of appeal against a death sentence.

The army used firing squads to set an example to soldiers who needed one. Proclaimed throughout the army, executions were often staged before troops of the condemned man's unit. It was thus made clear to his comrades that it wasn't only murderers and rapists who were executed, it was exhausted men who closed their eyes, and men who refused to do the impossible. As the war went on, and ever younger conscripts were sent to the trenches, parents worried about how their sons would endure the ordeal. As stories of executions gained wider currency, the under-secretary for war admitted that there was great public anxiety, and questions by members of parliament, about whether wounded or 'shell-shocked' men were being executed, were met by outright lies. In the debate on 17 April 1918, several members, including serving officers, urged the government to change court-martial procedures so that an officer with some sort of legal training should be available to defend a soldier accused of a serious offence, and to ensure that all presidents of the court had previous experience of evaluating evidence. Even these modest reforms were denied.[13]

In February 1919 the most senior of the official historians spent an evening with Douglas Haig, dining and studying the maps and papers. 'Why did we win the war?' Haig asked him.[14] No one knew. But after the war Haig had demanded, and got, a massive cash hand-out. He was also presented with a mansion overlooking the River Tweed, where he carefully revised his memoirs. No matter what lengths he went to in rewriting history, Haig was never forgiven for what he had done. Nor was it forgotten. There was no wild cheering in public places when war was declared on Sunday 3 September 1939. The 'Great War' and the dead in Flanders were still very much in the minds of the survivors from all nations.

THE WORLD AFTER THE FIRST WORLD WAR

Georges Clemenceau, the prime minister of France, said in 1917: 'War is a series of catastrophes which result in a victory'. For France that was true. As in the war to come, she emerged victorious only because the United States entered the war on the Allied side. Her provinces of Alsace and Lorraine were returned to her, and French troops occupied Germany's Rhineland and Saar. But the victory was a sham. The northern region of France had been the heart of its industrial strength, and after many battles had been fought there, it was devastated. France was bankrupt and deeply in debt. Jules Cambon, a French diplomat, saw the drastic decline in fortunes and wrote: 'France victorious must grow accustomed to being a lesser power than France vanquished'.

Germany had fought and survived the combined forces of Britain, France, the USA, Italy and Russia. The Fatherland was intact, and fighting had not brought destruction to any region of Germany, which even in defeat remained the strongest power in Europe. Germany's population of 70 millions was growing, while France's population of 40 millions was static. Within a decade of the peace treaty there would be twice as many Germans reaching military age each year as Frenchmen. Furthermore Germany's potential enemies were weakened; by internal strife (Russia), by division into smaller units (Austria-Hungary); by impoverishment (Britain and France), or by concern for their own affairs (USA).

The sacrifices they had made persuaded the French people that they alone had won the war, and their government did nothing to correct this false impression. The Canadians buried at Vimy Ridge, the British sailors lost at sea, Australians and New Zealanders who had fallen at Gallipoli, the Indian Corps which had frozen at Armentières in the first winter of the war, Americans killed at Champagne and Argonne, all these were forgotten. Her allies became bitter at what they considered a lack of gratitude, and the Anglo-Saxon nations moved into isolation and away from friendship with France. The French thought the world was being too kind to the Germans, and began to regard themselves as the sole guardians of the Versailles treaty. For this reason the French army was never to be short of men or money.

VERSAILLES—THE PEACE TREATY

The treaty the great powers signed in 1919 to end the First World War remains one of the most controversial historic documents of the twentieth century. The American President Wilson arrived in Europe with his own programme for a lasting peace. We will never know if his ideas were sound, for his Allies would have nothing to do with his 'Fourteen Points'. Georges Clemenceau said: 'Mr Wilson bores me with his Fourteen Points; why, God Almighty only had ten'. Some said Wilson's proposals were altruistic. Certainly there was nothing benevolent about the twisted political wrangling of the European politicians, but the treaty that finally emerged was not vindictive compared with Germany's peace with France in 1871 or the terms Germany inflicted upon Lenin's Russia in 1917.

In postwar Germany, politicians made much of the £1,000 million charged to Germany in reparations. Less was said about the £1,500 million loaned to her by Britain and the United States. The peace terms laid down that Germany could have an army no bigger than 100,000 men and must not build or buy tanks, submarines and aircraft. Few Germans recognized that this would aid their economic recovery; rather it was seen as an insulting and unreasonable order that had to be flouted and eventually rectified.

Perhaps the path to true democratic government would have proved more certain had the monarchy been maintained. Certainly a hereditary monarchy makes it more difficult for tyrants like Hitler to become the head of state.[15] As it was, Germany's postwar democratic government—the Weimar Republic—was ridiculed as a puppet regime that implemented the forceful terms of the victors.

The most far-reaching effects of the peace treaty were the frontiers it drew. Austria-Hungary was split into pieces by the victors. The lines scrawled across the map cared nothing about consigning large numbers of Germans to live under foreign governments. Eventually, in Czechoslovakia and Poland, these vociferous expatriate communities were orchestrated and used by Hitler as an excuse for invasion.

SOLDIERS GO HOME

At the end of the Great War the armies went home, and it was the attitudes and actions of these returning soldiers which created the world that went to war in 1939. Virtually all the men returning from the battlefields were to some extent cynical and embittered as they compared what they and their comrades had suffered with what others, less worthy, had gained. Most of the veterans' associations—from the Croix de feu in France to Oswald Mosley's Blackshirts in Britain—were anti-Communist. Communists had conspicuously associated themselves with pacificism and antimilitarism. Returning soldiers despised the men who had stayed at home preaching against the war.

Despite its new democratic government, a defeated Germany was convulsed in a series of localized revolutions as left-wing and right-wing political groups fought for power.

There were violent uprisings in many German cities and for a few days Bavaria had 'a Soviet Republic'. Many German institutions—the army, big business and the labour movement—had survived the war intact; now each threw its weight behind the factions it favoured.

The government of this fragile republic saw its prime tasks as protecting the government from Communist take-over and keeping public order. To do this it came to terms with the highly organized veterans' organizations: most notably the Freikorps, a huge patchwork of small armies, illicitly armed and ready to fight all-comers. Such units were used as an·armed frontier guard against Polish incursions and as a secret supplement to the army permitted by the peace treaty. At first Freikorps men wore their old army uniforms. Later they were issued with a consignment of shirts originally intended for German soldiers in East Africa. Dressed in them, these men became the brown-shirted Sturm Abteilung—storm-troops—who eventually allied themselves to Hitler's Nazi party to be its tough uniformed auxiliaries.[16]

Few of the veterans were looking for personal material gain. Life in the front line had shown them a special sort of comradeship, a world in which men literally sacrificed themselves for their fellows. The ex-servicemen were looking for such a new idealistic world in peacetime too. In Russia Lenin had not waited for an end to hostilities before harnessing the energies of the soldiers to his Communist revolution. In Italy Benito Mussolini offered such men a uniformed Fascist state. But it was Adolf Hitler, in Germany, who most skilfully designed a political party that could manipulate the ex-servicemen. The declared aims and intentions of the National Socialist German Workers' party swept away their cynical disillusion with politics and transformed such veterans into ardent Nazis.

ADOLF HITLER, EX-SOLDIER

Unlike their counterparts in Italy and Russia the German veterans felt that their leader—Führer—was an archetypal ex-soldier. There has been a mountain of contradictory material written about Adolf Hitler's wartime service. In fact he was a dedicated soldier who respected his officers and showed no cynicism about the war.

During the fighting Hitler was selected to be a 'runner' taking messages from the front line to the staff. It was a dangerous job usually given to intelligent and educated fit young soldiers. He won the coveted Iron Cross 1st Class in August 1918 when advancing German troops came under 'friendly fire' and his officer—Lt Hugo Gutmann—promised the award to anyone who could get a message back to the artillery. Hitler completed this 'suicide mission' and Lt Gutmann kept his promise. By that time Hitler had also won the Iron Cross 2nd Class, the Cross of Military Merit 3rd class with swords, and the regimental diploma. Details of Hitler winning his Iron Cross 1st Class—a notable award for a low-ranking soldier—were not widely publicized, leading to suggestions that it was never awarded at all. Probably Hitler felt his virulent anti-Jewish policies did not go well with receiving a medal from a Jewish officer.

Entering politics, Hitler's coarse regional accent and wartime lowly rank were appealing to thousands of ex-servicemen who heard their thoughts about war-profiteers and self-serving politicians voiced by a man with natural skills as an orator. The Communists kept blaming the soldiers for the war: Hitler's patriotic respect for the army was more to the taste of the veterans, and the relatives of those who had been killed and injured. The Nazis were fiercely xenophobic: Germany's troubles were blamed on foreigners. Socialists and Communists owed their true allegiance to Moscow, the Nazis said. Capitalists were equally unpatriotic, for they used cheap overseas labour for their imported goods and sent their profits to foreign banks overseas. Never mind that it wasn't true; in the harsh postwar climate it was the sort of explanation many Germans wanted to believe.

Hitler's anti-Jewish tirades were well received in Bavaria, the Nazi party's home, where both Lutheranism and the Catholic Church provided soil in which deep-rooted prejudice had flourished over hundreds of years. The Communists proposed a workers' paradise from which all 'privileged' Germans should be excluded; while Hitler's vision of a new Germany was designed to appeal alike to generals and tycoons, schoolteachers and physicians, as well as to workers and beggars.

HITLER AND ANTI-SEMITISM

Hitler was not the first politician to foment anti-Jewish hatreds for political ends. In 1887 an International Anti-Jewish Congress had been organized in Dresden. More such gatherings had taken place in Kassel and Bochum in 1886 and 1889.[17] By 1895 anti-Semites were virtually a majority in Germany's lower house, while in Vienna, Karl Lueger's anti-Jewish Christian Socialists had 56 seats against 71 Liberals. In France the persecution of Captain Alfred Dreyfus revealed anti-Semitism no less deeply seated.[18] A motion in the Senate that would have banned Jews from public service in France was defeated 268:208.

A native of Austria, Hitler centred his political activities upon Bavaria in southern Germany. Always deliberately vague about his political aims and intentions, he artfully used many local prejudices to win support. Berlin bureaucrats ruled the new unified Germany. He attacked the remoteness of the heartily detested central government. He blamed the generals—conveniently regarded as Prussian Protestants—for losing the war. In Catholic Bavaria, traditionally resentful of Prussian attitudes, these views found warm support.

Hitler's vaguely defined anti-Semitism enabled the small farmer to hate the bank to whom he owed money, the small shopkeeper to hate the department store against which he competed. More intelligent Germans were convinced that these rabble-rousing simplifications were temporary measures. They firmly believed that once the Nazis turned their eyes away from Munich, Bavaria, to focus attention on the real seat of power in Berlin, such vicious anti-Semitism would tone down and fade away.

These hopes that Hitler and his Nazis would become moderate and statesmanlike were illusory. Hatred of Jews was Hitler's whole motivation. His campaign against Jews became more and more murderous and demented right up to the time of his death. He fanned ancient irrational fears of Jewish international conspiracies. This gave him the excuse to put peacetime Germany into a permanent state of emergency. That 'war footing' was what gave the Nazi party such tight control of all aspects of the life of every German.

Albert Speer provides a revealing memory of Adolf Hitler:

> He jumped from one subject to another, frequently repeating words like 'fundamental', 'absolutely', 'unshakeable'. Then too he had a special fondness for phrases and words out of the days of the beer-hall brawls, such as 'club down', 'iron perseverance', 'brute force', or 'beat up', as well as scatological words like 'shithead', 'crapper'. In moments of excitement he also tended to phrases like: 'I'll finish him off myself'; 'I'll personally put a bullet through his head'; or 'I'll fix him'.[19]

THE MAGINOT LINE

While the French generals still regarded attack as the secret of success in war, plans were approved for a mighty series of

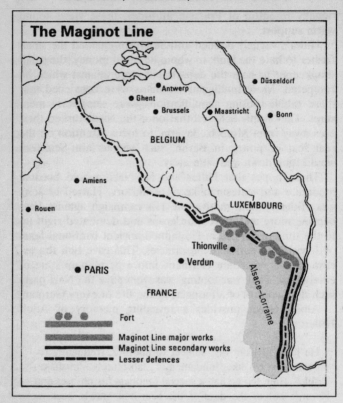

The Maginot Line

Düsseldorf

Antwerp
Ghent
Brussels
Maastricht
Bonn

BELGIUM

Amiens

LUXEMBOURG

Rouen

Thionville
Verdun

Alsace-Lorraine

PARIS

FRANCE

●●● Fort
━━━ Maginot Line major works
━━━ Maginot Line secondary works
- - - Lesser defences

fortifications along her frontier with Germany. This was not
incompatible with the military policy of attack; it would provide time for the reserve to be mobilized and for a naval
blockade to be established. Attack, using the best forces,
would follow.

The 'Maginot Line', as it came to be known, was born out
of the mighty battles that had raged round the French forts
at Verdun. These forts had been a part of the defences built
after the 1870 defeat. For ten months in 1916 the French and
German armies stood toe-to-toe there and countless men

died. Almost every French soldier served at Verdun at some time or other. Every family in France had cause to curse its name. After the war it became a shrine and a place of pilgrimage. Still today the echoing footsteps, and whispered words of school parties, can be heard in its monolithic blockhouses which even 42-cm Krupp shells failed to raze.

Liddell Hart's *History of the World War* suggests that it was luck that saved Verdun.[20] All the German 17-inch howitzers were destroyed by French long-range guns and 450,000 ready-fused artillery shells in a German artillery park near Spincourt blew up. Others say Verdun was saved when Haig's attack on the Somme diverted German resources. In France General Henri Philippe Pétain was given the credit for stopping the German advance at Verdun in 1916. He was hailed as the saviour of Western civilization. Doubly so when in 1917 he used his reputation and personal pleas to quell the mutinies that threatened the continued existence of the French army.

Until 1914 Pétain had been an undistinguished lecturer in infantry tactics at the Ecole de Guerre. Then General J.J.C. Joffre, who had been appointed commander-in-chief despite entirely lacking staff experience, remembered Pétain, his old teacher, and thought he might prove useful if employed on his staff. So when, after the war, the government wanted a soldier's opinion about permanent defences, Pétain, now inspector-general of the French army (and designated C-in-C in the event of hostilities), was an obvious choice. He had a theory about 'battlefields prepared in peacetime', a line of defences along the western bank of the Rhine, and to Thionville on the Moselle. The line would not be strongly fortified, neither would it continue along the Franco-Belgium border. Pétain believed that that part of the frontier could only be defended from inside Belgium.[21] From this time onwards it became a fundamental part of French strategy that Belgium remain an ally of France, and that the line of fortifications inside Belgium was a de facto part of French defences.

Some believe that the Maginot defences were deliberately positioned so as to ensure that any German attack would have to go through Belgium and bring Britain and the Dominions into the war as it had done in 1914. To the south, the main defences of the Maginot Line were built to include the provinces of Alsace and Lorraine. These provinces had been a part of Germany until 1918. The people there had grown up under German rule but the Maginot fortifications told them unequivocally that France would not allow this region to become German again. Thus the siting and building of the Maginot Line took political as well as military ideas into account.

The northern provinces provided special problems. The low lands flooded every winter, as had been discovered by the wretched frontline troops who served in waterlogged trenches there in the First World War. An urban-industrial region straddled the Franco-Belgian frontier and was growing as Europe recovered from the war. It would be difficult to build fortresses amid factories and houses. Any construction along the French side of this border would be a declaration that France would abandon Belgium in the event of war.

For all these reasons, and many more, the Maginot Line was not a continuous series of fortifications. It stopped and started; and in any case it was designed only as a barrier which would enable France to spread second-rate troops thinly behind the forts, and concentrate its best units elsewhere. Many people, including Winston Churchill, agreed that the small population of France, compared with that of Germany, made the construction of the Maginot Line a sensible precaution.

That the Maginot Line 'was an astounding feat of twentieth century engineering'[22] can be seen still today. It was designed however before the use of armoured mobile columns changed the textbooks. When the Maginot Line was being planned, whole armies of tracked and wheeled vehicles were no more than theoreticians' dreams that few soldiers took seriously.

In the long run the Maginot Line had more effect upon the French than it had upon the Germans. It lulled them into a false sense of security. When war began, at a time when the German army was fully occupied in Poland, the French had a wonderful chance to use their fortifications as a base from which to strike against the Rhineland. They did not do it. The 'Maginot mentality'—added to its political confusions and Hitler's fearsome propaganda—had hypnotized France and made it into a victim waiting for an end that many considered inevitable.

Neither did the magic of Maginot totally fade in 1945. At war's end, the French army immediately occupied and reconditioned the Maginot Line. It kept it maintained until 1964. Now its mouldering turrets and weedy entrances are to be found by curious holiday-makers who wander off the highways.[23]

8 FRANCE IN THE PREWAR YEARS

Peace is better than war, because in peace the sons bury their fathers, but in war the fathers bury their sons.

CROESUS TO CAMBYSES

(SON OF HIS ENEMY CYRUS THE GREAT)

It was not only the 'Maginot mentality' that rendered France so vulnerable in 1940. Although the generals failed to equip France's army for modern war, the nation itself during those interwar years became ever more demoralized and divided. Political extremists of both left and right had a powerful influence upon French society, as did the widespread corruption that so often procured fat government contracts. The French aircraft industry provided an example of the crippling effect of political theorists. In 1936 all the well established French aircraft manufacturers were nationalized by the Communist air minister Pierre Cot. The effect upon production was devastating, and the resulting chaos was still being sorted out when the Germans attacked in 1940. France's relationships with the rest of the world suffered as a result of its own dissensions. Although the French had remained Britain's close allies since before the First World War, the ties between the two countries had grown more and more uncertain. Even in November 1938—after the Munich agreement—the British prime minister thought it necessary to ask the French whether they would support Britain if it became the victim of German aggression. In the same cabinet meeting, Prime Minister Neville Chamberlain said he had been assured that France was not proposing to sign a non-aggression pact with Germany that would rule out help to Britain.[1] These were chilly words about Britain's closest neighbours immediately prior to a life-and-death struggle with a well armed and determined enemy.

HITLER'S NEW ORDER

In the eyes of many people, Adolf Hitler's regime was a success. Everything seemed to have improved since the waves of economic depression that rolled over Europe in the 1920s. Germans were thankful for the way Hitler's coming to power stopped the vicious and extensive street battles which were a regular ending to all Communist and Nazi political rallies. But the Nazi way of restoring law and order was to execute or imprison without trial all opponents. Equally drastic was the way Hitler reduced unemployment by means of massive public works projects and rearmament. In 1935 conscription was introduced. All German youth was called to serve twelve months in the armed forces following a term of manual work in the RAD, the State Labour Service. In September 1936 Hitler was able to announce to a party congress that the jobless had fallen from 6 million to 1 million. A strictly controlled economy caused living standards to rise sharply, so that Germans soon enjoyed the highest living standards in Europe.

The Nazi propaganda machine brought the arts, theatre, cinema, newspapers and radio under the direct control of the artful Joseph Goebbels. Parades with flaming torches, vast uniformed rallies on monumental stages and stadiums, massed flags and columns of searchlights had made Germany into a political theatre watched by the rest of the world.

As part of the rapid expansion of the German army, during training and exercises it employed motor cars fitted with flimsy wooden superstructures to represent tanks, with other mock-ups for artillery and so on. Such improvised vehicles gave rise to colourful rumours that were repeated every-

FIGURE 14:
Mercedes and Auto-Union racing cars

where abroad and even got into foreign newspapers. They
said the German army was no more than a sham force built
for parades, and designed solely to intimidate other nations.
A more accurate picture of the expanding war machine was
available to motor-racing enthusiasts.

During the Thirties the victories of the German motor-
racing team shocked and dismayed its competitors. Many, if
not most, British racing drivers were competing simply for
fun; using the same cars to journey to the circuits, race there
and then travel home. The Nazis were quick to see the propaganda benefits of international racing victories. German
cars—Mercedes and Auto-Union—were highly specialized
designs with engineering that was years ahead of their rivals.
The drivers—some of them non-Germans—and fitters were
highly trained and dedicated. The team organization was
managed with a professional resolution quite unlike anything from other European countries. It could be said that
the Germans invented the racing team as we now know it. In
every respect those victorious German racing teams of the
Thirties provided a glimpse of blitzkrieg to come.

It wasn't only racing cars that Germany was manufacturing: in the period 1930–38 German car production went

from 189,000 to 530,000 vehicles. Industrial production soared and unemployment plunged from its 1932 peak.

Hitler's defiant stance, and his violent speeches against the injustices of the peace treaty, gave Germans a new sort of pride. It was the 'stick and carrot' technique. Most Germans turned a blind eye to the persecution of the Jews, and all the other legalized crimes of the Nazis, when the stick might be a spell in a labour camp. Those who objected were arrested; many were never seen again. Article 48 of the Weimar Constitution legalized protective custody and enabled all the fundamental rights of a citizen to be withheld. Using this the Nazis sent thousands of opponents to concentration camps without due process of law. The lawyers found legal reasons to classify such prisoners as citizens assisting in upholding the law.

Here and there a brave German spoke up against the regime. The view that Nazi Germany—whatever its faults—had to be supported because of the 'protection' it provided against the spread of Russian Communism was echoed by the rich and powerful everywhere. It was certainly a view aired in the British cabinet. In Rome the Pope did nothing to stop the anti-Semitic excesses of the 'anti-Bolshevik' state Hitler had created as a bulwark against the Reds.

The German trade unions had been silenced by arrests and threats. The Nazi labour organizations which replaced them gave workers cheap vacations and luxury cruises but deprived them of the right to strike, demonstrate or make any kind of objection to the regime. It succeeded. Working-class Germans—like middle-class ones—offered no serious opposition to the Nazis.

It is difficult to give a balanced picture of the respective strengths of the great powers in that period immediately before the war. But in an attempt to provide some sort of estimate, Table 2 looks at three aspects of each nation. Manpower is a guide to the size of the army that could be put into the field. Annual steel-making capacity estimates the ability to build ships, submarines, tanks and artillery. Annual aircraft production is a guide to the potential production of such items as trucks, cars and infantry weapons, as well as aircraft.

TABLE 2

Relative strengths of the Great Powers in 1939

	Population (000s)	Steel (000 tons)	Aircraft
Britain	47,961	13,192	7,940
France	41,600	6,221	3,420
Germany	76,000	23,329	8,295
USA	132,122	51,380	5,856
USSR	190,000	18,800	10,382

British population figures do not take account of men in the Dominions. For steel, the figures given are the best for the 1930s, with German figures including Austrian production. Aircraft numbers take no account of size (tending to underrate UK and USA, which were building more large aircraft than the other nations).[2]

THE BRITISH AND THEIR PRIME MINISTER: CHAMBERLAIN

It has become convenient to think of the war as a confrontation between Adolf Hitler and Winston Churchill, but Britain's leader in the years leading up to the war was Neville Chamberlain. Although very much in the minority, there are still those who say that Chamberlain was an astute statesman. They prefer to believe that Chamberlain, by appeasing Hitler and letting him march into Austria and then Czechoslovakia, gained time for Britain to rearm. There is nothing to support this contention.

By 1937 Hitler had provided Germany with formidable fighting forces. His troops had reoccupied the demilitarized Rhineland in open defiance of the peace treaty. In Britain there were no signs of a resolve to confront Germany. According to the foreign minister, Anthony Eden, the elder men of the cabinet were not convinced of the need to rearm.[3] Chamberlain thought armaments were a wasteful form of expenditure and saw no reason to believe that war was bound to come.[4]

In the previous cabinet, Chamberlain had been chancellor of the exchequer. He knew how much a government's popularity depended upon keeping income taxes low. Opposition politicians were certainly not demanding rearmament. Clement Attlee, leader of the Labour (Socialist) party, had said in December 1933: 'We are unalterably opposed to anything in the nature of rearmament'. His party stuck to that line and campaigned against rearmament right up to the outbreak of war. Prominent churchmen and intellectuals said little about the persecution of German Jews, even though refugees brought ever more appalling stories of what was happening. Priests, politicians and writers combined in such pacifist organizations as the Peace Pledge Union, and the influential voices of Aldous Huxley, Siegfried Sassoon and Vera Brittain were heard arguing persuasively against any preparations for war.

Everywhere pacifism was coloured by the fear of what fleets of bombing aircraft might do to large cities. The writings of General J.F.C. Fuller and Bertrand Russell, and the H.G. Wells science-fiction book *Things to Come* (and the frightening Alexander Korda film based upon it), fanned fears of impending devastation and chaos by bomber fleets. It was against this background that Chamberlain made his decisions about rearmament.

Seen in photographs and cartoons, Chamberlain appears a wretched and ridiculous figure with drawn face and craning neck, but an American who met him in 1940 was impressed:

Mr Chamberlain was seated alone at his place at the Cabinet table when we were both shown in. He was spare, but gave the impression both of physical strength and energy. He appeared to be much younger than his seventy-one years. His hair was dark, except for a white strand across his forehead. His dominating features were a pair of large, very dark, piercing eyes. His voice was low, but incisive.[5]

Chamberlain was concerned with his personal popularity and he spoke of it frequently. The welcoming crowds he saw on his visits to Munich and Rome were reassuring to him. He even remarked that Mussolini did not seem jealous at being welcomed less warmly than Chamberlain and the British party. Chamberlain's ego led him to believe that his personal negotiations with Hitler were a statesman-like contribution to world peace. In fact he did little but give way to Hitler's bullying, and ratify and assist the aggressions he claimed to be stopping. In addition Chamberlain's well publicized meetings with Hitler encouraged the more extreme Nazis while demoralizing the few influential Germans who opposed Hitler's methods.

The persistent belief that war could be avoided by appeasement made Chamberlain reluctant to form an alliance with Stalin's USSR. He and his colleagues shared a well merited distaste for Stalin's violent and repressive empire, and yet an alliance with Russia—as the British chiefs of staff pointed out—might be the only practical way to stop Hitler. When, in the summer of 1939, General Ironside (inspector-general of Overseas Forces) returned from a trip to Danzig, Chamberlain asked him to confirm that it seemed impossible to come to terms with the Russians. Ironside would not confirm it; he said it was the only thing that Britain could do. Chamberlain was not pleased at this response and retorted: 'The only thing we cannot do'.[6]

Many military men said that the Red Army was worthless, and that an alliance with the USSR would be only an encumbrance. Britain's ambassador in Berlin added to Chamberlain's confusion with a ridiculous warning that a British alliance with Russia would provoke Germany into an immediate war. (To prepare peacetime Germany for a war against Russia would have taken many months.) While Chamberlain vacillated it was Hitler who saw the advantages that a pact with Russia would provide.

Hitler's occupation of the Rhineland and then Austria had been welcomed by virtually the whole population of those German-speaking regions. *Blumenkriege* the German soldiers called these occupations; flower wars in which the soldiers got kisses and posies, not bullets and shells. But the people of Czechoslovakia—apart from the vociferous Volksdeutschen who lived in the border regions—had no love for the Germans.

CZECHOSLOVAKIA—THE MUNICH CRISIS

Czechoslovakia had been created in ten minutes at the end of the First World War. The imperial governor of defeated Austria-Hungary telephoned the illegal Czech National Committee and told them to come up to Hradcany Castle and pick up his seals and keys.[7]

Within Czechoslovakia's boundaries remained many of the old Empire's munitions factories. With the newly minted Czech crown unwanted on the international money markets, the Czechs were pleased to find that their armaments could be sold for hard currency.[8] The new government strongly supported the armaments industry—Skoda at Plzen and Zbrojovka at Brno—and the chemical plants too. Within a decade Czech arms salesmen had 10 per cent of the world arms market. In the violent interwar years Czech arms were used by the Japanese and the Chinese, by the Ethiopians and by both sides in the Spanish Civil War. The British army's best light machine-gun was named the Bren because

FIGURE 15:
British Bren light machine-gun

it was evolved by the Czechoslovak factory at Brno and the British factory at Enfield.

The German army greedily eyed the Czech arsenals. Rightly so: tanks and guns of Czech design and manufacture were to serve that army throughout the war. Czechoslovakia's production of aero engines and aircraft components was to prove even more important. Hitler would now add all this to his empire. There was no one in France and Britain with the will and wherewithal to stop him, and yet this was the crisis that eventually signalled the war.

Hitler's claim to Czechoslovakia's Sudetenland was based upon spurious complaints that the German communities resident there were being harshly treated by the government in Prague. It was not true, but German newspapers, manipulated by Goebbels, told the story the way the Nazis wanted it told. The Sudeten Germans lived in the borderlands, an area well fortified against German attack. The Czechs stood firm and mobilized their army. Chamberlain, convinced that Hitler was a rational individual with whom an agreement could be reached, offered to meet him. Old and somewhat frail, he made his first flight in order to meet Hitler at the Führer's mountainside retreat near Berchtesgaden. There were more fruitless meetings and for a time outsiders began to think that war was inevitable. Then at the last moment

Chamberlain sent a secret message to Italy's leader, Benito Mussolini, asking him to intercede.[9]

In September 1938 Hitler, Chamberlain, Mussolini and Daladier, the French PM, met in Munich to discuss Hitler's claim. It was a fiasco that might call to mind a Marx Brothers comedy. The room was crammed with all kinds of officials and hangers-on, milling around and eating the buffet food. Hitler, Daladier and Chamberlain had no common language and their interpreters found it difficult to work in such a restless crowd. Mussolini delighted in the fact that he could manage all their languages. He strode about, turning the meeting into a quiz show in which he played question-master. Eventually, at twenty-five minutes past midnight, the Munich Pact was signed.

Chamberlain came back from Munich waving the agreement, and a supplementary joint declaration renouncing war, and saying that it meant peace for our time. The end had always been a foregone conclusion. The meeting was a futile attempt to preserve the dignity of France and Britain, while allowing Hitler to seize the Czech border regions. By occupying the fortified border the Germans rendered the rest of Czechoslovakia defenceless. The only consolation for the Czechs, who were given no say about the dismemberment of their land, was that Britain and France guaranteed the new frontiers against unprovoked aggression. Germany was also asked to do so, but never did.

Winston Churchill, a rebel back-bench member of Parliament with patchy influence, stood up in the House of Commons and said: 'We have sustained a total, unmitigated defeat. We are in the midst of a disaster of the first magnitude . . . And do not suppose that this is the end. It is only the beginning'. He was shouted down by his fellow members of Parliament.

Any last idea that Chamberlain, and his colleagues, were temporizing, permitting Hitler to march into the Sudetenland to give Britain time to rearm, is refuted by Chamberlain himself. When, after the Munich meeting, Lord Swinton (one-time secretary of state for Air) said to Chamberlain: 'I will support you, Prime Minister, provided that you are clear that you have been buying time for rearmament', Chamberlain would have none of it. He took from his pocket the declaration that Hitler had so cynically signed and said: 'But don't you see, I have brought back peace'.[10]

Most of the cabinet, in fact most of the British public, tried to believe that the joint Anglo-German declaration affirming that the British and German peoples would 'never go to war with one another again' meant the 'peace for our time' which Chamberlain promised. But, according to Chamberlain's account of that meeting, when Hitler went to sign the declaration there was no ink in the inkwell. A more wary man might have wondered about the sincerity of German preparations that didn't include filling the inkwells.

The German occupiers of the Sudeten region treated the Czechs spitefully. Families who had lived in the same house for many generations were expelled without household goods or farm animals. SS Einsatzkommandos—a newly formed unit which later, in occupied regions of Poland and the USSR, organized mass murders—were manning the checkpoints to be sure the Czechs took nothing with them. When Hitler, on a tour of inspection, noticed Czech refugees being given bread and soup from German field kitchens he asked General Reichenau: 'Why do we waste good German bread on those pigs?' In fact the bread was good Czech bread.

Some Germans were shocked at this first sight of the behaviour of Himmler's SS units. One Abwehr (Army Intelligence) officer wrote in his diary: 'The SS Standarte Germania has murdered, pillaged and evicted in a bestial fashion. I saw one unfortunate girl who had been raped nine times by a gang of these rascals while her father had been murdered . . . these troops believe all they have read in the newspapers about Czech atrocities against our brothers'.[11]

Those Sudeten Germans who had encouraged Hitler's claim, by totally unfounded complaints about the Prague government's treatment of them, gained no lasting advantage. After the war ended, all the Sudeten Germans were unceremoniously deported back into Germany at a few hours' notice.

APPEASEMENT

On 9 October 1938, only days after his triumph at Munich, Hitler made a speech at Saarbrücken in which he attacked the Western powers and forecast that soon warmongers would take control of Britain. It was a reference to Churchill and any others who objected to Chamberlain's appeasement policy.

In those days before worldwide electronic communications, such as satellite telephones, the role of an ambassador could be vital. It was unfortunate for all concerned that so many of the ambassadors involved were men of low calibre. America's man in London was Joseph Kennedy, father of the future US president. He was rabidly anti-British and had long since decided (not without some reason) that Britain would not long survive a clash with Germany. The American ambassador in Paris was a man who saw Bolshevik conspiracies everywhere he looked. As their ambassador in Berlin, Britain's cabinet had to depend upon Nevile Henderson, of whom William Shirer—an American journalist and historian who was at the time resident in Berlin—wrote as a footnote in his memoirs:

> I have tried to be as objective as possible about Sir Nevile Henderson, but it has been difficult. From the moment of his arrival in Berlin he struck me as being not only sympathetic to Nazism but to Nazism's aims. The ambassador did not try to hide his personal approval of Hitler's taking Austria and then Czechoslovakia—he seemed to loathe the Czechs as much as Hitler did.

But worse than Henderson's personal prejudices were his personal limitations. Sir L.B. Namier, the British historian, summed them up: 'Conceited, vain, self-opinionated, rigidly adhering to his pre-conceived ideas, he poured out telegrams, dispatches and letters in unbelievable numbers and of formidable length, repeating a hundred times the same ill-founded views and ideas. Obtuse enough to be a menace and not stupid enough to be innocuous, he proved *un homme néfaste* [a very bad fellow]'.[12]

By the end of 1938 the threat of war was giving the British government economic worries. In April that year Britain was holding a healthy reserve of £800 million in gold, but appearances were deceptive. The money belonged largely to foreigners seeking a safe haven for their funds. The threat of war and the fact that Britain seemed unready for it[13] caused some £150 million in gold to move out of the country between April and September. Britain's economy was not resilient enough to cope with such swings of fortune. The cost of the First World War was still a burden on the taxpayer, despite the fact that the war debt to the United States was never paid. The Treasury had repeatedly warned that Britain could not afford to fight a major war lasting three years or more. The armed services all needed money and the government's headache was made worse by the ever-growing cost of modern armaments.

The reluctance to spend money was most apparent in cabinet on 2 February 1939 when the secretary of state for war, Leslie Hore-Belisha, sought £81 million to re-equip six divisions of the Regular army and four divisions of the Territorials. Chamberlain was against spending such money, saying that Britain's financial strength would be a decisive factor in any future war. But the French, fearing that the British might be no more than spectators in a future war, had been insisting that the British prepare an army to fight on French soil. In the event, it was decided to re-equip all the twelve Territorial divisions but not the regular army.

Having occupied the Sudetenland, Hitler encouraged Slovakia—a large section of the dismembered country—to demand autonomy. Nazi demands upon the Prague government became more and more outrageous: Czechoslovakia must leave the League of Nations, reduce the size of its army, turn over part of its gold reserves to the Reichsbank, outlaw the Jews in line with the Nuremberg Laws the Nazis had passed. Inevitably, in March 1939, the Germans took over the whole of Czechoslovakia. Bohemia and Moravia were declared a German 'protectorate'. Hitler went to Prague and spent the night in the President's Palace, the castle which was to become the German administrative centre. Soldiers and Nazi party members wearing the red and black ribbon given to those who had 'rendered valuable service' in organizing the occupation of the Sudetenland, now got a 'Prague castle bar'—*Prager Burg Spange*—to put on it. Slovakia became a separate state.

The newly acquired riches made Germany the greatest industrial power in the world after the USA. All the Balkan nations, from Yugoslavia to Turkey, were equipped with Czech weapons. From this time onwards, all foreign powers using Czech armaments would depend upon Hitler's good will for spare parts and replacements. The British could certainly not help such foreign powers by supplying British equipment. British guns, tanks and artillery were in short supply, and they lacked the quality of Czech production. Czech steel was so much better than Britain's that during the Thirties Britain was importing Czech armour plate for building its warships.

In London the news that German troops had driven into Czechoslovakia and occupied Prague came as a shock. Under the terms of the Munich Pact, it was now time for Britain to fight for the Czech borders. The cabinet looked to Lord Halifax, Chamberlain's foreign secretary, for a reaction. He received the news calmly. Halifax was a tall autocratic figure who had taken over as foreign secretary when his predecessor, Anthony Eden, showed opposition to Chamberlain's policy of appeasement. Britain hadn't guaranteed the Czechs against the exercise of moral pressure, explained Halifax. In the circumstances which had arisen, Britain's guarantee had come to an end. Chamberlain agreed and blamed the Slovaks for wanting a separate state: that was what had precipitated the crisis, he said.

Yet despite these self-abasing reactions to it, the German occupation finally persuaded Chamberlain and his cabinet that Hitler might be seeking world domination. Chamberlain aired these thoughts in a speech. Now he began to look for allies who would actively oppose the next act of aggression. Britain's secretary of state for war, Hore-Belisha, pointed out that from the Czechs Hitler had just acquired the complete equipment of 38 infantry divisions and eight mobile divisions. (This might have been an exaggeration, but it was certainly enough for 20 divisions.)

Britain's foreign secretary was hardly the man to put backbone into Chamberlain. An intensely religious former viceroy of India, the first Earl of Halifax was an elitist of the old school, a snob who recoiled at any prospect of true democracy. As more and more was known of his behaviour, he was to emerge as the personification of appeasement. Halifax was prepared to go to extreme lengths to appease Hitler, even to giving Germany some African colonies. It was Halifax who tried to muzzle British newspapers which he thought too critical of the Nazis. It is certainly chilling to consider how near he came (in 1940) to getting the premiership instead of Churchill.

9 AN ANTI-HITLER COALITION?

If it will all be wonderful after the war,
Why didn't we have this old wo-er befo-er?

WARTIME DITTY BY A. P. HERBERT

Any coalition to resist Hitler would have to include Poland's formidable army and Romania's oil wells. Both countries shared frontiers with Germany and were likely to be attacked, but the Poles and Romanians were not friends and didn't want to be allies. Both felt closer in spirit to Germany than to Soviet Russia. Political creeds made it difficult to put together an agreement that included Russia with such anti-Communist governments as those of Spain, Portugal, Poland and Romania. The recurring problem was that countries with short-term fears of German military actions also had long-term fears about Soviet Communism.

The shape of Poland provided Hitler with an excuse for action. The Poland created after the First World War, with its 'corridor' through Germany to the sea, cut East Prussia away from the rest of Germany. Danzig (present-day Gdansk) was a coastal town on the corridor and the centre of the crisis. Largely German, it had been made a 'free city' under international control in the hope of avoiding such conflicts. In October 1938, even before his troops occupied Prague, Hitler was demanding that Danzig be incorporated into his Third Reich.

In March 1939 the British cabinet was receiving convincing reports that Hitler was planning to attack Poland. One came from America's ambassador in Warsaw and was delivered by the abrasive Joseph Kennedy, the US ambassador in London. Another came via Ian Colvin, Berlin correspondent of the *News Chronicle,* who had just been expelled from Germany because of his continuing contacts with anti-Hitler groups. Colvin's detailed report of German intentions was a mixture of hard secret information, inferences and wild exaggerations. Some of this material originated from General Franz Halder, chief of the army staff.[1] It had been concocted by someone with access to Hitler's 25 March directive to Brauchitsch, the army C-in-C, and was given to Colvin in the hope of provoking resistance to Hitler's aggressive plans.

On 29 March Colvin took his story to the Foreign Office[2] and was immediately asked to recount it first to Lord Halifax and then to Prime Minister Chamberlain, who decided that some sort of undertaking to aid Poland was needed while they continued to seek a coalition of anti-Hitler nations. An 'interim' statement was cobbled together by 31 March. It simply said that in the event of a threat to Poland which that country resisted by force, Britain would go to Poland's support. 'The French Government have authorized me to make plain that they stand in the same position', Chamberlain added, and a crowded House of Commons echoed with cheers at this more positive news.

Chamberlain looked sick. A mortal illness had begun to take its grip on him, and he seemed not to understand the extent of his momentous undertaking. In a letter dated 2 April, he told his sister: 'And it is we who will judge whether that independence is threatened or not'. Lord Beaverbrook, the newspaper tycoon, writing anonymously in his *Evening Standard,* interpreted Britain's obligations even more loosely. He saw no obligation for Britain to interfere in minor territorial adjustments: a German Autobahn might be constructed through Poland to connect Germany with East Prussia, or Danzig might be handed over to Germany, without any need to rush to Poland's aid.

Such interpretations were not supported by a Foreign Office statement of 3 April which said Britain would not seek to influence the Poles in any way if such pressure arose.

Clearly if the Poles asked for help they would get it. It was later discovered that the Polish foreign minister had threatened to cancel his visit to London unless Britain's obligation was clarified. For anyone looking for the moment when war became inevitable then this must be the date. Avoiding the embarrassment that a cancelled visit would bring to the Foreign Office was the trigger.

Less than a week after Chamberlain's momentous statement, news came that Italy—until this time regarded by Chamberlain as an opponent of German expansion—had invaded Albania, a small country that was in any case virtually an Italian mandate. The news sent a ripple of alarm across Europe. In those days European governments were even more secretive than they are today, and rumours mushroomed in the darkness of official silence. Concerted attacks by the German and Italian dictators were expected any minute. The scare-mongers said that war would start with bombing raids on London and Paris.

The attacks did not come, but during that winter of 1938–39 the mood in Britain changed. Way ahead of politicians, the British public was starting to believe that war was inevitable. Few people anywhere in the world realized that Britain lacked the financial resources needed for a major war. Everyone assumed that Britain, with the backing of a vast empire, must be strong and rich enough to play policeman to the world. In any case a future war would be fought in France, which possessed the world's most formidable army and the Maginot Line defences. 'Hitler has got to be stopped', was the prevailing opinion in Britain. Perhaps it was too often said with an air of frightened resignation but it was said nevertheless. There was little excitement. Too many men had vivid memories of the previous war for there to be widespread pleasure at the prospect of doing it all over again. And yet there was a spirit of grim resolve that is peculiarly British. Intellectuals and pacifists who preached peace at any price were finding it more difficult to get a sympathetic hearing.

In line with prevalent fears about the devastating effect of bombing, it was decided that a portion of the anti-aircraft defences should be manned every night. Londoners now saw the night skies criss-crossed by searchlights. Those who knew where to look saw the 3.7-inch guns sitting inside their sandbag emplacements and manned by soldiers in steel helmets. But the bulk of the defences depended upon out-of-date 3-inch guns,[3] and opposition to having guns nearby continued to come from golf club secretaries, farmers, park authorities, residents and the municipal councils. 'In nearly all cases the protests were entirely successful' said the C-in-C of Anti-Aircraft Command bitterly.[4]

On 11 April Lord Gort, chief of the Imperial General Staff, warned the secretary of state for war,[5] Hore-Belisha, that he couldn't keep the air defences at this state of readiness without more men. The government must call up the army reservists by partial mobilization. The only alternative was for Parliament to pass an Act drafting men for peacetime military service. Gort knew that Hore-Belisha was sympathetic to this need, having heard his speech on 31 March saying that conscription might be necessary.

Drafting civilians into the armed services was a painful step for the British. Compulsory military service had been used in the previous war, but it was very distasteful to them. Chamberlain was opposed to the draft because his predecessor had promised the voters that on no account would it come before the next election, and Chamberlain had repeated the promise. He also feared bitter objections from the largely pacifist Socialist opposition and the trade unions. In a last effort to avoid conscription the prime minister proposed an impractical scheme in which Territorials (part-time volunteer soldiers) would man the defences at the end of their day's work as civilians. The army was adamant: the Territorial Anti-Aircraft units were already overworked and finding it difficult to fulfill their civilian and military obligations. Finally, after Lord Halifax was also persuaded of the necessity for compulsory call-up, Chamberlain gave way.

Chamberlain now adopted the idea as his own, although the word conscription was carefully avoided, recruits were called 'militia men', and the draft was described as compulsory military training. The suggestion that the government should declare 'a state of emergency' was abandoned in case it had disastrous effects on the financial markets of the City of London.

In a triumph of party politics over common sense, the (Socialist) Labour party and the Liberals voted against this compulsory military training. The Tory party could muster more than enough votes in the House of Commons to secure the new measures by a large majority: 380 to 143. At least 30 MPs, most national newspapers and some demonstrators aired the view that the time had come for a new government to be formed from men of all parties. Chamberlain was not convinced by them.

By 23 April 1939 cabinet and Treasury approval for some of the army's urgent needs produced some money, but that was not the same as having the equipment to hand. The list of urgently needed items that could not simply be bought off the shelf makes chilling reading now that we can see how close Britain was to war. Tanks were in very short supply: even guns had to be borrowed from the Indian army.

DIPLOMATIC MANOEUVRES

In response to questions raised by the British ambassador in Moscow the cabinet was astonished to receive on 18 April a long proposal from Maxim Litvinov, Stalin's foreign minister. Litvinov, an urbane and widely travelled Jewish diplomat of long experience, had an English-born wife and was an advocate of stronger Soviet ties with Britain and France. Now he proposed a five- or ten-year military pact with Britain and France, providing for mutual assistance in the case of aggression by Germany. The British cabinet was thrown into disarray by such plain language. The British guarantee to Poland had deliberately not mentioned Germany by name; wouldn't a Russo-British agreement upset Hitler?

Surely it would upset all the other east European countries threatened by Hitler. The Poles would scorn a Russo-British pact: they had already made it clear that they would not permit Red Army units to cross their frontier, even to help fight German invaders. What about the Baltic states? What about the United States and the Dominions? An agreement with the Soviets would bring a change to just about every international relationship the British enjoyed.

The French government was ready to explore the Russian proposals, and try to find some form of words that would satisfy London, while Chamberlain was frightened that news of the Russian proposals would leak and become known to the British voters. When he told the leaders of the Labour party, he swore them to secrecy.

The Russian proposals challenged the intelligence and understanding of the men in the British cabinet. They consulted their army, navy and air force chiefs not once but twice. The military chiefs modified their views considerably for the second report but the cabinet ended up as baffled as they ever were. In a private letter Chamberlain said he had 'the most profound distrust of Russia'. As war drew ever closer, Lord Halifax summed up the dismal confusion of these men, to whom the British people looked for wisdom and leadership, with the words: 'we ought to play for time'.

The British got deeper and deeper into a quagmire of words, producing counter-proposals which seemed ever more complex and unsatisfactory to Stalin. The Foreign Office mandarins realized that if they continued to leave Germany unnamed in their agreements Britain could end up guaranteeing everyone in the world against everyone else. The Russians could see that the British were in no hurry and suspected that they were trying to keep the negotiations going ad infinitum. Stalin, who had traitors spying for him in the high levels of virtually every European government, became convinced that Britain and France would never fight anyone until they were directly attacked. He decided that Russia's salvation might after all be a pact with his declared enemy, Nazi Germany.

Whether Hitler or Stalin was first in suggesting a non-aggression pact is still disputed. Before Hitler came to power, Germany had been a major buyer from the Soviet Union and was supplying almost half of all their imports.[6] Hitler's doctrine and his noisy and vituperative propaganda had strangled that trade. Since then Hitler's rearmament programme had drained the German economy so that in January 1939 every director of the Reichsbank had signed a warning memo to Hitler. The German economy was dangerously over-extended and, for reasons both economic and political, it had become more and more difficult for Germany to get foreign credit.

The Soviet Union on the other hand had never ceased to hint that a return to the volume of trade they had enjoyed with pre-Hitler Germany would suit them very well. It was this mutual need to trade that drew the two great powers together. Some accounts, including those by Soviet historians, insist that the German-Soviet Non-Aggression Pact of August 1939 began as Hitler's idea.[7] They cite Hitler's lengthy conversation with the Soviet ambassador at a reception in Berlin in early January 1939.

New Year celebrations had been postponed to 12 January in order to greet the new year in a palatial new Reich Chancellory that Hitler's architect Albert Speer had built on Voss Strasse. It gleamed with marble, mosaics and bronze. Hitler's study, 80 feet long with a 60-feet-high ceiling, was designed to overawe and intimidate visitors as they walked the length of the room to reach the Führer's gigantic marble desk. At the celebration the Papal Nuncio, doyen of the foreign diplomats, gave a formal address wishing Hitler a happy and successful New Year. The brief ceremony over, Hitler watched by everyone present took the Soviet ambassador aside for a talk that lasted 30 minutes or more. Done in the glare of a diplomatic occasion this was a deliberate signal that Hitler wanted to change his foreign policy. In fact it was a response to a meeting of German-Soviet trade experts held in Berlin on 22 December,[8] and Stalin's subsequent approval of a 200 million Reichsmark credit deal.

It is hardly surprising that stories of a forthcoming Russo-German trade pact appeared in newspapers in France and England. In London the *News Chronicle* of 27 January ran a more detailed article saying that a German-Soviet agreement was imminent. The article was written by Vernon Bartlett, who was known to have close contact with Soviet officials, and it was reprinted in the Soviet Press without comment. Perhaps Hitler's calculations concerning the contribution that Austria and Czechoslovakia could make to the German economy lessened his enthusiasm for a pact with Stalin, for it was not until Good Friday 7 April that Joachim von Ribbentrop, Germany's foreign minister, told Peter Kleist, an expert on his personal staff, to make contact with the Soviet diplomats and push the negotiations along. Ribbentrop was widely regarded as lacking talent, knowledge and experience;[9] his work on the German-Soviet Non-Aggression Pact was to become the high point of his career.

Within a few days Kleist was drinking tea with Georgi Astakhov, the bearded Soviet chargé d'affaires in Berlin, who had the rarely granted power to receive a foreigner and be alone with him. Ten days later the Soviet ambassador in Berlin made his first visit to the Foreign Office. He asked if, in view of the fact that German troops had now seized Czechoslovakia, the arms contract with the Skoda works would still be honoured. It was, admitted the ambassador, a test case to see if Germany was sincerely interested in resuming trade with the Soviet Union.

At the May Day parade in Moscow, Stalin gave his foreign minister a noticeably chilly reception. Ivy Litvinov, the minister's English-born wife said 'Damn that fool Chamberlain!' and others capable of recognizing subtle foretokens of Soviet foreign policy changes guessed that Stalin's eyes were now turned toward Berlin. The delegation of French and British negotiators the Allies sent to Moscow confirmed all Stalin's fears. It lacked the sort of high-ranking figure that the Russians thought appropriate, and instead of travelling by air or fast warship it spent five days aboard an ancient passenger liner, the *City of Exeter*.

When Astakhov went to the Berlin Foreign Office to get the official answer about the Skoda exports he pointed out that Stalin's new foreign minister, Vyacheslav Molotov, was also prime minister, second in power only to Stalin himself. Unlike his predecessor he was not a Jew, and this too was a signal to the Nazis. In fact he did have a Jewish wife, and this became a closely guarded secret.

Molotov was a man of 'outstanding ability and cold-blooded ruthlessness' Churchill wrote in his war history,[10] adding that Molotov's 'cannon-ball head, black moustache, and comprehending eyes, his slab face, his verbal adroitness and imperturbable demeanour, were appropriate manifestations of his qualities and skill'. Molotov's real name was Scriabin, and, a nephew of the famous composer, he'd studied music before going into politics and becoming a slave to Stalin's ideas and opinions. His appointment was a sign that from now on the Nazis were dealing with Stalin himself.

The next sudden lurch forward in the negotiations came when Ribbentrop told Hitler that the Soviets might be considering a military pact with the British and French. The Nazis had never got beyond discussing trade, and this development caused Ribbentrop to again bypass the usual channels by sending a personal representative to hurry things along. Astakhov and a colleague accepted an invitation for dinner in a private room in a smart little Berlin restaurant called Ewest's, where steak Holstein had been invented and named after a famous diplomat of Bismarck's time.[11] Ribbentrop's envoy and his assistant talked until gone midnight and their discussions were no longer confined to trade but ranged widely and successfully over all manner of political and economic problems.

From now onwards it was the Germans who pushed the talks forward urgently, and the Soviets who met most of their wishes. When Astakhov became suspicious of German motives he was recalled and put into prison, where he remained until he died in 1941. There was good reason for German eagerness. The pact would have to be announced before a German invasion of Poland, and military action there would have to be complete before the winter rains started.

On 20 August Hitler sent a telegram to Stalin asking him to receive Foreign Minister Ribbentrop in Moscow. This direct personal appeal, and the way in which it recognized Stalin as head of state while technically he was only the secretary of the Communist party, arrived at exactly the right time. During that summer, for the second year, fighting had broken out between the Red Army and Japanese troops in the Far East. Stalin, like Hitler, feared a two-front war and to avoid it he was prepared to trust even Hitler.

Warnings about a forthcoming Hitler-Stalin pact, and the way in which the two dictators planned to slice Poland in two and gobble it up, were received in both London and Paris. General Karl Bodenschatz, a wartime comrade of Göring in the old Richthofen squadron and now his liaison officer at Hitler's headquarters, disclosed an outline of the German plans to the French air attaché in Berlin, and to the Foreign Office in London. Dr Karl Goerdeler, one of the most active anti-Nazis, also sent warnings. The Foreign Office ignored them, preferring to believe that these stories were planted to spoil Britain's negotiations with the Russians.[12]

Hitler was confident that Molotov would sign a non-aggression pact with him. Indeed so certain was he that on 22 August, at his mountain home in Berchtesgaden, he briefed his military chiefs about the coming attack on Poland: 'Our opponents [the French and the British] are little worms. I saw them in Munich . . . The victor is not asked afterwards whether or not he has told the truth . . . Close your hearts to pity. Proceed brutally . . . The stronger is in the right'.

On the following day the German-Soviet pact was signed in Moscow. In keeping with the devious and feudal nature of both powers, many of the pact's most important clauses remained closely guarded secrets. Ribbentrop was reassured by the warm welcome he and his team received from the Russians. 'It felt like being with old Party comrades', he said. There was a great deal of eating and drinking and Stalin toasted Hitler and said he knew how much the German people loved their Führer.

Like Chicago gangsters, Hitler and Stalin had split eastern Europe into two spheres of influence in which each could do more or less as they liked. Stalin's territory included the Baltic states and Finland, while Poland was to be invaded by both armies and divided down the middle.

When the pact was announced *Life* magazine cabled the exiled Leon Trotsky, who had lost to Stalin in the struggle to inherit Lenin's Russia, asking for his views. From Mexico City came a prescient reply: '[Stalin] sees clearly for a short distance, but on a historical scale he is blind. A shrewd tactician, he is not a strategist . . .'.

Stalin honoured the German-Soviet pact in a way that Hitler never did. Russian grain and oil soon began moving to Germany. So did iron-ore, manganese and cotton. All over the world, members of the Communist party (many of them secret members) obediently changed their political opinions and switched activities to line up with the new pact. From now onwards Communists would oppose all attempts to bring Hitler to heel. When war began, the Communists in France and Britain would marshal their considerable resources against the war-effort. Allied soldiers were told not to fight in the war against Hitler, for it was a betrayal of the workers.

HITLER ATTACKS POLAND

Hitler had arranged everything for action against Poland with uncanny skill. He had become convinced that Britain and France would never fight him, and his demands on the Polish government were based upon that belief. Some historians say that Hitler did not look for concessions from the Poles; what he wanted was a short sharp war that would establish his military skills.

When he heard that a Stalin-Hitler pact was about to be

ratified, Chamberlain summoned Parliament back from its summer recess. In a speech on 24 August he told the Commons: 'I do not attempt to conceal from the House that that announcement came to the government as a surprise, and a surprise of a very unpleasant character'. Chamberlain described how an Anglo-French mission had been welcomed in Moscow on 11 August while the Soviets were actually conducting their secret talks with the Nazis. Perhaps Chamberlain's indignation made Stalin smile. Double-dealing was Stalin's regular method of doing business. Perhaps Hitler smiled too. What chance was there now that 'the worms' would be stupid enough to declare war?

The Germans had failed to appreciate that even Chamberlain could not be pushed for ever. The time had come to stand firm and, if need be, to fight. Yet Britain was not prepared enough, strong enough or rich enough to fight; it was an insoluble dilemma. Chamberlain was worried about the way in which events had prompted a drain on the gold reserves; £30 million was withdrawn in one day. Currency exchange control (to prevent anyone converting sterling to other currencies) was discussed, but the government contented itself with doubling the bank rate to 4 per cent and asking businessmen not to purchase foreign exchange or assets, nor move capital out of the country.[13] Despite all his misgivings Chamberlain tried to make his position absolutely clear. To Hitler he wrote:

apparently the announcement of a German-Soviet Agreement is taken in some quarters in Berlin to indicate that intervention by Great Britain on behalf of Poland is no longer a contingency that need be reckoned with. No greater mistake could be made. Whatever may prove the nature of the German-Soviet Agreement, it cannot alter Great Britain's obligation to Poland, which His Majesty's Government have stated in public repeatedly and plainly and which they are determined to fulfil.

It has been alleged that if His Majesty's Government had made their position more clear in 1914, the great catastrophe would have been avoided. Whether or not there is any force in that allegation, His Majesty's Government are resolved that on this occasion there shall be no such tragic misunderstanding. If the need should arise they are resolved and prepared to employ without delay all the forces at their command, and it is impossible to foresee the end of hostilities once engaged . . . I trust that Your Excellency will weigh with the utmost deliberation the considerations that I have put before you.

Even this did not persuade the Germans that Britain was determined to fight. Hitler told Goebbels that Chamberlain would resign. Goebbels, always more devious, wrote in his diary: 'I think it is more likely the Polish government will resign under English pressure. This is England's only chance to get out of this mess halfway safe without a war'.[14] The German army was no less confident. General Halder, the army's chief of staff,[15] wrote in his diary: 'Face must be saved . . . General impression, England soft on the issue of a major war'.

BRITAIN AND FRANCE GO TO WAR

The German army invaded Poland in the early hours of Friday 1 September 1939. All through that day and the next London was pressing Paris to declare war. By Saturday afternoon rumours about more appeasement were being circulated. At 10.30 that evening, members of Parliament sought out Chamberlain as he dined with Halifax. While a thunderstorm raged overhead they demanded action of the prime minister.[16] On Sunday morning Chamberlain broadcast to the nation, telling them that war had begun and that 'It is evil things that we shall be fighting against, brute force, bad faith, injustice, oppression and persecution'. While he was on the air, the air-raid sirens sounded in London. The US ambassador went to his shelter with his wife and two sons.

Kennedy was convinced that Britain would not last long against German military power.

The personnel at the German embassy in London were not similarly alarmed by the air-raid sirens. It was during the air-raid alarm that the emergency switchboard at the Foreign Office received an urgent call from the German embassy asking for Lord Halifax. It produced some consternation, for this was only a couple of minutes after the declaration of war. Attempts to contact Halifax at the Cabinet Office failed because he had left there already. The Germans were told this, and asked if the under-secretary would suffice. Yes, said the Embassy official, they simply wanted to be sure that their elderly black dog, which could not be taken back to Germany with them, would be cared for in their absence. When Lord Halifax arrived the problem was put before him and he made the necessary arrangements to have the dog looked after.[17]

Winston Churchill, appointed to be first lord of the Admiralty that Sunday morning, went with his wife to the Westminster apartment of his son-in-law, a stand-up comic named Vic Oliver. They drank champagne and toasted 'victory', after which Churchill took a short nap and then went to the Admiralty to start work.[18]

With conscription as a way of life, France entered the war with an army of 2.7 million men. Most of these were draftees or reservists. Their job was to defend France, and many were being assigned to the subterranean fortresses of the Maginot Line, which were proving an uncomfortable and unhealthy environment. Neither draftees nor reservists were well trained or well equipped, and almost all were unhappy at their plight.

In 1939 the Hotchkiss and Somua tanks used by the French army were as good as any in the world, and the 4.7-cm gun mounted on the Somua was better than anything the Germans had in use. The French tank force was equal to the Germans in numbers too. But the French generals did not agree on how to use this weapon. In 1939 they were still experimenting, not only with the constituents of the ar-

FIGURE 16:
British, French and German tanks in use at the start of the war

moured division but also with the methods of its deployment. They spread tanks thinly, assigned them to scouting and reconnaissance duties, or gave them to infantry units. When in 1939 three real armoured divisions were formed there was an overreaction and the high ratio of tanks made these units unwieldy and vulnerable.

To form an effective armoured force it was vital to have the constituents mixed in the right proportions. The German armoured divisions were like very mobile miniature armies, incorporating infantry regiments, combat engineers, anti-tank guns (Pak), artillery and their own Flak.[19] Such wheeled or tracked elements were able to react quickly to the changing situations that battle brings. Germany had ten such divisions ready for action in Poland.[20]

France's professional army was quite different to, and mostly separated from, the mass of its drafted soldiers. The regulars were more likely to be stationed abroad in colonies, such as Africa or Indo-China, where careers were made. The officer corps was a small elite element of the population which did not consider it desirable that the army should distance itself from political ideas and political movements. Few officers thought the Socialist government that ruled France in the Thirties was in any way successful, and monarchist and extreme right-wing organizations had sympathizers in the highest ranks.[21] Many officers thought that eventually the army would be compelled to take a more active part in the nation's political life.

France was a divided nation where Fascists, Communists, Socialists and monarchists were numerous at all levels of society. Since the signing of the German-Soviet pact, in August, Moscow had been instructing Communists not to join the fight against Hitler. These differences of outlook meant that the French began hostilities without the sense of purpose that by this time had unified Britain to a remarkable degree. The French government went to war under pressure from Britain and with considerable misgiving. The National Assembly was not invited to vote on the matter of declaring war. Members were simply asked to vote credits to 'fulfil our treaty obligations' and no debate was permitted. Some leftist members who wanted to speak were silenced. As soon as war was declared, political extremists, and some not very extreme opponents of the war, were taken into custody.

When war began France's agreement with Poland called for substantial French military action in the west. This was an undertaking made by General Maurice Gamelin, the 68-year-old commander-in-chief of the French army, whose influence in shaping his country's foreign policy during the interwar years was disastrous. 'Small, plump, slightly puffy, with his hair tinted, he might, but for the uniform, be an abbé, a fashionable abbé . . .'[22] He had virtually forbidden any discussion of motorization and mechanization of the army, by saying that all lectures and articles dealing with such subjects must be submitted to authority.[23] Although those in contact with him found him lacking in both intelligence and 'guts', the wider world rated him as a high-grade military expert. For this reason perhaps he had decided to manage without the aid of a proper staff.

March 1936, when Hitler occupied the Rhineland in defiance of the Versailles treaty, had been the time to confront the Nazis. Despite the fears expressed by the British government at that time, France's Prime Minister Sarrault and Foreign Minister Flandin had urged Gamelin to eject the Germans, but he would not do so, explaining that Germany had 22 divisions on a war footing. In fact they had three. Afterwards, it was discovered that the Germans had orders to withdraw if they were opposed, and Eden's memoirs said that this was the act of appeasement he most regretted.

Gamelin decided what he wanted to do and invented the reasons afterwards. It was his low opinion of the Czechoslovak army that influenced the Allies to give way to Hitler at Munich.[24] He told his political masters, and the British too, that the 'West Wall'—Germany's concrete fortifications, which the British Press liked to call the 'Siegfried Line'— would possibly halt him and force him to withdraw to his Maginot defences. When asked about the strength of his army he boasted of what it could do, while artfully adding such alarming asides as 'initially [it] will be a modern version of the battle of the Somme'.[25] It was enough to make the politicians sign anything Hitler gave them.

But when the next crisis came Gamelin expressed no such reservations about the Polish army. He thought it was formidable, and this had persuaded him to agree that in the event of war he would attack Germany three days after France's mobilization. Such a two-front war was calculated to divide Germany's effort and give the Poles a chance to defend themselves. And on 7 September 1939, eight divisions of the

French army—including two motorized divisions and five tank battalions—moved forward into the region between the Maginot Line and the West Wall. The Germans pulled back, leaving unoccupied some 200 square kilometres of ground and about 50 German villages mined and extensively booby-trapped. Newspaper correspondents exulted, telling of great French victories and deep penetrations into Germany. Photographs and newsreel footage appeared to back up the claims.

As September ended the 'Saar offensive' could be seen for what it really was: a propaganda exercise. The French withdrew having suffered 27 killed and 22 wounded and the loss of a number of aircraft. By the end of October both sides were back in the positions from which they had started. From what we now know of Gamelin's spirit and mentality it seems not impossible that the 'Saar offensive' was staged to prove that the cautions he'd expressed to his government about going to war in aid of Czechoslovakia were correct.

Just one week into the war the British cabinet were told some harsh facts by the chancellor of the exchequer: Britain's financial position was desperate; far worse than it had been in 1914. Her ally France was also far weaker in every respect, and three other allies of that previous war—Russia, Italy and Japan—were now potential enemies. Britain's total resources were about £700 million with little chance of adding to that figure. And, because the government had defaulted on its First World War debts to the United States, purchases there would in future have to be paid for in cash.[26] Surely no one in the cabinet room that day could have missed the implication: America's entry into the war was the Allies' only chance of salvation. And it would have to come very soon.

For two weeks the world watched the Germans smash their way into Poland. Then there came a grotesque finale as the Red Army occupiers came rolling across Poland's eastern frontier. It was clear to anyone who looked at a map that if Germany and Russia were friendly enough to mount a combined attack on Poland, they would be friendly enough for the German army to leave only a token force along that Polish frontier when they regrouped and came clubbing their way westwards.

THE GERMAN CAMPAIGN IN POLAND

For the first time, the new German army was seen in action, using techniques and weapons old and new. The Polish campaign was decided by the fact that the German army went to war by railway. The railheads near the border had to be the jumping-off points for the invaders. The armoured and motorized units that spearheaded the assault constituted only about one-sixth of the invading force; the rest of it was the same plodding horse-drawn German army that had fought in the previous war. Of the whole army only about 10 per cent had been equipped with wheels and tracks.[27] Even this attempt to mechanize the army had been achieved only after 16,000 German civilian vehicles were commandeered in 1939. Germany's auto-industry was big but it never came near to supplying the quantity of vehicles needed. Neither was the quality good enough. Few, if any, German trucks were robust enough for military use. But in 'lightning war' such failures did not matter. By the time the hardware of war fell apart the enemy had surrendered.

The Germans used bases in Czechoslovakia to attack Poland from north and south, as well as from the west. Poland's geography, and the historic threat from both west and east, precluded effective defensive works. Like the French, the Poles would not build any defence lines that relinquished large areas of the country to the enemy, and they tried to hold the Germans along the frontier. It was hoped that this would provide time for the country to mobilize its army and mount a counter-offensive, and for France and Britain to attack Germany from the west.

For the first time, the world saw the sort of opening air attacks that nowadays are the way in which most wars begin.

German intelligence—both on the ground and by photo-reconnaissance—had prepared the target lists, and hampered as they were by bad weather, the Luftwaffe managed to destroy much of the Polish air force in the first hours of war. Medium-range bombing attacks on Polish towns disrupted mobilization of the army. At the fighting front Stuka dive-bombers served as efficient artillery, for the Stuka training schools produced men able to get at least 50 per cent of their bombs within 25 metres of the target. (Stuka is an abbreviation of Sturzkampfflugzeug, dive-bomber. The name could be applied to any aircraft used in this role, but was often used to refer specifically to the Junkers Ju 87.)

The Polish army, and its air component, proved a dauntless opponent, but it was not equipped to fight a modern war. The Germans used armoured divisions to pierce the front. Following them, conventional armies converged to surround the Poles in two vast encirclements, one inside the other. It was the seventeenth day of the campaign when the second set of pincers met at Brest-Litovsk in the middle of eastern Poland. On the same day, the Red Army moved across Poland's eastern frontier. The fighting continued but the war was decided.

The Germans, always ready to learn, studied their campaign. The supply of fuel and ammunition to the fast advancing units must be improved. Battalion and regimental commanders were urged to keep closer to the fighting men. Artillery must be pushed forward more quickly. The lighter tanks—the Mark Is and Mark IIs—had suffered 89 per cent and 83 per cent losses, while the heavier ones—Mark IIIs and Mark IVs—had suffered only 26 per cent and 19 per cent casualties.[28] The factories must shift to the production of heavier tanks. Lighter models could be adapted for reconnaissance and command duties; some were converted into self-propelled artillery and anti-tank guns. Every change was designed for striking harder and faster next time. For soldiers who believed that battle was to be revolutionized by mobile forces, the Polish campaign had been too orthodox. They wanted blitzkrieg.

LORD GORT

The 6th Viscount Gort, the hereditary Irish peer appointed
to command the British Expeditionary Force, was not unor-
thodox. He had spent much of the First World War as a staff
officer, but when he went to the front line with the Grenadiers he showed himself to be a fearless leader. He ended
the war with an amazing array of awards for bravery: a VC,
three DSOs, an MC. In 1937 Gort's record as a fighting
soldier had played a big part in his becoming Chief of the
Imperial General Staff, CIGS, Britain's top soldier. He was
the youngest man to get this job and he was jumped a rank
to pass many senior officers such as generals Brooke, Dill
and Wavell. Gort had been chosen by Leslie Hore-Belisha,
the war minister, to revitalize the army. There is little sign
that he did this.

In September 1939, Gort relinquished the role of CIGS
for the even more coveted job of commanding the BEF. By
this time he had made many enemies, including his political
chief Hore-Belisha. It was this rift between Hore-Belisha
and his most important general that enabled the army's top
brass to campaign against the minister. The fact that Hore-
Belisha was Jewish gave a specially unpleasant dimension to
this squalid intrigue. The end result was that the generals
were divided and Gort—whose subordinates, such as the ir-
repressible Alan Brooke, were less than loyal to him—made
no stronger. After Dunkirk, when Gort needed friends in
high places, none were to be found.

'Fat Boy' Gort—depicted by the British Press as 'Tiger
Gort'—was thought to be directly responsible to his king and
government for the British force he led. In fact he was no
more than the commander of an army; one of many armies.
In Paris, General Maurice Gamelin, the supreme commander, regarded the BEF as a minor element of his western defences but Gort did nothing without first checking

with London.[29] This ambivalence was to play a part in the final tragedy of the BEF.

THE BRITISH EXPEDITIONARY FORCE

In the first hours of war Britain sent RAF units to France and put together the British Expeditionary Force, consisting of all five regular home-based divisions. They were joined in the early months of 1940 by five divisions of Territorials (part-time volunteers now serving full-time). Their restricted prewar training schedule meant that drilling had been neglected in favour of more practical tactical and weapons training. But General Gort was a Guards officer, and the regular soldiers around him were distressed to attend parades alongside soldiers deficient in drill. The 'Terriers' soon found themselves doing quite a lot of marching and parading when they might have been training for combat.[30]

Britain's professional army was prepared to remedy other deficiencies it found in the civilian soldiers who joined up to help fight the Germans:

> The Colonel, the Adjutant told us, had been concerned and shocked on the previous evening—a guest night—to observe that some of the newly joined officers had been in doubt about the correct implements and glasses to employ for the successive courses. If we would be kind enough to pay attention and take notes, he would give us a practical demonstration. Without batting an eyelid this impeccable young man then sat down at the table and an equally solemn mess waiter served him first with token soup, then with token fish, then with token meat, then with token pudding and finally with a token savoury. The wine waiter went through the motions of pouring out sherry, burgundy, port and brandy.

'Somewhere I still possess the valuable notes I made', added Ralph Arnold, who shortly after this performance at the Infantry Training Centre became an aide with Lord Ironside, now CIGS.[31]

Another three divisions crossed the Channel in April but these were so ill-trained and ill-equipped that they were classified as 'labour' formations. Since the BEF spent more time digging and constructing defence lines than in any form of battle training the distinction made little difference at this stage. Although there were tank formations in the BEF, Britain's one and only armoured division was still not ready for action.[32]

The British force was criticized by the French as being an inadequate contribution. Its size was seen as evidence that the British were relying on the French to fight the war. They had some cause to complain: the British Expeditionary Force was smaller than the Dutch army, and only 40 per cent the size of the Belgian army, while the French fielded 88 divisions from a population smaller than Britain's.

The 150,000 British soldiers put at the disposal of the French were deployed along the frontier of neutral Belgium, where there was not even an enemy to face. It was logical to put the British along this northern part of France's western frontier, for it shortened their lines of supply, which came through Arras from England. There was also the fact that any German attack on France was likely to come this way.

The southern part of the front was defended by the mighty Maginot Line. The sector along the hilly Ardennes forest was almost universally regarded as impassable to armour. Therefore, said the experts, the Germans would have to strike at France by going through Belgium. When this happened, said Gamelin, who made the master plan, the Allied northern armies would swing forward to meet the enemy in Belgium and halt him there. The northern part of this 'door' would have furthest to swing, so the all-mechanized BEF was best equipped to do it.

The British were justifiably proud to field the world's first fully mechanized army. Unlike their contemporaries, the

British had relegated the horse to ceremonial duties, while Tommies went to war on wheels and tracks. And yet a closer look reveals that it wasn't all that the War Office Press releases claimed. One division commander, Bernard Montgomery, later wrote:

> The British Army was totally unfit to fight a first-class war on the continent of Europe . . . In the years preceding the outbreak of war no large-scale exercises with troops had been held in England for some time. Indeed, the Regular Army was unfit to take part in a realistic exercise. The Field Army had an inadequate signals system, no administrative backing and no organization for high-command; all these had to be improvised on mobilization. The transport was inadequate and was completed on mobilization by vehicles requisitioned from civilian firms. Much of the transport of my division consisted of civilian vans and lorries from the towns of England; they were in bad repair and when my division moved from the ports up to its concentration area near the French frontier, the countryside of France was strewn with broken-down vehicles.[33]

Gort, during his time as CIGS, had done very little to build the modern army that Britain needed to fight the Germans. The armoured division was not ready for war and tank experts had been given no chance to contribute their opinions to the top planners. And Gort had shown little concern about air support for his army. Army Cooperation RAF squadrons were neglected, and the army was permitted no say in the use of the 'Advanced Air Striking Force', the tactical bombing RAF squadrons sent to France to support the land forces.

But France and Britain had a breathing space. While concentrating their efforts on Poland, the Germans remained inactive, apart from a few air reconnaissance sorties, on their Western Front. The Allied politicians, and the soldiers too, breathed a sigh of relief and made sure their German enemies were not provoked. France asked Britain not to bomb Germany lest that brought retaliatory bombing attacks on French factories. Instead the RAF dropped propaganda pamphlets which Churchill sarcastically hoped might rouse the Germans to a higher morality. Only at sea was the phoney war real. Time is on our side, the optimists said.

WAR PRODUCTION

Had such optimists seen the German production figures they might have been even more complacent. In quantity, if not in quality, the Allies were outstripping the Germans. In the first six months of 1940, Anglo-French factories produced 1,412 tanks compared with German production of 558. The chaos of French aircraft production was being improved and brought Anglo-French aircraft production to 6,794, double that of Germany.[34]

The change of pace resulting from the Munich crisis began to show benefits in the opening months of the war. The organization of Britain's air defences—notably the radar chain—improved every day. The worry was that so many vital items, including Swiss fuses and Dutch and American radio valves used in the radar stations, had to be imported. So did many aircraft components, and as much as 25 per cent of Britain's wartime steel came from overseas.

Britain's steel-making was poor in both quality and quantity. Although German domestic steel production was not large, conquests provided a total of 212 million tons a year by the end of 1940. At this time Britain's annual output was a mere 18 million tons.[35]

Hitler was the most popular leader Germany had ever known.[36] Believing that the naval mutinies had brought Germany's downfall in 1918, and remembering the revolutions that followed, he was determined to avoid discontent at home. He would fight his wars while Germany continued to enjoy many of the luxuries of a peacetime-style economy.

During the prewar years Hitler had built a well equipped army while keeping German living standards as high as any in Europe. To further increase production he would have to do as the British were doing—increase working hours and draft women into the war factories. Hitler was reluctant to do either of these things. (In fact the proportion of women workers was about the same in both countries, but many German women were engaged in such inessential jobs as domestic service. Furthermore the generous allowances paid to the wives of German soldiers gave no immediate incentive for them to do war work.)

As the war continued, the Germans expanded their work-force by using foreign labourers, including those brought by compulsion or coercion, prisoners of war and slaves. Even these drastic measures did little to increase German war production. At no time did the Germans, together with the Austrian and Czech output, reach the level of production they had achieved in the First World War. During the first year of the German assault on Russia, they did not even reach a quarter of their 1918 production. Albert Speer, who became minister of war production in February 1942, had no doubts that bureaucracy—aggravated by the Nazi authoritarian system—was at the heart of the failure. As an example, he pointed out that the Ordnance Office employed ten times as many staff during the Second World War as they had in the First World War.[37]

No accurate estimates of German production were available to the Allied governments because the British intelligence services could not provide regular reliable and informative reports from even one agent in Germany. The Secret Intelligence Service had to depend upon refugees, escapers and what could be gleaned from foreign newspapers.

All the same Germany's victories convinced the world of its overwhelming strength. Even after the war Churchill still believed that, at this time, German munitions manufacture was much more 'fruitful' than that of the Allies.

NORWAY: THE ALLIES START FIGHTING

The essence of Anglo-French policy in these days of what an American journalist called a Phoney War, and Chamberlain termed Twilight War, was to go and fight somewhere else. The French proposed schemes for fighting in south-east Europe and wanted to bomb Russian oil wells in the Caucasus. Fortunately these crackpot ideas came to nothing. However another lunatic scheme did.

In November 1939 Stalin, quick to utilize his allotted sphere of influence under the pact with Hitler, effectively took control of Latvia, Estonia and Lithuania. Faced with demands for their territory, the Finns refused to fall in with Russia's demands. On 30 November 1939 the Red Army attacked with five armies, against which the Finns put up stout resistance.

Still smarting from the way in which Stalin had done a deal with Hitler, the men in London and Paris impulsively offered aid to the Finns. Without consulting the British, the French Premier Daladier said he'd send 50,000 volunteers and 100 bombers to Finland via northern Norway and Sweden. Britain followed suit and said it would send 50 bombers. Landing at the (iron-ore) port of Narvik, the troops would travel by railway through the mountains to the Swedish iron-ore region, and thus to Finland. Behind these altruistic offers there lurked a cynical plot. On the pretext of aiding the Finns, the Allies planned to seize neutral Sweden's iron-ore fields and prevent them exporting to Germany. It is strange to record that the same Allied leaders who were frightened to attack Germany's Western Front, and were forbidding their air forces to bomb German towns, were planning to send soldiers and bombing planes to fight the Red Army and bring Russia into the war against them. Before this ill-conceived operation could begin, the Red

Army, despite grievous casualties, broke through the Finnish fortified defences. The Finns asked for a cease-fire.

The Allied governments looked again at the map of Scandinavia showing the iron-ore fields. The Royal Navy was ordered to lay a minefield in neutral Norwegian territorial waters. This would block the ice-free route used by the ships carrying ore to German ports. Churchill wrote afterwards:

> As our mining of Norwegian waters might provoke a German retort, it was also agreed that a British brigade and French contingent should be sent to Narvik to clear the port and advance to the Swedish frontier. Other forces should be dispatched to Stavanger, Bergen and Trondheim, in order to deny these bases to the enemy.[38]

It was the same plan as before, but dressed up in new clothes: an Allied force would cross Norway, invade Sweden and seize the iron-ore fields. The plan is noteworthy, not just for its cavalier attitude to the neutral countries but in its revelation of top-level over-confidence and a profound ignorance of what fighting the Germans would entail.

There was an intelligence failure too, for Churchill thought that Swedish iron-ore provided the basis of the German war industry and this has been repeated in most histories of the war. But the idea that Allied seizure of the Swedish ore fields would have slowed the German war machine—let alone brought it to a sudden halt—is difficult to sustain. Germany had no urgent need of the ore. In the first year of war no less than 40 per cent of Germany's steel was still being allocated to civilian needs, and this figure excludes construction work and exports. Germany had immense stockpiles of steel. It was coming from Austria, the Protectorate (as German-occupied Czechoslovakia was now called) and Poland.[39] By the end of 1940 over 200 million tons a year was available to Germany. To what extent, then, was this *casus belli* real? Could it have been Britain's excuse for some other strategy, such as the occupation of Scandinavian naval bases? Or was it intended to provoke the Germans to a Scandinavian campaign that the Allied high commands were confident they could win?

Whatever the true motives, on 8 April 1940 the Royal Navy mine-layers began operations. For months Admiral Raeder had been warning Hitler of the consequences of British air and naval bases in Norway, while telling him too of the door to the outer oceans that Norwegian ports would give German shipping. Other Nazi leaders supported Raeder,[40] although the army thought an invasion of Norway too hazardous to contemplate. Göring's dislike of it came from the need to subordinate Luftwaffe elements to the army's command, but Erhard Milch, Göring's second in command, was happy to cooperate. Actually it was Göring's private intelligence service, blandly named the Research Office, Forschungsamt (FA), that provoked Hitler into action. Göring's men tapped any telephone that might provide useful information. They were helped since 1935 by the Magnetofen, a small recording machine from the laboratories of AEG and IG-Farben.[41] When the recorded voice of a neutral ambassador[42] revealed the British plan to sow mines in Norwegian waters, Hitler gave the invasion forces the go-ahead.

Having dabbled in the Polish campaign, Hitler took personal command of the Norwegian invasion. His plans were drawn up by his small OKW (High Command of the Armed Forces) office. Bypassing the normal channels, orders were funnelled through a corps headquarters where the day-to-day work was done. Much to their consternation, the high commanders of the army, navy and air force had no say in the planning: they were simply told to provide the units as needed for Hitler's campaign. The army's own planners were at this time working on 'Fall Gelb', Plan Yellow: the attack on France and the Low Countries.

The timing of the German invasion of Norway was vital. There were no landing craft: the ships would have to come alongside a jetty and put the troops ashore like passengers getting off a ferry.[43] All the landings would have to be made at exactly the same time because the first landing would warn the Norwegian defences and any delayed landings would attract fierce opposition.

Oslo was still at peace on the evening of Friday 5 April when the German ambassador invited distinguished guests, including members of the Norwegian government, to a film show. *Baptism of Fire* was a stark and horrifying documentary of the war that the Luftwaffe brought upon Poland. Its script and aerial sequences were the work of a former air ace[44] and his airborne camera lingered upon the gutted buildings and smouldering ruins of Warsaw. 'And remember', said the film narration, 'this is what happens when the German Luftwaffe strikes'. As the film's finale the song 'Bomben auf England', punctuated with trumpets and drum rolls, concluded with the spirited line: 'Bombs! Bombs! Bombs on England!' Just in case anyone in the audience had missed the implication, an end caption said that this outcome was something for which the Poles could thank their British and French friends. It was diplomacy in the true Nazi style: crude and bellicose. When the room lights came on there was no applause; no reaction at all. The audience was stunned.

Hitler chose the same date as the Royal Navy to begin his Norwegian expedition, and for the same reason. It was a dark night of the new moon period and the coincidence almost brought disaster to Hitler's armada. Four days after German supply ships embarked on 3 April the man at Bletchley Park responsible for 'traffic analysis'—interpreting the volume of signals rather than the content—warned the Admiralty's Operation Intelligence Centre of an unprecedented volume of German naval signals activity west of Denmark, and in the exit from the Baltic. It was the German invasion fleet moving to Norway,[45] and the Germans were at their most vulnerable. Yet the warning was dismissed and the British navy continued with its mine-laying as planned.

Even when the German shipping movements were confirmed, the navy failed to counter them. Churchill, first lord of the Admiralty, thought the naval movements were German warships heading north to break out into the Atlantic.

1. Before Munich—Winston Churchill talks earnestly in Whitehall to Lord Halifax, Secretary of State for Foreign Affairs, after returning from the Continent in March 1938

2. General Wilhelm Keitel, Hitler's Army Chief of Staff, in conversation with the Führer on a flight to Munich in March 1938

3. Hitler receives Prime Minister Chamberlain at Obersalzberg in September 1938—'the prime move in 'appeasement'

4. Admirals Erich Raeder and Karl Dönitz planning the German U-boat campaign in the North Atlantic, October 1939

5. Six days after becoming prime minister, Churchill flew to France for talks on the imminent collapse with General Gamelin and General Lord Gort, commander of the British Expeditionary Force, May 1940

6. General Erwin Rommel, after sweeping through France in May 1940, became the notorious 'Desert Fox' of North Africa

7. Hitler meets the fascist Spanish dictator General Franco, October 1940

8. General Thomas Blamey, commander of Australian forces in the Middle East, talks to troops just returned from Crete to Palestine

9. General 'Dick' O'Connor with the Commander-in-Chief of British forces in the Middle East, General Sir Archibald Wavell, outside Bardia, Libya, January 1941

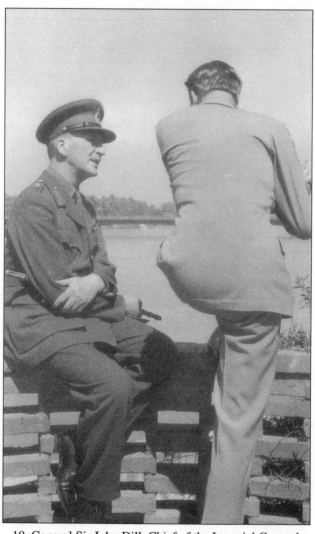

10. General Sir John Dill, Chief of the Imperial General Staff, with the Foreign Secretary Anthony Eden in Cairo, March 1941

FIGURE 17:
Junkers Ju 52/3m transport

The Royal Navy's warships were sent too far north to intercept the invasion. The first sign that the RN had been completely outwitted came when the Polish submarine *Orzel* sank a German troopship *Rio de Janeiro* to pitch men and horses into the cold Norwegian coastal water. At 6 am on 9 April, Hitler learned of his success: at Narvik, Trondheim and Bergen U-boats were guarding the port entrances. The bulk of his seaborne invasion force had arrived safely. Two and a half hours later Junkers transport aircraft were landing troops at Oslo's airport.

10 GERMAN ARMS OUTSTRETCHED

I grieve, not because I have to die for my country, but because I have not lifted my arm against the enemy . . . much as I have desired to achieve something.

CALLICRATES: DYING WORDS WHEN MORTALLY WOUNDED AT PLATAEA

When Germans marched into Denmark, resistance collapsed so quickly that it became the only occupied nation not to have a properly constituted government in exile. For a long time the Germans treated the Danes well, and Danish political parties, including the Communists, continued to function as before.[1]

Norway was not so quickly conquered, but it was a German triumph nevertheless and one in which the Luftwaffe played a vital role. At Oslo and Christiansand serious opposition by the Norwegian coastal defences had been overcome by the Luftwaffe. At Christiansand bombers attacked the harbour forts so that the invaders could land. Luftwaffe parachute troops captured Oslo airport, permitting the transport aircraft to come in. The seizure of airports, and the speed with which Luftwaffe squadrons moved into them, complete with maintenance and repair units, soon gave the Germans complete control of the air.

The muddled Allied reaction began at the embarkation port of Rosyth when the troops were separated from tanks, artillery and stores. They did not get to Norway until ten days after the German landings. The French contingent was no better organized: a ship loaded with vital supplies was found to be too large to enter harbour. Said General Sir Adrian Carton de Wiart:

The Invasion of Norway 1940

- ● Seaborne attack
- Ⓐ Airborne attack on an airfield

2,000 Men — Narvik

1,700 Men — Trondheim

1,900 Men — Bergen

Airborne landing 2,500 Men

1,100 Men

Airborne landing 3,000 Men

Oslo
Stavanger
Kristiansand
Skagerrack

2,000 Men

SWEDEN

FINLAND

NORWAY

DENMARK

Baltic Sea

■ Berlin

ENGLAND

NETHERLANDS

BELGIUM

GERMANY

FRANCE

BOHEMIA

MORAVIA

SLOVAKIA

LITHUANIA

EAST PRUSSIA

German conquered Poland

The French Chasseurs Alpins were a fine body of troops and would have been ideal for the job in hand, but ironically they lacked one or two essentials, which made them completely useless to us. I had wanted to move them forward, but General Audet regretted they had no means of transport, as their mules had not turned up. Then I suggested that his ski-troops might move forward, but it was found that they were lacking some essential strap for their skis, without which they were unable to move.[2]

In the north, the landing of British and French troops kept the battle going but there was never any doubt about the outcome. Everywhere the German air force was the decisive factor. It was air cover that permitted the Germans to keep pouring into Oslo the reinforcements that won the campaign. Neither the French nor the British were prepared for the closely coordinated operations of German air and ground forces. Despite grievous errors at the top, units of the Royal Navy fought with distinction and success but the vital damage to the German navy had been done by the Norwegians. And the RN had discovered that its ships could not operate safely in 'narrow seas'—waters within range of land-based enemy bombers. The RN's precious radar-equipped anti-aircraft cruisers (there were only three of them) were severely restricted by high-sided fiords which nullified the radar.

Within six weeks the Germans had Norway. The campaign had called for coordination of air, land and sea forces, and Hitler, having taken control of the invasion, took all the credit for its success. His generals, who had all advised against it, now had to listen to Hitler's humiliating lectures. Only Grossadmiral Raeder, who had pressed for it, was smiled upon.

Like the Polish campaign, it was a victory largely attributable to the efficiency—and sometimes improvisation—of the German supply services. Göring was not thanked for the Luftwaffe's contribution; all credit went to Erhard Milch, who, while retaining his other posts, had gone to Hamburg to take personal command of Luftflotte 5, which carried out the largest air transport movement ever seen up to that time. In over 3,000 sorties by the Junkers Ju 52 transports, almost 3,000 men were moved, together with 2,370 tons of supplies and a quarter of a million gallons of fuel.

The most serious German setback was the German naval losses. All ten destroyers used to ferry the invasion force to Narvik were sunk, along with their tanker refuelling force. The Oslo coastal guns sank the heavy cruiser *Blücher* and, at a time when the navy should have been husbanding all its resources, Raeder recklessly committed his battleships *Gneisenau* and *Scharnhorst* to unnecessary forays in the north where both were seriously damaged and out of commission for many months. So the German navy found itself with only three cruisers and four destroyers fit for sea duty. Admiral Erich Raeder needed all the good will he could get from Hitler. His navy was now quite unfitted to support and protect a seaborne invasion of England.

WINSTON CHURCHILL

The Anglo-French failure in Norway could not be glossed over. It caused considerable public disquiet, and Chamberlain's Conservative government came under fierce attack even from its own supporters. There was a two-day debate about the débâcle in Norway. Some of Churchill's backers cautiously ensured that their savage attacks upon Chamberlain's conduct of the war did not harm Churchill, but when one of them made excuses for him, he immediately jumped up and told the House: 'I take complete responsibility for everything that has been done at the Admiralty, and I take my full share of the burden'.

The Labour party were afraid to force a division in case a substantial vote of confidence consolidated Chamberlain's power. But some women members of Parliament, having retired to an all-party room of their own, resolved to force a vote, and this made the Labour party chiefs agree to divide the house.[3]

And so, on 8 May, Churchill found himself making the speech winding up the debate for the government. It was probably the most difficult performance of his career. Churchill had spent his life opposing the sort of policies that Chamberlain personified; and now he was making the key speech to defend the man and the policies. But, as first lord of the Admiralty, he was responsible for many of the misjudgements that brought the Norwegian fiasco and caused the widespread rage that was threatening to topple the government. After a two-day recital of German triumphs, and the resulting atmosphere of impending doom, his speech 'amused and dazzled everyone with his virtuosity'.[4] One of his secretariat later wrote:

> He was constantly heckled by the Labour opposition, and he tore into them vehemently and often angrily . . . Churchill knew that he was defending positions which were, in many respects, indefensible. He knew that if the bitterest critics had their way, Chamberlain would resign. He knew that, in that case, he would probably become Prime Minister himself. But throughout the entire political crisis he never spoke or acted except in absolute loyalty to his Prime Minister.[5]

The vote brought the government's majority down from more than 200 to 81. The way in which so many of his own party had either voted against him or abstained was enough to convince even the egoistic Chamberlain that he could not remain as prime minister. The Labour party, which most people now thought should be represented in the wartime government, refused in any circumstances to serve under Neville Chamberlain. Many thought his replacement would have to be Lord Halifax, and yet several people noticed that feeling in the House was veering towards Winston Churchill.[6] Chamberlain, who had been the target of so much of his criticism, had no affection for Churchill. King George

VI, who consistently tried to influence political decisions, declared Halifax to be his preference. Fellow Conservatives had no great love for Churchill, who had changed his political allegiance more than once, who had attacked them again and again with uncomfortably accurate warnings of the need for rearmament, and had in the end proved right. The (non-elected) members of the upper House remembered him saying that their chamber was 'filled with doddering peers, cute financial magnates, clever wire-pullers, big brewers with bulbous noses. All the enemies of progress are there'. The Socialists had made him into their bogey man for using troops in the Welsh mining strikes of 1911, and for his role in the General Strike of 1926. Anyone who listened to the debate could see that many of the failures of the Norwegian campaign had been Churchill's fault.

So why did Churchill get his position of ultimate power? His speech had proclaimed him his own man; endearingly loyal to the wretched Chamberlain, fiercely combative with his political opponents, ready to admit mistakes but bending his knee to no one. Certainly a large section of the British public thought that a man who had, during the 1930s, constantly opposed Hitler, and had urged rearmament to stop him, must be the best man now to confront him. But the opinion of the man in the street does not count for much in such a situation. At one time it was widely said that Lord Halifax—who would have had technical problems running the country from the House of Lords—was gentlemanly enough to give way to Churchill on this account.[7] Nowadays more convincing explanations have emerged.

It seems that Chamberlain favoured Churchill as the lesser of two evils. For him to say this openly would have brought the displeasure of his party, so he conspired to get Churchill into the job. Possibly Chamberlain hoped that Churchill's tenure would be short, and he himself would return before long to number ten Downing Street. Some said that the cabinet seat, and the job as party chairman, that Churchill let Chamberlain keep was the offer that tipped the balance. Chamberlain's remarks to his colleagues suggest that he knew that Churchill's elevation to the premiership had been only a matter of time once war began. One recent history says Chamberlain feared that if Lord Halifax gained power he would immediately start armistice negotiations with Hitler.[8]

There is plenty of evidence to support such allegations. Britain's acute financial difficulties meant that continuing the war would involve going to the United States cap in hand. This was not a task that would appeal to Halifax, who had grave doubts about the wisdom of continuing the war in any case.

Winston Churchill never showed any doubts about confronting dictators of the left or of the right. He championed individual freedom to the point of being a maverick. Having an American mother, the daughter of a tycoon, provided Winston with a realistic view of the disposition and power of the United States at a time when most of those around him were patronizing and smugly superior about that nation.

Winston Leonard Spencer-Churchill was born on 30 November 1874 in Blenheim Palace, built and named by Churchill's ancestor the 1st Duke of Marlborough to celebrate the battle he had won. Winston's father was a cynical, irascible and unpredictable politician who spent most of his adult life suffering the agonies of syphilis, from which he eventually died. Churchill's mother was reputed to have had 200 lovers and his brother Jack was probably fathered by one of them.[9] Churchill saw very little of either parent, being attended by a nanny until, still not eight years old, he was sent to boarding school. Lining up in alphabetical order at Harrow, one of England's most exclusive private schools, Winston noticed that he would be nearer to the front if his name began with C. He liked being near the front of everything so he dropped the hyphenated name and became plain Churchill. His performance at school was so lamentable that the housemaster wrote to his mother saying: 'his forgetfulness, carelessness, unpunctuality, and irregularity in every way, have really been so serious, that I write to ask you, when he is at home to speak very gravely to him on the subject'.[10]

The decision to send him to Sandhurst Military College was taken as much because of his poor academic performance as because of his interest in things military.

As a cherubic golden-haired lieutenant in the fashionable 4th Hussars, with five months' leave every year, he excelled in polo, steeple-chasing and hunting. Using his father's influence to the full, and subsidized by an allowance from his mother, he chased after wars and made no secret of his determination to win medals. In 1895, on his twenty-first birthday, he came under fire from rebels while visiting Cuba and was awarded a Spanish medal. A sniffy English newspaper said: 'Spending a holiday in fighting other people's battles is rather an extraordinary proceeding even for a Churchill'.[11] He won a coveted 'mention in dispatches' fighting Afghan tribesmen in northern India. At Omdurman on the Nile, he took part in the last great cavalry charge made by the British army.

Churchill supplemented his pay by contributing articles to newspapers and writing books about his adventures. He also showed no reluctance to address political meetings. But a lieutenant who dabbled in politics, and fluently criticized the strategy and tactics of his senior officers, was not universally popular. He left the army and went as a war correspondent to South Africa, where in 1899 he was captured by the Boers. He escaped, and the warrant for his arrest provides this snapshot him: 'Englishman 25 years old, about 5 ft 8 in tall, average build, walks with a slight stoop, speaks through the nose, cannot pronounce the letter S'. It would still do to identify him half a century later. So would the habit of smoking cigars and drinking at all hours of the day.

In 1900 Churchill embarked on the long and restless political career that was to bring him infinite joy and pain. He was elected to Parliament as a Conservative but four years later his beliefs in free trade took him over to the Liberals, who in 1911 made him first lord of the Admiralty (a post which he held again in 1939). His decision to keep the fleet mobilized after exercises in the summer of 1914 was an important one and widely applauded, but he took the blame for what proved a disastrous attempt to seize Turkey's Gallipoli Peninsula in 1915. Some said his ideas had been changed too much for him to be the guilty party. But dejected and almost 40 years old, he resigned from office and went to serve as an infantry colonel on the Western Front. Later he had other important jobs, secretary for war and colonial secretary, before rejoining the Conservative party in 1922. They made him chancellor of the exchequer from 1924 until 1929. But after that his political past caught up with him and he became an obstinate outcast whose career seemed to have ended. All through his life he suffered from the bouts of melancholy that he referred to as 'The Black Dog', but his capacity for reading, writing and working was undiminished.

Churchill's restless political history, and radical ideas, had left him with powerful enemies and few friends. Yet in practical terms he was never an extremist: extremism was more likely to be revealed in his critics. As a Liberal minister in 1909 he'd attacked the gulf between rich and poor, and 'the absence of any established minimum standard of life and comfort among the workers, and at the other end, the swift increase in vulgar, joyless luxury'. In 1918 he demanded lenient terms for the defeated Germans. His official biographer observes: 'A most remarkable feature of Winston Churchill's career is the way in which almost every action of his was interpreted by contemporaries in the worst possible light'.[12] In the interwar years, when lethargy crippled the thought processes of voters and politicians alike, it was Churchill's energy that frightened everyone and excluded him from office. In May 1936 he asked the House: 'Is there no grip, no driving force, no mental energy, no power of decision or design?'

It was an extraordinary coincidence that Chamberlain's enforced decision to step down should come at the same hour that the Germans attacked France and the Low Countries. Churchill, sixty-five years old, came to power at the moment of Britain's direst peril. 'I have nothing to offer', he told the nation on 13 May, 'but blood, toil, tears and sweat'.

He told the House of Commons: 'You ask what is our aim? I can answer in one word: victory, victory at all costs, victory in spite of all terror, victory however long and hard the road may be; for without victory there is no survival'. Then he left the Chamber, eyes brimming with tears, but remarked to an aide: 'That got the sods didn't it?'[13]

In fact these orations cut little ice with his fellow members of the House of Commons. One eyewitness said his speech on the 13 May was not well received, and remarked upon the far warmer welcome given to Chamberlain that day. Although Churchill was popular with a large section of the general public, the cold reception he got from the House provoked journalists to complain (to Chamberlain) that the hostility shown to Churchill was having a bad effect abroad.[14] Only after that did the chief whip persuade backbenchers to rectify their manners. From then onwards Churchill was dutifully cheered and applauded.

THE GERMAN DRIVE WESTWARD

On 10 May 1940, with the battle in Norway still raging, the German armies facing France and the Low Countries moved forward to carry out Plan Yellow. Supported by fierce air attacks, two German Army Groups—A and B—were deployed in a plan devised by General Erich von Manstein. Army Group B, in the north, using largely horse-drawn units, rolled across the frontiers into the Netherlands and northern Belgium. These neutral countries, which had gone to extreme lengths to avoid giving Hitler any excuse to attack them, resisted the invaders. Meanwhile Army Group A was threading its way unseen through the narrow forest roads of the Ardennes. This was a region that the Allies had officially proclaimed to be impassable to tanks. And yet this Army Group included the greater part of Germany's armoured divisions.

Although the Allies were caught completely by surprise,

the northern attack was the sort of development that the French and British generals expected. Gamelin's contingency plans were taken out and dusted off while the newspaper photographers provided pictures and platitudes about the sons of Tommy Atkins meeting the daughters of Mademoiselle from Armentières. The British and French armies in the northern section of the front plodded forward to join up with the Belgian and Dutch defenders. They were pleasantly surprised to find how little they were harassed by German air attacks.

In 1940 the kingdom of the Netherlands was, in some ways, the most foreign land in Europe. The Dutch stood apart from other Europeans. Their language was a challenge even for Germans. Their clocks and watches were set to a different time (2 hours and 40 minutes ahead of Germany, 40 minutes behind Belgium, France and Britain, and 20 minutes ahead of Greenwich Mean Time). Their worldwide colonies provided oil and raw materials: Indonesia (at that time the Dutch East Indies of Java and Sumatra) was the 'spice islands' so many early explorers had sought. Neutrality in the First World War had further enriched the Dutch, who had hoped to remain neutral in the Second World War.

They were an easy target. In no way prepared for a European war, their tiny army was trained and equipped only to police a colonial empire. No one seriously considered the possibility that their towns might be bombed and they had not organized the sort of 'air-raid precautions' to be found in France, Germany and Britain. Their military defence plan consisted of falling back into the part of the Netherlands that the Dutch call 'Holland' and manning trenches with infantry supported by a few light tanks and armoured cars.

The German attack on the Dutch, like others, came without declaration of war. To speed up the crossings of the Dutch waterways, German airborne troops were dropped to seize bridges for the advancing columns. Tricks and deception were used: Dutch Fascists dressed as Dutch military policemen helped to capture key bridges over the Juliana

Canal. Many of the nation's vital objectives were taken in the first hours of war.

Belgium was only marginally better prepared for the German onslaught. Like the Dutch, the Belgians had refused to coordinate their defence plans with those of France and Britain lest Hitler use that as an excuse to invade them.

FIGURE 18:
German DFS 230 4.1 glider

The Belgian border and the Albert Canal's bridges were guarded by the mighty defensive fort of Eben Emael. This huge citadel was soon overcome by German infantry. To everyone's amazement, the soldiers came from gliders towed by Junkers transports. They sailed out of the dawn sky to settle gently on the thick concrete roofs, disgorging specially trained men who were able to subdue the garrison by dropping explosive charges down the air vents.

Bitter charges by the French government immediately after the Belgian capitulation have left in French and British history books the convenient story that the Belgians gave up

virtually without a fight. This fiction was given further cre-
dence by the self-serving memoirs of General Alan Brooke,
one of Gort's corp commanders. The Germans did not share
these estimates. 'It was astonishing to see that the Belgians
fought with increasing tenacity the nearer the end approached', said one German officer.[15] The more one delves
into the history of this fatal month, the more clearly it
emerges that soldiers, sailors and airmen of all nations
fought with tenacity when they were properly led. The Belgians were certainly no exception.

Nevertheless within a short time the Dutch and the Belgians found it more difficult to put up a spirited defence
when the British and French armies were in retreat. The
Germans were nowhere met in full-scale battle nor seriously
delayed. Army Group B had followed Manstein's plan and it
had worked.

By 13 May it was becoming apparent that the Germans
fighting in Belgium and Holland were only one half of the
German invading force. Spearheads of Army Group A
emerged from the Ardennes forest and were seen along the
banks of the River Meuse near Sedan. This unexpected sight
did not panic the French, who were well set up in defensive
positions on their side of the river. The military textbook
said a river would hold the enemy. It said that the Germans
would need a long time to bring up their artillery. Then they
would subject the French positions to a lengthy bombardment before starting the infantry assault and river-crossing.

The Germans had thrown away that textbook early in the
1914–18 war. Initiative, speed and surprise was the new German technique. Richthofen's Stuka dive-bombers were their
artillery. With the defenders taking cover from continuous
air attacks, the Germans got their tanks across the Meuse in
a matter of hours. Determined and valiant attacks by RAF
light bombers did little beyond demonstrating the deadly effectiveness of the Flak with which the Luftwaffe defended
the crossing places.

The Germans were not dismayed by tanks in the way that
the Allied soldiers were. Rommel, like any good factory

manager, liked to be where the hard work was done. He crossed the Meuse in one of the first boats. With a small number of his men on the far bank, he showed what could be achieved by determination and little else:

> I then moved up north along a deep gully to the Company Enkefort. As we arrived an alarm came in: 'Enemy tanks in front'. The company had no anti-tank weapons, and I therefore gave orders for small arms fire to be opened on the tanks as quickly as possible, whereupon we saw them pull back into a hollow about a thousand yards north-west of Leffé. Large numbers of French stragglers came through the bushes and slowly laid down their arms.[16]

Maps showing the German movement across the Meuse have to simplify the crossings with a few arrows. In fact the German army filtered across the river man by man, unit by unit. At Leffé, near Dinant, some of Rommel's men captured a footbridge, others paddled across in tiny inflated boats. Elsewhere men dragged motor-cycles along a narrow stone weir to get to the far bank. At Houx they clambered over a lock gate. Light vehicles were ferried across on big rubber boats. At Bouvignes soldiers put their armoured cars on to pontoon rafts. Here and there a bridge was captured, or a damaged bridge repaired. When enough pontoons arrived the engineers fitted them together to make a bridge. Constantly under fire, groups of Germans improvised their crossings to the far bank of the river in increased numbers before they joined up and moved forward.

By nightfall on 15 May a 50-mile gap had been torn into the French defences. Through it came the armour and trucks crammed with infantry, pressing onwards in a long curving route alongside the River Somme, heading for the Channel coast.

And yet this does not tell the whole truth. Many French units contested the advance, fighting bitterly to halt the Germans for a few hours. Follow the routes of the invaders, and you will find the plaques and war memorials where brave

Frenchmen died. Read the German diaries to see that many of these tiny actions were fought to bloody conclusions.

'Plan Yellow', the German assault upon France and the Low Countries, was notably different to the attack on Poland. There the Germans had stretched two arms forward before closing them around the enemy in a battle of encirclement. Such envelopments, that embraced the opposing army, were as old as war itself. But Plan Yellow was not that sort of envelopment. Army Group A was a single knife that cut a long sweeping gash—the 'sickle cut'. They didn't need another arm, for the coast provided enclosure enough. Panzer divisions swung away from the southern part of Army Group B to join them and add more steel to the cutting edge. This determined German thrust would quickly separate the Allied armies in the north from their support and supplies. Using good roads the movement was the most perfect example of what blitzkrieg could do.[17]

The German Armoured Offensive

BELGIUM

● Calais

R. Lys

● Boulogne

R. Escaut

Douai

21 May British armour
attempts breakthrough

6. Pz. Div reacts
to British attack

Cambrai

Canals

▲△▲△△▲▲
Ardennes
Forest

Novelles

Doullens

Albert

St Quentin

Planned
Allied movements

Abbeville

Péronne

German
bridgeheads

Amiens

R. Somme

FRANCE

Defensive air cover was continuously provided to the columns. To lessen congestion on the roads men, fuel and spare parts for them were brought forward by Junkers Ju 52 transports. Luftwaffe fighter squadrons kept up with the advance by moving forward into newly captured airfields. Within nine days the Germans had reached Abbeville. So quick and expert had this 'sickle cut' proved that the Allied armies in the north took time to realize that they were now surrounded. The beleaguered armies had to move fast to reorganize themselves and man their defences on all sides.

THE ALLIED REACTION

It took many days for anyone on the Allied side to recognize the German attack for what it was. At first it was supposed that the invading columns would not get far. They would hammer away to produce a huge dent in the Western Front, and this great salient would then be contained by the Allied armies and the war would settle into stalemate.

Hitler's Directive of 14 May reported:

> The progress of the offensive to date shows that the enemy has failed to appreciate in time the basic idea of our operations. He continues to throw strong forces against the line Namur-Antwerp and appears to be neglecting the sector facing Army Group A.

By the evening of 15 May General Maurice Gamelin, commander of Allied land forces, realized that he had been completely out-manoeuvered, but still he misunderstood the German intentions. The American ambassador was at the French War Ministry when Edouard Daladier received a phone call from Gamelin to say that he had not a single corps of soldiers between Laon and Paris. Gamelin had still not recognized that the German thrust was not aiming for Paris. It was heading for the Channel and so cut Paris, and its command and supplies, away from the Allied armies in northern France and the Low Countries.

When the sickle cut was recognized for what it was, the counter-move was obvious to everyone. Coordinated thrusts from north and south would cut the German armoured spearheads away from their supporting infantry. The Germans would be sliced up, deprived of essential supplies, and defeated.

No such counter-offensive was launched, because the prime failure of the French army was not of equipment, manpower, nor even generalship. It was a failure of communications. The French army could not have mounted such a counter-attack in anything less than three weeks. A new commander—Weygand—was called to replace the exhausted Gamelin, but by the time he had travelled from Beirut in the Lebanon, collected his thoughts, and evolved ideas for the counter-attack, the Allied armies in the north were besieged.

The poor communications were reflected in the disposition of the French commanders. General Gamelin, who commanded soldiers as far away as North Africa, was to be found in the gloomy Château de Vincennes, near Paris. He had no general staff. Operational control of the armies in northern France was given to General A. L. Georges (although even his chief of staff was not sure where Gamelin's powers ended and Georges' began). Georges had his headquarters about 35 miles from Gamelin's but spent a great deal of time at his 'personal command post' near his residence and some twelve miles from his HQ. In any case, most of Georges' staff, under General Doumenc, were somewhere entirely different: GHQ Land Forces, a Rothschild mansion at Montry, lay halfway between Gamelin's and Georges' HQ. Together with some of his subordinates, Doumenc habitually spent his mornings at Montry and his afternoons at Georges' HQ, whether his general was there or not. There were no teleprinter connections between these places. At Gamelin's HQ there was not even a radio. Messages were usually sent by motor-cycle, and Gamelin's usual way of communicating with Georges was to visit him by road.

When the German attack came, motor-cycle messengers left Montry HQ every hour. Several of them were killed in traffic accidents said André Beaufre, an officer who was there at the time. He went on:

Late that night [13–14 May] when I had only just got to sleep I was awakened by a telephone call from General Georges: 'Ask General Doumenc to come here at once'. An hour later we arrived at the Château des Bondons, at La-Ferté-sous-Jouarre, where General Georges and his staff had their command post. In the château, which was rather more a big villa set in a park on a hill, the large salon had been made the map room. Around a long trestle table the staff officers answered the telephone and made notes.

When we arrived at about three o'clock in the morning all was dark except in this room which was barely half-lit. At the telephone Major Navereau was repeating in a low voice the information coming in. Everyone else was silent. General Roton, Chief of Staff, was stretched out in an armchair. The atmosphere was that of a family in which there had just been a death. Georges got up quickly and came to Doumenc. He was terribly pale. 'Our front has been broken at Sedan! There has been a collapse . . .' He flung himself into a chair and burst into tears.

He was the first man I had seen weep in this campaign. Alas there were to be others. It made a terrible impression on me.[18]

French armies on the southern side of the German sickle cut tried to slice through it. On 17 May at Montcornet a collection of armoured elements under the command of Colonel de Gaulle made a determined assault, but German air attacks decided the day. Although de Gaulle tried again, his force of about three battalions was not big enough, or good enough, to have any effect on the German advance. De Gaulle did not give up. He led other attacks and was promoted to the rank of general.

On 19 May General Gort learned from radio intercepts that he was surrounded. The Germans were pressing against his perimeter which was shrinking by the hour. His lines of communication were severed, the railway system was collapsing and all movements had to be made by road. This was particularly hard on the tanks; the endurance of their tracks was limited, and shortened still more by any paved surface. Mechanical problems were common.

Gort moved quickly to form defence lines along the only obstacle available, the Aa Canal, while continuing to fight the main German forces of Army Group B. His ammunition and other supplies were spread thinly. There was little left for any counter-offensive southwards, yet one did take place.

On 21 May a hastily contrived collection of British units—two territorial battalions, a motor-cycle battalion and 74 mixed tanks—was poised for a counter-attack from Vimy in the direction of Arras. They were to advance in conjunction with a larger French force which was still moving into position. The French asked for extra time but the British didn't wait for them. Nevertheless this encounter showed what a well organized, well equipped counter-attack might have achieved. Cutting through the armoured tail of Rommel's 7 Panzer Division they caused consternation akin to panic. Their success was short-lived as the Luftwaffe came into the action and Rommel brought his dual-purpose 8.8-cm guns into use against the thick-skinned Matilda tanks. After 48 hours of combat—as the French were coming up to start fighting—the British force had only two Matildas battleworthy. They began to withdraw. The history of one of the participating regiments said:

> After some initial success the attack broke down under the increasing strength of the enemy. This determined the fate of the BEF. It was clear that an aggressive role was now far beyond its powers and that its extrication from Arras would be of itself a perilous operation.[19]

A coordinated Anglo-French action at this time might have caused the Germans to recoil. As it was, these uncoordinated swipes brought them only to a temporary halt. Valuable time was gained: the Arras attack delayed the Germans by two and a half days while Rommel's men paused to rest and refit.

The BEF was not trained, supplied or equipped for full-scale attack. No one properly informed could doubt that any effective counter-offensive would have to come from the larger French resources to the south of the German thrust. But few people were so informed. There were endless discussions, telegrams, orders and instructions between Paris,

London and the BEF (which eventually was driven to using public cross-Channel phones to speak to London).

Despite the long period for preparation that the 'phoney war' had provided, the British army, like the French army, was not ready for modern battle. Tank crews were half-trained, tanks lacked radios, sighting telescopes and even armour-piercing ammunition. Reinforcements were hurried to France but even these units were not ready to fight. The 3rd Royal Tank Regiment landed at Calais on 22 May and was ordered to drive straight for St Omer. It was delayed by 'disorderly loading and the loss of much ancillary equipment [which] led to chaos in the French port'.[20] By 26 May this regiment had lost every tank.

While France fielded some excellent tanks, there were few good British designs. In the 1930s works of fiction and non-fiction depicted arms manufacturers as venal and un-scrupulous villains, but the truth was that few factories wanted such government contracts. This was especially true of tanks. So British tanks were built by agricultural engi-neers, locomotive factories and shipyards, at times when those contractors could get no other work. Old techniques, such as riveting, were used even though it had been demon-strated at Woolwich, back in 1934, that welded armour plate was essential for modern tank manufacture. When the test of battle came these failings were evident: their crews de-served better. As a recent official British publication says:

> From this point the histories of all the British cavalry [tank] regiments seem to tell the same story, a repetitive saga of withdrawal from river line to river line, holding on for a while, blowing bridges then falling back. It is a tale of endless duels with German anti-tank guns that sliced clean through thin armour, of suicidal charges to destroy these guns by running over them, and even of scout carri-ers dashing into action like tanks.[21]

British generalship suffered from conflicting ideas about the role of armour. Heavy tanks were designed to plod alongside the infantry as they had done in 1918. Lighter, thin-skinned models were to gallop about like cavalry. Such specialized roles led to the tanks being spread around, and shared throughout the Allied armies, at a time when the Germans proved that tanks were far more effective if used in armoured divisions. The tactical failing of Allied tank warfare was to send tank against tank; the Germans knew that armour should be used against vulnerable targets, while mobile batteries of high-velocity anti-tank guns dealt with enemy armour. Allied tank experts also knew all this, but tank experts were not consulted by the higher commands. Now Gort had cut back his headquarters to the minimum scale, so that during the fighting in May there was no tank expert at his GHQ and no intelligence staff. It was a severe limitation.

Perhaps intervention by military intelligence could have lessened the hysteria about secret agents which gripped almost all Allied soldiers. Rumours about the successes of German paratroops, and the isolated use of Dutch uniforms, had grown into ever more vivid stories; such as Germans in high-ranking Allied uniforms ordering troops to their deaths. Locals who did not understand English were likely to be categorized as saboteurs; those who did speak English were suspected of being spies. Signals and messages, artfully cut into growing crops, were seen everywhere. The slightest flicker of light, like that through a briefly opened door, was believed to be signalling by German agents. The stories became more and more bizarre. A typical account appears in the otherwise more sober regimental history of the Grenadier Guards:

One example of this carefully planned [spying] organisation made a great impression on the Battalion. The occupants of the farm where their headquarters was lodged decided to leave the building as the German shelling became more intense. Madame, who had greeted the Grenadiers two days before with warmth and a flood of passable English, now bade farewell to her cows, horses and guests, and left in tears. Two hours later the headquarters was very heavily and accurately shelled. Their suspicions aroused, the Grenadiers searched the immedi-ate neighbourhood and found that arrows, pointing di-rectly towards the house, had been ploughed into all the adjoining fields . . . Germans dressed in British uni-forms added to the danger and the strain.[22]

Its regimental history reports that on 20 May this same battalion executed seventeen 'ubiquitous civilian snipers' in one day! There is no evidence that the Germans employed foreign snipers—they needed no help—nor that they had secret agents laboriously ploughing messages in fields. But such summary executions of local people were common, and may well have spread an urge for revenge amongst the friends and relatives of the bereaved. The grave shortage of British soldiers fluent in any foreign language hampered re-lations with local populations and with Allied units.

In overview it is difficult to refute the criticism made by the French and others that the British were too eager to quit the Continent. Gort had never allowed his army to become an integrated part of the Allied line. His counter-attack at Arras lasted only 48 hours and was the only offensive the British staged. The casualties suffered by the BEF were not severe when compared with the other armies which fought alongside it.[23] The French argued that Gort had pulled back at times when they most needed him to stay put. As they saw it the BEF did nothing but stage an orderly advance, a rag-ged retreat, and then improvise a sea evacuation to save themselves while the French army defended the evacuation.

11 RETREAT

Berlin. 25 June 1940.
I have the impression that we are rushing for a common currency for the whole of Europe. That would be progress, of course, and, one would hope, of lasting significance.

LETTER FROM HELMUTH VON MOLTKE
(MILITARY INTELLIGENCE)[1]

As early as 19 May 1940 the British army had begun to prepare to evacuate its Expeditionary Force from the Continent of Europe. General Lord Gort, its commander, sent an officer to London to discuss pulling out through Dunkirk.[2] At this stage it was only a contingency plan, but on that same day, headquarters troops—not required in battle—were moved to Dunkirk by train. Soon the ships bringing supplies to France took such non-combatants back to England.

On 21 May Gort started pulling his army back to ensure that it occupied a piece of coast from which his force could be lifted off. It was a controversial decision, the more so because of the way the British deliberately kept their Allies in the dark about what they were doing, and what they intended. At Gort's headquarters there was little faith in General Blanchard,[3] who commanded the neighbouring French divisions, while Billotte, commander of the Army Group to which the BEF belonged, had that day been fatally injured in a car crash.

By some bizarre arrangement, Gort's orders had until now been coming from the supreme commander Gamelin, who had just been replaced.[4] Earlier that day, with the Germans racing through France, the newly appointed supreme commander, Weygand, went to judge the situation on the spot.

Gort was not summoned to the meeting until the discussion came round to using British troops in a counterattack. By the time Gort arrived Weygand had departed. The French, who found their flanks exposed by British withdrawals, demanded that Gort stay in position but the BEF kept moving.

By Saturday 25 May there were reports about the Germans capturing the Channel port of Calais, as well as Boulogne. At Dunkirk the bombing had deprived the port of electricity, so that dockside cranes were out of action. Unloading had to be done by small ship's cranes. Time was running out and the section of front held by the Belgian army was vital. They had now become the focus of the German attack and the Luftwaffe was giving them pitiless attention. If they yielded ground, or asked for a cease-fire, Dunkirk, and the British army's only chance of salvation, would be lost.

Sir John Dill arrived in France on a visit. He was the CIGS, Britain's top soldier, and perhaps Gort had hoped to get a direct order from him.[5] Dill was an affable man of courteous disposition, but he brought no news or official instructions for Gort. His only message was that there was 'criticism at home that the BEF, 200,000 fighting men who claimed to be better fighters than the Bosche [sic], were not doing enough'.[6] Coming from the genial Dill, this was a slap in the face for Gort.

That evening Gort was sitting alone wondering how long the Belgians could keep fighting. Suddenly he got up and went to the office of his chief of staff. He ordered him to move two British divisions (the 5th and the 50th) to reinforce the line the Belgians were holding. Gort's sudden impulse probably saved the BEF from destruction, but he was using the men General Blanchard had been promised for the much-discussed Allied counter-attack. That night Gort's chief of staff recorded Gort's reasoning in this diary entry about the Belgians:

If they go from that [line], Dunkirk is taken from the north and we are bust. If the Belgians need help to hold that, only we can give it . . . a beleaguered garrison must first be sure of its perimeter before it can indulge in sorties.[7]

The two divisions travelled all night to move into position facing eastwards on the line of the Ypres-Comines canal. The regimental history of the Royal Scots Fusiliers recorded the crucial outcome of Gort's decision:

> Their arrival was narrowly timed. The Germans attacked after dawn on May 26. The battle raged all day, and so furiously that the three battalions of the 1st Division which had been held in reserve, were drawn in. . . . The Belgians collapsed completely on May 27. Their capitulation was made without previous consultation and at very short notice.[8]

In fact the Belgians had taken the weight of the German attack from the north. For a week King Leopold had been warning the Allies that his army's capacity to hold out was limited. It was the British who had let their ally down. The Belgians were never informed that the BEF was abandoning them. When the surrender came the French premier Paul Reynaud immediately broadcast a vitriolic diatribe in which he called the Belgian king a traitor. Churchill knew that this abuse was a scandalous untruth because he'd had a special liaison officer at Leopold's headquarters, but he was too anxious about upsetting Reynaud to issue a denial, so King Leopold was widely condemned as a traitor.[9]

For the British everything was happening at great speed. One British artillery officer said after being handed a new map:

> I took mine without paying much attention to it. We were already up in the corner of our last sheet, so I had expected we'd soon get a new issue. Suddenly glancing down at it, I noticed that a great proportion of the new sheet was occupied by the sea. Another look showed me a

strip of coast. And the principal name on this strip was Dunkirk. It was the first time the word had struck us with any particular significance.[10]

The BEF was in full retreat. Gort believed the French had been told that he was pulling out of the continental fighting, but when Paul Reynaud went to see Churchill in London on Sunday 26 May, still the news was kept from him. For the British soldiers in France, the planned evacuation was all too evident. Said the same artillery officer:

Into this pancake of land it seemed as if the whole of the BEF was pouring. Every road scoring the landscape was one thick mass of transport and troops, great long lines of them stretching back far to the eastern horizon, and all the lines converging towards the one focus—Dunkirk. Ambulances, lorries, trucks, Bren-gun carriers, artillery columns—everything except tanks—all crawling along those roads in well-defined lines over the flat featureless country in the late afternoon sunshine, provided an impressive and memorable picture of two modern armies in retreat. Under their greyish camouflage paint they resembled from a distance slow-moving rivers of muddy-coloured lava from some far-off eruption.

It was now that I saw for the first time, regiments in the doleful process of wrecking their equipment. New wireless sets, costing perhaps £20 apiece, were placed in rows in fields, twenty in a row, sometimes, while a soldier with a pick-axe proceeded up and down knocking them to pieces. Trucks were being dealt with just as dramatically. Radiators and engines were smashed with sledge-hammers; tires slashed and sawn after they had been deflated. Vehicles that were near the canals were finally pushed in. Some of the canals were choked with the wrecks, all piled on top of each other.

To reduce congestion, the British posted military police on the roads to prevent trucks and transport of any kind entering the beach area. This led to angry clashes as the French soldiers objected to leaving behind their ammunition trucks or losing other elements of their fighting force. For the British, Dunkirk was the end of the road; for the French it was one of their towns to be defended with all the means at their disposal.[11]

The German Blitzkrieg and evacuation of Dunkirk.

Direction of German Advance   Allied Line

Perhaps a fierce German assault upon the Dunkirk perimeter would have eliminated the chances of a seaborne evacuation, but it did not come. The armour was halted for a respite and the Germans took their time. Afterwards the 'halt order' became a subject of controversy, but at the time it seemed normal.[12] Paris, and the greater part of France, had still to be conquered by Germany's limited armoured forces. No one, least of all the Germans, thought that the bulk of the British army could be rescued from the beaches by a ragtag collection of ferry boats, privately owned yachts manned by civilians, and RN warships risked in shallow waters as HM ships have never been before or since. But it was time for the British to pull a rabbit out of the hat. Largely due to the ad hoc skill and foresight of a few naval officers the seemingly impossible was achieved.

DUNKIRK

Perhaps the first indication the Germans saw of British determination to continue the war was the fortitude of the RAF fighter pilots covering the Dunkirk evacuation. Men do not readily expend their lives for a cause that is already lost. It was the belief in Winston Churchill that German fliers encountered over Dunkirk. 'The enemy has had air superiority. This is something new for us in this campaign' said the German 4th Army's war diary on 25 May.

The RAF fighter pilots lacked the range to spend much time patrolling over the beaches and there were times when the Germans had the air to themselves. For the most part the RAF tried to intercept the German bombers before they reached Dunkirk. The Allied soldiers fighting a brave rearguard action in the streets, and the infantry patiently lining up on the mole from which most were rescued, seldom saw the RAF. Neither did the men dug into holes on the beaches, or scrambling across beached ships or over lines of vehicles that had been run into the sea to make piers. They were more apt to remember the enemy bombers that got through time and again, and the German fighters that came roaring out of the haze with their machine-guns blazing. The survivors of Dunkirk did not emerge as admirers of the RAF fliers who had fought to give them air cover. On the contrary, in the English summer of 1940 many men in light blue uniforms were singled out for abuse by angry soldiers with vivid memories of the Luftwaffe's successes.

One RAF Flying Training School commanding officer felt so anxious about the growing hostility that he contacted the nearby army commander in North Wales about the bad effect of BEF troops hissing newsreel pictures of the RAF in local cinemas. He also sent a signal, classified Secret, on the subject to his Group HQ. Churchill was also aware of the problem. Addressing Parliament he gave special emphasis to the contribution the RAF made to the sea evacuation despite the fact that they were above the clouds and out of sight.[13]

In the ports of harbours of southern England yachtsmen and fishermen of all ages were asked to help evacuate the British army from France. Some declined, but many civilians crossed the Channel to help with the rescue. The small boats could not carry many men but they played a vital role in repeatedly ferrying the soldiers out to the larger boats. The *Seasalter,* a smack arriving back from dredging the oyster beds near Burnham-on-Crouch in Essex, was asked to go and help. The skipper said:

> The soldiers were coming off the beach clinging to bits of wood and wreckage and anything that would float. As we got close enough we began to pick them up. We saw a row-boat coming off loaded right down with troops. And with this we went to and fro, bringing as many as it would dare hold, and in the meantime we went round picking up as many as we could. When we got a load we would take them off to one of the ships lying off in the deep water.[14]

All that was good and everything that was bad about men could be found on the Dunkirk beaches. It was a sense of fair play that made men wait their turn, even when it looked as if their turn would never come. But it was a time of cowardice and lies as well as selfless heroism. Allies were deceived, comrades abandoned. Officers trying to organize unruly crowds of weary soldiers sometimes had to draw their pistols. Looting and rape were not unknown. Some men died unheroic deaths. But all in all the Dunkirk evacuation worked because heroism, discipline, self-sacrifice and common sense prevailed. It became the sort of heroic failure that the British cherish, and celebrate for longer than their victories.

Soldiers arrived in England at the same south coast resorts that many of them knew from peacetime holidays. At Dover, Deal, Folkestone, Margate, Sheerness and Ramsgate there was tea and biscuits, apples and oranges, cigarettes and matches, doctors and nurses, coaches and trains. Crowds gathered at the London railway terminals to watch the arrival of subdued, tired and dirty men. A few arrived complete with packs and rifles, some brandished souvenirs, most had only the barest clothes. By 4 June 338,226 had been rescued and of these 123,095 were French. On this day Churchill told the House:

> We shall not flag or fail. We shall go on to the end. We shall fight in France, we shall fight on the seas and oceans, we shall fight with growing confidence and growing strength in the air, we shall defend our island, whatever the cost may be. We shall fight on the beaches, we shall fight on the landing grounds, we shall fight in the fields and in the streets, we shall fight in the hills; we shall never surrender.

Portentously he added: 'in God's good time, the new world, with all its power and might, steps forth to the rescue and liberation of the old'.[15]

The significance of Operation Dynamo cannot be over-emphasized. Although almost all the French rescued went back to fight for a still undefeated France, the British survivors provided the cadre of a new and better army. Had a quarter of a million British men languished in German captivity, it is hard to believe that public opinion would have been in favour of continuing the war.

As the British departed from the Continent, there remained a vast scrapyard of military equipment, the more so since the British Expeditionary Force had been a mechanized army. A German officer[16] wrote home saying:

Just before La Panne we passed the first collecting point for wrecked vehicles. There were hundreds, possibly thousands, of cars, trucks, armoured vehicles of all sizes. Almost all of them were burnt out, because the British and French had put fire to all the vehicles they had to abandon. In La Panne itself, a harbour which had served for embarkations, there was merely a vast amount of war matériel, all useless. Anti-aircraft guns, machine-guns, motor bicycles, anti-tank guns, etc. From the place where we stopped on the beach we could see a sunken British warship.

Gort was sent to become inspector-general to the forces for training. It was an inappropriate job for a man brimming over with courage who had already demonstrated that training for modern war was not something he understood. One of his subordinates, Alan Brooke, who had not enjoyed being subordinated to Gort in France, became Commander in Chief Home Forces. His version of the events of May 1940 was that he had shown exemplary skill in covering the withdrawal to Dunkirk while Gort had been found wanting. In December 1941 Brooke's striding energy and sincere ambition gained for him Dill's post of CIGS. Gort, Ironside and Dill had held the job in quick succession, but now it had been given to a man who would never let go. Sir Arthur Bryant, a distinguished writer, used Brooke's war diaries and autobiographical notes to write a history of the war. As proof that the pen can be mightier than the sword, Field Marshal The Viscount Alanbrooke ended up widely regarded as the man who'd won the war almost single-handed. Gort faded into military oblivion.

THE END OF FRANCE

On 5 June the regrouped German armies launched a concerted offensive southwards. Weygand, the new French commander, tried to hold a front to the north of Paris, but by 8 June had begun to retreat to the River Seine. Two days later the French government fled Paris, and on that same day Italy declared war on Britain and France. 'A great day in the history of the German Army!' said General Franz Halder, chief of the army general staff, on 14 June. 'German troops have been marching into Paris since nine o'clock this morning'.[17]

Now the German drive southwards fanned out both east and west. A week later 32 Italian divisions attacked the six Alpine divisions that manned the French south-east frontier. This was Mussolini's last-minute bid for a seat at the peace conference and a share of the spoils.

Many French units fought hard and well but as Telford Taylor, an American military historian, summed it up: 'The trouble was that those who fought were woefully hampered by those who did not, and fatally handicapped by those who failed to prepare'.[18] Soon the Germans had the French armies pinned against the rear of their Maginot Line, while other spearheads reached the Spanish border.

On 16 June, Marshal Pétain, the 84-year-old hero of Verdun, the war minister whose decisions had played an important part in creating the Maginot Line and the disaster that now befell the French army, came forward to negotiate with the Germans. Hitler simply dictated terms to him, and with a childish and vindictive sense of theatre arranged for the armistice to be signed in the same railway coach in which the Germans had been made to sign the armistice of 1918.[19]

Success always wins friends, and Hitler was not lacking in admirers. Casting aside his feelings about freedom, in the Indian newspaper *Harijan* on 22 June, Mahatma Gandhi wrote: 'Germans of future generations will honour Herr Hitler as a genius, as a brave man, a matchless organizer and much more'. In Moscow Foreign Minister Molotov cast aside his feelings about Fascism and summoned the German ambassador to convey 'the warmest congratulations of the Soviet government on the splendid success of the German armed forces'. The democratically elected government of Denmark, which the Germans had kept in place, allowed gratitude to overcome its respect for democracy and announced: 'The great German victories, which have caused astonishment and admiration all over the world, have brought about a new era in Europe, which will result in a new order in a political and economic sense, under the leadership of Germany'. The Aga Khan cast aside his feelings about alcohol and promised to drink a bottle of champagne 'when the Führer sleeps in Windsor Castle'.[20]

PEACE FEELERS

Hitler and his generals had never anticipated the Dunkirk evacuation, principally because they were men of a continental land power. For them the coast was the end of the road. For the British, with their 'island mentality', the sea was an open door. The poor impression Hitler had formed of Chamberlain made him confident that the British cabinet would come to him seeking peace terms.

Such an opinion was not without foundation. Lord Halifax, who had so nearly become prime minister in May, certainly did not rule out talks with Hitler. As France collapsed, Halifax was hinting to the still neutral Italians that Britain would be interested in the prospect of a conference to decide the fate of Europe.

Britain, like France and many other European countries, was subject to the influence of aristocrats and land-owning gentry who worried about the spread of Communism, and the social upheaval that a major European war would bring.

They even feared a British victory: Germany weakened by war would open the floodgates to a tide of Soviet expansion. For such people, appeasement of Hitler had been the only sensible prewar policy. Even after war began, there were a great many men of influence who thought that Britain should admit its error and quickly come to terms with the Nazis. So did those in the Foreign Office and the Treasury who anxiously watched the steady depletion of their country's financial resources.

During the period of the 'phoney war' contacts with pre-war personal British friends convinced highly placed Nazis that the British were irresolute. German diplomats and secret agents were alerted to the possibility of making peace with Britain. The armistice sought by Marshal Pétain on 16 June 1940 gave new urgency to British peace feelers, which were now being extended in Spain, Switzerland and Sweden.

There is no known verbatim record of the conversation that took place when on 17 June 1940 R.A.B. Butler (Halifax's deputy) met Björn Prytz, Sweden's minister in London. But long after the war Prytz published the telegram he sent to Stockholm as a result of that meeting.[21] According to Swedish records, Butler told Prytz that 'no opportunity of reaching a compromise peace would be neglected if the possibility were offered on reasonable conditions'.[22] Butler was seeking peace terms on behalf of his boss, and in an unmistakable reference to Churchill and his supporters he added that Lord Halifax specifically promised that 'no diehards would be allowed to stand in the way'.

Churchill was unable to attend a meeting of the war cabinet at 12.30 pm the following day. One item has since been deleted from the official minutes of that cabinet meeting but the diary notes of Alexander Cadogan, head of the Foreign Office, who was present, provide a tantalizing clue to what the closely guarded secret might be. 'Winston not there—writing his speech. No reply from Germans'.[23] It seems that Churchill's authority was flouted by men determined to sue for peace.

Halifax and Butler were not alone in their quest. Lloyd

George, who had been prime minister in the First World War, had seen little chance of a British victory in the Second. The Americans would not enter the war, he said, and he made no secret of his readiness to take over his nation in defeat, as Pétain had now taken over France.[24] How many others were of like mind can only be guessed. The Duke of Windsor—who as Edward VIII abdicated from the throne in 1936—and his wife, the infamous Mrs Wallis Simpson, were outspoken admirers of Hitler and his Third Reich. Bitterly divided from his family on account of his marriage, there are suggestions that Edward hoped to assume the throne of a defeated Britain with Hitler's blessing.

But nothing came of the peace feelers. At 9 pm on 17 June Churchill spoke on the radio for two minutes before the evening's news bulletin. In a hastily prepared response to the French collapse he told the world: 'The news from France is very bad, and I grieve for the gallant French people who have fallen into this terrible misfortune'. He went on: 'We shall defend our island, and, with the British Empire around us, we shall fight on unconquerable until the curse of Hitler is lifted from the brows of men. We are sure that in the end all will be well'.[25]

At 3.45 the following afternoon, while the Germans were still considering how to react to the hints, questions and off-the-record conversations, channelled through their ambassadors in neutral capitals, Churchill stood up in the House of Commons and delivered the speech that he had been writing when he was absent from the cabinet:

> The whole fury and might of the enemy must very soon be turned on us. Hitler knows that he will have to break us in this island or lose the war . . . if we fail, then the whole world, including the United States, and all that we have known and cared for, will sink into the abyss of a new dark age made more sinister, and perhaps more protracted, by the lights of a perverted science.
>
> Let us therefore brace ourselves to our duty and so bear ourselves that if the British Empire and its Com-

monwealth lasts for a thousand years men will still say 'This was their finest hour'.[26]

It was one of Churchill's finest hours too. At that time there were no recording or broadcast facilities in the House of Commons, and so the prime minister was prevailed upon to deliver the speech again over the radio at 9 pm before that evening's BBC news bulletin. The radio performance did not communicate the Churchill fire that a live audience had produced in the afternoon. Some of his colleagues thought his voice sounded unusual over the air and put it down to emotion, or the imperfections of broadcasting. Less charitably, the publisher Cecil King wondered if he was drunk. Harold Nicolson at the Ministry of Information remarked that a speech that sounded magnificent in the House of Commons 'sounded ghastly on the wireless'.

John Martin, private secretary to the prime minister, said that Churchill's 'halting delivery at the start seems to have struck people and we had a letter from someone saying that evidently something had gone wrong with his heart and he ought to work in the recumbent position. The fact was, I gather, that he spoke with a cigar in his mouth'.[27]

In recent years an elaborate myth has grown up around speculation that maybe the 18 June speech was not broadcast by Churchill at all. The rumors spread when the BBC repertory actor Norman Shelley, who played Winnie the Pooh and Toad of Toad Hall in the BBC Children's Hour, revealed that, with the prime minister's permission, he had recorded Churchill's speeches for American audiences. But there is no real evidence to support the view that Shelley had imitated Churchill's voice on the BBC in June 1940.[28]

In the face of Churchill's fiery rhetoric, the Germans decided that Lord Halifax, Butler and their many peace-seeking friends were no match for him and shelved their hopes of total victory. Hitler's prewar experience with Chamberlain was no longer a guide to Britain's mood. Winston Churchill had brought a psychological change to Britain that could never have taken place under his predecessor's direction.

A 'SUCCESSFUL LANDING'

The tragedy, comedy and confusion that reigned on both sides is illustrated by what happened to Britain's Channel Islands in this summer of 1940. These small islands, part of Great Britain but not of the United Kingdom, are self-governing communities under the British crown. They are all near to France, and by 19 June 1940 Whitehall had decided that they should be demilitarized and declared 'open towns'. However with that reticence for which bureaucrats are noted, the men in Whitehall did not announce this decision, probably because the humiliation of publicly yielding British territory could not be faced.

FIGURE 19:
Heinkel He 111 bomber

To test whether they were being defended the Germans sent aircraft to fly very low across the islands. As one roared across St Peter Port on Guernsey, someone aboard the Southern Railway steamer *Isle of Sark*, sailing from Jersey to Southampton, fired ancient twin-mounted Lewis machine-guns at it. The Germans decided that there was a military force on the islands. As a result Heinkel He 111 bombers bombed and machine-gunned the two principal towns of St Helier in Jersey and St Peter Port, Guernsey, on the evening of 28 June. There were many casualties, and only after this did Whitehall announce that the islands had been demilitarized.

The German monitoring service missed the demilitarization announcement put out by the BBC, and it was the United States ambassador in Paris who made sure the Germans knew of it. The commander of the German naval forces in northern France was engaged in a conference on the subject of the Channel Islands when he received the news by telephone. It was decided that occupation would be a propaganda coup. Luftflotte 3 assigned ten Junkers Ju 52 transport planes as well as fighter, bomber and reconnaissance units to the task. Army Group B were to provide soldiers, and naval craft were prepared for the assault on the beaches. Most importantly film camera-men, photographers and writers were sent to Cherbourg and attached to all the participating units.

Meanwhile a Dornier Do 17P—a version of the somewhat outdated 'flying pencil' relegated to reconnaissance duties—landed, apparently on a whim, at Guernsey airport. Locals told the pilot that the islands were undefended. When the Dornier returned to its base, a few Luftwaffe personnel were given rifles and flown across to the island formally to take it over. The next morning another Dornier—piloted by Oberleutnant Richard Kern—flew to Jersey airport. He took over there armed with nothing more than his pistol.

These enterprising men of the Luftwaffe had, of course, completely spoiled the propaganda invasion. To make things even more humiliating for the assembled invasion force, their own start was delayed by fog.

The Channel Islanders' first sight of the rank-and-file German occupation forces was good enough to persuade them that they were specially selected as disciplined, polite and good-looking. In fact these troops were a company of Infantry Regiment 396 (216 Infantry Division) and were simply the nearest available unit.[29]

MEN AND WEAPONS

In a six-week campaign the Germans had conquered all of western Europe. Their casualties were remarkably few (see Table 3):

TABLE 3
German and Allied casualties, 1940

	Dead	Wounded	POW/Missing
German	27,074	111,034	18,384
French	90,000	200,000	1,900,000

Other (total) casualties:
BEF (approx. 40 days fighting) 68,111; Belgian (17 days fighting) 23,350; Dutch (5 days fighting) 9,779.

The German army displayed ingenuity and adaptability in the invasion of the Low Countries. In the heart of Rotterdam, Heinkel float planes landed infantry which paddled ashore in inflatable boats. Infantry-carrying gliders had been towed behind transport planes to land on the roof of Belgium's titanic Eben Emael fortress. On the Luxembourg frontier, German soldiers posing as tourists and dressed in civilian clothes went ahead of the main force to disconnect the demolition devices. The invaders used Dutch uniforms and an armoured train to take the bridge at Gennep. Parachute troops came tumbling out of the sky to seize the mile-long undefended bridges at Moerdijk. Three-engined Junkers airliners crammed with infantry were crash-landed on Dutch roads.

Most of this 'exotica' was used against the Netherlands,

Luxembourg and Belgium by the Germans of Army Group B. There was not very much of it and its actual contribution was small. These gimmicks were not a portent of wars to come, they were a stage conjuror's trick to hold the attention of the audience while Army Group A brought the rabbit from the Ardennes woodlands.

At the time it was salve for the wounds to believe that the Germans had won by massive force, and revolutionary new weapons. A relative of mine, freshly arrived home after the Dunkirk evacuation, rhetorically asked my father: 'What chance do you have with a bolt-action rifle against a man with a tommy gun?'

Most of the techniques of 1940 could have been seen in the German offensive of March 1918. In that 'Kaiser's Battle' lightly burdened shock-troops had pushed deep into enemy territory spraying rounds from 'machine-pistols' almost identical in size, shape and performance to the MP 38 guns used in 1940.[30] And there was nothing new about the skilled 'combat-engineers' deployed at the very front of the attack. German close-support aircraft had been used in the First World War, as is evidenced by the widespread use of the term 'ground-strafing' at that time. All of these elements could have been anticipated by the Allied generals had they cared to study the previous war.

In 1940 virtually the whole German army was horse-drawn and equipped with the Mauser Kar 98k, a bolt-action rifle, dating, as its name implies, from 1898.[31] The British army faced them with an almost identical rifle: the Lee-Enfield introduced at the end of the Boer War (when the Boers had been using the Mauser 98!). Even the German tanks were orthodox developments of the machine the British invented in 1915.

But unlike the Allies, the Germans learned from their defeats and their victories too. After the 1940 fighting they modified their equipment in light of their experience. Lightweight tanks, armed with only machine-guns, were phased out in favour of heavier models.[32]

The fundamental change in light weapon manufacture

FIGURE 20:
German Mauser Gewehr 98

that took place in this period is as significant as the one that jet propulsion brought to flight. All the major powers abandoned fine craftsmanship—the blued steel and polished walnut of another age—and turned to truly mass-produced

FIGURE 21:
German MG 34 machine-gun

weapons. The MG 34 was the sort of gun a collector cherishes, a Rheinmetall development of a Swiss gun, but its time was past. Mauser produced its replacement, the MG 42, composed of simple sub-assembled units; its machined parts kept to a minimum. The cost was reduced from 310 Reichmarks for the MG 34 to 250 RM for the MG 42, and even half a century later, the MG 42 is widely used.[33] In 1941 Britain produced the first throw-away machine-gun: the

Sten, a lightweight weapon that was accident-prone but suitable and cheap enough to drop in thousands to guerrilla forces.

On the whole, the British army's equipment had proved only marginally inferior. If their trucks succumbed to tough treatment, so did many German ones. European armies depended upon the railway system, and this had ensured that few good heavy-duty trucks were built anywhere except the United States, where customers expected trucks to repeat thousand-mile journeys over poor roads for decades.[34] The British army's Bren light machine-gun proved effective and reliable; it could be fired from the hip and it kept firing even when the barrel glowed red hot. Some British tanks acquitted themselves well enough when deployed skilfully on the battlefield, but after the BEF had abandoned 2,472 guns, 63,879 vehicles and over half a million tons of supplies in France, Britain could not afford the luxury of redesigning, or seriously modifying, the heavy equipment. British factories were put into high gear even when the products coming off the line were obviously inferior.

The production crisis of 1940 helped to ensure that, throughout the war, there never was a well designed British tank.[35] The British forces became more and more dependent upon American equipment sometimes modified to British requirements. When American tanks arrived they were properly packed and weatherproofed and fully equipped. Spare parts fitted without being hammered, filed and bent. They proved reliable[36] and the crews liked them. For many in Britain there came the startling revelation that mass-production methods could be superior to the hand-fashioned low-technology that was called craftsmanship.

The Allied defeats in 1940 were not due to a failure of quality or of quantity. Their air forces were very big and had many well designed aircraft. The French air force had well over two thousand modern fighters, more than twice the number deployed by the Luftwaffe.[37] The French army had excellent tanks and more of them than the Germans and British put together!

Some said it was a victory won by the close coordination of air and ground forces, a triumph for radio communication and ruthless aggression. But the collapse of Britain and France was mostly the outcome of the West's profound failure in political, industrial and military leadership. The men with the authority to write specifications had not done it well enough: and the designers were not skilled enough. Education at all levels of British society was not good enough. Those who had become used to easy profits from outmoded factories failed to meet the nation's needs. There had been no political will to stop Hitler at a time when he would not have dared to go to war. The military leadership, from top to bottom, had been totally outclassed on the battlefield.

The British army's very subjective interview system of officer selection had not stood the test of battle. Young men from esteemed public schools automatically accepted into the regiments of their fathers and grandfathers were not always the best leaders, and the prevailing system discouraged suitable men of other social backgrounds applying for a commission. With up to half the officer candidates failing their wartime training courses, and high levels of psychological breakdown, the Adjutant-General, General Sir Ronald Adam, decided to bring psychologists into the selection process. It became more difficult for commanding officers to commission anyone they thought would prove convivial in the regimental mess. The 'leaderless group test' was one of the new exams. Teams, randomly gathered, were provided with barrels, ropes and planks of wood and given complicated physical tasks to perform, while their actions were evaluated. Examiners looked for the ability to both give and take orders. This method provided a much higher rate of successful officer candidates as well as increasing applications for commissions by 25 per cent.[38] The British army, fast becoming more democratic and more effective than ever before, prepared itself for a return engagement.

In 1940 the European land war ended in stalemate. Germany had expanded its frontiers in all directions and Europe was permanently changed, but Britain was far from defeated. Meanwhile the Germans could celebrate a victory for the German educational system, professionalism, coordinated arms and realistic training. It was also a victory for a malignant dictatorship, and for a people who valued their material standard of living above the personal freedom of themselves and their neighbours.

BRITAIN'S SPY NETWORK

As Britain looked back upon a seemingly endless succession of unpleasant surprises, some taxpayers asked what help had come from the vaunted Secret Intelligence Service. The answer was very little. Until the French and the Poles supplied their work to the British, the cracking of Germany's Enigma coding machine had got nowhere apart from an occasional lucky guess.

In the first weeks of the war the chief of the SIS, Admiral Sir Hugh Sinclair, died unexpectedly in King Edward VII Hospital for Officers, London. His memorial service, held at St Martin-in-the-Fields church in London, was attended by every senior intelligence officer who had ever come in contact with him—'a very full congregation', remarked the head of MI5.[39]

Sinclair's death came shortly after the signing of the German-Soviet pact, and the secret protocol by which Stalin would occupy half of Poland. As Chamberlain had admitted to Parliament, the pact came as a grave shock to the British government. This failure of the intelligence service was discussed in an emergency session of Parliament on 24 August, and feelings were running so high that Chamberlain felt bound to offer his resignation.

The death of Sinclair provided an opportunity, as well as a reason, to put the service on a modern and more competent footing. Their personnel might have been drawn from a wider section of the population, and been subject to careful vetting, but Sinclair's successor, Sir Stewart Menzies, was a candidate put forward by Lord Halifax, and he preferred to retain the traditional recruitment methods. Men from good families who had private incomes and had attended expensive private schools seemed to be the most appropriate people to be trusted with secrets, even secrets prised from foreigners. Such men invariably came into the service by personal introduction which seemed sufficient recommendation without inquiries into their previous activities.

Within days of Sinclair's death, the SD (Sicherheitsdienst), the intelligence arm of the Nazi party, showed itself to be far less gentlemanly. Himmler's men put out feelers to London pretending that they were army generals about to stage a coup against Hitler. On 9 November 1939 two top-level executives of Britain's SIS attended a rendezvous at Café Bacchus, an eating place right upon the Dutch frontier at Venlo. One was a flamboyant 55-year-old, Captain Sigismund Best, and the other one Major Richard Stevens, an accomplished linguist but otherwise an inexperienced member of the service who had been appointed 'our man in The Hague'. In broad daylight the two men were seized by a detachment acting under the orders of the German SS officer Walter Schellenberg, who physically resembled Best. He described the arrival of a Buick containing the two British agents and Dirk Klop, a Dutch officer:

At this moment the SS car came skidding around the corner into the car park. Coppens [Klop], recognising it as the greater danger, turned and fired several shots into the windscreen. I saw the glass shatter and crystalline threads spreading from the bullet holes. [An SS man] had also drawn his pistol and a regular duel developed between him and Coppens. I had no time to move and found myself between them. Both men shot with deliberation, aiming carefully. Then Coppens slowly lowered his gun and sank down on his knees.

I turned and ran round the corner of the house towards my car. Looking back I saw Best and Stevens being hauled out of the Buick like bundles of hay.

. . . I suddenly found myself face to face with a huge SS subaltern whom I had not seen before. He grabbed hold of me and thrust a huge pistol under my nose. It was obvious that he mistook me for Captain Best . . . I pushed him back violently, shouting, 'Don't be stupid. Put that gun away!' . . . whereupon he aimed his gun at me, but in the same second that he pulled the trigger his hand was knocked to one side and the bullet missed my head by about two inches. I owed my life to the second SS leader's alertness. He had noticed what was happening and intervened just in time. I did not wait for further explanations, but got into my car as quickly as I could and drove off, leaving it to the SS detachment to finish the operation.[40]

The Dutch officer died, while Best and Stevens were dragged over the border and taken to Berlin to be interrogated in customary SS fashion. The victims were chosen with commendable skill. Between them they provided a complete description of the personnel and departments at SIS headquarters in London, as well as the names of all the western and central Europe station chiefs, and other information about staff and their sexual activities.[41]

The Germans had a score to settle with Sigismund Best. During the First World War he had secured personal permission from Lloyd George the prime minister to set up as a drug-dealer in Holland, smuggling morphia tablets and cocaine—thirty or forty pounds at a time—to German officers across the border in return for military secrets.

At this time the idea that Germany was on the point of economic collapse was well rooted with the British government and the public at large. The German collapse would bring the overthrow of Hitler and a new government that would sue for peace. There is no evidence that the SIS tried to correct this totally unfounded belief. On the contrary, they clearly were themselves deceived by it, for the 'Venlo incident' had been effected by dangling before the SIS a story about a group of highly placed Germans who were about to overthrow Hitler.

As the German army overran continental Europe the British secret service men—based mostly in British embassies—packed their bags and moved out. The British armed services, more than ever in need of intelligence material, found little of substance coming from the SIS. As winter turned to the spring of 1941, and the possibility of a German invasion increased, the chiefs of staff turned to the SIS for hard facts. Churchill wanted to send reinforcements overseas: were the Germans still intending to invade England or not? All the SIS could come up with was their view that maybe the Germans just wanted to keep the British guessing. The chiefs of staff said they didn't want strategic appreciations, they wanted answers, and they didn't pull their punches: 'the SIS should take every possible step to remedy this extremely unsatisfactory state of affairs'. At a meeting at the Foreign Office on 31 March, Sir Alexander Cadogan, head of the Foreign Office, noted that the armed service intelligence chiefs failed to reach any agreement with Menzies.[42] Cadogan noted in his diary: 'He [Menzies] babbles and wanders, and gives the impression he is putting up a smoke screen of words & trying to put his questioners off the track'.[43]

In fact Menzies and his secret service were remaining in business only by assuming credit for the gradually improving performance of the codebreakers at Bletchley Park. From early 1941 Menzies visited Churchill each day at about 9 am, taking with him as much interesting BP material as he could muster. Often the meetings became cosy chats in which Menzies provided Churchill with Whitehall and clubland gossip and 'indecent jokes'. It was these meetings, said the biographer of Menzies, that enabled SIS to survive rather than be absorbed by its wartime rival organization, Special Operations Executive (SOE). Indeed the relationship helped Menzies to keep control of Bletchley when four of its most important cryptanalysts staged a 'mutiny' against bad management and the chronic staff shortage that was holding up their vital work. Having failed for months to get improvement through the usual channel, they went over the heads of Menzies and his men and got someone to put their letter on the prime minister's desk. The next day, 22 October 1941, Menzies received a caustic message from Churchill:

> ACTION THIS DAY.
> Make sure they have all they want on extreme priority and report to me that this has been done.[44]

The Special Operations Executive had come into being as a result of the collapse of France—not to be primarily an intelligence-gathering operation but to organize movements in enemy-occupied territory. Hugh Dalton, who ran the SOE in its early days, said they had to be comparable to 'the Sinn Fein movement in Ireland, to the Chinese guerrillas now operating against Japan, to the Spanish irregulars who played a notable part in Wellington's campaign or—one might as well admit it—to the organizations which the Nazis themselves have developed'.[45] Churchill simply told them to set Europe ablaze.

Setting Europe ablaze proved a lengthy and difficult business, though they certainly lit a fire under Whitehall. The bureaucrats of the Foreign Office were furious to hear that they were not the only ones to run a spy service. Menzies complained endlessly that the SOE took from him the sort of recruits he wanted. In fact the mixed bag of male and female linguists, foreigners, soldiers and adventurers recruited by SOE were a far cry from the sort of men to be found in Menzies' quiet corridors of power. Perhaps even Menzies came to see that, for he later concentrated his complaints upon the way the SOE was given the use of planes, boats and money.

SUMMER 1940—BRITAIN GOES BUST

With the Swastika fluttering from the Eiffel Tower, and German staff officers investigating the wine cellars at Maxim's, Britain's leaders set aside their hopes of imminent German economic collapse. It was the German army which now had nothing to do while waiting for Britain's collapse. As things stood, it looked as if they would not have long to wait.

Only in Göring's vast Air Ministry building in Berlin was there any real activity, for there were those who felt a need for the Luftwaffe's bombers to fly to England and teach the British one final lesson.

The British prime minister's speech on the 18 June 1940 had already given the forthcoming battle a name. 'The Battle of France is over', he'd said. 'I expect the Battle of Britain is about to begin . . .'[46] Churchill always had the right words on his tongue. In him the nation had found its leader, its chronicler and its orator. The world's memory of the Second World War is largely formed by Churchill's view of those events. His richly worded speeches provided to the English-speaking world a folk memory: the narration to a horrifying scratchy grey newsreel film where perpetually ships sank, cities burned and bodies were shovelled into mass graves.

Both Churchill and Hitler strove always to get a tighter rein upon the day-to-day conduct of the war. Hitler took control of the Armed Forces Office, the OKW, and from there issued orders to the services. Churchill declared himself minister of defence, carefully not saying what powers that gave him. He took over direction of the Chiefs of Staff Committee when he had a mind to do so and had access to the Joint Planning Staff. Since he was chairman of two defence committees, supply and operations, he had control of the entire nation. But Churchill always had to answer to the war cabinet and to Parliament.

Hitler was a teetotal vegetarian while Churchill was a bon

vivant whose consumption of alcohol, according to one witness, 'could be described as unique, for it continued at quite regular intervals through most of his waking hours'.[47] While Hitler was a short-sighted and vindictive 'soldier', who became ever more obsessed with the tactical deployment of smaller and less vital units, Churchill is recorded as a broadminded and far-sighted 'statesman'. His protracted negotiations for 50 ancient US navy destroyers reveal the clarity of his thinking. Churchill told Roosevelt he wanted them for the Atlantic routes, to release modern escort ships for use against a German invasion fleet. But his true motives were more important ones. He wanted to establish precedents: the release of war equipment by the US armed forces, and the supply of such material without payment. Even when it seemed to be agreed that the destroyers would be swapped for 99-year leases on military bases, Churchill insisted that the wording of the agreement should be changed so that the leases could not be measured in terms of cash. The final deal was said to be part 'gift' and part exchange.

It was not simply a matter of pride. Until the summer of 1940 the United States Treasury had been unyielding in demanding dollars for every item the British received. (A law of 1934 decreed that countries, such as Britain, which had defaulted on their First World War debts could not be given credit.) The British cabinet was faced with the grim outcome of this obligation when on 22 August 1940 the chancellor of the exchequer brought to the meeting his report on the 'Gold & Exchange Resources'. In the first six months of 1940 Britain's total gold and dollar reserves, including US holdings, had fallen from £775 million ($3,100 million) to £156 million ($624 million). Taking into account orders placed by the French government, which the British had now taken over, Britain would have no resources left by Christmas 1940.

At the centre of this crisis were the two schemes put forward by Lord Beaverbrook, a dynamic Press baron who had taken over as minister of aircraft production. One scheme to buy American aircraft would eventually spend £300 million a year, the other £800 million a year. In fact as Kingsley Wood (the chancellor) told the cabinet, 'There is no prospect of our having dollars to pay these sums, nor of our ever paying these amounts, if lent to us by the USA'. He added that it was doubtful if money would be found to pay the £75 million that would be needed by the end of that year.

Beaverbrook urged them to keep ordering war material at such a rate that, when British money ran out, the United States government would be forced to provide aid or else risk a severe jolt to the US economy just as it was feeling the benefit from the war orders.

The cabinet came to no conclusion but, in effect, Beaverbrook's advice was taken, for there was no reduction in the ordering of machine-tools, aircraft, aero-engines and motor vehicles. In all goods worth $3,200 million were ordered over the next twelve months. In addition, steel became the principal Atlantic cargo in the second half of 1940.

Churchill watched the calendar as the time for presidential elections approached, for he was anxious to see Roosevelt reelected. With the American public about to pronounce upon the European conflict, it was becoming more and more evident that propaganda was playing a vital part in the progress of the war. Churchill, believing that the Americans liked nothing so much as a winner, changed his theme from that of 'the English-speaking cousin in mortal peril' to the plucky fighter who, given the tools, will finish the job. Both Germany and Britain were giving ever more facilities, and greater and greater attention, to neutral radio and Press reporters. Fighting men had their photos on the front pages; so did admirals, generals and air marshals. From the smoke and dust of the May fighting in France and the Low Countries three 'star' personalities emerged: Erwin Rommel, Alan Brooke and Bernard Montgomery. None of them merited the attention given to them. It was a sign of the changing times that all three were somewhat more adept at self-publicity than skilful in the conduct of warfare.[48]

ISOLATIONISM AND THE USA

Perhaps it explains something of Chamberlain's prewar appeasement policy that he believed America could not be depended upon for help in resisting the European dictators. 'It is always best and safest to count on nothing from the Americans but words', he said. Britain's ambassador in Washington, Lord Lothian, did not do a great deal to improve the transatlantic relationship. One American writer said of him:

> He was an old-school-tie product of the British Foreign Office, with manners fit for the days of dominance. He was six feet nine inches tall and had the bulging eyes, walrus moustache and the austere arrogance of the English clubman. He had little interest in anyone in Washington: a boring and provincial town he thought. He associated with almost no one but the socialites of New York, Newport and Palm Beach.[49]

When Churchill became prime minister a new ambassador was appointed to tackle the difficult task in Washington. In 1939 a poll found that 67 per cent of Americans opted for the United States to remain neutral; only 12 per cent wanted aid sent to the Allies and a mere 2 per cent thought Americans should do battle against the dictators. An organization calling itself 'America First' held rallies and made headlines; it's supporters believed that an Axis victory would not menace US security. Some cynics pointed out that the British and the French, who claimed to be fighting a war for democracy, had colonies where millions of people were not permitted to choose their own form of government.

The German victories in Poland and western Europe changed the opinions of some Americans about whether they should fight. Newsreels and newspaper accounts revealed the ruthless methods of the Wehrmacht and the Nazi regime which controlled it. France fell and Britain became the only outpost of democracy in a Nazi Europe. Without Britain, there would be no base from which the United States could ever confront Hitler. And there was the economic effect. The European war brought orders to US factories, and this was welcomed by both capital and labour. Unemployment went down and stayed down; the 1941 jobless percentage was not again reached until 1975.

Yet expressing disapproval of the totalitarian regimes was not the same as wanting to fight them. Isolationists were to be found everywhere; isolationism did not follow social or geographical lines. Neither did it follow party-political lines: Communists and Republicans stood side by side in opposition to Roosevelt's Democratic policies. Roosevelt gave full recognition to this fact when in June 1940 he appointed a Republican as secretary of war and another as secretary of the navy.

The American peacetime army had become a refuge for the unemployed, and a social club for poorly trained officers. Its headquarters was a temporary wooden building dating from the First World War. For the first year of the European conflict, America's secretary of war—who lacked any sort of military background—did nothing to equip or train the US army. He was a dedicated isolationist who opposed any aid to Britain. Roosevelt's replacement for him—Henry L. Stimson—began a long-overdue programme of change. In September 1941, as a dramatic symbol of America's new role in the world, work began on the mammoth Pentagon building. Three hundred architects were at work in an abandoned aircraft hangar trying to keep blueprints coming for 13,000 construction workers working round the clock.

Roosevelt was opposed in the presidential election of 1940 by Wendell Wilkie, who had been a Democrat all his life but was chosen as the Republican candidate. During the lead-up to the election, Roosevelt took care to get Wilkie's support for such warlike actions as transferring the 50 old destroyers to Britain and passing a Selective Service Act that would draft Americans in peacetime. It was difficult to judge the mood of the voters and Roosevelt used his position in the White House to be photographed with the evidence of the expanding economy. Such pictures showed the president with tanks, planes and ships, so enabling Wilkie to warn the voters that Roosevelt would push America into the European war. This campaign strategy backfired. Roosevelt won a third term, with 27 million votes against Wilkie's 22 million.

It was time to look at Britain in a realistic light. Roosevelt found it hard to believe that the mighty British Empire, which seemed to cover most of the globe, could be on the point of bankruptcy, and felt sure that the British must have billions hidden away somewhere. For this reason his response to ever more desperate pleas for help from the British was a demand for a complete breakdown of Britain's assets. On 23 December 1940 the president notified London that he had sent the cruiser *Louisville* to Simonstown naval base in South Africa to collect £42 million worth of gold, which was Britain's last negotiable asset. Now British-owned companies in North America were sold at giveaway prices. The Viscose Company, worth $125 million, was liquidated to eventually fetch $87 million. Some businessmen thought such deals disgraceful, but only when they were satisfied that Britain was penniless did the Americans agree to supplying all future war material as gifts.

In January 1941 Roosevelt introduced the Lend-Lease Bill that authorized the president to sell, transfer, exchange, lend, lease, or otherwise dispose of war equipment and other commodities to the government of any country whose defence the president deemed vital to the defence of the United States.

Britain, which had never recovered financially from the First World War, was saved just in time by Roosevelt's Bill. On 1 March, ten days before the Lend-Lease Bill became law, debts of $540 million were due for settlement—some of the money was owed to foreign countries other than the United States. It was double the amount of money Britain possessed, and her gold and dollar reserves had shrivelled to less than £3 million. Churchill asked the Dutch and Norwegian governments in exile to sell Britain gold for sterling; both said no: Britain was saved from disaster only when the Belgian government in exile lent Britain £60 million from the gold reserves which it had managed to get out when the Germans had overrun the Low Countries.[50]

The Lend-Lease Bill was not unanimously welcomed. Joseph P. Kennedy, former ambassador to Britain, and father of the man who later became president, opposed it. So did the famous aviator Charles A. Lindbergh, as well as Wendell Wilkie. Some feared that Roosevelt would send abroad armaments that America needed for its own defence. Others warned that such a Bill would give the president dangerous powers. The Act became law on 11 March 1941, and Congress authorized him to lend an initial $7 billion worth of war matériel to any nation. On 27 May Roosevelt proclaimed an unlimited national emergency and, three weeks later, suspended diplomatic relations with Germany and Italy and froze all their assets in the United States.

In July the president sent US troops to build and maintain military installations in Iceland.[51] If the Germans were allowed to create military bases there, US sea routes would be threatened. Only two senators protested. American public opinion was changing as the Axis successes could be seen as a threat to even the US mainland, and Washington became involved in Britain's conduct of the war. At first the Atlantic campaign against the U-boats was the prime concern, but more and more US army, and army air force, 'fact-finding observers' were to be seen in London just as British military men were found in Washington DC, where eventually all the big decisions would have to be approved.

The Allied top brass made an Anglo-American Combined Chiefs of Staff Committee dominated by General George C. Marshall, chief of staff of the US Army. His opposite number was General Sir Alan Brooke, newly appointed chief of the Imperial General Staff and thus military adviser to Churchill and the government. Brooke was a prima donna who considered himself above the humdrum tasks of planning and management that Marshall was using to transform the US army. He saw himself as a battle-hardened master of strategy and regarded the Americans as inexperienced newcomers who should be attentive to his teaching. The Americans saw Brooke as the commander of a poorly organized, ill-equipped army that since war began had never beaten the Germans in battle. So it was remarkably good fortune for the Allied cause that Brooke spent so much time in London and George Marshall became friends with General Sir John Dill, an Englishman to whom he could relate. Dill had to heal the wounds that Brooke frequently inflicted upon his allies and doubtless Marshall did the same when Roosevelt got rough. The two men conspired to evade the interference that came from every side. So closely did they cooperate, that each would confide in the other memos and communications that were not even available to their closest colleagues. They regularly lunched before the committee meetings, sometimes with their wives at lunch with them, and by the time the meeting opened the most tricky matters were already agreed.

When, with the war still unfinished, Dill died of anaemia the cortège went along a route lined with thousands of US soldiers. The US Joint Chiefs of Staff acted as honorary pall-bearers and there was a gun carriage drawn by six grey horses. General Sir John Dill was buried with pomp and ceremony in that most sacrosanct ground for American warriors: Arlington National Cemetery.

THE DEVELOPMENT OF THE ATOM BOMB

Had the United States not gone to war it seems probable that the atomic bomb would never have been made at all. Fiction writers had from time to time scared readers with the idea of an ultimate weapon, and by 1939 most Western nuclear physicists agreed that building such a device was theoretically possible. In the summer of that year leaders of some of the great powers were also told of it.

In August Leo Szilard wrote a letter urging the American president to investigate the use of atomic energy in war. Although Albert Einstein, the most famous scientist in the world, was an ardent pacifist he added his immense authority to the plea by signing the letter. A few weeks earlier, Professor Hentsch of Hamburg had alerted the Berlin War Ministry to the same possibilities and the Reich Ministry of Economics started at once to look for uranium. That summer, Raoul Dautry, the French minister of armaments, also became interested in nuclear research. In Britain, government research was already being done at the universities, and by May 1939 enough was known for Britain's Air Ministry to order one ton of uranium.[52]

At first only Britain and France took the scientists seriously. As the German invaders arrived, in the summer of 1940, French scientists were well advanced. The French secret service had already bought the whole of the world's stock of 'heavy water' for use as a moderator for slowing down neutrons in a controlled chain reaction using uranium. As France fell this work was transferred to Cambridge, England, where work on the isolation of plutonium continued. At the same time two American physicists published an account of their work on the same process. It was becoming clear to all the scientists that further work would be far more demanding; it would require a great deal of money and national backing.

In March 1940 two scientists[53] in England—both refugees from the Nazis—wrote a short description of how a bomb using uranium 235 might be made. They convinced Professor Lindemann that a few more costly experiments would confirm that making an atomic bomb was perfectly feasible. Lindemann, later Lord Cherwell, was an eccentric man who is as well remembered for his bad scientific judgments as for his good ones. But Churchill seemed to believe everything Lindemann told him, and now the atomic project was given all the resources that Britain could spare. In July

1941 those supervising the research (the MAUD Committee: a camouflage title)[54] reported that the bomb definitely could be made and should be hurried forward 'in case the Germans got such a weapon first'. German physicists received no such encouragement, and nuclear research there came to nothing.[55]

In the United States research was proceeding slowly and without much emphasis on the military applications of fission, when E.O. Lawrence, at Berkeley, discussed the conclusions of the MAUD committee with Vannevar Bush, who was close to President Roosevelt.[56] As a result Roosevelt contacted Churchill and suggested that there should be some sort of coordination of efforts, or even a joint atom project. Told by his advisers that Britain could soon have a bomb of its own, Churchill declined the offer.

It was only in July 1942 that Churchill learned that building a nuclear bomb would be so costly that Britain could not possibly do it alone. But by then it was too late to link up with the Americans, who were ahead of the British in theoretical work, in experiment and in production. The English historian R. A. C. Parker wrote:

> [The Americans] thought the help of British scientists, and that of refugees in Britain, might save perhaps a few weeks of valuable time, especially in devising a plant for separating uranium-235 by gaseous diffusion.

The Americans considered a few weeks of time too high a price to pay for British interference, and some feared that the British would turn the results of the American work to their own commercial advantage. Roosevelt agreed but added that America must ensure that postwar Britain had nuclear energy as a way of helping an ally with an ailing economy. (President Truman did not honour this pledge.) Only after Churchill had renounced any commercial benefits did the Americans agree to a limited exchange of information, and this was restricted to what the Americans decided was needed to produce a bomb. Postwar Anglo-American cooperation was not helped when, in 1950, it was discovered that Dr Klaus Fuchs—one of the scientists sent by the British to work on the bomb—had all along been spying for the Russians.

By the time it was ready, it had become evident that no nation but the United States had anything like the resources to solve the problems that arose from building the first such bomb. (The bomb was built in the Soviet Union far more cheaply after spies such as Fuchs had turned the results of the American work over to Moscow.)

Part Three

THE
MEDITERRANEAN
WAR

12 THE WAR MOVES SOUTH

I have a tremendous admiration for Caesar. But . . . I myself belong rather to the class of Bismarcks.

MUSSOLINI IN CONVERSATION WITH EMIL LUDWIG

The war that Germany fought in Northern Europe was grey. Solemn grey-faced civilians, in dark three-piece suits, made the decisions. Hordes of men in Feldgrau flooded the Continent of Europe until they reached the grey waters of the Atlantic, where grey-painted ships fought their grim grey wars.

The war in the Mediterranean was different. It was more varied and complicated than in any other theatre. Mussolini's Italy provided bravura passages for battles fought in the sunshine, with a more vocal scenario. Operatic uniforms and florid speeches sustained a war that was really a series of adventures. A feudal emperor, desert Arabs, a poet soldier, undersea chariots, illustrious noblemen, armies that floated from the sky and landed amid monuments of the classical world. That was the Mediterranean war.

BENITO MUSSOLIN: 'BELIEVE! OBEY! FIGHT!'

Despite a certain hypnotic charisma, Adolf Hitler was an embittered man of banal tastes and predictable opinions. Benito Mussolini was a far more complex personality. One of the most intimate portraits of him is to be found in the diaries of his son-in-law, Count Galeazzo Ciano, who became Italy's foreign minister. Ciano promised that his published diary:

> records the mental processes, sudden rages, lechery and sentimentality, flashes of insight, inconceivable stupidities, ingenuousness and shrewdness of the buffoon who for a quarter of a century imposed himself on the Italian people . . . There is the man in all his folly and humanity.[1]

An American sent to speak with him provided a harsher portrait:

> It should never be forgotten that Mussolini remained at heart and in instinct an Italian peasant. He was vindictive and would never forget an injury or a blow to his personal or national prestige. He admired nothing except force and power. His own obsession was the re-creation of the Roman Empire.[2]

In the years before the First World War, Mussolini was one of the most respected and well-informed Marxists in Europe. He edited *The Class War*, a paper which advocated violent revolution with such slogans as 'He who has steel has bread'. He saw the coming of war in 1914 as the event which would bring worldwide Socialist revolution. Lenin, who went some way to proving this theory correct, wrote enthusiastically of Mussolini in *Pravda*, and the two men saw eye to eye on most important political matters. Both wanted to be rid of parliaments and all the inconveniences that multi-party politics bring to men who wish to wield centralized and permanent state power.

Italy entered the war in 1915 as an ally of Britain and France in spite of a treaty binding the country to Germany. The war gave Italy—a unified nation only since 1870—an expectation of greatness and enlarged its borders. Opportunism paid off and the war changed Mussolini's ambitions: 'he sniffed the nationalism in the air and drew down great lungfuls of it. It was intoxicating'.[3]

Mussolini was vain and excitable; he needed the adoration of the people. Above all he was very human, and his evident love of uniforms and abundant sex life appealed to the Italian crowd. He was quite unlike the cruel and inhuman Lenin or the narrow-minded Hitler. Embracing nationalism and the 1914–18 war, Mussolini relished the territorial gains that came from it and eventually came to despise Lenin for making a separate peace that conceded so much Russian soil to the Germans.

In March 1919 Mussolini and his friends invented a new political party, adopting costumes, symbols and ideas for social reform from many different political groups. Their speeches were angry and dynamic, if not to say violent in their promises. Black-shirted men, using the military terminology that all revolutionaries relish, vowed to take over capitalism rather than destroy it. In passing, they pledged to seize Church property, give land to the peasants, abolish the monarchy and give the government absolute control of the economy. Nowadays it sounds like a recipe for disaster, but at that time the prospect was new, and the failure of the revised Soviet Russian economy was not yet apparent.

Mussolini was an essential ingredient of the new era. He understood the value of history and how to use its poems, myths and legends. Blood was invoked as an element of Italian heritage and also as something to be spilled in 'the struggle'. Machinery and technology would revitalize Italy.

In Russia and Germany, comparable political ideas had arisen when battle-weary soldiers returned to an angry and bewildered homeland. It can be argued that the Italians were a victorious nation and the Germans a defeated one but it was not easy for the working man to distinguish victor from vanquished. Anyway the Italians had suffered crushing defeats on the Austrian front, and the German army contended that their defeat had come not on the battlefield but at the peace conference table.

The German and Italian experience can be more closely compared, for in both lands soldiers returning from the battlefields were vilified by Communists, Socialists and pacifists. Ex-soldiers, and those who resented the treatment meted out to them, formed the core of the Fascist and Nazi parties. In both countries the middle classes were understandably fearful of the bloody terror that Russia's Communist revolution had demonstrated. Violent clashes between political parties fomented these fears, persuading the middle classes, including ex-soldiers and local police forces, to put their weight behind anti-Communist organizations. As the Fascists and Nazis took power, most people accepted a loss of freedom in exchange for the restoration of law and order.

Italy had joined the Allies in the First World War in the hope of becoming a great power. At the peace conference the Italians were treated with contempt. The permanent under-secretary at Britain's Foreign Office, Sir Charles Hardinge, called them odious colleagues, well known for their 'whining alternated by truculence'. Italian claims to the port of Fiume at the head of the Adriatic Sea were dismissed out of hand.

This treatment unified Italians in a way the war had failed to do. A thousand war veterans, under the poet Gabriele D'Annunzio, marched into Fiume in September 1919 and refused to go away. The victorious Allies were nonplussed by their bellicose stance and did nothing. In 1924 Italian possession of Fiume was ratified. Mussolini, leader of the largest veterans organization, learned the lesson: force pays when words fail.

Fascism (of which Nazism was a later German variant) was Italian in origin. Mussolini organized fasci, or groups of working men, to agitate for social change. A *fascio* is a bundle or a pack. In Ancient Rome *fasces*—a bundle of rods bound together (unity is strength) and containing an axe— had been carried before magistrates as an emblem of official power, and the symbol was adopted in the French Revolution. For Mussolini this classic symbol was perfect, and he used it extensively to promote Italy as a mighty and warlike nation. In 1921 the Fascist party was formed. It wore the all-black uniform of the Arditi, the Italian army's storm-troops.

The word 'totalitarianism' was invented by Mussolini. It decreed (as did the Marxism that Lenin and Stalin inflicted upon Russia) that everyone and every activity came under the direct control of the state. Under both regimes, to be apolitical was a punishable offence.

As he came closer to power Mussolini revised some of his ideas to suit new allies. A thousand deals were done with politicians, businessmen and people of influence who believed that the Fascists would be able to furnish votes enough to win. In October 1922 King Emmanuel III asked Mussolini to form a government, and arriving in Rome in his Fascist uniform he announced dramatically that he had just come from the battlefield. It was to become a well-propagated myth that the Fascists marched on Rome and seized power by force of arms. In fact Mussolini turned up on the overnight train, his wife exclaiming: 'What a character!'

Having forgotten all ideas about ending the monarchy, he abandoned another pledge by eventually coming to terms with the Pope and the Roman Catholic Church. It was an important move, for the Church and the Italian state had been on bad terms for many years. Now Mussolini put a crucifix into every schoolroom and gave his soldiers chaplains. He was, the cynics said, merely displaying the traditional Italian reverence for religion, family and graft.

The black-shirted Fascists chanted *Credere! Ubbidire! Combattere!* (Believe, Obey, Fight) and called Mussolini *Il Duce* (the Leader). The complex uncertainties of democracy were scorned. Death, Violence and Will were among the favoured words as they discovered that the prospect of miracles was easier to sell to the electorate.

Opponents were imprisoned or fled abroad. Newspapers and radio stations were controlled. Local government was made a part of the new movement. 'Our mayor was suddenly wearing a smart uniform and giving Fascist salutes', an Italian friend of mine remembered. 'And when we went to the next village their mayor was also in uniform'.

In the 1920s his Fascist economy flourished: unions were tightly restricted, the workforce was disciplined and obedient, and industry cooperated. As Italy slowly recovered from the war Mussolini promised not the peace and rebuilding that was so obviously needed, but more war. He told his countrymen that, to stay healthy, Italy needed a war every 25 years. Perhaps they did not take him literally (in the same way that Hitler's anti-Jewish diatribes were not taken literally), or else thought that such 'wars' would be overseas colonial adventures.

EASY PICKINGS: ABYSSINIA AND ALBANIA

Ever since records were first kept, large numbers of Italians had been going overseas to live. In many Mediterranean towns—Tunis, Beirut and Tripoli—they had outnumbered other Europeans, yet Italian possessions overseas were few. Apart from Tripolitania, which in 1911–12 the Italians had wrested from the Ottoman Empire and renamed Libya, they had Eritrea and part of Somaliland. These two slices of Italian territory in the 'horn of Africa' were separated by Abyssinia, a primitive kingdom ruled by Emperor Haile Selassie. Said to have been founded by a son of the Queen of Sheba in the tenth century BC, it was remembered by the Italians for the town of Adowa, where in 1896 an invading Italian army had suffered terrible destruction at the hands of the native defenders.

Mussolini was determined to enlarge his overseas possessions. He liked to declare his admiration for Julius Caesar and an African empire smacked of Ancient Rome. Mussolini relished the idea of erasing the shame of Adowa and teaching the Abyssinians a lesson by occupying their land. That would unite the two Italian colonies into one large 'Italian East Africa'.

When in 1934 Mussolini invaded Abyssinia (present-day Ethiopia) he was confronted by huge lakes, scorching desert and formidable mountains. To bring the war to a successful conclusion, he used bombers—the first town bombed was Adowa—and even poison gas against barefoot native soldiers armed with nothing more lethal than spears.

Hitler took advantage of the world's dismay at the Italian atrocities by marching into the demilitarized Rhineland, and so began the military expansion which led to the Second World War. As Hitler became more and more bellicose the other major powers, which might have restrained the Italians, began vying for Mussolini's friendship. An attempt to cut off Italy's oil was frustrated by the United States, which feared that such a blow to the Italian economy could lead to a Communist revolution there.

The Italian victory in Abyssinia brought Mussolini great popularity with his own people but made him many enemies abroad. A world prepared to support his political experiments in his homeland could not stomach pictures of gassed and bombed native villagers. But international disapproval only served to unite Italians behind Mussolini. The Italian king was acclaimed emperor, and his empress was presented with a golden rose by the Pope.

Mussolini's next adventure was to send troops to assist General Franco's nationalists fighting the civil war in Spain. In Britain and America this bitter struggle was widely portrayed as the extinction of democracy by Franco's entirely evil Fascist forces, although history's verdict on the Spanish Civil War is nowadays less simplistic. Mussolini became isolated and identified with right-wing extremism, yet for him the Spanish fighting was no more than an adventure. He told his son-in-law, Count Ciano, who was also his foreign minister, that it was to mould the character of the Italians. 'When Spain is finished, I will think of something else', he promised.

Perhaps Mussolini took to reading his own Press releases,

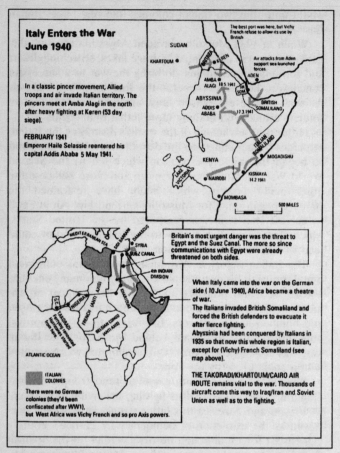

**Italy Enters the War
June 1940**

In a classic pincer movement, Allied troops and air invade Italian territory. The pincers meet at Amba Alagi in the north after heavy fighting at Keren (53 day siege).

FEBRUARY 1941
Emperor Haile Selassie reentered his capital Addis Ababa 5 May 1941.

The best port was here, but Vichy French refuse to allow its use by British

Air attacks from Aden support sea launched forces

SUDAN
KHARTOUM •
ERITREA
KEREN
AMBA
ALAGI 18.5.1941
ABYSSINIA
ADDIS
ABABA
ADEN
FR.
SOM.
BRITISH
SOMALILAND
17.3.1941
ITALIAN
SOMALILAND
KENYA
LAKE
VICTORIA
• NAIROBI
MOGADISHU
KISMAYA
14.2.1941
• MOMBASA
0   500 MILES

Britain's most urgent danger was the threat to Egypt and the Suez Canal. The more so since communications with Egypt were already threatened on both sides.

MEDITERRANEAN SEA
RED SEA
DAMASCUS
SYRIA
SUEZ CANAL
4th INDIAN
DIVISION
KHARTOUM

When Italy came into the war on the German side (10 June 1940), Africa became a theatre of war.
The Italians invaded British Somaliland and forced the British defenders to evacuate it after fierce fighting.
Abyssinia had been conquered by Italians in 1935 so that now this whole region is Italian, except for (Vichy) French Somaliland (see map above).

NIGERIA (ANTI AXIS)
TAKORADI
reached by
freighters
from here
FRENCH (ANTI AXIS)
BELGIAN CONGO (ANTI AXIS)
ATLANTIC OCEAN

ITALIAN
COLONIES

There were no German colonies (they'd been confiscated after WW1), but West Africa was Vichy French and so pro Axis powers.

THE TAKORADI/KHARTOUM/CAIRO AIR ROUTE remains vital to the war. Thousands of aircraft come this way to Iraq/Iran and Soviet Union as well as to the fighting.

an ailment for which even Hollywood has no remedy, and began believing that he commanded a formidable fighting machine. On 30 November 1938 Ciano hinted in the Fascist Chamber at Italy's 'natural aspirations'. It was enough to get the parliamentarians on their feet shouting 'Corsica, Tunis, Nice!'—which did not go down at all well in Paris. It must have reconciled many French voters to the Franco-German

Declaration of Friendship which was signed a week afterwards.

As the Romans of the classical world had found, the Mediterranean is an unfriendly lake. Even at the height of Roman power, the Italian mainland was often invaded. Mussolini had not chosen well in conquering Abyssinia, for it was far away, and lay beyond the Suez Canal which Britain jealously controlled. Italy's other great colonial possession, Libya, was on the far side of the Mediterranean, a stretch of water which the Royal Navy and the French fleet could make dangerous for sea traffic.

Bismarck is reputed to have said that Italy had a good appetite but poor teeth. One historian added that Mussolini 'put a lot of effort into national dentistry'.[4] He did, but the teeth Mussolini provided were false ones.

If Mussolini's exhortations had helped to pull Italy into the modern world, it was still far from being a prosperous country, and scarcely even a developed one. It depended upon imported raw materials such as oil, coal and iron ore. Italy's shape, with the mountainous spine that extends its entire length, gives it problems of communications even in peacetime. Italian genius for exquisite design and innovative engineering was there for all to see; its naval architects unsurpassed. But genius and strength do not always go hand in hand. Except for a few showpiece units the Italian army was not mechanized. Its air force consisted largely of out-of-date biplanes. Although the navy was the most impressive of its armed forces, it was by no means adequate to face the combined navies of Britain and France.

In July 1938 5 billion lire were assigned to modernization of the Italian armed forces. Two new battleships were designed and there were to be monoplanes for the airmen. But wars—even small wars—cost money. The fighting in Abyssinia had cost about 13 billion lire and there were still 300,000 Italian troops engaged in occupation duties. The intervention in Spain's civil war had written off many tanks and aircraft, and 50,000 men were still there. As Mussolini's need for money took large bites out of the taxpayer, the population lost some of its enthusiasm for war, although few complained aloud now that the secret police were listening.

Then, as the Spanish Civil War drew to an end in 1939, Mussolini thought of the 'something else'. With little preparation, he sent an invasion force against Albania, a small kingdom that faced the heel of Italy across the Adriatic Sea. The occupation was effortless: Albania had been an Italian protectorate since 1934.

UNEASY AXIS

By this time the Western powers had come to see Italy as a close partner of Hitler's Germany, and almost as dangerous. Mussolini thought of the Führer as the only ally who would let him continue his policy of selective aggression. Hitler willingly became Mussolini's accomplice, while keeping his own plans secret until his armies moved. As one crisis followed another, Mussolini became fearful that his partner would involve them in a major war for which Italy was unprepared. It was Mussolini who contrived the Munich Pact to give Hitler what he wanted and avoid war. When the Western powers stood firm against Hitler's demands upon Poland, Mussolini urged caution upon his partner. On 12 August 1939 he sent Ciano to talk to the Führer at the Berghof near Berchtesgaden in Bavaria. Ciano found the atmosphere icy and was shocked to discover that the Germans intended to invade Poland come what may.

> Hitler is very cordial, but he, too, is impassive and implacable in his decision. He speaks in the large drawing room of his house, standing in front of a table on which some maps are spread out. He exhibits a truly profound military knowledge. He speaks with a great deal of calm and becomes excited only when he advises us to give Yugoslavia the *coup de grâce* as soon as possible. I realize immediately that there is no longer anything that can be done. He has decided to strike, and strike he will.[5]

The next day Ciano reported to Mussolini at the Palazzo Venezia:

> And in addition to reporting to him what happened, I also make known my own judgement of the situation, of the men and events involved. I return to Rome completely disgusted with the Germans, with their leader, with their way of doing things. They have betrayed us and lied to us. Now they are dragging us into an adventure we do not want and which may compromise the regime and the country as a whole.

Mussolini was alarmed, and even began to wonder if Britain and France might be better partners for Italy. Meanwhile he sent Hitler a 'shopping list' which detailed all the guns, vehicles and raw materials that Germany would have to supply to make Italy ready to fight a war. It was clearly intended as a way of getting off the hook. Blandly Hitler promised a few of the items but 'he proposes to annihilate Poland and beat France and England without help'.[6] Hitler asked only that Italy should not declare its neutrality in advance, but Ciano immediately told the British ambassador 'we shall never start a war against you and the French'. Secret police reports revealed that the Italian public did not remotely desire a war and didn't like the Germans.

As Ciano realized, the Germans were determined to invade Poland and the British equally determined to oppose them. On 1 September Hitler's attack on Poland began and two days later Britain and France declared war. For months Italy remained neutral while Hitler divided up Poland with his new ally Stalin and then struck at Norway. In May 1940, as German Panzer divisions pushed across France, Italy's position as an ally of Germany was still not established. At that desperate time Churchill wrote Mussolini a letter, expressing the hope that Italy would not join in the war. But it was to no avail: Mussolini wanted a seat next to Hitler at the peace conference, and that meant he must start fighting before the French asked for peace. According to Sumner

Welles, the American president's personal representative in Italy: 'One man and one man only, the Dictator Benito Mussolini made the decision'. By 1940 there was no way 'whereby the will of the Italian people could combat the fatal determination of their dictator'.

Ciano was courageous but he quailed before Mussolini, and even the king did not dare oppose him. 'The Italian race is a race of sheep', said Mussolini, '. . . we must keep them disciplined and in uniform from morning until night. Beat them and beat them and beat them . . . This is what I shall do'. He was quite sure that, as soon as France fell, Britain would have to sue for peace, and that promised rich pickings. He made no secret of what he wanted—Malta and Cyprus would become Italian islands, Egypt and the Sudan would be joined to Italian East Africa and Libya to make a vast Italian protectorate. Iraq, with its oil, would become another protectorate and provide the Italian fleet with fuel. Gibraltar would be an international port.

On 10 June 1940 Mussolini sent his troops across the frontier to fight 'against the plutocratic and reactionary democracies'. He was only just in time. France was at her last gasp, but even a mortally wounded France was too much for the Italian army. Five demoralized French divisions found renewed strength and fought back against 32 Italian divisions of the invading army. French Premier Reynaud said: 'What really distinguished, noble and admirable people the Italians are to stab us in the back at this moment'. In faroff Charlottesville, Virginia, President Roosevelt heard the news and, bravely disregarding his Italian voters, said: 'the hand that held the dagger has plunged it into the back of its neighbour'.

Ciano was reported as saying that Italy's chance (to fight an already defeated France) was one that comes only once in five thousand years. Winston Churchill dryly commented that rare chances are not necessarily good ones. In Rome the French ambassador told Ciano: 'The Germans are hard masters. You too will learn this'. Not many Italians needed the reminder: fighting their French neighbours was not a popular task.

When the 84-year-old Marshal Pétain became French president and sued for an armistice, France was split into the occupied north and the unoccupied 'Vichy France' that declared itself neutral. With France out of the war, and Italy a combatant, the balance of force was radically changed. The frontier where the British forces in Egypt faced the Italians in Libya became a battle front. So did the small enclave where British Somaliland was faced on three sides by Mussolini's Italian East Africa. From here an enemy could menace Khartoum, and even Nairobi to the south in British colonial East Africa. Bereft of French warships, the British naval forces in the Mediterranean suddenly looked very small. There was no sign that French overseas possessions, with their military forces and naval bases, would remain in the war. A French general, Charles de Gaulle, escaped to Britain and become a rallying point for any who wanted to continue to fight. But most Frenchmen felt they owed their duty to the only legitimate government of France, that of Marshal Pétain in Vichy. They were no longer at war with the Germans.

A GLOBAL WAR

During 1940 the war changed from being a strictly European conflict to being one of potentially global proportions. The Vichy authorities in French Indo-China (part of which later became Vietnam) passively gave extensive facilities to the Japanese military. These bases were to play a vital part in Japan's manifold attacks at the time of Pearl Harbor. This twelve months, starting with the Battle of Britain in the summer of 1940, was the most complex period of the war. Now began a series of battles and events, each triggering another, leading inevitably to the German-Soviet contest before Moscow in December 1941, and to the Japanese attack on the American fleet at Pearl Harbor.

The Mediterranean was vital to British strategy. It provided the short sea route to India, Australia and the Far East as well as being the door to Egypt and the oil-rich Persian Gulf. Without the aid of French warships the Royal Navy faced a formidable Italian naval presence. The Italians had 6 battleships, 19 cruisers, about 50 destroyers and over 100 submarines. It was partly the threat of Italy's submarines that prompted Churchill to ask Roosevelt if he could spare 30 or 40 reconditioned US navy destroyers. The grim prospect of the sea war was made worse by the nightmare possibility of the Germans taking over the mighty French fleet, either as a part of the peace treaty or simply by force of arms.

THE RN FIGHT THE FRENCH

In the desperate days after the French collapse the British could obtain no information about the terms likely to be agreed for the French surrender, nor of the messages that were being sent to French naval commanders. Churchill and his naval chiefs had not yet fully understood the threat of the U-boat, despite paying lip-service to it. They believed that the surface raider was the real threat to Britain's sea supply lines. The Royal Navy were concerned about France's modern battle-cruisers, *Dunkerque* and *Strasbourg,* and also about two unfinished battleships: *Jean Bart,* which was at Casablanca in French Morocco, and *Richelieu,* at Dakar in French West Africa. The Admiralty thought the *Richelieu* was the most powerful ship afloat.[7]

Churchill ordered that the navy's Force H, based in Gibraltar, be sent to threaten the French at their various North African stations, while French warships in the United Kingdom were taken over by boarding parties. Admiral Andrew Cunningham, the Mediterranean commander-in-chief, protested and the whole Royal Navy was horrified by the order. Churchill prevailed, and on 3 July Force H, consisting of the battle-cruiser HMS *Hood,* the aircraft-carrier HMS *Ark Royal* and the old battleships *Valiant* and *Resolution,* stood off shore at Mers-el-Kébir in French Algeria, where most of France's fleet was at anchor. A message from this powerful force demanded that the French should either scuttle or join the British side flying the Free French flag, or else sail to the French West Indies.

Negotiations lasted for many hours, but the French admiral finally refused and the British opened fire at point-blank range. The battle-cruiser *Dunkerque* was hit by a salvo of 15-inch shells, the old battleship *Bretagne* was hit in the magazine, capsized and was lost with 977 of her crew. The old battleship *Provence* ran aground, but with exemplary seamanship the battle-cruiser *Strasbourg,* a sea-plane-carrier, *Commandant Teste,* and five destroyers got up steam and escaped past the British force. They reached Toulon in southern France. The next day *Ark Royal* sent torpedo bombers to the anchorage to finish off *Dunkerque.* When they hit a lighter laden with depth charges, the resulting explosion killed another 150 sailors.

A couple of days later, French naval units at the Atlantic ports of Dakar and Casablanca refused to comply with the British instructions. They were attacked by motor torpedo boats and torpedo planes. The two unfinished battleships, *Richelieu* and *Jean Bart,* were damaged.

At Alexandria the RN took a more subtle course. Patient negotiations included displaying the offered terms to all ranks by means of placards mounted on small boats. A blind eye was turned to an ill-timed hurry-up message from the Admiralty in London. The good will of the respective admirals—Cunningham and Godfroy—survived even after news came of the Mers-el-Kébir tragedy. The result was an agreed demilitarization of the French ships: the battleship *Lorraine,* four cruisers and some torpedo boats. Fuel stocks were sent ashore and breech blocks and torpedo detonators put into the care of the local French consulate.

The French navy's wartime role at Alexandria was a relaxed one. The French commander, Admiral Godfroy, was permitted to use Vichy French codes and communicate with his masters. His men were paid by the British and, unlike the Free French, were able to send money home to France. They were permitted to take shore leave in Alexandria, and also in Vichy-ruled Syria and Lebanon. The Royal Navy fought a desperate war while these French ships—a battleship, four cruisers and three destroyers—remained unscratched. 'The French ships looked brazenly sleek and shiny compared to the battered British fleet'.[8]

Could the same peaceful agreement have been achieved at Mers-el-Kébir had Churchill shown patience and allowed the local Royal Navy commander more latitude? Certainly all three RN flag officers concerned in these actions thought so, but one of them who expressed that view in a letter to the Admiralty was eventually relieved of his command. Publication of some of the papers of Admiral Cunningham, the Mediterranean C-in-C, revealed the depths of Cunningham's antipathy for Churchill and for this order in particular.[9] Some historians claimed that the record of these exchanges had been deliberately distorted to protect Churchill's reputation.[10]

While Anglo-French relations sank to an all-time low, at least the Royal Navy's shocking action served to show the world that Britain was not just playing for time: Britain was going to continue the war, whatever the cost.

The cost notably and immediately beset the Royal Navy. The central position of Italy, and its shape, provided for the Axis powers naval and air bases that could command the central Mediterranean. Whereas a British convoy sailing from east to west would inevitably come under sustained attack, the short sea crossing from Sicily to Tunisia made it possible to keep open Axis sea lanes to North Africa. Malta's naval dockyard and well equipped harbour was in the perfect position to harass the Italians, but that meant it was an easy short-range target for Italian bombers, and would be difficult to defend against an invading force. A number of drastic strategies were considered by the British, including the truly desperate one of abandoning the Mediterranean and using all their resources to guard Gibraltar and Suez.

Men, munitions and supplies destined for Egypt and other Middle East countries garrisoned by Britain could no longer pass through the Mediterranean. They were sent all the way round Africa. Only supplies for Malta or urgently needed equipment were put into fast well defended convoys to run the Axis gauntlet in the Mediterranean. The Royal Navy's response to this grim situation was to demonstrate in the Mediterranean the same aggressive spirit that the German army had shown on land. Although its original forces had been depleted by the needs of the Norwegian campaign, the threat of invasion of the British Isles, and the battle of the Atlantic, by May 1940 ships drawn from the East and West Indies, China and Australia had restored the Mediterranean fleet to a considerable fighting force.

Resisting the tentative Admiralty suggestion that perhaps the RN should withdraw from the eastern Mediterranean, Admiral Cunningham took his whole fleet to within sight of the Italian coast, where on 9 July 1940 there was a clash with a strong enemy force of 2 battleships, 16 cruisers and 32 destroyers. But the end result was to be counted more in the morale boost it gave to the Royal Navy than in damage inflicted on either side. On 19 July the Australian-manned light cruiser *Sydney* encountered two Italian light cruisers off Crete and sank one of them. These actions established the aggressive way in which the British would sail the sea, and the Italians would sally out to attack or bomb them.

A plan to abandon Malta to the enemy was changed. It was decided that Malta should be reinforced. The aircraft-carrier HMS *Argus* was sent through the Mediterranean with Hawker Hurricane fighters for the island's defence. It was the beginning of a long hard struggle to keep Malta fed and defended.

DISASTER AT DAKAR

It was General de Gaulle who became convinced that the French colonists of French West Africa, as well as those of North and Equatorial Africa, were keen to join him. He proposed to send an expedition to Dakar and, just in case his countrymen failed to recognize him as a liberator and friend, it would be an armed expedition.

Dakar was on the extreme tip of the West African coast. A naval presence there would have safeguarded the sea routes around Africa, and a 'Free French' West Africa coloured in as part of Allied power would look good on the map. The British consul-general in Dakar told London that local civil and military leaders were anxious to continue the war on Britain's side. Such unfounded wishful thinking persuaded Churchill to support the idea. After British intelligence told them of German plans to establish a military base in Dakar, the war cabinet agreed. On 31 August 1940 a force of Royal Marines and French and British soldiers was dispatched.

Codenamed 'Menace', the Allied plan of attack was largely dependent upon the state of defences the French had prepared in the First World War remaining unchanged. An up-to-date French defence scheme had been given to the War Office in June, only to be lost.

The expedition was a failure in every way: politically, because the French colonists certainly did not wish to continue the war as a part of de Gaulle's Free French Forces; in security, as through French sources in London plans of the attack were deliberately leaked to Vichy and to all manner of other parties; through intelligence, because the Germans were not about to establish a base there; in organization, due to the Admiralty not making it clear in Gibraltar whether Vichy French warships should be permitted to pass unopposed; in communication, leading to the landing force not knowing where to land; in naval gunnery, where one hundred 15-inch shells from the RN battleships did not stop the defenders' guns damaging three RN ships; in aviation, where attacks by carrier aircraft were largely ineffective; in anti-submarine tactics, which led to the battleship *Resolution* being torpedoed by a French submarine.

A far from minor benefit to arise from this tragic and absurd fiasco was that his lengthy stay aboard one of the expedition's troopships provided a mature Royal Marine officer named Evelyn Waugh time enough to complete a rough draft of his book *Put Out More Flags*.[11]

13 A TACTICIAN'S PARADISE

'What is happening?' [Hag Latif] asked one day
of his great-grandson.
'It is el Harb—the war'.
'Who makes this war?'
'El nussara—the infidel'.
'Against whom? And why?'
'It is infidel against infidel. Who knows why?'

PAOLO CACCIA-DOMINIONI, *AN ITALIAN STORY*[1]

Early in November 1940 the Royal Navy struck again.
Admiral Cunningham took the attack to the Italian
anchorage at Taranto. Torpedo-carrying Fairey Swordfish biplanes, flying at night off the carrier *Illustrious,* sank three
Italian battleships.

The engagement was historic in its implications, for this
was the first time that aircraft had crippled an enemy battle
fleet and changed the balance of naval power. The Italian
fleet anchorage was a tempting target, and the navy had
prepared contingency plans for attacking it as long ago as
1938. However the primary reason for the raid on Taranto
was that British intelligence could think of no other place to
look for the enemy fleet. Signals intelligence, at any level
from Enigma to low-grade ciphers, provided no clues to the
movements of the Italian warships.

Martin Maryland aircraft newly arrived from America
and based in Malta confirmed that the big ships were at
anchor. The air photos, flown to the carrier *Illustrious* from
Malta, revealed that a balloon barrage and anti-torpedo nets
were now in use, and these demanded last-minute modifica-
tions to the plan.

FIGURE 22:
Fairey Swordfish biplane from HMS *Illustrious*

A LITTLE PEARL HARBOR

Five aircraft from HMS *Eagle* were included in the raid. Two waves of Swordfish aircraft, twenty in all, were divided into a first strike with six torpedo aircraft, four with bombs and two with both bombs and flares. The flares were to illuminate the whole anchorage, the cruisers would be bombed while the torpedo aircraft went in at sea-level to attack the battleships. The 18-inch torpedoes had magnetic pistols which would make them explode under the hulls to do maximum damage.

The usual three-man aircrews were reduced to two in order to accommodate extra fuel tanks. Flying 170 miles from the *Illustrious* to the target, the open cockpits exposed the flyers to freezing cold.

These Fairey Swordfish biplanes had been first delivered to the Fleet Air Arm in 1936. The configuration followed the prevailing policy that carrier aircraft must have low wing-loadings, slow landing speeds and air-cooled engines. Obsolescent when war began, its replacement, the Fairey Albacore, was even less satisfactory. Phased out of operational service, the Albacore was relegated to training, leaving the Swordfish to soldier on. Any word of criticism or sympathy with its crews is likely to be indignantly answered with loyal tributes to the nimble flying qualities of the 'Stringbag' and a claim that Swordfish sank a greater tonnage of shipping than any other Allied aircraft used in the war.[2]

With its braced wings and fixed landing gear, it could fly as slowly as 50 mph without risk of stalling. This proved a useful facility that night when negotiating the almost invisible balloon cables. One pilot remembered asking: 'Where's that bloody balloon barrage?', and his observer answering: 'We've been through it once and are just going through it again'.[3] The slow speed made it possible to spot the defence booms at sea-level. The underwater anti-torpedo nets went down to 25 feet and the torpedoes ran at 30 feet. To run accurately an aerial torpedo must be put into the water gently and from very low altitude. One Swordfish went so low that its wheels touched the water and sent up a great sheet of spray.

A second strike of five torpedo aircraft, two bombers and two flare carriers flew off about thirty minutes later. They left behind a plane which had been slightly damaged in a collision, but the pilot managed to get his plane airworthy and hurried after the others. He arrived fifteen minutes after the second strike had departed and made a solo bombing attack with every gun in Taranto firing at him.

It will come as no surprise that the only two bombs that hit, failed to explode. The torpedoes, however, sank three battleships, one of which never sailed again. For such a small operation, and the loss of only two aircraft, it was a great victory, and early proof that the aircraft-carrier had become the master weapon of naval warfare. Three men survived from the two lost Swordfish, and the Italian navy magnanimously treated their captives with impeccable courtesy. The carrier *Illustrious* turned and sped to rejoin the fleet where, by Cunningham's order, all ships displayed the signal 'Manoeuvre well executed'.

The well executed manoeuvre was not lost on the US navy. Its chief of operations sent a warning to Pearl Harbor telling Admiral Kimmel that the British operation proved aerial torpedoes could be made to run true in shallow water. But no anti-torpedo devices were installed at the American moorings, on the excuse that they would narrow Pearl Harbor's ship channel and cause inconvenience. Admiral Kimmel told Washington that he would make no changes until a light and efficient net was developed.[4]

THE WESTERN DESERT

The desert is a virtually uninhabited region about the size and shape of India. It stretches from the River Nile to Tunisia about 1,200 miles away to the west, and 1,000 miles south to the place where there is enough light rain to produce scrubland. The western part of Libya was called Tripolitania. Here stands Libya's largest city, Tripoli, through which most Axis supplies passed. In eastern Libya, which was called Cyrenaica, the port of Tobruk was equally vital for the supply services. The British held Tobruk for most of the war.

Bordering the Mediterranean there is a flat coastal strip from Alexandria in Egypt to Cyrenaica. The seashore, made of limestone sand, is of a memorable whiteness, especially in the summer when the sea is blue. Few and far between, there are towns and villages with miserable palms, bushes and patches of cultivated ground. Many of the names on the map in this region—El Daba, Fuka and Buq Buq—were no more than names: no houses, no people, no drinking water. Here in summer it becomes too hot to fight. In winter there can be a heavy rainfall which turns the dust-like sand into sticky mud. Most of the fighting took place in this northern strip of the desert, which is about 40 miles wide. But the strip was not manned; this was not a war of fixed fronts, rather a war of forts—secured by barbed wire and vast minefields—and moving columns. There were no civilians to get in the way, just rodents and reptiles and dense clouds of flies. 'The Desert', said General Rommel, 'is a tactician's paradise and a quartermaster's hell'.

The coastal region is higher than the desert behind it. Sooner or later anyone travelling southwards encounters the Great Sand Sea. In some places there is an escarpment which drops away steeply, forming an obstacle that makes movement south difficult for wheeled and even tracked vehicles. This is why the El Alamein region became so vital for the defence of Egypt; for here the Qattara Depression and the sea produce a narrow strip where an army can stand and fight without fear of being outflanked.

At El Agheila the Great Sand Sea comes near enough to the coast to provide another place where an army can rest its flank. Except at these two spots, an army can find long-term security only by means of a fortified perimeter around a water supply, and a port through which supplies can come. So it was that the entire North African campaign was fought for possession of three places: El Alamein in Egypt, El Agheila in Cyrenaica, and the port of Tobruk about halfway between them.

Along the Libyan coast there was a good road; the via Balbia. The section of the road the British built in Egypt was a simple layer of asphalt which could not withstand the continuous weight of heavy vehicles.[5] Alongside their road the British built a very useful railway, but by the end of 1940 it didn't go beyond Mersa Matruh (almost 150 miles short of the Libyan frontier).

Other roads in the desert were just tracks leading over

broken stone and pebbles or various sorts of sand. Most of the sand is powdered clay that produces clouds of white dust, making even half a dozen walking men visible for miles. It gets in your eyes and your hair and your clothes and your drinking water. It gets through even the finest dust-filters, and nothing you see or eat is without a coating of it.

Despite the discomfort, most of the soldiers soon got used to the desert. They revelled in the informality that prevailed in this inhospitable place, and it became normal in most units for officers and men to dress as they wished. Sun helmets were soon discarded, along with all the myths about the noonday sun that the Empire's Englishmen had enshrined in dress regulations for a hundred years. It became fashionable for officers to be seen brandishing fly-swatters and dressed in corduroy trousers, coloured scarfs, suede boots or even sandals. In the hot weather many other ranks wore nothing but khaki shorts and boots and, despite the endless tinned food, remained healthy.

Most of the desert could be traversed by motor vehicles, and hard sand made good 'going', although there were always horrifying rumours of parked tanks disappearing into quicksand after a shower of rain. But along the western frontier of Egypt and sprawling westward, unmapped and ever-changing, there stretched the 'Great Sand Sea'. About 600 miles long and 150 miles wide, it is probably the greatest continuous mass of sand dunes in the world, and some of the dunes are 400 feet high. Thus, for all practical purposes, the Libya-Egypt frontier is only about 200 miles long. However the 'sand sea' is not impassable for dedicated travellers. 'To get a heavy truck up 200 or 300 feet of loose sand at a slope of 1 in 3 you have to charge it very fast . . . But it takes a lot of confidence to charge at full speed into what looks like a vertical wall of dazzling yellow', said Brigadier Bagnold while lecturing at the Royal Geographical Society.[6] To an expert the colour, curvature and ripple marks in sand reveal good going. Soon after war began, a group of soldiers—many of them given ranks overnight—started modifying and equipping Chevrolet trucks for the purpose of exploring and outflanking the Italians in Libya.

This small band of New Zealanders, led by men who had known the open desert for many years, was named the 'Long Range Desert Group' and their strange and dangerous war became something of a legend. They came out of the southern desert at first to observe, and later to attack. By studying the vehicle tracks, they could read the movements of enemy traffic as a Bedouin can estimate the age, breed and condition of every camel that has left a print. In the desert the LRDG found tracks that had been left by Fords of the Light Car Patrols of 1916. And still today the marks of Second World War armies can be seen right across the southern desert.[7]

Their journeys in the south took men far from medical aid or supplies, and required a special sort of nerve. The climate was more extreme than anything known in the coastal strip. There were winds so hot that they could cause collapse. One matter-of-fact report described dead or dying birds in the shade of every rock.

Distances were vast. One patrol went south far enough to make contact with French outposts in Equatorial Africa and found there Frenchmen who wanted to fight Germans. A wounded soldier was taken 700 miles in a truck for treatment at a French post in Tibesti. After that he went 3,000 miles by air to Cairo. Water and fuel were treasured; a truck was towed more than 1,000 miles to get it repaired. By the same measure, patrols would destroy all Italian transport at an outpost and sever it from the world. Sometimes things went wrong. Sharing only two gallons of water and one tin of jam, two Guardsmen and a New Zealander walked across the desert for 10 days, covering 210 miles.

GENERAL WAVELL

Britain's share of this region was ruled by Lieutenant-General Archibald Percival Wavell, one of the more interesting military personalities of the Second World War. More potentate than army commander, his position as commander-in-chief Middle East gave him control over British forces in Egypt, Sudan, Palestine, Transjordan and Cyprus. When war came his armies fought in East Africa, Syria, Lebanon, Greece and Crete, and the fighting in Iraq brought the Persian Gulf into his field of responsibility. These countries were not Dominions or Empire countries. Egypt, where he had his headquarters in Cairo, remained neutral until the final few days of the war. His soldiers were usually subject to a treaty with, or invitation from, a local ruler. He was not subordinate to British political representatives—ambassadors, high commissioners, governor-generals and so on—but neither were they subordinate to him. These officials reported back to London, some to the Foreign Office and others to the Colonial Office. These Whitehall departments did not coordinate their policies with the army nor with each other. Neither did they try very hard to understand the problems Wavell had fighting the enemy.

No other man was ever given the equal of Wavell's immense territorial responsibility.[8] With scanty resources he often found himself fighting several battles at once. The political, geographical, climatic and military constraints within which he worked called for a diplomat with sharp political sense, a soldier's training and the patience of a saint. Above all he had to please Churchill, whose deep distrust of generals was matched only by Wavell's doubts about politicians. Churchill was ebullient and aggressive, Wavell taciturn and an exponent of mediation. Wavell was by nature hesitant, and his humility encouraged him to think that his enemies would at least be equal to his skills and resource. Churchill's ego persuaded him that an enemy could often be overcome simply by bold action. Churchill's sympathies were Zionist; Wavell was always fearful lest he provoked an armed Arab rebellion.

Wavell has been described as the best-educated soldier of his time. Poetry was 'his strongest and most lasting solace' his biographer wrote. So outstanding was Wavell's prose that, when Churchill talked of sacking him, he was warned about the possible effect of Wavell's postwar memoirs (which in fact were never written). Wavell's lectures at the Staff College are still quoted, yet he attended the Royal Military College, Sandhurst, only briefly and his schooling at Winchester, like most British education, took no account of science, engineering or technology in any form.

Perhaps it would be more accurate to say that Wavell was the most cultured soldier of his time. Even so, we must be cautious, for he shared his time with an immense number of soldiers. He attracted loyalty and affection as few men do. A stocky figure in leather gaiters and with a wrinkled face that almost matched them, he was not a publicist who flaunted the eccentricities of dress and manner that other generals so artfully contrived. Perhaps it was his love of poetry that ensured he wasted no words, although this directness of manner could be disconcerting. A very junior officer seated next to Brigadier Wavell at a regimental dinner in 1931 tried to respond to Wavell's 'good evening'.

'Good evening, sir', he ventured. 'I think you know Major X, of the Y regiment?'

'Yes', said Wavell. 'I don't like him'.[9]

His wartime job wore Wavell out. When he left it, on the very day of Hitler's invasion of Russia, he was replaced not by one man but by several. His reputation as a general is legendary, despite Churchill's criticisms, but this is partly due to the way in which he has been given credit for every successful campaign fought under his command and seldom blamed for the avoidable failures. Praise for Wavell has over the years become a method of depicting Churchill as an ignorant, uneducated and dictatorial figure whose understanding of war never progressed beyond his precocious experiences in South Africa. It is difficult to believe that such writings would have given Wavell any pleasure.

Archie Wavell, the son of a general, said he went into the army only to please his father. When the Boer War crisis brought a sudden demand for officers his course at Sandhurst was cut from eighteen months to two terms. By September 1901, Wavell, an eighteen-year-old lieutenant of the Black Watch, was on his way to a war in Africa. In the First World War he served in Egypt and Palestine and returned to Palestine in 1937. Now, back again in Cairo, he was at the height of his career.

GENERAL O'CONNOR ALMOST CONQUERS LIBYA

The Italian army in Libya had been at war with the British in neighbouring Egypt ever since June 1940, when Mussolini attacked southern France. Here in Africa it was too hot to fight. Cautiously the Italians waited to see if the French forces in Tunisia and Algeria to the west of them were in a mood to fight. They were not. Wavell had already decided that a show of belligerence along the Egyptian frontier wire would be his best form of defence. Three days before Italy declared war Major-General R.N. O'Connor had been called from Palestine, complete with his divisional staff, to command what was called the Western Desert Force. (The misnomer 'Western Desert' had started in the First World War to distinguish it from the Sinai, which was called the Eastern Desert.)

O'Connor was a quiet, modest man, remembered at the staff college for his poor performance as a lecturer. In the First World War he'd fought alongside the Italians and they'd awarded him the Silver Medal for Valour. He was usually shabbily dressed in a very ordinary style, and detested publicity or show of any sort. He was seldom known to smile, and one of his subordinates said he had never seen him laugh. Despite this stern demeanour, O'Connor was a popular general of the old school. For students of warfare he is one of the most successful commanders of his time.

Two days after war began, a patrol of the 11th Hussars, equipped with Rolls-Royce armoured cars dating from the 1920s, crossed the frontier into Libya and captured two Italian officers and 59 other ranks. More such raids followed and the army adapted itself to harassment and hit-and-run patrols:

> It attacked not as a combined force but in small units, swiftly, irregularly and by night. It pounced on Italian outposts, blew up the captured ammunition, and ran away. It stayed an hour, a day, or a week in a position, and then disappeared . . . Fort Maddalena fell, and Capuzzo. Sidi Aziz was invested. British vehicles were suddenly astride the road leading back from Bardia, shooting up convoys.[10]

O'Connor took a personal interest in studying the enemy at close quarters. A patrol of the 11th Hussars, pushing well into enemy-occupied territory, saw a staff car heading from the west but lowered their guns as the car got close enough for them to recognize General O'Connor. 'I did not like this', said one of the Hussars.

Those who encountered the desert for the first time found the climate alone to be a daunting experience. One young officer newly arrived from England described a khamsin or sandstorm:

> A darkness would come over the land and a hot wind—as if a gigantic oven door had been suddenly opened— would rush in, bringing with it a hot fog of sand. The khamsin was on us. This howling fury, blowing at a steady pace, might keep us occupied for days, filling our eyes and ears with sand, penetrating everywhere . . . and filling the mind with melancholy and foreboding. These depressing sandstorms, we were to learn later, were about the only things that could halt the war.[11]

But for the old soldiers the desert was as familiar as the weapons they used. Little had changed since the First World War. Biplane fighters flew across the barbed-wire, watched by infantrymen equipped with Lee-Enfield rifles. The machine-guns were Vickers and Lewis designs of long ago, and so were the guns: 18-pounders and 6-inch howitzers. When Marshal Italo Balbo—an internationally famous aviator before governing Libya—was killed in an airplane crash, the RAF flew over the Italian lines and, in a scene straight out of Hollywood's *The Dawn Patrol,* dropped a note of condolence.

The Italian armed forces were even more outmoded, with armoured cars dating back to 1909 and tanks that Rommel described as 'totally obsolete'. Marshal Rodolfo Graziani (who took over the Italian forces in Libya and the governorship after the death of Balbo) had gained a considerable reputation fighting in Italy's colonial wars but he had no experience of fighting a modern enemy.

Mussolini ordered Graziani to attack, and in September the Italians advanced about 60 miles, with the British offering only slight resistance. At Sidi Barrani he halted to extend the metalled road and water pipeline, and build a series of fortified camps. The chain of forts, which stretched 50 miles inland, were not built for all-round defence. No two were mutually supporting (with fields of fire that would provide for a neighbour's defence) and there was a gap of 20 miles in the line.

Rome radio proclaimed a victory. 'All is now quiet in Sidi Barrani', said the announcer. 'The shops are open and the trams running again'.[12] And yet one doesn't have to be a general to see the possibilities offered by a gap in the defences. A force could be marched through the gap and then attack the Italians from the rear. Artillery fire upon the whole camp area would create confusion and panic, while heavily armoured Matilda tanks, almost impervious to light anti-tank gunfire, moved in along Italian vehicle tracks (mapped by means of aerial photographs), thus avoiding minefields and getting right into the compounds. More infantry would follow the tanks in open trucks.

The 'Western Desert Force' was made up of an armoured division and an experienced Indian division which, like most Indian divisions, incorporated British infantry battalions.[13]

O'Connor's plan was for a large-scale raid, lasting five days, which would penetrate the enemy line of forts after an approach by night. No-man's-land was about 70 miles wide, so supplies were taken forward and concealed there. In support the RAF was to destroy enemy aircraft on the ground while the Royal Navy bombarded coastal targets.

Security was tight. Troops were not given notice of the offensive, leave was not stopped, the forward dumps were described as precautionary, and even the medical services were not alerted to the possibility of extra casualties. Since O'Connor was planning no more than a five-day raid, he was surprised, shortly beforehand, to know that Wavell had hopes of a big breakthrough. 'It is possible that an opportunity may offer for converting the enemy's defeat into an outstanding victory', wrote Wavell, adding:

> I am not entertaining extravagant hopes of this operation, but I do wish to make certain that if a big opportunity occurs we are prepared morally, mentally and administratively to use it to the fullest.[14]

On the night of 8 December 1940—in well remembered moonlight and under a starry sky—the attack started. As the artillery fire began, the heavy tanks trundled forward and Cameron Highlanders followed the sound of the bagpipes. The Rajputana Rifles found themselves confronting sleepy and bewildered Italians, some still in pyjamas.

In contrast to the desert fighting portrayed in oil paintings, on this cold night the soldiers wore heavy underwear and woollen sweaters. Many were bundled up in overcoats and laden with three days' rations, lots of grenades and as much ammunition as they could carry.

Many of the Italians fought hard but the plan of attack was a good one. The forts fell and Sidi Barrani was taken. Anyone who'd heard the previous announcements on Rome radio might have looked in vain for its shops and streetcars. Sidi Barrani turned out to be no more than 'a few mud huts and a landing strip'. The British pressed on as the Italians retreated back along the fine coastal road they had built for supplies.

The five-day raid soon turned into a full-scale offensive that captured the coastal strip all the way to Tobruk. By now the 6th Australian Division was in action pressing along the coast, while the 7th Armoured Division struck inland to fight an inconclusive action against a big Italian tank force at Mechili. With considerable skill, the Italians at Mechili withdrew intact into the Jebel Akdar (Green Mountains) during the night of 26 January.

The Jebel was an upland region where some hills were as high as 2,500 feet and where good soil and adequate rain had produced an agricultural area favoured by Italian colonists. In this lush region the Italian colonials rushed out with eggs and gifts for the invading soldiers. They complained that as the Italian army had withdrawn, local Arabs had attacked their farmhouses, looted their possessions and raped their women. The Arabs didn't deny it, but looked to the British for praise and encouragement: the Italians were the enemy of the British, weren't they? 'We could only hope for the best and drive on', said the war correspondent Alexander Clifford.

While the Italians were retreating along the coastal road, closely followed by the Australians, O'Connor pondered about sending his armoured division on a short-cut. By going across the desert, keeping to the south of the Jebel, they might get to the sea at Beda Fomm ahead of the retreating Italians. The patrol sent to explore the route came back to say that the country was 'impossible'. This report was ignored. O'Connor decided not to wait for new tanks or supplies, and instead transferred armour from other units to make one full-strength brigade. So this much depleted armoured division, followed by every available supply vehicle, set a compass course and headed south-west into a land the maps showed as blank white space. It was not just a matter of getting there intact: the whole operation would be futile unless they reached the coastal road at Beda Fomm before the retreating Italians. Clifford said:

The advance patrol had not lied . . . For mile after mile they juddered over great slabs of sharp, uneven rock. Then they crossed belts of soft, fine sand which engulfed vehicles up to their axles. Sandstorms blew up, and the trucks had to keep almost touching if they were not to lose one another. Whole convoys lurched off into the gloom and only re-established contact hours later. It was freezing cold, and the latter half of the division had to contend with fierce, icy showers. All kit had been cut to the bone, and there were no extra blankets or great-coats, and scarcely more than a glass of water per man per day . . . Thus it was that early in the afternoon of February 5 the Seventh Armoured Division cut the road in two places some fifty miles south of Benghasi. And they found they had straddled the entire remaining Italian army, sandwiching it between their two prongs.[15]

'They can't do it', the Italian commander had said of the short-cut across the desert, 'and even if they do do it we still have two days to spare'. In fact if the Italians had passed through Beda Fomm two hours earlier they would have escaped.

The battle began with the leading Italian trucks being wrecked by gunfire. Now the road was blocked to form a traffic jam that snaked back for miles on the hard land that was flat except for a bitterly contested knoll that the British called the Pimple.

For 36 hours the British fought a battle of constant movement against a superior Italian force by which they were far outgunned. One squadron of British tanks shot its way along the ten miles of fighting, replenished its shells and fuel, and then fought all the way back again. The cooperation between tanks, guns, infantry and engineers was exemplary. When the Italian tanks formed up for a counter-attack, sappers moved forward and laid a minefield in front of them. In another remarkable action, infantry of the Rifle Brigade moved fast to prevent a break-out by means of a track leading down to the coastal road.

All day, with tanks and artillery, the Italians made fierce attempts to break through. Accounts of the battle seldom give sufficient importance to the fact that many Italian civilians were with the retreating army, and this created distressing problems. Their army commander, General Tellera, was mortally wounded. In the early morning of the second day the Italians made one last desperate counter-attack with their armour, but it suffered heavy casualties and that was the end. There were no more tanks and the infantry had been fought to a standstill. At about 9 o'clock in the morning white flags were shown.

O'Connor went to a farmhouse at Soluch where half a dozen Italian generals were held prisoner. There he found senior Italian officers smartly dressed in clean uniforms and polished boots while he appeared in his usual corduroy trousers, leather sleeveless jerkin, tartan scarf and sagging cap.

'I'm sorry you are so uncomfortable', said O'Connor. 'We haven't had much time to make proper arrangements'.

'Thank you very much', said Generale Cona. 'We realize you came here in a very great hurry'.

For years afterwards passers-by saw the wreckage of that day: miles of tanks, guns, lorries, fuel drums and debris in such abundance that even the local Arabs found it too much to carry away.

O'Connor wasted no time. Within hours of the Beda Fomm victory armoured cars of the 11th Hussars were speeding along the road to El Agheila. Apart from a few men surrendering, there was no sign of the enemy. It was February 1941 and Wavell's 'five-day raid' had lasted 62 days. The 4th Indian Division, the heart of the army, had been snatched away to fight in East Africa and the Australians had replaced them. The advance had continued for 500 miles and destroyed Graziani's army. Ten Italian divisions were shattered, 133,295 of their men made prisoner, about 400 tanks and 1,240 guns captured. The British force was exhausted too. Virtually all the transport of the Western Desert Force was either written off or would be when the workshop staff saw it.[16] But its human casualties were few: 500 killed, 1,373 wounded and 55 missing.

Whatever the condition of the Western Desert Force, there was nothing to oppose them. The generals were agreed, the men could smell victory and, while the distances were great, only the soft rear areas remained to be conquered. Supplies and replacements were on their way, the port of Tobruk was in operation and the port of Benghazi, although too shallow for big ships, would soon be an even nearer place for supplying the advance. The navy was fully operational and the RAF would destroy any last remnants of the Italian air force. Everything was ready for the final push that would sweep the Italians out of North Africa.

O'Connor's remarkable campaign was one for the military textbooks, and is to be found there, but it didn't sweep the Italians out of North Africa, for at that crucial moment everything was stopped. Churchill, in what is now almost universally recognized as one of the worst military decisions of the war, halted O'Connor's victorious army and ordered

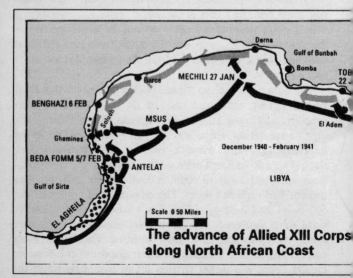

The advance of Allied XIII Corps along North African Coast

Wavell to detach an armoured brigade and three infantry divisions for shipment to Greece, which the Germans were expected to invade at any moment.

HITLER'S GREAT TRAIN JOURNEY: OCTOBER 1940

To follow the chain of events that led to the crisis in Greece, we must go back to October 1940, when Marshal Rodolfo Graziani was still building his forts in the desert, and laying a road and pipeline to supply them. There was no hint of O'Connor's offensive and Hitler had every reason to hope that Graziani's promised attack upon the British would carry him through to Cairo. With the Italians occupying Egypt, the Italian fleet would be able to move up to Alexandria, gain control of the Suez Canal and open the way to the oilfields of the Persian Gulf.

MEDITERRANEAN SEA

BARDIA
Sollum Sidi Barrani
ALEXANDRIA
EL ALAMEIN
EGYPT
KEY   ROUTES TAKEN BY BRITISH FORMATIONS
7TH ARMOURED DIVISION
6TH AUSTRALIAN DIVISION
COAST ROAD
RETREATING ITALIAN TENTH ARMY
FRONTIER

With such hopes in mind, the German army had sent a notable armoured warfare expert, General Ritter von Thoma, and a small staff, to assess the Italian army in Libya. Von Thoma was due to report his findings to Hitler on 3 November, but Hitler was already confident 'that the Italians were capable of holding their own in Africa'. Although they might need a little German help.[17]

While Mussolini's armies threatened Egypt, Hitler was looking at ways of seizing Gibraltar and sealing up the other end of the Mediterranean. In his luxury train Amerika, he went to Hendaye, a French town close to the Spanish border, to meet General Franco, Spain's head of state. Hitler asked Franco to join the war, or at least allow German troops to move across Spain to capture Gibraltar.

Franco made no response to Hitler's bountiful inducements of arms and raw materials, some French colonies and Gibraltar too. Even oil was offered, for in French storage depots the invading Germans had found countless tons of it, enough to fuel their Battle of Britain and their first campaign against Moscow. Franco and his advisers had their answers ready. Spain had been torn to pieces by the civil war and Franco was not persuaded that a foreign war would now weld it together. Moreover, his bitter struggle against his own countrymen had been an anti-Communist crusade: how could anyone trust this man who was now the ally of Joseph Stalin? So cold was Franco and his party that eventually Hitler got to his feet and said that there was little point in continuing their talk. Franco made no response. But Hitler was not a man who gave up easily; he talked on and eventually the two dictators retired to the dining car for a meal. Hitler was not used to such indifference and after Franco's train departed to the tune of the Spanish National Anthem at 2.15 am, he ranted about Franco and the 'Jesuit swine' of a Spanish foreign minister who had interrupted him in a way that no German would have dared to do. Hitler had grown used to having his own way. Later he told Mussolini: 'I would rather have three or four teeth extracted than go through that again'.

In June 1940, after France collapsed, many people had expected that Italian troops would march into the French African colonies. Such a vast extension of Italian power would have made Mussolini the powerful statesman that he always wanted to be. The reason why this did not happen is to be discovered in the text of a secret document which Hitler signed while his train was at Montoire, 25 miles north of Tours, the next day.

Here the Führer met Marshal Pétain, the man who now ruled Vichy France. Pétain, a stately old man with large white moustache, arrived wearing the uniform of a general to remind everyone that he was a hero of the First World War. Hitler, who understood such vanities, provided a guard of honour for the old man to inspect. Pétain, equally cunning, ignored the honour guard, knowing full well what the German propaganda service would make of the photographs, and went straight to business—the signing of a secret undertaking with the conqueror.

> The Axis Powers and France have an identical interest in seeing the defeat of England accomplished as soon as possible. Consequently the French government will support, within the limits of its ability, the measures which the Axis powers may take to this end.

It sounded good to Hitler, and Pétain's quiet dignified manner impressed him enough to persuade him that it was best to leave the colonies in French hands and allow Pétain to bring them more and more in line with German needs. Hitler had been 'greatly cheered' by the way a few French colonists at Dakar had repulsed the Anglo-French force and the Royal Navy. French colonists handed over to foreigners such as Franco or Mussolini might not be so anti-British. In a directive arising from this meeting, Hitler mentioned 'the urgent duty' of French West and Equatorial Africa to act against Britain and resist the Free French.

Back aboard his private train, Hitler was all ready to return to Berlin to meet Russia's foreign minister when a long coded teleprinter message arrived from Mussolini, warning him that Pétain was secretly conniving with the Free French in London and that the British were about to invade Greece. The latter danger would be forestalled, Mussolini suggested archly, with pre-emptive action by the Italian forces in Albania striking against the Greeks. Both warnings were groundless and self-serving.

Hitler was alarmed enough to change his plans. He requested a meeting with Mussolini, who suggested the following Monday 28 October at Florence. When his train passed through Bologna, Hitler received the news that the Italians based in Albania had invaded Greece that morning. It was of course a demonstration that Mussolini could spring upon his partner the sort of *fait accompli* that he had suffered in the past. Hitler was not pleased, but his objections were not fundamental. He would have preferred the Duce to have waited until after the American presidential elections, which were only one week away. He would have liked to show him the best routes for the invading forces and to have coordinated the move with a German invasion of Crete. Hitler accepted the new situation but it was not easy to look happy when, in Florence, Mussolini came striding up to him calling: *'Führer, wir marschieren!'* and waited to be congratulated.

Hitler liked surprises only when he was springing them. He was furious that not one of the German attachés, or liaison officers attached to Italian units, had warned him of this development. In fact the Italians were not that skilled at keeping secrets: it was German incompetence. Many warnings had been sent about the Italian preparations for the invasion of Greece but none of them had reached Hitler.

While Hitler pondered, the British moved. Only five days after the Italians crossed the frontier the British occupied Crete and the island of Lemnos farther north. On the mainland the Greek army fought fiercely and the Italians retreated. Some rejoiced at the Greek victories but others saw that Italian reverses would draw the Germans into the fighting in Greece. That in turn might bring the British there.

On 15 November, long before the Italian failure was evident, General Thomas Blamey, commander of the Australian forces in the Middle East, wrote an informal letter to his prime minister.[18] The Australians had become a major part of the British resources in North Africa and Blamey said that they must spend all their time and energy in preparation 'if international developments, for example in the Balkan countries, do not force us into the extremely dangerous position of participating piecemeal in land warfare'.

MONTOIRE

Hitler's
train journey

HENDAYE

BOLOGN

FLORE

SPAIN

OCTOBER 23, 1940
Hitler meets Franco, asking
him to help seize Gibraltar.
This plus an Italian victory in
Egypt would seal off the
Mediterranean and perhaps
bring the British to the peace
table.

GIBRALTAR

MEDITERRANEAN SEA

SICILY
(ITALIAN)

SPANISH

ORAN
MERS EL KEBIR
July 1940 Royal Navy
Bombard French Warships

MALTA
(BRITIS

TUNISIA

ALGERIA
(VICHY
FRENCH)

MOROCCO

(Vichy
FRENCH)

Tripoli

TRIPOLITANIA

14 FEB 1941
The first German tr
arrive in Tripoli

The Mediterranean Theatre 1939 – 40

USSR

APRIL 6, 1941
Germans attack Yugoslavia

HUNGARY

ROMANIA

YUGOSLAVIA

7

4
NOVEMBER
Hitler forces Rumania and Bulgaria into the Axis.

BLACK SEA

APRIL 8-21, 1941
Greece attacked

ALBANIA

BULGARIA

GREECE

LEMNOS

TURKEY
(NEUTRAL)

2
OCTOBER 28
Without consulting Hitler, Italy invades Greece from her captured territory of Albania.

3
NOVEMBER 3
British occupy Lemnos and Crete, and thus could bomb Rumanian oil fields.

CRETE

CYPRUS
(BR)

SYRIA
(VICHY FRENCH)

8
MAY 27, 1941
Crete captured by Germans in first airborne invasion of history.

MEDITERRANEAN SEA

PALESTINE
(BRITISH)

Tobruk

Benghazi

CYRENAICA

5
Dec 9 Sidi Barrani
British inflict crushing defeat on Italians

EL ALAMEIN

Alexandria

Cairo

SUEZ
CANAL

EL ARGHEILA

LIBYA
(ITALIAN)

GREAT
SAND SEA

GREAT SAND
SEA LIMITS
MOVE CONSTANTLY

THE GREAT SAND SEA

QATTARA
DEPRESSION

EGYPT
(BRITISH)

14 DOUBLE DEFEAT: GREECE AND CYRENAICA

In trouble to be troubled
Is to have your trouble doubled.

DANIEL DEFOE,

THE FURTHER ADVENTURES OF ROBINSON CRUSOE

Britain's obligation to Greece was based upon a promise made by the Chamberlain government in April 1939 and was made to discourage Hitler's aggressions. Those circumstances were quite unlike the desperate early days of 1941 with the British fighting for their lives. Now that Greece was at war Churchill told himself, and anyone who would listen, that sending a British expeditionary force to Greece might bring Turkey and Yugoslavia into the war against the Axis and thus create a major new southern front. A better intelligence service might have persuaded Churchill that Turkey had neither the will nor the resources to enter the war on either side, that Germany had 150 divisions and a massive air force all ready to fight, and that his strategic notion was just wishful thinking.

But the British intelligence service was not capable of providing very much useful information apart from the material coming from Bletchley Park, where in early February 1941 they cracked the Reichsbahn (German railways) Enigma. In those days most movement of goods and passengers was made by railways, so BP began to get reliable evidence of German movements, such as those of box-car transports that took Jews to the extermination camps and the flatbed wagons that took Panzer divisions to their assembly areas. A sudden increase in signals indicated the movement of Luftwaffe equipment, supplies and, more significantly, ammunition, to southern Bulgaria where the Germans were busy building airfields. This suggested imminent German invasion of Greece from the eastern side, well away from where the Greeks were fighting the Italians.

Churchill's correct interpretation of those Enigma signals led to the Defence Committee's decision, on 11 February, to order General Wavell to intervene in Greece, and to give this expedition priority over his advance on Tripoli and clearing the Italians out of North Africa. It was one of the most fateful decisions of the war.

Wavell should have refused. He had a sufficiently independent command, and enough authority, to say no to Churchill. The failure of the Allies in France, and the whipping suffered in Norway, showed that control of the air was vital to such operations, and there was no hope of obtaining that with the inadequate RAF squadrons at Wavell's disposal. Wavell didn't say no. He stripped his armies bare to find four divisions to send to Greece. No one seems to have asked where replacements and reinforcements would be found.

After the Germans had conquered Greece, with seemingly effortless skill, many diaries and memories were conveniently changed. The history books leave an impression of Churchill pushing everyone screaming and objecting into a Greek war they did not want.[1] But look at the opinions filed away before the débâcle, and a different picture emerges. Words of caution abound, but it is difficult to find many senior figures steadfastly opposed to the British intervention in Greece. A friend of Wavell's, who was in his headquarters at this time, wrote:

There were plenty of wiseacres afterwards to say that the intervention in Greece was madness; but in point of fact there was only one responsible staff officer at GHQ who opposed it from the start and consistently, and who can legitimately say: 'I told you so' . . . Both Wavell and Wilson maintained afterwards, and in cold print, that in the light of their then knowledge they would do it again.[2]

This staff officer who was strongly opposed to sending a British army to Greece was Francis de Guingand, on Wavell's Middle East planning staff. In his memoirs he wrote about the Greek campaign:

> As far as I can remember the Planners were not asked to produce a paper giving their views as to the feasibility of the project. We certainly held some very decided ones. The DMI, Brigadier Shearer, did produce a paper drawing attention to the great dangers of this campaign in view of the German resources and methods. I remember this paper coming back from the C-in-C, General Wavell. There was a short note written in his own hand across the top—it said: ' "War is an option of difficulties."—Wolfe. A.P.W'. We admired the spirit but questioned—in so far as junior officers are allowed to question—the judgement![3]

Apart from Wavell, there was probably only one man in the Middle East who had enough authority to veto the plan to send men and material to Greece, and that was General Thomas Blamey, commander of the Australians. Blamey was a big jovial 57-year-old who liked to wear a broad-brimmed bush hat and seemed to enjoy his reputation as a ladies' man. He was under orders from his government to prevent any part of his Australian forces being 'detached or employed apart' to serve under British commanders. His government was determined not to allow Australians to be sacrificed in the way they had been in the First World War.

Blamey had already had some confrontations with Wavell. The previous September, when Blamey refused 'Jumbo' Wilson's order to detach an Australian brigade from his force, renewed commands had come from Wavell and then from Churchill, who 'insisted' that the order be obeyed. Blamey stood firm and it was Churchill who backed down. Now on 18 February, having come directly back from his forward headquarters, he listened to Wavell's plans for sending to Greece an expedition consisting largely of Australians and New Zealanders. Blamey's views about the wisdom of such an operation were not sought.

Blamey replied that he would have to refer to his government before the Australians could be committed. Wavell said he had already spoken with Robert Menzies, the Australian prime minister, and in any case the proposal had come from a meeting of the British war cabinet which Menzies had attended. Blamey gave his agreement, feeling that the decision had been made for him, but on 9 March, after another meeting with Wavell, he wired a detailed and despondent report to his government. He told them that he did not relish the prospect of his men facing overwhelming enemy forces completely equipped and trained, and said that the Greek operation was extremely hazardous in view of the disparity between opposing forces in numbers and training.[4]

Menzies and the Australian government read the report and were alarmed. They said they thought that Blamey had been asked about the expedition and approved of it. Without the Dominion troops it would be impossible to mount the operation, but all agreed that it was too late to withdraw now.

Blamey did not want to see his men under British command. 'Past experience has taught me to look with misgiving on a situation where British leaders have control of considerable bodies of first-class Dominion troops', he said, 'while Dominion commanders are excluded from all responsibility in control, planning and policy'.[5]

Australia and New Zealand would furnish all the fighting troops sent to Greece, apart from an armoured brigade and artillery, but they would not be commanded by Blamey or the New Zealander Sir Bernard Freyberg. Instead command was to be given to a British general, Sir Maitland 'Jumbo' Wilson, who commanded in Egypt and was in effect Wavell's right-hand man. Wilson was not universally popular. He was well remembered for having an acrimonious public shouting match with one of the British army's few armoured warfare experts—Major-General Percy Hobart—and having him sent home in disgrace.

Blamey protested that with so many Dominion troops in the expedition, command of it should be offered to him. Wavell did not deny that he envisaged an Australian and New Zealand component of 42,000 but said that additional supply and 'line of communication' personnel would bring the total force to 126,000 so that Dominion soldiers would be only a third. Blamey backed down on his claim but soon began to suspect that Wavell had deceived him by using a figure for the British troops that was no more than a forecast. 'Some is on its way and some of it is not even in existence', he wrote. Blamey's suspicions seem well founded: 17,125 Australians and 16,720 New Zealanders were actually sent to Greece, which comprised more than half of the grand total.[6]

If Wavell was being dragged into the fighting in Greece, he was certainly good at hiding his feelings. One of his junior staff officers, de Guingand, was with him in Athens when the British delegation made a definite offer to send a force to help. He wrote:

When the time came for an expression of opinion on the military prospects, and the chances of success of British intervention, Eden [Britain's foreign secretary] turned to General Wavell and asked him to say his piece. It was a tense moment and you could have heard a pin drop as Wavell climbed to his feet and prepared himself for his reply. I remember almost praying that he would voice some doubt as to the outcome, and when he had completed his exposé I felt a hot wave of anger surge over me, for I failed to understand how it was possible for an experienced soldier to say the things he did say. In a low and subdued voice Wavell told the negotiators that it was his considered view that the assistance being offered held out every chance of permitting the Allies to withstand a German advance into Greece.[7]

It was said by Wavell's supporters that he thought the Greek army much stronger than it really was, and that he thought the mountain landscape of Greece would make it easy to defend. But the final decision made that day, like all strategic decisions, was a political one. It was the foreign secretary, Anthony Eden, who led the delegation to Athens, and led the enthusiasm for getting into the fight in Greece. On the plane to Athens he prepared a long detailed list of guns and tanks and men that he would promise to the Greek government. The Greeks would decline help if they considered the expedition inadequate, and one of Eden's Foreign Office men had the figures 'swelled' upwards. 'I felt that this was . . . bordering upon dishonesty', de Guingand confided in his memoirs. He went on to describe Eden when the conference ended, and the decision to send troops to Greece was made:

> Eden came in looking buoyant. He strode over to the fire and warmed his hands, and then stood with his back to it dictating signals to his staff. They in turn looked nearly as triumphant as he did, and were positively oozing congratulations. Presumably he had done his job, and accomplished what he had set out to achieve.[8]

That the launching of an impromptu invasion of Europe from the south was even considered is astounding. Leaving aside the lack of air support, which played such a part in the British defeat that the shocked survivors talked of nothing else; discounting, too, the lines of support, supply and communication that stretched right across the Mediterranean; forget that the British Middle East forces were being supplied from the United Kingdom by convoys that had to travel right round Africa to the Suez Canal or through the shooting gallery of the Mediterranean—consider how any British army, let alone four divisions of its 1941 forces, could have been expected to withstand the immense force that Germany held poised to attack Russia.

Wavell acquiesced. Starting on 5 March 1941, convoys from Alexandria to Piraeus in Greece carried an army of 60,000 men, with inadequate weapons and virtually no air cover, to fight a battle already lost. Three weeks earlier O'Connor had been told that continuing his advance in Libya was out of the question. On 12 February the ambitious General Erwin Rommel spent his first night on African soil, having already flown over the front line before going to bed. He was determined to push the British back to Cairo and make his mark on history.

Without the Greek campaign Wavell could have held on to his desert gains, perhaps captured Tripoli and also have held the vitally important island of Crete. The verdict of Correlli Barnett is appropriately severe:

> Thus the Greek episode lengthened the campaign in North Africa by two years—a campaign that sucked in the major ground efforts of the British Commonwealth, and left the Far East almost undefended against the Japanese.[9]

AIR AND SEA

The war was demonstrating the almost insurmountable burdens brought by long supply lines and the vital importance of air superiority on the battlefield. Air superiority had little to do with long-range bombing operations under cover of darkness. It meant commanding the air over the enemy's head, and behind his fighting front, so that he was subjected to relentless bombardment and his supplies and communications seriously impeded. Soon the meaning of the old Roman word 'interdiction' was extended to describe this new dimension of war.

To be successful, interdiction must be relentless and so it needed airstrips—with all the maintenance facilities—near the fighting, permitting relays of aircraft to operate. Such air cover could not be provided at long range, or across a sea.

The regularity of Axis sea traffic between Italian seaports and Tripoli, the only good deep-water port available to them, was a triumph and a tribute to the Axis merchant crews and their naval escort forces. In theory the Royal Navy should have been able to cut off the supplies by sinking the merchant ships, but dark nights and the short sea route enabled the Axis convoys to evade interception. In the second half of 1940 these convoys had moved 690,000 tons of shipping to North Africa with less than 2 per cent losses.

As British shipping to Crete and Greece increased, there was a chance for the Italian fleet to turn the tables by attacking the British troop and supply convoys. The Italian navy was less than ready to oblige. The 1,800,000 tons of fuel oil available at the start of the war had been used at the rate of about 100,000 tons per month, and by March 1941 ship's fuel was carefully rationed.[10] The German promises of oil had never materialized beyond a meagre average 21,166 tons a month. No wonder the Italian chief of staff was moved to say: 'I have two major preoccupations—oil and Malta'.

Any British convoys would undoubtedly be escorted by as many warships as the Royal Navy could spare, and if the Italians intercepted them a naval action would result. The Italian navy had no aircraft-carriers and it was by now becoming clear that ships without air cover were sitting targets. In addition, Mussolini believed that warships, especially big ones, must not be put at risk.

But despite all the objections, the Italian navy was persuaded that it should send out its fleet to attack the British convoys. To help them to this decision the Germans said that the Luftwaffe would provide air support and added that German bombers had, in mid-March, already weakened the Royal Navy by sinking two of its battleships.

Enigma intercepts were at the heart of British counterplans. Regularly monitored Luftwaffe signals provided information about fighter cover for this operation, and included details of Italian submarine movements. Italy's main naval book ciphers (used by the fleet for important communications) were never broken by the Bletchley Park analysts but on this occasion the Italian navy's Enigma codes, used for only one or two messages a day, provided a vital clue to

Italian plans. The mighty *Vittorio Veneto* from Naples, three cruisers from Messina, three cruisers—*Fiume, Pola* and *Zara*—from Taranto and two cruisers from Brindisi, with many destroyers, were to coordinate sweeps along the coast of Crete.

In light of the Enigma messages, all British convoys were directed away from the danger area. This had to be done with discretion in case the Italians realized that their plans were known. Admiral Cunningham went to considerable trouble to conceal his intentions. On the day he sailed, he went to his golf club and arranged overnight accommodation in such a way that the Japanese consul-general (a fellow golfer and well-known Axis collaborator) knew about it. Then Cunningham doubled back to his ship and took his fleet to sea.

Contact with the Italians was made by a light force of four cruisers and four destroyers which tried to lure the Italian ships into range of the main British battlefleet, which included the aircraft-carrier *Formidable*. The Italians didn't take the bait, so the Royal Navy staged air attacks instead. Flying through intense gunfire the naval airmen dropped torpedoes that damaged *Vittorio Veneto* and forced the cruiser *Pola* to stop. *Fiume* and *Zara* were ordered back to protect *Pola* against what the Italian admiral thought to be only light cruisers.

The night was dark and the sky overcast. HMS *Ajax*, the only radar-equipped ship in the light force, found *Pola* on the radar. Cunningham thought this stationary ship must be the *Vittorio Veneto* and closed in with his battleships. Towards midnight HMS *Valiant* made radar contact and began firing. Searchlights probed into the darkness to reveal the Italians, completely unaware of the impending danger, and trying to get the crippled *Pola* in tow. Despite a gallant defending action by Italian destroyers, all three Italian cruisers were sunk. At what came to be called the battle of Cape Matapan the Italians had been beaten by intelligence, air power and radar. In all these aspects of war the British were improving faster than their enemies.

But meanwhile the Royal Navy's campaign in the Mediterranean was proving wearying and costly. As the Germans moved southwards on land, their air force was more and more active over the water. Proof of the Luftwaffe's southwards deployment came on 10 January 1941 when dive-bombers of X Fliegerkorps scored six hits on the carrier *Illustrious* at sea and followed it back to Malta to bomb it again and again until it limped away to Alexandria, and eventually to the United States for major repairs.

The expedition to support Greece would add new dangers and difficulties. The plan called upon the navy to escort convoys, safeguard landings and evacuations, and supply, defend or bombard positions on the coastline, as well as being always prepared for an engagement with the Italian fleet. It was an almost impossible undertaking.

THE BALKAN CAMPAIGNS

Having crossed the Adriatic Sea and occupied Albania, Mussolini looked greedily at its neighbour Greece. The Greek dictator General Ioannis Metaxas was a Fascist and pro-Axis in sentiment. Mussolini thought the Greek population, if not Metaxas himself, would welcome Italian occupation. At dawn on 28 October 1940, from bases in Albania, two unsuitably equipped Italian armies crossed the frontier. The Greeks speedily mobilized and within two weeks the invaders were outnumbered and fighting for their lives. Mussolini's choice of season condemned his men to torrential rain and mud, soon followed by temperatures that fell to 20 below zero. By 3 November the Greeks had gone over to a general offensive along the length of the frontier, and were soon taking thousands of prisoners and pushing the invaders back into Albania. The humiliating defeats forced Marshal Pietro Badoglio, the Italian army's chief of staff, to resign, as did Admiral Domenico Cavagnari, the commander of the navy. In Menton, an Italian-occupied town on the French

Riviera, a daring joker printed leaflets saying 'Greeks, this is a French town, stop your advance!'

General Metaxas declined all offers of a British expeditionary force going to the aid of his country, believing that such a force would provoke a German invasion and not be strong enough to resist it. He did however permit the British to occupy the Greek island of Crete, and he accepted the offer of RAF squadrons to help him fight the Italians. By mid-November, aircraft together with 3,400 troops and airfield personnel arrived in Greece.

While the Italians struggled in Greece, and were routed by O'Connor's offensive in North Africa, Hitler demanded that the Balkan states of Hungary, Bulgaria and Romania come into closer alliances with Germany. With varying enthusiasm, they did so.

As the fighting continued through February 1941, the Greek government had a change of men and minds, and said it would accept a British expeditionary force to help fight the Italians, providing it was a large force. Eden assured them it would be large enough. With Mussolini in ever deeper trouble, Hitler saw that he would have to send a German force to join in the war against Greece. To move it and supply it, he would need the roads and railways across Yugoslavia.

Yugoslavia was created at the end of the First World War: an artificial combination of at least six very different nations who were consumed with deep hatred of each other. They were divided by race, religion, culture, history and aspiration. They did not even share the same alphabet. 'Such indeed were the divisions in Yugoslavian society that after 1929 the country had been ruled by a royal dictatorship as the only practical alternative to civil war', wrote one historian in 1989 shortly before the Communist dictatorship collapsed and a vicious civil war ripped Bosnia, Serbia and Croatia apart.[11]

In 1941 Yugoslavia resisted Hitler's demands. Prince Paul, the regent, had been educated at Oxford and was sympathetic to the British. Married to a Greek, he had no desire to help Hitler conquer Greece. But by March 1941, with

German armies threatening them from Hungary, Romania and Bulgaria, the Yugoslavs signed an agreement with Hitler.

On the night of 26–27 March, however, Serbian officers denounced the agreement and took control of the capital Belgrade. This romantic and impulsive act, encouraged by the British secret service, was doomed from the beginning. Hitler could probably have toppled the new regime by peaceful methods, but he had spent months in patient negotiations and now he was in a hurry. 'I have decided to destroy Yugoslavia', he told Göring, Brauchitsch and Ribbentrop on 26 March. Plans for the campaign had been prepared months before. Yugoslavia, with over 1,000 miles of frontier to defend, was attacked from all sides, with Italian and Hungarian armies coordinating their movements with those of the Germans. The German 12th Army in Bulgaria, with a Bulgarian division attached to it for good measure, invaded northern Greece.

The Yugoslav army was primitive compared to the German armoured columns that advanced down the river valleys, and deep into the heart of the country. The Luftwaffe bombed Belgrade, targeting the city centre, where the government was located, and severing all communications with the field armies. Estimates of the civilian casualties vary from 3,000 to 17,000.[12] (In 1946 the Luftwaffe's Colonel Martin Fiebig was executed as a war criminal for this bombing.)

The German attack revealed the fragmentary nature of the contrived Yugoslavian kingdom. Mostly Serbian, the army put up little resistance. Some of the Croat army units mutinied and went over to the Germans, who in the whole Yugoslavian campaign suffered only 151 dead.

The German victory unleased a frenzy of slaughter. The widespread cruel and arbitrary killing done by the German and Italian occupying forces has to be compared to the way in which the Fascist Croat militia murdered 250,000 people in three months. The Muslims of Bosnia decimated the Christian population while the Serbs, dividing into Monarchist and Communist guerrilla bands, indulged in the same sort of massacres as the Hungarians did in Vojvodina and the Bulgarians did in Macedonia and Thrace.[13] As the war progressed, torrents of blood were shed while various paramilitary partisan groups fought each other more fiercely than they fought the German occupiers.

Hitler's armies now turned all of their force upon Greece. The Luftwaffe did the same, and it was the assault from the air that most of the survivors remembered vividly. Against the Italians the RAF flyers held their own and provided sufficient air cover, but when the Germans came they were totally overwhelmed.

The RAF had 192 aircraft, of which only about 80 were serviceable on any one day, to combat combined German and Italian air strength of about 1,000 machines.[14] Obsolete Gladiators, obsolescent Hurricanes and inadequate Blenheims gallantly took off to face a well equipped and expert enemy which brushed them aside. An official account describes six Bristol Blenheims which 'took off from their mountain valley, circled above the olives and the grey cliff where they used to watch the bears, flew into the north-east and none returned. For the slow bombers were no match for Messerschmitts in daylight'.[15]

Few RAF airfields had any anti-aircraft guns and there was not one all-weather airfield anywhere in Greece, while the enemy's newly built airfields in Albania and Bulgaria were heavily defended and had the logistic support of home bases that were only a short flight away. The legacy of the Air Ministry's prewar obsession with strategic bombing was once again bringing about disaster. An official historian remarked with uncharacteristic bitterness:

In 1938 the Chamberlain government had authorized the Air Ministry to order virtually all the aircraft the British aircraft industry could produce. Large sums had been spent on the development of a bomber force which was almost useless for its intended purpose of attacking industrial targets in Germany. Yet in 1940 the British were painfully short of high-performance aircraft with which to support their naval and land forces in the Mediterranean and the Middle East.[16]

Once again it became clear that weapons played a large part in deciding battles. The obsolete tanks the British had taken to Greece were no match for the Germans or even for the rough terrain. One British tank regiment lost only one tank to enemy action; its other 51 tanks broke down and had to be abandoned.[17] And without air cover an army in the field faced inevitable defeat. On 17 April, the day that Yugoslavia capitulated, Churchill agreed that the British should begin to evacuate their forces from the Greek mainland. Defeated in the field, the British had to stage another 'Dunkirk' and abandon all their precious heavy equipment. Tanks, artillery and unserviceable aircraft were all lost to an army which needed every single item. But this was no retreat across 21 miles of English Channel to a homeland with radar and fighter squadrons. It was a long hard haul to safety, and many failed to make it.

One of the few consolations of the disaster had been the spirit shown by the Greeks. It survived even as the British army was pulling out. A colonel of the 1st Armoured Brigade said:

No one who passed through the city with Barrowclough's brigade will ever forget it. Nor will we ever think of the Greek people without the warm recollection of that morning—25 April 1941. Trucks, portées [wheeled guns in trucks] and men showed plainly the marks of twelve hours battle, and the hundred and sixty miles march through the night. We were nearly the last British troops they would see and the Germans might be on our heels; yet cheering, clapping crowds lined the streets and pressed about our cars, so as almost to hold us up. Girls and men leapt on the running boards to kiss or shake hands with the grimy, weary gunners. They threw flowers

beside us crying: 'Come back—You must come back
again—Goodbye—Good luck'.[18]

As Greece vanished over the skyline it was the British
who were shown to have a good appetite but poor teeth. By
May the Luftwaffe was ready to show how it should be done.
They would swallow the strategically vital island the British
had used as a staging post for the movements to Greece.

CRETE: 'IF YU LEI YU UILL BI SCHOTT'

This is the first sentence printed in a phonetic English
phrase book given to German paratroops sent to invade
Crete. This machine language seems apt for warriors who
would drop from the air under a silken canopy and shoot
anyone they thought was lying.

Like so many flawed ideas of the 1930s, it came from
Soviet Russia. In 1936 a small British delegation in Moscow
was invited to watch the Russian army manoeuvres. The
large-scale drop of parachute troops included a military
band which picked itself up 'and began to play like men
possessed'. One of the delegation was Archie Wavell who, in
1941 on the Mediterranean island of Crete, was to suffer
history's only defeat by an unsupported parachute army.

It was awesome to see on artistically shot newsreel films
the Red Army's parachute troops descending from the
clouds. Schoolboys said they would be shot coming down.
Perhaps it was all a propaganda bluff. In the war the Red
Army did not use parachute soldiers except in very small
numbers for clandestine operations. But the Germans were
impressed. The German air force was not like those of other
nations. Göring's vast and bureaucratic Luftwaffe also
manned most of the anti-aircraft defences and performed
many other functions. He made sure that a parachute army

was a part of his Luftwaffe, and in this way he expanded his empire.

In 1940 the Germans had used parachute troops to support their invasions of northern Europe. So when, on 26 April 1941, German Reichsbahn Enigma revealed that Germany's only paratroop unit, Fliegerdivision 7, was moving to the Balkans this attracted immediate attention. British intelligence staffs had been trying to guess the next German move. Now a Luftwaffe decrypt of the same date mentioned Crete by name. So Crete was the place; but how much time was left?

Hitler himself chose Crete in preference to Malta. There were not enough resources to hit both. Most high-ranking German officers said Malta was the most desirable target, but General Kurt Student, who would be commanding the airborne attack force, said that Crete was more vulnerable. Student, a First World War fighter pilot, had become a tireless worker on behalf of his airborne army. During the fighting in Rotterdam a Dutch surgeon had prised a sniper's bullet from his brain, but now fully recovered and raring to go, Student explained that Crete, a long island with only one road, would be less well defended than Malta, which had been a British base for many years. German troops were already in nearby Greece. Hitler backed Student. He wanted to avoid coordinating his arrangements with Mussolini, and using bases near Malta would have forced him to do that.

Crete is a mountainous island about 160 miles long and 36 wide. Although it now had three airfields, its ports were fit only for fishing boats, its roads very poor and too narrow for trucks. Much of the island was inaccessible to motor vehicles. Its position on the map, however, made it a desirable base for operations by either side. Waiting for the Germans there were 42,640 men, of whom 10,258 were Greeks.

Karl Student's force consisted of an Air Division (three parachute regiments and a glider regiment) reinforced by parachute engineers, parachute medics and parachute antiaircraft personnel. Elements of a mountain division were added to make about 25,000 men in all.[19] At his disposal there were 493 three-engine Junkers Ju 52 aircraft, each capable of carrying 14 paratroops or 15 infantrymen, although the weight of machine-guns and mortars meant that some planes carried only one six-man weapons team. Student also had 85 DFS 230 gliders which could hold eight infantrymen or freight. His task was twofold: he had to capture the island and air-supply his fighting men. General Freiherr Wolfram von Richthofen's bombers and fighters were to provide air support, which meant suppressing all action by the RAF and the Royal Navy.

Bletchley Park, always prompt with Luftwaffe Enigma signals, provided a complete German order of battle (strength, position and movement of all the units involved) and the decrypts went directly to Crete. Enigma was unusually precise. It listed exact stages of the German plan, unit by unit and sector by sector. It even gave details of the equipment that would be supplied by sea.

At about 7.30 in the morning on 20 May 1941, in the silence that followed a ferocious air attack, the defenders of Crete heard a faint buzzing in the morning air, like the sounds made by the swarms of flying insects that sometimes infest the island at that time of year. As the sound increased in volume it became possible to see the troop-carrying aircraft quite low against the horizon and heading towards Máleme airport. The island of Crete was being invaded by airborne troops. In the small hours of the morning Student had been warned of the possibility of concentrated anti-aircraft fire from Royal Navy warships placed offshore for that purpose.[20] It had not come; neither did any fighter planes take off to attack the vulnerable troop-carriers. After losing 29 of the 35 fighters it had based on the island, the RAF had withdrawn the six surviving ones the previous day.[21]

The air-raid warning was sounded for the last time: from now on the raids would be unceasing. The gliders arrived first; silent except for the faint hiss of their wings. Then came thousands of parachutes: green, yellow, red and white. The voices of the Germans calling to each other in mid-air could be heard as they sailed down. 'Beautiful little kicking dolls', said one who saw them coming. 'Slipstream and wind carried them indeed like dolls', said the military historian John Keegan, who added that their American and British contemporaries would have viewed the German equipment 'with horrified incredulity'. They were suspended under their chutes by a single strap to the middle of their back, so that they dangled and twisted. Jump injuries were numerous.[22]

The glider troops were landed close enough to seize specified vital positions—bridges, anti-aircraft batteries and so on. The parachute soldiers were then dropped well away from the defences so that they could form up and go to the support of their comrades. As soon as the invaders gained a foothold on an airfield, transport planes filled with infantry landed on it. Most of them came under fire.

Paratroops were dropped from 400 feet, connected to their planes by 20-feet-long static lines which ripped the covers from their parachutes so that they opened in the air stream. Each paratrooper stretched his arms wide to prevent any chance of his swinging through the lines of a neighbour's parachute. As they floated down, at 16 feet per second, each soldier was about 16 feet below, and 150 feet behind, his successor. Thus 36 men from a three-plane formation arrived in a patch about 120 yards by 500 yards. Each glider was towed to the target zone by a three-engined Ju 52 which would have been specifically loaded for its task with, for instance, a five-man mortar team, two riflemen, ten boxes of bombs and a handcart. A glider might contain combat engineers with special demolition equipment, or only infantry with a good supply of ammunition. The first wave of the German assault had no transport except what it could capture.

The defenders were Greeks, Australians, New Zealanders and British, most of whom had been evacuated from the Greek mainland without their trucks, artillery and anti-aircraft guns. Commanding them was Sir Bernard Freyberg, who was surely one of the most remarkable men to command an army.

Trained as a dentist in New Zealand, he was also a champion swimmer. In 1914 he went to fight under Pancho Villa in the Mexican Revolutionary War. When the First World War began, he deserted Villa and went to London. He became a lieutenant in the Hood Battalion of the Royal Naval Division and served alongside some notable poets, including Rupert Brooke. He fought at Gallipoli, winning the DSO, and then in France. He ended the war with the VC and a bar to his DSO. He had been wounded nine times. By 1919, at the age of thirty, he became one of the youngest generals in the British army.

By the time of Crete Freyberg had been appointed commander of the New Zealand Expeditionary Force. In his biography of his father, Freyberg's son emphasized that Freyberg's prime responsibility was to the government of New Zealand and not to Wavell (GHQ Middle East), whose handling of Dominion troops was open to criticism.

Freyberg was a fighter, a good choice to command the defence of Crete—he was wounded ten more times!—and his men fought very hard indeed. On the first day the German attack seemed like a failure. Scattered and disorganized, many parachute troops were killed before they could get to the canisters which contained their mortars and machine-guns. Rank offered no immunity. In the first hours of fighting, the Air Division's commanding general was killed when a tow cable broke and his glider crashed into the sea. Another German general was gravely wounded by machine-gun fire soon after landing. The 3rd Parachute Regiment, assigned to capture Rétimo airfield, found itself surrounded by almost a brigade of Australians and was shot to pieces. Most Germans found themselves forced to fight in small groups without their own officers and NCOs. A great number were killed before they touched the ground. One eyewitness recalled how:

> The platoon returned to find the battalion area littered with crumpled parachutes, their gay colours lending an air of macabre festivity to the scene of carnage. On all

sides lay the bodies of the dead Germans, most of them still in their harness, the sheets and cords entangling them in death like a strange earth-bound sea-weed.[23]

The same observer—I. McD. G. Stewart, a medical officer of the 1st Welch Regiment—saw how vulnerable the paratroops were to immediate counter-attack. They were equipped only with grenades and a hand-gun, a 9-mm Luger pistol, with two extra 8-round magazines. All their other weapons—machine-pistols, rifles, machine-guns and mortars—were dropped in canisters. Their stubby machine-pistols were originally designed for trench warfare. At close range they were an excellent weapon but at longer distances they were inaccurate and ineffective.

Trained infantry, using old-fashioned rifles, could pick off newly landed troops easily. But overall the defence showed a distinct lack of urgency. Counter-measures were discussed at length. Orders were slow to arrive from battalion, and from company level too. Junior officers were all too often prepared to wait for them. Yet what could be done was demonstrated by 60 soldiers from the Field Punishment Centre near Modhion who, released from imprisonment and told to go after Germans, killed 110 within an hour.

The British, Australians and New Zealanders, proud of their individualism, found it very difficult to believe that the Germans might outdo them in initiative and improvisation. But everywhere there was evidence that the Germans excelled at both. One New Zealand battalion commander soon encountered the hidebound attitude of his commanders. He asked that a mixed collection of RAF and Fleet Air Arm personnel—339 officers and men—should be officially placed under his command. Some attempt had been made by the New Zealanders to instruct these men in musketry, but they had not wanted to learn: 'They played cards and hoped for the best'. The colonel's urgent request that these men be put under his command was refused by high command. Stewart commented sardonically that 'nothing could be held to justify so revolutionary a liaison of arms'.

On the afternoon of the first day, the same New Zealand colonel, a First World War veteran and winner of the Victoria Cross, came face to face with German resource and determination. His position overlooked Máleme airfield. Two detachments of a German assault regiment, led by a first lieutenant and the regimental surgeon, took Hill 107 using only pistols and hand-grenades. The German medico, who had a reputation for warlike deeds, was awarded the Knight's Cross for this action, although some say he did nothing but occupy ground already vacated.[24] In any case Germans were now holding a position that commanded the airfield.

With their radio out of action, the New Zealanders withdrew to their reserve position, a piece of high ground where the colonel believed he would be reinforced the next day, and so be able to mount an attack that would regain the lost ground. When daylight came the handful of Germans were still on Hill 107. Kurt Student had chosen the airfield at Máleme as his *Schwerpunkt,* main point of attack, and with that determination for which Germans are noted, he now stubbornly continued to land more planes there into what soon became a meatgrinder. It was one of the most reckless battlefield decisions of the entire war. Riddled with shell fragments and bullets of the defenders as they came into their approach run, 40 or so Ju 52s were crash-landed on to the airfield. The Germans scrambled over slumped dead and wounded comrades to get out of the planes and fight. These men were not even trained airborne troops; they were Gebirgsjäger of the 100th Mountain Rifle Regiment. By 5 o'clock that afternoon the town of Máleme and the airport were in German hands. One account says that:

It is not too much to say that this tiny movement [by the New Zealand colonel] lost the Allies the Battle of Crete. By noon on May 21 so many more German paratroops had dropped safely, so many gliders come in, so many Ju-52s had crash-landed on the slowly expanded space, that overwhelming strength had been packed into it. In the

afternoon it burst out, and the Fallschirmjäger could follow Student's orders to 'Roll up Crete from the west'.[25]

Crete was not easily conquered. For a week bitter fighting
continued. Food, supplies and even ammunition were left
behind so that the Junkers could bring more and more combat troops. But by the end of that week the battle was decided. Freyberg was granted permission to start the British
evacuation. The Royal Navy played its part to the end. Not
only did it cover the withdrawal, taking severe losses in the
process, but it prevented the Germans bringing in supplies
and reinforcements by sea. Until the end of June all German
supplies were brought in by air.

Almost fifty years afterwards, two books took up the issue
of the Crete fighting all over again.[26] One said that Freyberg
misread the Enigma intercept he was given, and believed
that the main German attack would be from the sea. With
this in his mind, the writer said, Freyberg saw no reason to
squander men in a bitter fight for the airfields.

The other, by Freyberg's son, said that Freyberg was given
the complete German battle plan nine days before the attack. It was passed on to every senior commander and staff
officer in Crete in an intelligence appreciation dated 12 May
1941. But, added Paul Freyberg, commanders in the field
were never allowed to act on information derived solely
from Enigma. Wavell was not empowered to vary this order
and stopped Freyberg from changing his dispositions at
Máleme.

Perhaps it would have made a difference. But the failure
to hold Máleme airfield, and indeed the loss of Crete, was
largely due to the determination of the elite German paratroops and their willingness to take devastating casualties
and go on fighting:

> In flexibility of mind, and speed of decision and action,
> the German battalion and brigade commanders had out-
> done the officers who had opposed them. The fact is not
> surprising, nor anything to the dishonour of men leaving

their peace-time occupations to make war against opponents whose every thought and ambition for many years
had been devoted to nothing else.[27]

However, there were other factors. Little had been done
since the army arrived to prepare the island against invasion.
Six successive commanders of varying competence and energy had come and gone while Wavell's headquarters had
failed to impose any defence plan. Enigma intelligence was
not used to the full because so few British commanders
knew that it was a flawless glimpse into the enemy's mind.
The defenders failed to appreciate that possession of the
airfields was the sole decisive factor. Had they understood
that, the Germans would probably have been fought to a
point where their losses were too severe for the drops to
continue.

German commanders were less impressed with the performance of their soldiers. The paratroops suffered very
heavy casualties. Of 8,500 men dropped on the first day,
3,764 were killed and 2,494 wounded. Freiherr von der
Heydte, commander of the paratroops at Máleme airfield,
attributed the high losses to insufficient training and tactical
experience, especially among the junior officers. The casualties, and the losses of transport aircraft, helped to ensure
that Germany never again used a parachute army for an
airborne attack. A plan to follow success in Crete with an
immediate airborne invasion of Cyprus—and thoughts of a
similar invasion of Malta—were abandoned. Most of the
veterans of the Crete battle died fighting as infantry on the
Italian or the Russian fronts.

At sea the Royal Navy had attacked convoys bringing
seaborne reinforcements, and covered the evacuation too. It
was a battle between German bombers and RN warships.
The total losses were three cruisers and six destroyers sunk;
three battleships, an aircraft-carrier, six cruisers and seven
destroyers damaged. Once again it was demonstrated that
warships could not operate without effective air cover. Admiral Andrew Cunningham, C-in-C of the Mediterranean

fleet, said that three squadrons of fighter planes would have been enough to save Crete (and his warships too, no doubt). But there were no fighters available. The Air Ministry continued to devote the greater part of its energies to strategic bombers. There was no indication that any lessons were learned by the men in London who decided these matters. Little wonder that after the war an official history sardonically quoted Cicero's maxim: 'An army is of little value in the field unless there are wise counsels at home'.

There was a bitter after-taste to the battle. Motivated by a rumour that German prisoners had been mistreated, the victorious paratroops formed firing parties and executed Cretan hostages (200 in one town square alone). The German inquiry that followed said the rumour was groundless. Kurt Student was condemned to five years imprisonment at a postwar war crimes trial for killing British POWs at Máleme but the sentence was not confirmed.

No matter what disillusion with paratroops the Crete battle brought to the German high command, the British and the Americans were thrilled by the idea of parachute armies and began to form and train their own units. Some were used in close support on D-Day. At Arnhem in Holland in 1944 a parachute army was dropped behind the enemy lines. It was not a success.

In strategic terms perhaps the German sacrifice was worthwhile. Crete was a fine prize, as one glance at a map will show. It provided a base from which the Germans could attack the whole eastern Mediterranean—such a good base that some critics of Wavell said that a commander with a better grasp of strategy would have abandoned Greece and used all the available resources to fortify Crete.

The fighting on Crete had revealed the limitations of Enigma and other high-grade decrypts. The Luftwaffe had always been the most vulnerable user of Enigma, largely due to careless mistakes and lack of signals discipline. But a prize-fighter out of training can be told that his opponent weighed in at 250 pounds, and is a great exponent of straight rights, and still get hurt when the punches land. The Enigma interception was passive, just as radar and asdic were passive. These facilities could report the presence of an enemy or reveal his intentions; you still had to find a way to hit him. After Crete, the British were able to reflect upon the German methods while they were full-length on the canvas.

15 TWO SIDE-SHOWS

Diverse paths lead diverse folk
the right way to Rome.

CHAUCER, *A TREATISE ON THE ASTROLABE*

The East African Campaign has been called a 'side-show' by men who were not there. Perhaps it was. Every confrontation seemed like a side-show to someone, and yet what at the time was called 'The Abyssinian Campaign' has all the ingredients of a great battle, and a unique place in the strategy of the Second World War.

The story begins a few weeks after Italy declared war. On 3 August 1940 three battalions of the Italian army and fourteen battalions of colonial infantry, together with pack-artillery, medium tanks and armoured cars, moved across the border into British Somaliland, in the 'horn of Africa'. It was a small country compared with neighbouring Abyssinia, which the Italians had conquered in 1936, and its defence force consisted of a battalion of the Black Watch, two Indian and two East African battalions and the Somaliland Camel Corps. After two days of heavy fighting the British force was evacuated on 15 August 1940 under a strong rearguard action by the Black Watch.

Churchill was angry. He felt that defeat at the hands of the Italians—for the one and only time on record—would boost the morale of the Italian army in Libya just when 'so much depended on our prestige'. Italy's propaganda service made the most of the British expulsion from its African holding. It was a black mark for General Wavell, and Churchill's black marks were accumulated like trading stamps: when you had a certain number of them, you were traded in for someone else.

To make matters worse for Wavell, he had Abyssinia's Emperor Haile Selassie sitting in Khartoum, waiting for the British to restore his country to him. He had arrived in Egypt by flying boat as long ago as 25 June. The Foreign Office in London had packed him off on one of the last cross-Europe flights before France collapsed, without warning anyone that he was on his way back to Africa. With the British defeat in Somaliland, he had become an even more embarrassing encumbrance with whom all communication was difficult, since the emperor insisted upon speaking Amharic. The only available interpreter of Amharic spoke only Arabic and, on at least one occasion, the Arabic interpreter spoke only French, thus requiring a third interpreter.

THE STRUGGLE FOR EAST AFRICA

In January 1941, after General O'Connor's victories at Sidi Barrani in the Western Desert, the 4th Indian Division was taken from the fighting and brought 2,000 miles south to East Africa. The 5th Indian Division was brought to Khartoum. West African troops and some South African brigades were moved to Kenya. There were several reasons why Churchill bullied Wavell into a three-pronged assault upon this million-square-mile rectangle of land. Beside his obvious chagrin at having been ejected from British Somaliland by the Italians, and the wish to remove, once and for all, the Italian dream of joining East African possessions to Libya by conquering Egypt, there was a broader strategy behind the move.

Churchill wanted to bring South Africa into a fighting war, and by taking South African army and air force units northwards into areas of greater strategic importance (instead of using them as garrisons, which is all the South African government had promised) there was a chance of blooding them and granting them a victory not too far away from their homeland. Removing the Italians would be a popular action at home in South Africa. The South Africans were not entirely sure about the wisdom of engaging in war against Germany, but Jan Christiaan Smuts—their premier and C-in-C—had won the vote in Parliament by a narrow margin. A victory for the South African fighting men would reinforce pro-British Smuts in his present shaky political position.

Wavell was not privy to Churchill's thinking on the matter. He was no politician and not, in the global sense, a strategist. Wavell did not want to attack Abyssinia; he preferred to wait until the rifles he had supplied to the natives brought about a popular revolt against Italian rule—or at least to wait until the rainy season had ended. Wavell sent a specialist in guerrilla warfare, Captain Orde Wingate, to get a revolt started, but Churchill was not prepared to let large bodies of fighting troops stand idly by, waiting for a revolt to start. He wanted this battle won and the troops—South Africans included—moved north into Egypt to face whatever proved to be the next crisis.

Few campaigns can match this Abyssinian one, either for the fierceness of its fighting or the colourful nature of its combatants. The 5th Indian Division, arriving at Keren, included such units as the 5th Mahratta Light Infantry Regiment, 3/2 Punjab, Skinner's Horse, the Worcesters, motor machine-gun companies of the Sudan Defence Force and the 1st Transvaal Scottish with its own pipe band. On the Italian side there were Blackshirt Legions, the Savoia Grenadiers, and Alpini units.

The landscape was equally exotic. In this land of precipitous mountains, high plateaux, gorges and ravines as well as tropical lowlands, Keren was a road and rail junction and the key to the north. Standing at 4,000 feet above sea-level, the country surrounding Keren was like a lunar landscape. To seal the mighty gorge the Italian engineers exploded charges under 200 feet of cliff and blocked the road. 'Keren', one account, describing that moment when the defenders sealed themselves inside, 'was like a great medieval castle whose portcullis has fallen'.

The 4th Indian Division had been chosen because of their experience of mountain warfare.[1] Facing them were crack troops of the Bersaglieri battalion of the Savoia Grenadiers, commanded by a young and energetic colonel. Five days of fighting cost the Italians nearly 5,000 casualties, including 1,135 dead. The Allied casualties were no fewer. The siege of Keren lasted 53 days and the British commander had to pause and bring in another division before finally taking the town.

None of the Allied troops who fought at Keren would dismiss Italian troops as lacking the ability to fight. Some of the most bitter fighting of the whole war was seen in East Africa. The RAF, the South African Air Force and Rhodesian squadrons were using antiquated planes such as Gloster Gladiators, Westland Lysanders, Vickers Wellesleys and Vickers Vincents. Without the air superiority they gained with these machines the Allied forces would never have been able to take Keren. The Italian commander was the Duke of Aosta, who was married to a French princess. He was described by Churchill as 'a chivalrous and cultivated man, partly educated in England'.[2] Churchill may have intended to say 'educated partly in England', but with Churchill you can never be sure.

Other Allied components included a battalion of the French Foreign Legion and the Highland Light Infantry. Exotic names abounded: a mobile force was called 'Flit' (after a well-known brand of insect repellent) and the commanding general's aircraft was called 'Mrs Clutterbuck'. The official war artist Edward Bawden depicted the campaign in several superb watercolour paintings now to be seen at the Imperial War Museum in London.

One column, 'Gideon Force', was commanded by 'Gid-
e Wingate, who said he was given nothing but 'sick
d the scum of the Cavalry Division'. With them he
he 'Lion of Judah', otherwise known as Haile Se-

lassie, back to his capital over some of the worst going in the world. The Force included 700 camels, 200 mules and some horses, the emperor and his guard, together with a propaganda unit which had its own printing press, Amharic typefaces and many coloured inks. The emperor's party was said to be able to follow the trail without a compass, using just the smell of the dead camels. Fifty-seven were counted on one day alone. One officer of the Cavalry Division wrote:

> Slowly, at the rate of about two miles an hour, we passed on over desolate ridges where the scrub had been burnt away by the fires of earlier hamlias [camel caravans]. The sun rose hot over a blackened landscape. Dead camels lay stinking in the heat at the foot and top of every khor where the broken ground had proved too much for them. The blood of crippled camels, newly slaughtered, was drying on the rocks. Frightened living camels shied away from the corpses; their drivers sometimes vomited. Hundreds of vultures, gorged with flesh, lurched heavily around.[3]

On 5 May 1941 Haile Selassie was back in his capital at Addis Ababa. It had been a campaign of remarkable chivalry which recorded no rape, murder, plundering or bombing of civilians. In defence of Keren the Italians fought fiercely and their final withdrawal from there was deft and skilful. The final skirmishes of the campaign in East Africa went on for seven months after the fall of Addis Ababa. It would provide time enough to reflect upon the strangely mixed quality of the Italian army. Some units proved brave and efficient while others were either unwilling to fight, or too disorganized to be formidable adversaries. Some said the Italians suffered from a shortage of the sort of officers that a large educated professional middle class could supply.[4] German liaison officers remarked on the low standards of training and the lack of initiative of junior officers. In part it was a matter of weapons. Italy lacked a strong industrial base and had failed to improve weapons which, although good enough in the early 1930s, were outmoded by the 1940s. There was a prevailing feeling amongst all Italian soldiers, except perhaps those in the elite Fascist regiments, that they were fighting on the wrong side; that the English, French and Americans were traditional friends, and the Germans and Austrians Italy's implacable foes.

As the mopping-up continued Churchill's reasoning proved sound. Italian East Africa was Italian no more. It was the first Allied strategic victory of the war, and came at a time when the Allies desperately needed victory of any sort. Here was a clear demonstration of what air superiority over a battlefield could achieve and how unity among disparate forces could win the day. South African, East African, West African, British, Indian, Sudanese and Cypriot troops had taken part and South African soldiers, once committed to serving in only southern Africa, were now a part of the main Allied battle forces. But the campaign had done nothing to ease Churchill's doubts about Wavell. When the two men met for the first time in August 1940 it had been clear to everyone that they were totally incompatible in temperament and outlook. The record suggests that Wavell, taciturn, wary and professional, probably thought Churchill an interfering politician who knew nothing about generalship. Churchill, exuberant, bellicose or laudatory as the mood caught him, certainly found Wavell uncooperative and narrow-minded. The subsequent exchanges between them had done nothing to change these first impressions.

The victory brought a vital change, enabling President Roosevelt to declare the Red Sea to be no longer a 'war zone'. This meant that United States shipping was once more permitted, by government and insurance conditions, to sail to Suez. American tanks, guns and planes could now be shipped around the Cape of Good Hope to Egypt.

The war had widened. With cool nerve, the 4th British Indian Division had been pulled south after the battle for Sidi Barrani and used for the assault on the Italians in Keren, where the fiercest fighting took place. Afterwards it was rushed north to fight the Vichy French at Damascus in

Syria. With equal facility, the 5th South African Brigade was sent north to Egypt as soon as victory in East Africa was assured. A further indication of the growing scale of the war was the way in which precious Hawker Hurricane fighter planes were being brought to Takoradi in the Gold Coast, some in crates to be assembled ashore, others flown from the decks of aircraft-carriers. From Takoradi the little planes made an astounding journey right across the continent, landing in northern Nigeria, and again in Khartoum in the Sudan before reaching Cairo. They were usually escorted by one twin-engined Bristol Blenheim as an 'insurance policy'.

HABBANIYAH AND AFTER: IRAQ AND SYRIA

For anyone who considers the campaign in Italian East Africa a side-show, the skirmish at RAF Habbaniyah in Iraq must rank as insignificant. But let us suspend judgement for a moment.

Iraq has held a place in the history of the RAF since the First World War, when Australian and New Zealand pilots flew Maurice Farman Longhorn biplanes to cover a British army advancing up the River Tigris to fight the Turks. A postwar mandate put it under British control and Winston Churchill (then secretary of state for the colonies) and Sir Hugh Trenchard (the 'Father' of the RAF) proposed that this huge area of desert, a barren place of stone and sand, could be policed successfully with a few fighter planes and bombers converted to carry soldiers. It would save the British taxpayer the cost of twelve infantry battalions, a cavalry regiment, a pack battery and engineers which it was estimated would otherwise be needed to keep order among the Arabs.

This was the time when Giulio Douhet published his influential book *Command of the Air;*[5] a time when the American flier Billy Mitchell demonstrated that his bombers could sink battleships. So why not make Iraq the first country to be garrisoned from the air? The idea seemed to work. Villages that harboured trouble-making Kurdish tribesmen were bombed. Flyers worked in conjunction with RAF Rolls-Royce armoured-car crews which were supplied from the air. One air force officer, Hugh Dowding, thought that punishment without bloodshed would be equally deterrent. After his commander had gone on leave, Dowding ordered that before a bombing raid all the villagers should be warned by leaflet, in time for them to escape to safety, and this became the standard practice.[6] By the time the mandate ended in 1932, a pro-British monarchy was installed in Baghdad, oil-drilling had started in the north and concessions had been granted. The RAF remained behind: a treaty provided them with two bases, defended by locally recruited 'levies', and the right of passage in time of war. The levies were mostly loyal and disciplined Assyrians who hated the Arabs with a deep passion and made a vital contribution to the British presence.

By 1941 this almost landlocked country, with just a tiny strip of coast on the Persian Gulf and a small fertile region watered by the mighty rivers Tigris and Euphrates, was pumping oil through two big pipelines to the Mediterranean. One of these pipelines crossed Vichy French Syria, and its use was denied to the British. The other pipe went through pro-British Jordan, and its outlet at Haifa in Palestine was used to fuel British forces in the Middle East. For some the oil brought great changes and political turbulence as military coups became commonplace. The warring nomadic tribes still fought barbarous skirmishes using Lee-Enfields and Turkish rifles left over from the First World War, while the rich lived quiet lives in fine houses with servants, silk and silver. Successive Iraqi governments always found enough money to keep a small army and air force well equipped with guns and planes.

The Germans had always shown interest in the region. Their archeologists and explorers have written some of the standard works on the desert and its history. Some of its most breath-taking wonders are still to be seen in Berlin's Pergamon museum. But the German interest had been political and military too, and their espionage network was well entrenched in the area and ready to encourage anti-British Arab nationalism. It came as no surprise that Rashid Ali's clique, which seized power in April 1941, was supported by Germany or that the coup should come immediately following Britain's humiliating defeats in Greece and Cyrenaica. Unlike previous coups this one hoped to get rid of the British altogether and May was the month of high floodwater when any British relief force would find its movement impeded.

That Rashid Ali took power from the pro-British regent Emir Abdullah Illah (who ruled in the name of the young King Faisal II) was no great surprise. That it was done without killing him was more a matter of good luck than of good will. The doctors who arrived at the regent's Baghdad home with a death certificate endorsed 'heart failure' were too late. The intended victim had left in the back of the American minister's car and the RAF flew him out of their nearby airfield.

Rashid Ali el Gailani was not the young sleek Arab the name might suggest but a plump bespectacled man of middle age who, while serving as prime minister, had acquired a reputation for duplicity in a region where duplicity was seldom remarked upon. He was known to be a Nazi sympathizer and the British were alarmed by his coup. Britain's proprietorial feelings towards the Suez Canal, about Iraq's oilfields, and communications between Egypt and India, prompted a quick reaction to the Baghdad palace revolution. Garrisoning from the air was temporarily suspended. The 20th Indian Infantry Brigade, waiting in Karachi for embarkation on ships to Singapore, was suddenly given an about-turn and rushed to Basra in southern Iraq. Faced with Iraqi objections, the British blandly denied that the newly arrived men had come to seize control back from the pro-German clique; the Indian Brigade was just passing through Iraq 'en route to Palestine'.

About 60 miles from Baghdad, and close to the River Euphrates, there was a lake used by Britain's 'Empire' flying boats which hopped from water-landing to water-landing all the way to India and beyond. Here too, within a steel fence, were comfortable bungalows with lawns and flower beds, a polo ground and a golf course that the RAF had built in an attempt to forget that just a stroke or two away lay a sandy bunker that stretched to the horizon. This was Habbaniyah: RAF No. 4 Flying Training School. There were no up-to-date fighting planes here—the RAF had none to spare—only 27 Airspeed Oxfords and 32 Hawker Audaxes, as well as some Gloster Gladiators and such remarkable museum pieces as Fairey Gordons and Vickers Valentias.

As one of his first political moves Rashid Ali said he would permit no further landing of troops in Basra. He wanted to limit the number of British troops in Iraq at any one time. Let those passing through pass through, he said, before any more arrive. In London it became known that Rashid Ali had signed a secret treaty with the Germans and the Italians on 25 April. A variety of intelligence material indicated that Rashid Ali was waiting for German armed assistance and that the disembarkation of British troops at Basra had proved an unwelcome impediment to his plans.

In a climate growing ever more tense, it was decided to move British women and children to safety. Some went to the American Legation, some to the British Embassy, and some were to be flown out of the country altogether. On leaving Baghdad, they were held up by Iraqi soldiers, but eventually were allowed to proceed to RAF Habbaniyah, where there were now 1,000 RAF personnel. These were mostly ground crews, administrative staff and flying instructors, as well as 1,200 Iraqi levies—Arabs, Kurds and Assyrian Christians—employed by the British. In addition 350 infantrymen of the King's Own Royal Regiment had been flown in.

At about this time Rashid Ali's men occupied the oilfields and switched the pipeline controls so that all the oil would flow to (Vichy) Syria and none to (British) Palestine. Red lights flashed: this was a serious threat. The British had persuaded Shell and Anglo-Iranian Oil to build at Haifa a refinery capable of supplying 2 million tons per year. This fuel was required by the Royal Navy's Mediterranean fleet. Additionally the refinery was supplying high-quality oils that were vitally important since the war had cut off Romanian supplies.

Iraqi army units (an infantry brigade accompanied by a brigade of mechanized artillery) soon arrived at Habbaniyah and occupied high ground outside it. The RAF cleaned up and oiled two ancient howitzers, relics of the First World War, which had been used to ornament the lawn outside the depot. In addition there were 18 armoured cars and the infantry's mortars and machine-guns. They fitted some of their Audax biplane trainers, and Oxford twin-engined trainers, with bomb racks, and the theory of bomb-dropping was hastily taught to pupil pilots. It was sobering to remember that the Iraqi air force was equipped with American bombers and Italian fighter planes.

On the morning of 1 May the Iraqis were to be seen siting their pom-pom anti-aircraft guns and bringing their armoured cars as close as possible to the RAF runways. A message from the Iraqi commander dictated that all flying was to cease on pain of aircraft being fired upon. The British replied that the training schedule would continue normally and reprisals would follow any such act of war. An RAF plane did a circuit without incident. The British then sent a note to the Iraqis saying that they must move, as the present disposition of Iraqi troops constituted an act of war. That night, the British decided that if the Iraqis were still there at dawn they would improvise a bombing raid.

The Audaxes and Oxfords were wheeled out under cover of night and took off so as to be in the air by 5 am. They were joined by eight twin-engined Vickers Wellington bombers of 37 Squadron from Shaibah near Basra. These 'Wimpys' were the only modern effective aircraft that took part in the fighting in Iraq. Twisting and turning without any proper formations, and narrowly missing mid-air collisions, the British planes bombed the Iraqi positions. As Iraqi pom-poms shot at the planes, Iraqi artillery bombarded the RAF station. One Oxford was shot down in flames and a Wellington was hit by shells on landing. The rest got down safely, though many were riddled with bullet holes.

The base was subjected to attacks throughout the day and was bombed by Audaxes of the Royal Iraq Air Force. No vital damage was done before RAF Gladiators chased them away. The artillery fire was a greater threat. 'But though the station church sustained some damage, owing to the powerful attraction invariably exercised by places of worship upon indifferent gunners, the water tower was never hit', said an Air Ministry account.[7]

Transport aircraft were loaded with women and children and climbed away while RAF Audaxes staged diversionary attacks. When they landed the Audaxes were moved to the polo ground where trees hid them, but take-offs now had to be negotiated through the main gates! Wear and tear on the aircraft was becoming severe, so that only four Oxfords of the original 27 were serviceable, and it was decided that only instructors should fly the remaining aircraft. But the arrival of some Bristol Blenheims persuaded the British to bomb the columns that supplied water, fuel and ammunition to the Iraqi positions. Then they went to make bombing attacks against nearby Iraqi airfields.

Suddenly, and without warning, on the fifth morning of the siege the plateau was empty. The Iraqis had gone. The 'Habbaniyah air force' pursued them, and motor buses which the Iraqis had seized from Baghdad streets to move their infantry were bombed on the road. The announcement that successful operational flights by pupils would mean a remission of further training set the pupil pilots demanding an opportunity to fly, and they were needed.

The British success at Habbaniyah did not deter Rashid Ali. On 12 May he went, together with his ministers and other dignitaries, to Baghdad airport to await the arrival of a German liaison team led by Major Axel von Blomberg (a son of the famous field marshal). Blomberg was to set up a headquarters to direct forthcoming Luftwaffe operations against the British in Iraq. Iraqi police levies on airfield defence duties had not been briefed about the visitors, and when a Heinkel bomber flew into view they opened fire at it. One bullet went through the fuselage, and in a bizarre stroke of fate mortally wounded Blomberg.[8] The following day Baghdad heard the exiled Mufti of Jerusalem broadcast a call for all Islamic countries to join the fight against the British.

More fighting broke out in Basra, where disembarked Indian troops were somewhat piqued to find themselves subjected to the brutal fire of 2-inch and 3-inch mortars that the British had supplied to the Iraqi army. They were still waiting for theirs, as were most other Indian units. Fighting spread even to the civil population and the British disarmed the police force.

The next day, an RAF Bristol Blenheim at Mosul in northern Iraq was fired upon by a German plane. There were reports that many German aircraft were operating from Mosul and that supplies of arms and ammunition were arriving there on the railway from Syria. Clearly the Vichy French were not only permitting transit facilities but actively supporting German intervention on the side of Rashid Ali.

There were worries about what sort of intervention the Germans might mount. On 20 May the Luftwaffe parachute troops began the assault on the faraway island of Crete. If the Germans were serious about reinforcing Rashid Ali, such airborne forces would be the ones needed. But by 29 May, the Crete fighting ended with Karl Student's Air Division decimated and the wrecks of 151 Junkers transport aircraft scattered across the Cretan landscape. A small collection of transports were scraped together and assigned to support the Iraqi revolt[9] but it had come at the wrong time as far as the German airborne forces were concerned. Rashid Ali and his associates, together with the Italian and German ministers and the ex-Mufti of Jerusalem, fled to Persia. The coup was over and the British reinstalled the regent in Baghdad.

But the story doesn't end there. Before the outcome of the Habbaniyah fighting was settled, some RAF flyers reported back to H 4 (a desolate RAF landing strip on the oil pipeline) in Transjordan after a routine reconnaissance over Syria. (Like those in its neighbour Lebanon, the French in Syria had declined all invitations to join in the war against Germany and Italy.) A big German transport plane was parked on Palmyra airfield. It seemed to be in the process of refuelling for an immediate take-off, its destination undoubtedly Iraq.

The RAF flyers had noticed that the refuelling was being carried out by hand, and pouring from cans of fuel was a slow procedure. One of the pilots suggested to his superior that, given a fighter plane with some incendiary ammunition, he could make sure the German aircraft never took off again.

'Are you two young gentlemen aware that we are not at war with Syria?' asked the man behind the desk.

'Yes, sir', the flying officer replied, 'I know, sir; but I think it would be a bloody good idea if we were'.

That was in fact how the British went to war with Syria. Permission was granted, and after eating a hasty lunch while an aircraft was prepared they flew off with two supporting Tomahawk fighters to attack the Germans.

In fact London knew well what was happening. Enigma decrypts had revealed that unmarked Heinkel He 111 bombers and twin-engined Messerschmitt fighters were flying to Syria. London judged the German commitment to be strictly limited, but took no chances. A British column set out from Palestine and the troops in Basra were summoned into action.

In the confused and terrible fighting that followed—sometimes in temperatures of 120 degrees (49 C)—Frenchman fought Frenchman and Arab fought Arab in a deeply felt struggle. And, at a time when the British fortunes were very low, Emir Abdullah of Transjordan sent his small but efficient Arab Legion into the battle on the Allied side. Feelings ran even higher when German aircraft bombed (Vichy)

Beirut and hit a school and a mosque. Whether this was a navigational error, or a deliberate attempt to have the RAF wrongly blamed for it, has never been established.

On 27 June Luftwaffe Enigma signals revealed that Vichy France was about to send infantry reinforcements to Syria. The troopships were to be escorted by units of the French fleet: one battleship, four cruisers and up to six destroyers. Air cover was to be supplied by the Luftwaffe. It looked as if the war was about to intensify, and France become a full ally of Germany. The Admiralty sent Royal Navy submarines to concentrate against the troopships and the escorting warships. Then, on 2 July, news came that the plan was cancelled. A deep sigh came from those who saw what a catastrophic clash had been so narrowly avoided.

The fighting ended with the British taking control of Syria and Lebanon, but the wounds would never heal. The defeated French servicemen were invited to join de Gaulle's Free French and fight the Germans, but almost all chose to go back to France. De Gaulle, taking seriously his self-declared role as head of state in exile, and pressured by the British (and unofficially by the Americans too), promised the people of the French mandates of Syria and Lebanon their independence.[10] There was uproar. De Gaulle's announcement not only upset the Vichy government, which felt that such decisions were theirs, but also made his Free French soldiers ask why they were fighting and dying for territory in order to give it back when it was taken.

It all ended in farce. In breach of the armistice terms, the Vichy French tried to spirit their prisoners of war back to Germany. This resulted in some senior Vichy officers being put under arrest in their hotel until the POWs were found and handed over. At the signing of the armistice a drunken Australian photographer fell over a cable and put out all the lights. In the darkness and confusion someone stole the gold-decorated képi of a French general.

Afterwards Churchill remarked that: 'Hitler certainly cast away the opportunity of taking a great prize for little cost in the Middle East'. Wavell never saw it in that light. When ordered to send a relief column from Palestine to Iraq, he let it be known that Palestine (with its ruler in league with Rashid Ali, and much anti-British feeling prevalent) could not spare soldiers from its garrison. Showing no sympathy for Britain's problems in Iraq, Wavell irritably replied: 'Your message takes little account of realities. You must face facts . . . a settlement should be negotiated as early as possible'.

Having intercepted an Italian diplomatic message saying that Rashid Ali had used up all his bombs and shells, London (chiefs of staff) replied testily: 'Settlement by negotiation cannot be entertained except on a basis of climb-down by the Iraqis . . . realities of the situation are that Rashid Ali has all along been hand in glove with Axis Powers . . .'[11]

'I am deeply disturbed at General Wavell's attitude', wrote Churchill, who felt that the essence of war was the rapid movement of forces.[12] He had urged Wavell to exploit the situation and break into Baghdad 'even with quite small forces . . . running the same risks as the Germans are accustomed to run and profit by'.[13]

Only grudgingly had Wavell obeyed the direct order to send a column to Habbaniyah, which he thought was 'a non-vital area'. Even then he pointed out that 'it is not capable of entering Baghdad', and repeated his advice to find a political solution for Iraq. He had always, he said later, 'disliked Iraq, the country, the people and the military commitment'.

Wavell's dislike of Iraq seems to have led him to underestimate its importance. In a telegram dated 25 May, he said that his main task was the defence of Egypt and Palestine and added that this 'would be made more difficult but would not be greatly jeopardized by hostile control of Iraq'. His opinion is difficult to sustain: Palestine and Egypt would have been outflanked by an Axis-controlled Iraq, and Wavell's army, navy and air force depended upon Iraq's oil wells and the pipeline.

Wavell's concern in Syria, Palestine and Iraq, just like his caution in East Africa, came from his belief that all military action, and even cross-country movement, required 'the co-operation of the local population and tribes'. Whatever the morality of this assumption it is not always the case in reality. This was proved when Churchill pressed Wavell into action.

That Churchill took any threat to Iraq very seriously is indicated by the way in which British military intelligence in Palestine sought out the extreme Zionist Irgun Zvai Leumi. They recruited Iraqi Jews to penetrate and spy upon the Rashid Ali organization. One of the volunteers was David Rashiel, Irgun chief of staff, who came from a prosperous Baghdad family and who, in the course of the revolt, was caught and executed by the rebels.[14]

When Wavell was sacked the following month, June 1941, most people put it down to his military failure in North Africa. The reasons for that failure and the injustice of Churchill's decision have been picked over many times, but there can be no doubt that the roots of Churchill's discontent were sunk much deeper.

16 QUARTERMASTER'S NIGHTMARE

Victory is a mirage in the desert created by a long war.

B. H. LIDDELL HART[1]

'Crete gave a great name; Africa gave a greater'. The words of the Roman poet Martial describe the rival bids for glory made by Karl Student and the even more ambitious Erwin Rommel, who was appointed to command the Deutsches Afrika Korps on 12 February 1941: 'In the evening the Führer showed me a number of British and American illustrated papers describing General Wavell's advance through Cyrenaica. Of particular interest was the masterly co-ordination these showed between armoured land forces, air force and navy'.[2]

Events moved quickly. A British intelligence summary dated March 1941 said: 'Detachments of a German expeditionary force under an obscure general, Rommel, have landed in North Africa'.

Stripped of much equipment and transport (which had been sent to Greece), tired, depleted and untested units made up much of the British army facing Rommel in North Africa. Wavell and his staff in Cairo were not unduly worried. They comforted themselves with the belief that the Italians in Tripolitania could be disregarded and that German reinforcements would not be sufficient for any attack to be started in the near future.

The codecrackers at Bletchley Park were keeping tabs on Rommel. When Churchill asked what was happening, he was supplied with German OKW, High Command of the Armed Forces, signals showing the approximate arrival dates of components of the Afrika Korps. Although Cairo frequently complained of Bletchley Park's slowness, this time there was no delay in passing on these figures to Wavell.

By early March Wavell's director of intelligence was telling him the Afrika Korps might attack very soon. He showed Wavell the sort of plan he thought might be on Rommel's desk. Wavell dismissed it. Without disputing the figures from London, his staff—guided by the way the British army did such things—calculated that Rommel could not be ready before May. His supply line was long and he would need considerable time to prepare reserves and dumps before going into action.

In Berlin the German army's C-in-C, Field Marshal von Brauchitsch, came to the same conclusion as Wavell. He told Rommel that there could be no question of staging an offensive in Africa in the near future. The Italian high command took the same view. But Rommel was aggressive and ambitious. He saw that Berlin was hoping that the Western Desert fighting might lull into a stalemate, and he had no intention of letting his command become a backwater. He was determined to make war, and he was in a hurry. When his ships arrived he kept the dockside lights on, and worked all night unloading despite the danger of air raids. The armoured cars that were swinging from the cranes in Tripoli in mid-February were in action ten days later.

The remarkable General O'Connor had been sent away to rest and the fighting army was now commanded by General Philip Neame, a man of outstanding valour, as his VC indicated, but lacking experience of mechanized desert fighting. Rommel knew from intelligence and air photos that British units were short of transport, which meant uncertain supply lines all the way back to their depots in Egypt. He saw them building defences, and that proved they had no intention of attacking him. In fact Rommel was in a situation exactly like that of General O'Connor when he had faced the Italians a short while before.

Still unconcerned, on 30 March Wavell told Neame that the enemy could not 'make any big effort for at least another month'. At 0944 hours the next day, armoured cars of the Stahnsdorf 3rd Reconnaissance Unit—having already advanced to El Agheila—led the attack. Behind them were the tanks of the 5th Panzer Regiment. The following day Stuka dive-bombers and Rommel's 8.8-cm dual-purpose guns were seen in action. The use of these Flak guns in an artillery role was a great surprise, just as it had been at Arras, before Dunkirk, and in Spain during the civil war. The chronic failure of British military intelligence to record that the 8.8-cm gun was a dual-purpose weapon is in sad accord with a signal Wavell sent to the CIGS in London estimating that Rommel's armoured division was equipped with 400 tanks, when its true strength was 168 tanks and 30 reconnaissance cars.[3]

DESERT WARFARE

The desert was an uninhabited empty space within which 'forts' were held. Capture one of his forts and your displaced enemy flounders and falls back. You outflank him and he tries to find another place to hold fast. This is what happened as Rommel pressed on, sending out the Luftwaffe to see what was happening. The aerial photographs soon showed the British in full retreat.

When Rommel tightened Italian field signals discipline, British listening units, which were not yet taken very seriously, could make nothing of the enemy radio traffic. Rommel on the other hand, gave great importance to his signals intelligence. He used it in combination with air reconnaissance, and armoured car patrols, to follow the movements of the retreating British.

British headquarters now knew the sort of confusion that had earlier hit the Italian staff officers. And exactly as they had done, the British rationalized their failure by larger and larger estimates of the forces ranged against them. On one thing only did the British commanders all agree; what was happening was incredible, if not to say impossible.

The commander of an Australian battalion in full retreat ordered his men to stop for breakfast. Those men who obeyed were known in the prison camp where they spent the next four years as 'the breakfast battalion'.

Still assessing the Germans on his own army's methods and performance, Wavell remained calm. He had personally assured Foreign Secretary Anthony Eden, and told the generals in Whitehall, that the Germans could not attack before mid-May. Now it was April and Wavell's generals reflected his unflustered optimism. They were convinced that Rommel's advance would quickly falter and fail of its own accord: where would he get water? Where would he get fuel? These two vital questions were answered as he captured water, and took fuel forward on trucks. And the Germans had brought excellent containers for water and fuel, made from welded pressed-steel. The British soon named them 'Jerricans' and seized every one they could find. They tossed aside the 4-gallon British cans, aptly known as 'flimsies'. The official history quotes a report dated December 1941 which said that 30 per cent or more of the fuel carried in flimsies to fighting men in the Western Desert was lost by leakage.[4] From an account given by one RASC driver carrying fuel, 30 per cent loss was an understatement:

> When we reached [the petrol dump] the 70,000 had been reduced to 30,000 gallons during the desert journey. Much to our surprise, we were told this was a good effort. This wastage was because of the 'flimsy' petrol containers which leaked badly, a state of affairs not eradicated until the introduction of the 'Jerrican' copied from the Germans.[5]

Suddenly Wavell interceded personally in the battle. He countermanded the orders of Neame, his army commander, to cover both the inland and coastal roads. Wavell assumed that Rommel would keep to the via Balbia, the tarmac road along the coast, and so sent all the armour to block it. It was not a good idea to underestimate Rommel. The Germans were just as capable as the British of taking a short-cut across the desert, following the route that General O'Connor's men had proved to be negotiable.

By the end of that day, 3 April, the Germans were moving into Benghasi, where the British had set fire to all their stores. Wavell decided that General Neame had lost control and ordered Major-General O'Connor to go and replace him. O'Connor asked Wavell to reconsider his decision, pointing out that one should not introduce new tactics in the middle of a battle. He said he didn't know the troops and would be better occupied preparing defensive positions to ensure Rommel didn't sweep right into Egypt. Wavell compromised by asking O'Connor to stay at Neame's headquarters for a few days, and offer advice when asked. This was the worst possible decision, and Wavell more or less admitted as much afterwards.

The British army was falling to pieces, and two heads were not better than one. Panicking troops had burned petrol and other stores at Msus long before the Germans got near them. The 3rd Armoured Division ran out of fuel. The 2nd Armoured Division, sent to protect the Australians, disintegrated to a point where it simply relinquished its tanks and joined the retreat. This 'complete disobedience of orders' was, said O'Connor, 'absolutely incomprehensible'.[6] But the problems that came from the shared responsibilities of Neame and O'Connor were soon to be solved. On 6 April, when moving their joint headquarters back a few miles, O'Connor, lacking his own transport, accepted the offer of a ride in Neame's car.

> Shortly before dusk it became obvious that they had missed the way and were on one of the northern tracks, but as this seemed anyway a safer route, Neame handed over to his driver and told him to carry on towards Derna. Well after midnight, O'Connor and [Lt-Col.] Combe, who had been asleep in the back of the car, were woken to

find the car stationary and voices shouting in front. Combe got out to investigate, quickly realized that the voices were not British and on asking the driver what was happening, received the classic answer: 'I expect it's some of them bloody Cypriot drivers, sir!'[7]

Not quite. The generals had been captured by a motorcycle reconnaissance unit, those probing patrols that Rommel kept pushing forward. Curiously enough a brigadier in a car ahead of the two British generals reached his destination without a hint of the fate that overtook the men in the car behind. Only early next morning, with his two generals nowhere to be found, was their loss discovered.

Rommel was out-thinking his adversaries at every turn. This was the sort of warfare at which he excelled. He told his air force to concentrate upon destroying the British supply lines. 'Rommel panic' spread. By 7 April the three prongs of Rommel's advance converged on Mechili, where the Indian Motor Brigade had been moved forward to make a stand. Surrounded, the whole brigade surrendered. A more forceful war had now come to the Western Desert.

When all is said, Rommel did little more than repeat O'Connor's methods. In an impudent replay, he had taken O'Connor's 'impossible' desert road south of the Jebel Akdar in order to surprise the British retreating along the coast. But the Germans added a spirit of blitzkrieg to the desert war. One German general ascribed the success of this period to the cooperation and versatility of his units. Batteries of anti-tank guns always accompanied the German tanks and targeted only tanks. Field artillery was there to bombard enemy anti-tank batteries. The general wondered why the British 3.7-inch anti-aircraft gun was not adapted to the anti-tank role. He noted that 'the British regarded the anti-tank gun as a defensive weapon, and they failed to make adequate use of their powerful field artillery, which should have been taught to eliminate our anti-tank guns'.[8] The armour of the heavier German tanks— Panzer III and Panzer IV—was vulnerable not only to 25-pounder field guns but also to the

2-pounder tank and anti-tank guns, providing you got close enough.

GENERAL ERWIN ROMMEL

Rommel was not one of the war's great generals. Many Germans express surprise that the British and American public know his name: they think of him as a product of Nazi propaganda. Rommel led from the front and his style suited divisional command. He became a hero for Allied front-line soldiers who seldom—if ever—saw their own top commanders at the front. British generals preferred to have their HQs about 60 miles behind the fighting fronts.[9] Besides, Rommel had for his Afrika Korps exceptional leaders such as Cruewell, Nehring and Bayerlein. But all that said, few other men could have inspired this mixed and demoralized German-Italian desert army in the way that Rommel did. He revelled in popularity and delighted in the sort of informality that the desert provided to both sides. In his paper *Modern Military Leadership* he wrote:

> The commander must try, above all, to establish personal and comradely contact with his men, but without giving away an inch of his authority . . . when an attack is ordered the men must never be allowed to get the feeling that their casualties have been calculated in advance according to the laws of probability.

The deciding factor in Rommel's North African campaign was the shipping and the ports. Even Tripoli was in no way equipped for the massive traffic that such armies demanded. Had the Axis coaxed the French for use of Tunisian facilities and used Tripoli and other less good Libyan ports with impeccable efficiency, and given proper attention to their road transport, they might have mustered the strength to capture Egypt. Then, having captured the port of Alexandria and got it working, they might have fed through it reinforcements enough to occupy Egypt and the Canal Zone. Even then such a strategy would almost certainly have faltered; German factories after the summer of 1941 were to be hard pressed by the demands of the Russian front.

Such a scenario was never a real possibility. Rommel's fatal flaw was his inability to see the importance of logistics. He liked to blame the Italian navy for his shortages, and historians have too readily accepted this judgement. In fact, Italian merchant seamen were nothing less than heroic in their performance. John Ellis reckons that the Axis forces were getting an average 800 tons per division per day, and points out that 'voracious US armoured divisions in North West Europe required only 600 tons of supplies per day, including fuel . . .'[10]

It was Rommel's own land-supply movements that brought him down. In fact his troubles arose from a combination of his own daring and improvisation and a disregard for the terrible problems such impulsive decisions made for his supply staff. He is quoted as saying that he left logistics to his staff officers.[11] It is significant that his supply officer in 1941 had the lowly rank of major.

As an indication of this major's problems, the trucks taking 1,000 gallons of fuel from the docks at Tobruk to Alamein consumed 120 gallons of fuel plus 9.6 gallons of other lubricants. Wastage and spillage in the hot climate would account for at least 10 per cent. Deduct fuel needed for the return journey, and they will have brought no more than 636 gallons to the front. But still more fuel was needed to bring up ammunition and food and all the other supplies. The map reveals that Tobruk, 300 miles from the front, is the key to supplying the desert war. It spent much of the war in British hands, and when in German hands it was a favourite target for the RAF bombers. Tripoli—Rommel's main port—was often 1,500 miles from his front! For their supplies the British used whenever possible the coastal railway out of Alexandria. It was economical and efficient. When

Rommel captured 300 miles of it (in 1942) he did little to keep it functioning.

There can be no doubt that much of Rommel's reputation as a general was due to his skilful use of intelligence. Many tactical moves were based upon secrets picked up by his highly efficient Fernmeldeaufklärung. This mobile radio monitoring service listened to everything it could pick up; casual battlefield chat, tank to tank calls, headquarters messages and supply depot reports. Rommel's traffic analysts reaped a rich harvest, for British units in 1941 had not learned of the dangers that poor radio discipline brought. In addition to this tactical intelligence, Rommel was receiving something even better than the British Enigma intercepts: the intercepted messages sent to Washington by the United States military attaché in Cairo.

At this time the British were showing this American everything and anything that he wanted to see. Not only did his messages contain details of British armour strengths and positions, they also reported forthcoming operations such as commando raids. Instead of the spotty information from the Enigma intercepts, Rommel was getting material about air, land and sea operations and getting it with a speed and continuity that BP could never equal. The most knowledgeable historian on this subject remarks:

> And what messages they were! They provided Rommel with undoubtedly the broadest and clearest picture of enemy forces and intentions available to any Axis commander throughout the whole war.[12]

Determined defence of Tobruk by Australian infantry and British artillery denied that port to Rommel even when the remainder of the British army had retreated back to the Egyptian border. Now Rommel came to a stop and concentrated on Tobruk.

Rommel's unexpected advance in April 1941 surprised Berlin and prompted the high command to send a senior observer, General-leutnant F. Paulus, to find out what this upstart Rommel was doing. Tall and slim, Paulus was one of the army's brightest staff officers and an expert on mobile warfare. His work as chief of staff for the 6th Army during its victorious campaigns in Poland, Belgium and France had resulted in him being selected to be deputy chief of the general staff and told to produce a strategic survey for invading the Soviet Union. Paulus, nicknamed 'the noble lord', was an old-fashioned but meticulous theoretician, who bathed as often as possible and wore gloves to protect himself against dirt. He had been Rommel's company commander in the 1920s and did not care for his cavalier way of waging war. Arriving on his inspection tour on 27 April, Paulus voiced great reservations about Rommel's proposed attack on Tobruk, which had now become a fortress. His scepticism proved well founded after concentrated bombing and shelling made no more than a dent in the Tobruk perimeter and both sides settled into a state of siege punctuated by bloody clashes at night. The Tobruk perimeter consisted mostly of rock-hard ground, so digging trenches or foxholes was not easy. Given the lack of cover, the Australians had to endure baking heat where a careless movement brought accurate sniper fire. On the night of 5–6 May, the defenders were given new hope when for the first time a ship brought supplies into the beleaguered port. From now onwards destroyers would make regular nightly visits, and each week reinforcements would be exchanged for wounded men.

The caustic report resulting from Paulus's inspection tour said that Rommel's supply lines were overstretched, his men exhausted and his reserves inadequate. He was told to forget about reducing Tobruk and withdraw to Gazala or Mechili and operate within his resources.

The Enigma experts at Bletchley Park sent the intercepted signal to Churchill, who reasoned that if Rommel was weak and over-extended this was the chance to knock him reeling back to Cyrenaica. It was especially urgent since Enigma signals also revealed that 15 Panzer Division would soon be reinforcing Rommel. Ignoring the warnings of everyone around him, Churchill took all the fighter planes and tanks to be spared in Britain and loaded them onto a convoy which, against more advice, he sent through the Axis-dominated Mediterranean. Four of the five freighters got through with 238 tanks and 43 Hawker Hurricane fighter planes and docked in Alexandria in mid-May.

While this newly arrived equipment was distributed and made ready, a limited offensive, codenamed Brevity, was launched. Its object was to capture key areas in preparation for a major offensive to come.

One account of the desert war, says: 'Operation Brevity began at dawn on May 15, and it soon became evident that neither Rommel nor his local commander . . . were either aware of or in agreement with the conclusions drawn by Paulus'.[13] The British attack captured one of its objectives, Halfaya Pass, but was otherwise a failure. Rommel's signals intelligence had given him good warning of what was coming, and even a weak and over-extended Afrika Korps was too much for the British as he staged a counter-attack that recovered the Halfaya Pass.

And when the British armour was unloaded from the convoy that had come through the Mediterranean at such risk it proved to be a mixed collection. Eight out of twenty tanks required a complete overhaul. Many of the others were already halfway through their effective life and some of the Matildas were in need of major repairs. All of them required 'tropicalization' and painting. Long before the armour was fit for battle, Rommel's 15 Panzer Division reinforcements had arrived.

On 15 June, in the terrible desert heat of summer, the promised British offensive, Operation Battleaxe, began. Repeatedly the Germans enticed the British tanks on to their well concealed guns. Only thirteen 8.8-cm guns were in action but their role was decisive. The British stuck to their 'naval battle' tactics, sending in tanks to fire broadsides at enemy tanks. Despite the consequences, some of the tank units—many of them smart cavalry regiments—preferred this dashing style and didn't want support from infantry and guns. There was no sign that the British, at any level, were learning lessons from their chronic losses. After only three days' fighting Wavell sent Churchill a cable: 'I regret to report the failure of Battleaxe'. Churchill sacked him.

The Germans were getting acclimatized to the desert. In the first few months they were given a monotonous diet of black bread, tinned sardines, tinned meat and grated cheese. This sort of diet led to medical problems, particularly jaundice. It also spurred them into action. British stores were coveted if only for the change of menu they provided. 'Our black bread in a carton was handy', said a German war correspondent, 'but how we used to long to capture one of your field bakeries and eat fresh white bread! And your jam!'[14] When finally ovens came, fresh bread remained scarce; the German quartermaster supplied the Afrika Korps with the standard field bakeries fired by logs. In most of Europe logs were easy to find, but they are not common in the desert. Fresh bread remained scarce.

Though the desert war seemed to come to a stop, this was an illusion. In fact the whole war was changing. There were changes of men, of methods and of machines. On 22 June Germany invaded Russia. It would be months before this took full effect, but from now on the Eastern Front would always dwarf the North African fighting. Henceforth Rommel's calls for men, armour, transport and fuel would be subordinated to other more urgent needs.

Wavell was dispatched to India. The day-to-day demands upon him had been greater than anyone could have imagined. He had been fighting too many battles—hundreds of miles apart—with skimpy resources. Sir Claude Auchinleck came to Cairo as the new commander-in-chief for the Middle East. The appointment of a number of subsidiary commanders ensured that he would never have the power that Wavell had wielded. New aircraft arrived and Bostons, Marylands, Beaufighters, Tomahawks and tropical Hurricanes were to be seen flying over the desert. There were new Crusader tanks, new ideas and even a new name for the desert army: the Eighth Army.

THE SIEGE OF TOBRUK

Rommel tried to eliminate the Tobruk garrison which remained like a festering sore upon his rear. He needed the port. He was always desperately short of road transport and supplies landed at Tobruk would be much nearer his front line. Bombed by relays of Stukas, shelled by day and night, the British garrison of Tobruk stayed in place. So efficiently was it resupplied by the Royal Navy that troops manning the perimeter went on leave and came back to duty there again. Nimble destroyers were used for the supply run, as regular raids by the Luftwaffe made negotiating the wrecked ships in the harbour increasingly difficult. Yet nothing was permitted to delay the loading and unloading:

> One stick of bombs screams down on the south shore of the harbour; the next is closer—in the water five hundred yards away. The old hands continue working, unworried, but some of the new ones, like us, pause momentarily, shrinking down behind the destroyer's after-screen. From the man with the megaphone comes a sharp rebuke—'What are you stopping for? Those bloody bombs are nothing to do with you'.[15]

Manned largely by Australians, Tobruk was, by October 1941, celebrating six months of siege. The curious life they led became the stuff of endless newspaper stories back home in England and Australia. It was General Blamey rather than General Rommel who eventually moved them. The Australian government felt their men had taken the brunt of the fighting long enough and insisted that they should be relieved. Most of the Aussies were replaced by British troops together with men of the Polish 1st Carpathian Brigade.

SUPPLY AND DEMAND

By November 1941 the British had made ready a large number of tanks, and launched another offensive. Facing them was the newly named Panzergruppe Afrika: Germans and Italians under Rommel's command. Operation Crusader was designed to get around Rommel's inland flank, cut off his armoured units, and push on far enough to relieve Tobruk. It was a fast-moving battle that resulted in some of the fiercest and most confused fighting in the history of the North African campaign. Any doubt about the worth of the Italian soldiers was removed when the British 22nd Armoured Brigade was mauled at the hands of the Ariete Division. Everywhere the battle became a slogging match in which tanks were usually the decisive factor. Newly arrived Honey tanks with high profile, short base and smelling of fresh desert-coloured paint could travel at 30 or 40 miles an hour. The Honeys charged the German Mark IIIs and Mark IV tanks, passed them, turned round and charged them again. It was a desperate tactic invented by a commanding officer who knew that the little 2-pounder guns on his tanks would have to get within 800 yards to have any effect on the enemy steel. The 5-cm and 7.5-cm guns on German tanks could rip the Honey open at 1,500 yards. Some of the Honeys never got close enough to even fire a shot.

The 5-cm gun proved more valuable to the Germans than did their big 'eighty-eights'. These smaller guns were ballistically superior to any British tank armament. More than half of the German tanks had them, and there were plenty more used as anti-tank guns.

The British started with 748 tanks against Rommel's 395 tanks, of which half were very inferior Italian models, but the Germans were frugal. At night, British wounded, lying out on the battlefield, were surprised to hear foreign voices and spot so many people walking around in the darkness.

They were the German tank salvage teams: recovery units bringing towing vehicles to drag their crippled steel monsters home for repair. For those even more badly damaged, huge tracked and wheeled transporters were brought up to the wrecks. The Germans worked hard, but here and there they managed to spare a blanket or a hot drink for British wounded suffering exposure in the chill November night. Anyone back in headquarters disbelieving these stories of the German recovery teams was in for a further surprise when they saw them moving around on the battlefield in the daytime, salvaging German and British vehicles while the shooting continued.

Around an airfield at the top of the Sidi Rezegh valley, a notable battle went on for some days of separated and confused fighting. The Germans discovered that an attack very early in the morning could catch the British half-asleep, and that in the fury of battle some of the inexperienced British units became lost and confused. As the battle came to a climax, commanders on both sides were seen standing up in their small cars, amid the furious gunfire and burning tanks, shouting and waving their men into action. A Rhodesian survivor of the 2nd Black Watch, which was almost annihilated, recalled:

> The enemy held his fire until we were past the wire. And then his machine-guns let go. Such of us that survived fell flat to take what cover we could; but our Adjutant, who had been wounded, crawled to where we were lying and got to his feet. 'Isn't this the Black Watch?' he cried. 'Then—charge!' He waved us on with his stick and was instantly killed.[16]

The Germans also sustained heavy losses of men and machines. The 23 November, marked on the German calendar as *Totensonntag*, when prayers are offered for the souls of the dead, not only saw the destruction of the 5th South African Brigade but also became a day of mourning for Panzer Group Africa. By the end of the battle the British tank force was reduced to less than 150 while the Germans could field 170. In the fighting further to the north, New Zealand infantry pushed forward and captured Afrika Korps headquarters.

Always an opportunist, Rommel used the confusion of the battle to press his Panzer divisions forward towards 'the wire', the Egyptian frontier. More Rommel legends were created as the tanks crashed through the British rear. Support personnel, clerks, dentists and men of mobile bath units saw Rommel's fighting men at close quarters, and related their stories of it ever after. Rommel thought victory was almost in his grasp, but in fact he was making a grave mistake. His fuel ran low, his men grew tired, the British lines through which he had come went back to work again, and most important of all the New Zealanders continued their advance along the coast road to Tobruk.

Demoralized by the destruction wreaked upon his force, the British Eighth Army's new commander, General Alan Cunningham, began to plan a dramatic withdrawal. When the new C-in-C Auchinleck arrived at his headquarters Cunningham explained that he was ordering the army to pull back out of Libya and form a screen that would prevent Rommel from getting to Cairo. Auchinleck sat down and wrote out a long careful analysis of the situation. The offensive would continue, and that was an order; a written order. Auchinleck's resolve saved the day but it marked the end for Cunningham. He was rested in hospital and sent back to command the Staff College while his replacement tried to sort out the confusion of the fluid fighting.

Rommel, enjoying the excitement of front-line action, could not be found to be told that forward elements of the New Zealanders had reached the Tobruk perimeter and made contact with the defenders. In his absence his subordinates took matters into their own hands. They pulled back from Egypt. When he surfaced Rommel greeted their insubordination with astonishment and rage, but when they showed him the maps he slowly recognized the dangers of leaving behind him substantial British forces that were already regrouping.

'He greeted nobody', one of Rommel's personal staff recalled, 'but stalked silently into the operations bus and looked at the battle maps . . . Rommel suddenly announced that he was tired and was going to lie down'.[17]

Rommel had received no tanks since June. On 5 December, with Germany's Eastern Front in the grip of a Russian winter and the German high command looking again at its long-term supply position, he was told not to expect early replacements of his losses of tanks and men. Now he devoted all his efforts to the capture of Tobruk, but his understanding of the part played by his supplies had come too late. Tobruk resisted doggedly.

By mid-December, while Rommel was pulling all the way back to El Agheila, the Italian navy made an all-out effort on behalf of the African armies. Despite their chronic shortage of fuel oil, they sent four battleships, three light cruisers and twenty destroyers to escort a convoy to Libya. That represented 100,000 tons of warships to escort 20,000 tons of merchant shipping.

Signals concerning such sea movements were being intercepted by Bletchley Park, and it was known that Convoy No. 52 was taking tanks to Rommel. Such was the urgency of his needs that the convoy was split. Three ships went to Tripoli, while the *Ankara*—carrying 22 heavy tanks (Panzer III and Panzer IV)—docked at Benghasi, an inferior port but one much nearer to the fighting.

In Cairo, British military intelligence reckoned that, as Benghasi had no dockside cranes capable of offloading such heavy tanks, it was safe to disregard the warning. Subsequent sightings by the Long Range Desert Group of German Mark IIIs and IVs travelling along on the coastal road, and a corresponding report from 4th Indian Division, did nothing whatever to change the minds of the men in Cairo.

Two days after Christmas, 60 German tanks tore into the British spearhead and knocked out 37 British tanks for the loss of seven. With little but light armour left, the British 22nd Armoured Brigade was withdrawn from the fighting.

The German ship *Ankara*, which had been built to carry railway locomotives to South America, did not need quayside cranes; its own derricks swung out the heavy tanks without trouble. On 30 December another tank action knocked out 23 more British tanks for a German loss of seven.

The British were always at a grave disadvantage. While all German tanks had a family resemblance, the British were coping with an amazing collection of different designs that crews had to learn afresh to operate. German tanks were delivered ready for use. When British tanks arrived, they needed overhauling and modifying for the desert, and this took a long time. 'Workshops worked at a leisurely pace with lots of breaks for tea', said the Eighth Army's inspector of military equipment, J. K. Stanford, who investigated slackness, waste, mismanagement, misappropriation and theft of military equipment on a scale unequalled until the Vietnam war.[18]

Military paperwork was done in Cairo offices which all closed down from 1.15 pm to 5 pm. The whole British supply route from factory to desert workshops has to be blamed for any shortages of fighting equipment. In the rear areas Britain's army showed all of the bloody-mindedness and pernicious practices of prewar trade unions. Stanford said: 'officers, sent down to Suez for tanks spares needed urgently, had to wait a day because ten tons of beer was number one priority for unloading'. British ships were incompetently loaded. Armoured vehicles were known to be transported in ships' holds under five hundred tons of flour. American ships were packed beautifully but British ships, said Stanford, were 'haywire'.

The laxity of all concerned was revealed when a message from Egypt complained about two recently arrived samples of the new Churchill tanks.

These vehicles were stowed on forward well-deck, unsheeted and unlocked. In consequence vehicles were exposed to seawater, and when received both tanks had water on floors and showed rust markings nine inches up the walls.

The damage to electrical and wireless gear required four-teen days' expert attention before the tanks could run. The message added: 'All American tanks are dispatched with all crevices and doors pasted up with masking tape . . .'[19]

A follow-up report said that no one from the manufacturers saw the tanks loaded aboard. The Ordnance officer at the port did not inspect them. His staff sergeant entered one tank and noticed that it wasn't properly 'greased up' but reported the fact to nobody.

In addition to the wholesale thefts by local people, the troops in the rear areas stole all manner of equipment that was needed by the fighting men. Compasses and binoculars were coveted. Cigarettes, food and whisky from army stores were supplied by the truckload to local traders by army de-serters in bandit gangs. Cars and trucks disappeared by the hundred. Stanford mentions 6,000 missing trucks in connec-tion with one enquiry by his inspection team. The misuse of smaller items was equally damaging to the war effort:

Anything up to thirteen blankets, stretcher pillows, or hospital sheets were purloined to soften beds. Blankets were used as curtains, carpets, or table-cloths, or nailed on walls to hang uniforms against. By the time 250,000 base details [soldiers] had equipped their beds, had bor-rowed ammunition boxes to hold their toilet sundries, or mess tins as soap dishes, a torch or a car inspection lamp for night use, a Tannoy set to listen in to a mess radio, and a W.D. padlock to secure their kit-bags, they had a great deal of stuff . . .[20]

Despite the inefficiency of supply services, and the sui-cidal tactics of the British commanders, there were still plenty of tanks left. The Eighth Army had started the Crusader battle with three times as many medium and heavy tanks as Rommel could field. Held in reserve (some in

Egypt, some nearer the front) were 216 heavies, 129 mediums and 150 light tanks. It has been calculated that the British could lose medium and heavy tanks at the rate of four to every German tank lost *and still maintain a superiority of four to one over Rommel's armour.*[21]

There was no drastic change in the methods of British commanders. Always slow to respond to German moves, they failed to understand that, even with endless supplies of armour, cavalry-style charges made by tank formations would end in failure. Rommel had his army intact, and from his bases in Tripolitania he was prepared to continue the war in North Africa for a long time to come.

But while the army repeated its mistakes over and over again, the Desert Air Force was undergoing a remarkable transformation. The RAF had improved its maintenance services beyond recognition and was receiving more and more aircraft. The Luftwaffe's fortunes were waning, as lack of road transport allowed them to retrieve fewer and fewer of their damaged aircraft. By mid-December 1941 fuel shortage had reduced the Luftwaffe to one sortie per day,[22] and the Afrika Korps was getting occasional tastes of fighting an enemy with air superiority.

THE THREAT TO CAIRO

Rommel threatened Egypt in a way that the Italians had never done. In 1941 this was the only land battle in which the British confronted the enemy with the determination to win. The British, in the words of one historian:

> still saw the Middle East as the epicentre of their struggle. The Suez Canal had become, if not in fact at least in theory, the fulcrum of their power in the world: their oil supplies, their links with India, their dominance of the Arab land mass—all seemed to depend upon their power in Egypt.[23]

Before the war Britain's only standing expeditionary force was one designed to go to Egypt, not France. Even in mid-1940, with an invasion army threatening across the Channel, Churchill sent an armoured brigade and 100 aircraft to Egypt and sent them via the Mediterranean at a time when the army and the navy brass advised him against doing so.

In 1940 and 1941 Cairo—as much as London—became the place from which Britain's war was waged. Technically Egypt was still neutral. Its plump young King Farouk had inherited the throne in 1936 and concerned himself with schemes of economic development and agrarian reform. Now he sat in his palace, surrounded by an entourage of Italians, and was bullied intermittently by a British agent, who confessed to his diary how much he enjoyed the baiting. In these exchanges between king and Foreign Office bureaucrat, British foreign policy was ill-informed and totally devoid of foresight or imagination. Present-day problems throughout the Middle East were created by such men of Whitehall, whose gunboat mentality was in the 1940s a century out of date.

Cairo in 1940 and 1941 provided the world's diplomats with a comfortable ringside seat for the heavyweight bout of the century. The world's Press could get cable facilities, whisky and hot baths in the city when they retired from the front line. In his map-room in Cairo the C-in-C listened to a stream of advice from Churchill and directed warriors in Libya, Greece, Yugoslavia, Crete, Italian East Africa, Persia, Syria, Iraq and on the high seas.

Every kind of imperial uniform was to be spotted in Cairo, in the first years of the war. There were kilts and turbans and tarbooshes, slouch hats and jodhpurs. There were Kenyan pioneers, and Indian muleteers, and Australian tank crews, and English gunners, and New Zealand fighter pilots, and South African engineers. There were scholarly staff officers straight from their Oxford colleges, and swaggering extroverts back from secret missions in the Balkans, and rumbustious troopers of the sheep station and the surfing beach.[24]

To lose Egypt would be for the British to lose the war. This is why such thoughts never surfaced in the military offices, bars, brothels, dance halls, nightclubs, open-air movie theatres, gambling salons, expensive restaurants and exclusive clubs of the amazing city of Cairo which, even before the war, had been the gossip capital of the world.

CASUALTIES OF THE DESERT

Perhaps this desert war was not modern enough. Few of the gadgets and gimmicks that were necessities by war's end were to be seen in the desert in 1941. Even tank transporters were rarities, and without them tank tracks wore out quickly, causing further supply problems. Engines and all the other machinery of war suffered from the abrasive effect of the sand. The Germans showed the way with mobile workshops, and engineers and repairmen who worked on the battlefield to salvage tanks.

Preliminary bombardments caused a high proportion of the casualties. Neither side had penicillin or sulphonamides. The extensive minefields were a constant menace, and it was in the nature of fighting in this 'tactician's paradise' that men were constantly on the move. Thus their whole bodies were exposed to bullet, mortar and shell. This led to multiple wounds and medical complications. Tank crews, of course, suffered a high percentage of burns, and for wounded men the distances to succour were an added torment:

An average medical chain at this time could involve successive journeys of 8–12 miles from the Regimental Aid Post [Battalion Aid Station] to the Advanced Dressing Station [Collecting Station]; 80–90 miles further to the Main Dressing Station; another 80 miles to the Casualty

Clearing Station, and anything up to 250 miles more to a General Hospital. All these miles had to be covered in lorries with no suspension worth the name, in extremes of heat or cold, and in constant danger of air attack.[25]

Retreating armies have to leave injured men to die, and so retreating armies always show high casualty figures. In the fighting around Sidi Rezegh in November 1941 two New Zealand battalions lost 450 men, 120 of them killed, which was one of the highest casualty rates of any action in the war. Dominion units suffered higher casualty rates than did the British (or later, American) units because they consisted mainly of front-line fighting soldiers, with only a few men serving in the rear.

SUBMARINES AND THE SEA SUPPLY LINES

In the Mediterranean campaign both sides depended upon supply convoys, and so submarines played an important part in the outcome. The 100 submarines of the Italian fleet were relatively ineffective, but in September 1941 six German U-boats entered the Mediterranean, and on 13 November one of them sank the carrier HMS *Ark Royal.* Less than two weeks later the *U-331* hit the battleship HMS *Barham* with three torpedoes. Still steaming ahead the great ship capsized and her magazines blew up in a titanic explosion that, captured on movie film, is one of the most horrifying sights in a terrible war.

The full-size Italian submarines scored fewer hits than did their tiny two-man electric 'chariots' ridden by frogmen in scuba gear. About 20 feet long, they had two propellers driven by an electric motor. The front section of the device the Italians called a *maiale* or pig was a warhead containing 550 lb of high explosive. The driver steered and dived by means of a control stick, and to guide him he had a compass

and simple instruments. Behind him the other member of
the team operated the diving-tanks to maintain trim. This
daring, dramatic and individualistic form of naval war suited
the Italian temperament. On the night of 18 December 1941
the Italian submarine *Sciré,* commanded by Prince Borghese,
navigated through a minefield to launch three of them. They
followed two Royal Navy destroyers through the anti-
torpedo nets into Alexandria harbour. The frogmen teams,
led by Tenente Luigi de la Penne, dismounted from their
pigs and affixed warheads to the battleships *Queen Elizabeth*
and *Valiant* and also to a naval tanker. Captured and held
aboard one of the doomed ships, the Italians refused to talk
and went down with their victim, but there was only six feet
of water under the keels.[26] To keep the successes secret, the
Royal Navy carried on as if nothing was wrong with its ships.
On Christmas eve there was even a ball aboard *Queen Elizabeth.*

Many months later, when the Italians had changed sides,
Admiral Morgan, who had been captain of the *Valiant* at the
time of the attack, was present when de la Penne was
awarded the Italian Gold Medal for Valour. In a sporting
gesture, Morgan stepped forward and pinned the medal
upon the man who had sunk his ship.

The Royal Navy submarines depended upon Malta as a
base from which to attack the Italian supply lines to Africa.
As well as being a submarine base, Malta was often described as an unsinkable aircraft-carrier, but after two weeks
in which the inhabitants counted 115 air raids, they began to
wonder whether the Axis bomber crews knew that.

The five islands of Malta, totalling 125 square miles of
land, are 220 miles away from Tripoli in Libya and 60 miles
south from Sicily. Ships approaching the island in wartime
often spotted the rising smoke and dust of a bombing raid
while still far out at sea. Back in history, chambers and gal-
leries had been cut into the limestone beneath the capital
Valetta, and these were enlarged to make shelters where
many of the inhabitants spent every night. Some families
moved in complete with clothes and furniture.

When Malta or the desert army needed supplies urgently, a convoy would be speeded through from Gibraltar under heavy escort. Seen from afar such convoys looked like a jam-jar at a picnic as the carrier-borne fighters battled against endless bombing and torpedo attacks. When they arrived, half the Maltese population seemed to be crowding the harbour for a glimpse of them, counting the ships, knowing that every packing case that came ashore was an assurance of next week's food ration.

The history of war provides many examples of the stubborn pride and determination that attack brings to a besieged population. In the manner of most garrison towns, Malta had learned to live with the Royal Navy but not to love it. As the bombardment continued for month after month, the Maltese showed no sign of wanting to give up the struggle. By war's end they calculated they had received 16,000 tons of bombs, and the harbour was filled with wrecks. Malta had the unenviable reputation for being the most bombed place in history. In a curious and unprecedented gesture of respect, the whole island was awarded the George Cross, Britain's highest award for valour.[27]

British air and sea operations from Malta and Egypt kept Rommel's supply lines under constant attack. In the autumn of 1941 Rommel blamed his failures on Italian sailors, persuading his masters in Berlin that the desert war was being lost at sea, but the figures do not support this excuse. Although there were desperate days like those in late October when his losses at sea were 75 per cent, such figures testify to the courage and determination of the Italian seamen. Take a broader view and we see that over the second half of 1941 Rommel's losses of fuel at sea were 16.4 per cent and of other supplies 26.8 per cent of the total dispatched. Severe losses, but not more than any prudent staff work would allow for supplies crossing seas where the Royal Navy was relentlessly active.

One can easily imagine how the army high command in Berlin reacted to such messages from Rommel, the Führer's impulsive protégé. The staff assessment from the meticulous

Paulus had advised Rommel to be restrained and not over-extend himself. It had proved entirely correct. To prove Paulus wrong, Rommel would have had to husband his fuel, give great attention to his transport and supply line, then capture Tobruk to shorten that line. Rommel failed to do any of those things.

And if Berlin showed less than infinite faith in Rommel's decisions, doubt was also displayed by some of the men under his command. His immediate subordinates had had to pluck the Panzer troops out of Egypt where Rommel's ill-judged advance had landed them, while the rank and file had seen too many of those orderly but demoralizing retreats to think their commanders infallible. On New Year's Morning 1942, General von Vaerst, commander of 15th Panzer Division, went to check his outposts in person.

From each slit trench the soldiers reported in the pre-scribed manner. Only one sentry had his field-glasses to his eyes and did not report. 'You must improve in the New Year', said the general to encourage him. 'I hope Herr General will do the same', was the reply. Old Vaerst laughed.[28]

If Rommel's crucial battles were being fought by Italian seamen on the supply routes, then the night of 8–9 November 1941 brought a notable defeat for him. Steaming out of Malta, two Royal Navy cruisers and two destroyers fought a night action against a convoy, sinking all seven merchantman and one escort. This, and an attack upon another convoy two weeks later, forced the temporary halting of the convoys.

By this time, Berlin had taken drastic action. Field Marshal Albrecht Kesselring had been sent to restore Rommel's sea supply line. 'Smiling Albert' was appointed Southern Commander (Oberbefehlshaber Süd) and given control of Luftwaffe units in Libya, Greece, Italy and Sicily. He was reinforced with an Air Corps from the Russian front, where winter had now lessened air activity. This experienced force included five bomber wings, Stukas, night fighters and long-range escorts. Kesselring's task was to gain total control of the air and sea lanes between Italy and Africa.

This would have been the moment for a German air assault and occupation of Malta, the key to Rommel's supply route. But it was already too late; the Luftwaffe's parachute army was decimated beyond recovery by the invasion of Crete. Germany's struggle with the Soviet Union was looking less like a blitzkrieg with every day that passed. Kesselring was bound to fail. To some extent his campaign would be lost in the shipyards (where for every ship the Axis build the Allies would build ten), but ships were of little use without trucks to carry supplies to the fighting men. Rommel's pleas for 8,000 trucks went unheeded in Berlin at a time when every German unit on the Eastern Front was crippled by a shortage of transport.

Once Rommel's November advance on Cairo was brought to a halt, it spelt the end of Hitler's ambitions in Africa and the Middle East. One distinguished military history concludes:

> Had Rommel, in November 1941, been fifty percent stronger than he actually was, the probabilities are that he would have taken Tobruk; that Auchinleck would never have dared to attack him; and that, after Tobruk had been eliminated, Rommel would have won Egypt.[29]

If! In fact the North African ports under Rommel's control did not have sufficient capacity to supply an army of the size he needed to take Cairo and hold it.[30] His road transport—which might have swung the balance—was inadequate in quality and quantity, and every reinforcement he received, every mouth, every gun and every tank, made his supply situation worse!

Rommel knew that history books bulge with the names of commanders who captured great cities, but he should have closed his ears to Cairo's siren song that repeatedly enticed him so far from his home and left him to languish. Rommel provides a perfect example of the 'Peter Principle' (that a person competent in certain tasks will be promoted to others he is less able to fulfil).[31] Rommel was a daring, and in every way exceptional, divisional commander, but he needed a superior who could keep him under control and make him understand the less glamorous realities of supply and maintenance.

MUSSOLINI: NO MORE TRIUMPHS

Every senior Italian commander knew that the appointment of Kesselring marked the end of Italy as an independent power. Mussolini went to war in June 1940 believing that the British were on the point of surrender. It was, he thought, simply a matter of dividing up the ships and overseas possessions of Britain and France. But after eighteen months, the real loser was Italy. There were grave shortages of cereals and oil and by the end of 1941 foreign exchange was so scarce that Italy's diplomatic corps had to be paid partly in lire. The fine Italian fleet—in which every Italian took such pride—had taken a battering and German U-boats roamed the Mediterranean. Italian East Africa had been conquered by the British and the Greek army had given the Italian army a bloody nose. Troops in Italian Libya were commanded by a German general, and Kesselring's appointment meant that the Germans had their army and air force based on the sacred soil of Italy. Count Ciano, Italy's foreign minister, wrote in his diary on 5 November 1941:

> Mussolini has swallowed the toad. He realizes the meaning of Kesselring's arrival in the general war situation, and within the country, but, like a good player, he takes the blow, and pretends that he doesn't feel it.[32]

By this time Mussolini had become so disillusioned that he engaged in regular anti-German outbursts to his followers, relishing the German setbacks in Russia, and telling them that if Germany could not be vanquished by arms, it would surely collapse in the end. At this time many Italians viewed the prospect of some sort of revolution in Germany as inevitable. The Germans thought the same about Italy, and also about Britain. The British thought that their bombing of German cities would soon precipitate revolution in Germany. It was a time of wishful thinking.

On 3 December 1941, the Japanese ambassador told Mussolini, who had been dragged into a war with Soviet Russia, that, under the terms of the Tripartite Pact, Italy would now have to declare war upon the United States. Mussolini accepted calmly the idea of war with America, but when he spoke from his balcony the crowd was 'not very enthusiastic'. It was three o'clock in the afternoon, Ciano reflected in his diary, the people were hungry and the day was quite cold. 'These are all elements which do not make for enthusiasm'.

THE FUTURE

The 'unenthusiastic' crowd listening to Mussolini declare war on America were more perceptive than the Duce. Many Italians with relatives settled in the New World had a better knowledge of the United States and its resources than Mussolini, the King and Ciano would ever have. Soon they would all have a chance to meet and know Americans at first hand. Victorious Anglo-American armies would mass in North Africa and invade the Continent of Europe by sea from the south, and that meant Sicily, and then Italy. Italy would change sides and every mile of it would suffer. Its monuments and treasures and its people would not emerge intact. Mussolini was to be shot by Italian partisans and, with his mistress, to hang upside-down, like a carcass of meat, in a public square in Milan.

In mid-1942 Rommel's battlefield listening service, Fernmeldeaufklärung, was overrun and its chief killed. From captured papers the British saw how much intelligence material Rommel had received from their careless use of radio, and as a result radio discipline was tightened. Messages employed new codes and all sorts of false messages were inserted into the daily transmissions. It was also in the summer of 1942 that the US ambassador in Cairo was recalled and Rommel lost that incomparable source of intelligence too. From then onwards Rommel's genius was more severely tested.

The hardest fighting was yet to come. Germany's titanic assault upon Soviet Russia had shown, to those who wanted to see it, how puny were the forces Britain deployed. Until the end of 1942 Britain never faced more than four weak divisions out of Germany's total of 200. But the last words about events still to come should be those of the men fighting in the desert. The official British medical history gives an intimate glimpse into the minds of the soldiers in the Middle East in 1941:

> There was a general expectation amongst men in the M.E.F. that they would suffer much the same fate as their fathers, who had been glibly promised a 'country fit for heroes to live in' and had subsequently spent many years drawing unemployment benefits . . . Men worried about their pay and the pay of their dependants; they had no confidence in the help dependants would receive in the event of their own death in the service of their country, and they frequently pointed to the vastly superior amenities enjoyed by soldiers from other parts of the British Empire and by American soldiers.[33]

Notes and References

In book references, publishers are British unless otherwise stated. Full publication details are given with first reference to a work and in short thereafter.

Introduction

1 Harry E. Figgie Jr, with Gerald Swanson, *Bankruptcy 1995* (Boston, Mass., Little, Brown, 1992).
2 Japan's non-defence R&D is at time of writing 2.8% of gross national product compared with about 1.8% in the USA. This and other comparisons from *US News & World Report*, 12 April 1993.
3 Hans A. Schmitt, *Lucky Victim* (USA, Louisiana State University Press, 1989).

1 Britannia Rules the Waves

1 Jacques Mordal, *Twenty-Five Centuries of Sea Warfare* (New York, Bramhall House, 1959).
2 *Proletariat, Culture and Lifestyle in the 19th Century*, edited by Dietrich Mühlberg (Leipzig, GDR Edition, 1988).
3 Including those building there were 62 Royal Navy battleships compared with the rest of the world's 96. See Paul Kennedy, *The Rise and Fall of British Naval Mastery* (HarperCollins, 1976).
4 In 1890 the populations of some key countries were: Britain 37.4 million; Germany 49.2; USA 62.6; Austria-Hungary 42.6; Japan 39.9; France 38.3; Russia 116.8. Only Italy, with 30 million, had a

smaller population. See Paul Kennedy, *The Rise and Fall of the Great Powers* (New York, Vintage Books, 1989).

5 Robert K. Massie, *Dreadnought: Britain, Germany and the Coming of the Great War* (Jonathan Cape, 1992).

6 Admiral Sir Reginald Bacon, *The Life of Lord Fisher of Kilverstone* (Hodder and Stoughton, 1929).

7 Richard Hough's excellent book *Dreadnought* (Michael Joseph, 1965).

8 *The Economist* in its 'Survey Britain', 24 October 1992, said, 'The irony is that Britain just missed having one of the best education systems around. In 1868 the government dithered then squashed a Royal Commission's recommendations for a twin-track school system broadly similar to the German Realschulen and Gymnasien. The government of the day found it too Prussian for English tastes. The Scots sensibly thought otherwise and have fared better ever since'. On the other hand, Scottish children were still leaving school at the age of 14 even until the Second World War.

2 Days of Wine and Roses

1 James Morris in *Farewell the Trumpets,* vol. 3 of the superb *Pax Britannica* trilogy (Faber, 1968).

2 The first lord was Eyre-Monsell. The initial impulse for the agreement came from the foreign minister, Sir Samuel Hoare. See Richard Lamb, *The Drift to War* (W. H. Allen, 1989).

3 By 1954 the Admiralty staff had grown to 33,788. See C. N. Parkinson, *Parkinson's Law* (Penguin Books, 1970).

4 Five million is the overall number. Only 1,300,000 served overseas. In the case of India 3,698,000 served in the army, of which 398,613 served overseas. These figures from John Ellis, author of *Brute Force* (André Deutsch, 1990) etc.

5 The two main types of U-boat—the Type VII and the Type IX—were usually referred to in Allied documents as the 500-tonner and the 700-tonner.

6 Lothar-Günther

Buckheim, *The Boat* (New York, Knopf, 1975).
7 As above.
8 As above.
9 David Kahn, *Seizing the Enigma* (Boston, Mass., Houghton Mifflin, 1991).

3 Exchanges of Secrets
1 The number almost invariably given is 57, because this was the number that had been commissioned, but *U-18* sank after a collision in 1936 and, after salvage, was commissioned a second time. See J. P. Mallmann Showell, *U-Boats under the Swastika: an Introduction to German submarines 1935–1945* (Ian Allan, 1973). The official history, *British Intelligence in the Second World War*, says that documents secured from *U-49* 'proved that Germany had entered the war with 57 U-boats completed', which is wrong, but in a footnote on the same page calls it the number of U-boats commissioned, which is of course correct.
2 The US navy had similar problems: its torpedoes ran too deep and the magnetic pistols failed. The Royal Navy had more success with its magnetic pistols but was apt to switch to contact pistols when the outcome was vital.
3 Mrs Elizabeth Turner of Toronto, quoted in *The Battle of the Atlantic* by Terry Hughes and John Costello (Collins, 1977). These authors give the figure of 118 deaths after the *Athenia* sinking.
4 After the war—at the Nuremberg War Crimes Tribunal—Dönitz testified on oath that Lemp's attack on the *Athenia* was the only instance of falsifying a war diary. In fact, we know that the captain of the *U-123* was also ordered to fake his war diary after sinking the neutral ship *Ganda* on 20 June 1941 off the coast of Morocco. *Ganda*, a Portuguese freighter, had taken two torpedo hits and then been shelled with the 10.5-cm gun. With two lifeboats smashed, fuel poured out of the broken hull and ignited on the sea. The U-boat reversed engines to get away.

When *U-123* returned to Lorient, Dönitz personally ordered the captain to fake his diary to show no action of any kind on that date, and he was ordered to tell no one of the sinking. Five doctored copies of the diary were filed in the normal way, but no one remembered to falsify the Schussmeldungen—shooting report—which went to Torpedo command. See Michael Gannon, *Operation Drumbeat* (New York, HarperCollins, 1990). Gannon interviewed the captain at length for his book about the *U-123*'s operations off Florida.

5 Germany's highest awards for valour were based upon the Iron Cross. As well as being awarded for individual acts of heroism—or in one case to a female test pilot—the Eisernes Kreuz 1 Klasse could be awarded en masse, as happened to the 1,300 crewmen of the *Admiral Scheer* in April 1941. By war's end about 300,000 EK1s had been awarded together with 2.5 million of the EK2 or Iron Cross Second Class. Winners of the EK2 usually wore only the ribbon.

The Knight's Cross, Ritterkreuz, was a much higher award. It was worn at the collar, and 6,973 were awarded during the Second World War. It could be earned over a period by a points system: adding up the tonnage sunk by U-boat captains or the aircraft shot down by fighter pilots. It could also be awarded to high-ranking officers for military leadership.

Small metal additions distinguished higher awards. In ascending order the Knight's Cross could be won with oak leaves (853 awarded), swords (150), and with diamonds (27). The highest category was the Knight's Cross with golden oak leaves, swords and diamonds. This was awarded to only one man—Col. Hans Rudel—who made 2,530 sorties as a Stuka pilot and was credited with the destruction of 532 Red Army tanks and two Russian warships.

6 Churchill, *The World Crisis* (Sandhurst edition, Thornton Butterworth, 1933).

7 Merlin Minshall, *Guilt*

Edged (Bachman & Turner, 1975).

8 The only time, according to the specialist naval historian Antony Preston in *Navies of World War II* (Bison/Hamlyn, 1976). Preston, author of several naval histories, was a research assistant in charge of Admiralty records at the National Maritime Museum, Greenwich.

9 Correlli Barnett, *Engage the Enemy More Closely* (Hodder & Stoughton, 1991).

10 More strictly speaking (although still a rough rule) codes are in letters; ciphers in numbers.

11 The first lord of the Admiralty was a politician, in effect the navy minister. The first sea lord was the senior naval officer at the Admiralty.

12 Conversations with Merlin Minshall.

13 An award somewhat like a medal usually given for gallantry.

14 To complete the story: Hans-Thilo Schmidt's treachery was revealed to the Germans by the man who recruited him—Rodolphe Lemoine—in March 1943. In German-occupied Paris, Lemoine, by now 73 years old, was plied with kindness by his German interrogators, first the Abwehr, then the SD and Gestapo. He admitted to being an intelligence officer and told the Germans that he had received information from Schmidt, but the Enigma machine was never mentioned by his interrogators. Lemoine's superior, Bertrand, was captured and interrogated in January 1944 but he too avoided any mention of the Enigma machine. By the time he was arrested in May 1943 Hans-Thilo Schmidt had taken to carrying cyanide tablets, concealed in his hernia belt. He died—probably by suicide—at Lehrterstrasse 61, Berlin, on 16 September 1943 while in SS custody.

In April 1943 Colonel General Rudolf Schmidt—who had secured his brother's engagement in the top-secret Cipher Office in Berlin but had no notions of his work as a spy—was now commanding the Second Panzer Army on the Eastern Front. It was obvious that much of Hans-Thilo's military information had come from confidences the general shared with his brother. He was relieved of his command. He survived the war, to be imprisoned in Russia until he was released after the intervention of Chancellor Konrad Adenauer. Rudolf Schmidt died in 1957.

15 By David Kahn, *Seizing the Enigma* (Boston, Houghton Mifflin, 1991).

16 The most interesting and reliable material about the French and Poles comes from Hugh Skillen's three books, *Spies of the Airways* (1989), *Knowledge Strengthens the Arm* (1990), and *Enigma and Its Achilles Heel* (1992). All published by Hugh Skillen, 56 St Thomas Drive, Pinner, England HA5 4SS. The quote is from General G. Bertrand's book *Enigma ou la plus grande Enigme de la Guerre 1939–1945*. See also Kahn, *Seizing the Enigma*.

17 Kahn, *Seizing the Enigma*.

18 Gordon Welchman, *The Hut Six Story—Breaking the Enigma Codes* (New York, McGraw-Hill, 1982). This is a good description of the Bletchley Park work, and highly recommended to anyone interested in detail.

19 Brian Johnson, *The Secret War* (BBC Publications, 1978). BBC TV built a 'bombe' based on descriptions of those who had seen them. Kenneth Macksey, in *Technology in War* (Arms and Armour Press, 1986), says the bombes used 'punched-hole sheets of paper' of the sort used in calculating machines. Welchman gives a better description of the sheets. So far the British government has refused to release details of the bombes, or of the breaking of the even more secret Siemens Geheimschreiber encoding machine. Welchman suggests that postwar British silence on the subject was due to the British selling coding machines like Enigma and not wanting their overseas customers to know they were vulnerable.

20 Ralph Bennett, writing in the periodical *World War*

II Investigator, September 1988.

21 Welchman, *The Hut Six Story.*

22 Some accounts talk of 'fingerprints' as the identification of a 'fist' or sending style of a Morse key operator. German ships could, and often did, leave their radio operators ashore in order to fool enemies who could recognize the 'fist'. The unique value of Minshall's innovation was that it identified the transmitter itself.

23 I took this irresistible description from David Kahn's *Seizing The Enigma.*

24 Gannon, *Operation Drumbeat.*

25 Kahn, *Seizing the Enigma.*

26 This story, and some details of the Tracking Room, from Donald McLachlan, *Room 39* (Weidenfeld & Nicolson, 1968).

27 Gannon, *Operation Drumbeat.*

28 McLachlan, *Room 39.*

29 Minshall, *Guilt Edged.*

4 Science Goes to Sea

1 J. G. Crowther & R. Whiddington, *Science at War* (HMSO, 1947).

2 Captain Kenneth Langmaid, *The Approaches are Mined!* (Jarrolds, 1965).

3 Ronald W. Clark, *The Rise of the Boffins* (Phoenix, 1962).

4 Langmaid, *Approaches.*

5 Sir Charles Goodeve in conversation with Guy Hartcup. See Hartcup's *The Challenge of War* (David & Charles, 1970).

6 Crowther & Whiddington, *Science at War.*

7 Wolfgang Frank, *The Sea Wolves* (New York, Rinehart & Co, 1955).

8 I am indebted to Michael Gannon's wonderfully researched *Operation Drumbeat* for some details of day-to-day naval activity.

9 Admiral Dönitz, *Memoirs* (Weidenfeld & Nicolson, 1959).

10 J. P. Mallmann Showell, *U-Boat Command and the Battle of the Atlantic* (Conway Maritime Press, 1989).

11 This instructor was a US navy ensign: Leonard Smith, of Missouri. He was

forever after called 'Bismarck' Smith.

12 *Coastal Command* (HMSO, 1942).

13 Although, using a VLF (Very Low Frequency) receiver, a submarine could receive messages if not submerged deeper than 65 feet.

14 Chambers Dictionary defines a boffin as a 'research scientist, esp. one employed by armed forces or government', but offers no source for the name. *A Dictionary of Forces Slang 1939–45* edited by Eric Partridge (Secker & Warburg, 1948) suggests that it derives from a series of books for children called Boffin Books. Certainly the term does not appear before the Second World War.

15 The contraflow of warm water and cold water through the Strait prevented the U-boats diving deep.

16 Hartcup, *The Challenge of War*.

17 Donald MacIntyre, *The Battle of the Atlantic 1939–1945* (Lutterworth, 1970).

18 These figures from Gannon, *Operation Drumbeat*.

19 Commander D. A. Rayner, *Escort* (Kimber, 1955).

20 A for Ausland—or foreign country—because the U-boat had originally been built for Turkey in 1938 and designed as a mine-layer.

5 War on the Cathode Tube

1 *Tirpitz*, 42,900 tons, and *Bismarck*, 41,700 tons, together with *Gneisenau* and *Scharnhorst*, 31,800 tons, were classified as battleships. *Admiral Graf Spee* and *Admiral Scheer*, 12,100 tons, and *Deutschland* (renamed *Lützow*), 11,700 tons, were at first called Panzerschiffe and then reclassified as heavy cruisers. The Western press called these three ships 'pocket battleships'. *Prinz Eugen*, 14,800 tons, *Blücher* and *Admiral Hipper*, 13,900 tons, were heavy cruisers. *Nürnberg, Leipzig, Köln, Karlsruhe, Königsberg* and *Emden* were light cruisers of less than 7,000 tons. This list (it is not a complete one) is based upon *Die Schiffe der*

Deutschen Kriegsmarine und Luftwaffe 1939–45 by Erch Gröner (Munich, J. F. Lehmanns Verlag, 1954).

2 HMS *Norfolk* had Type 286 radar, a development of the ASV Mark II, an old fixed-antenna set.

3 Lt-Commander T. J. Cain RN on HMS *Electra*. From *HMS Electra* (Muller, 1959). Quoted by John Winton in *The War at Sea* (Hutchinson, 1967).

4 Ian Cameron, quoted in *In the Cockpit,* ed. Anthony Robinson (Secaucus, New Jersey, Chartwell Books, 1991).

5 According to the inspection of the wreck in June 1981.

6 Dr Douglas H. Robinson, 'Normandy and After', unpublished MS.

7 William L. Shirer, *The Sinking of the Bismark* (New York, Random House, 1962).

8 G. Bennett, *Naval Battles of World War II* (Batsford, 1975).

9 Details of this inspection done by Dr Robert Ballard in June 1981, supplemented by drawings, photographs of the wreck, and other research aided by German and British survivors of the encounter, were published in what must surely be the final word on the subject in the US Navy's *Proceedings,* June 1991, 'Who Sank the Bismarck?' by William H. Garzke Jr, and Robert O. Dulin Jr. It concluded that the *Bismarck* was sinking because of uncontrolled progressive flooding, exacerbated by the flooding of magazines. German use of scuttling charges rapidly diminished the reserve buoyancy and caused the ship to begin to sink at 10.40.

10 A. and G. Franklin, *One Year of Life: Prince of Wales* (Blackwoods, 1944). Quoted in Winton, *War at Sea.*

11 Gannon, *Operation Drumbeat.*

12 It is often written that Britain's wartime oil came from Persia (Iran) and Iraq. Such oil was used by forces in the Middle East, including the Royal Navy in the Mediterranean, but almost all Britain's fuels came across the North Atlantic.

13 Capt. Gwilym D. Williams, letter to author.

14 A. J. P. Taylor, *The Second World War* (Hamish Hamilton, 1975).
15 Harris was not the only person to do all he could to prevent the Atlantic sailors getting the air cover they so desperately needed. America's Admiral King (who inexplicably in 1942 allowed the U-boats to massacre US coastal shipping for six months before agreeing to start a convoy system) also stubbornly denied air cover to the sea lanes. At a time when Coastal Command had only 23 of the very long-range Liberator aircraft in use, King controlled 112 of them. Seventy of these were flying in non-combat areas, but King would not spare the handful needed to fly out of Newfoundland and close the 'Atlantic gap'.
16 John Ellis points out in *Brute Force* that the US navy's submarines in the period 1942–45 sank 8,616,000 tons of Japanese shipping, which cut the Japanese merchant fleet by 75 per cent. The Allies during the same period lost 12,590,000 tons, while their merchant fleet increased in size from 32 to 54 million tons.
17 J. P. Mallmann Showell, one of the most reliable historians of the U-boat war, in *U-Boats under the Swastika*.
18 It is not easy to find reliable figures. Dönitz in his memoirs says of 1,170 U-boats 863 became operational, 603 were lost at sea through enemy action, 20 at sea causes unknown, and 7 at sea by accidents. In port 81 were lost by air attack and mines and 42 by all other causes. Another 215 were destroyed by crews at war's end (some were refitted and used). During the war 38 were scrapped either because they were badly damaged or obsolete. Eleven boats were handed over to foreign navies or interned in neutral ports after sustaining damage. At war's end 153 were handed over in Allied ports.

6 Germany: Unrecognized Power
1 See Frank S. Pepper, *Dictionary of Biographical Quotations* (Sphere, 1985).

2 The Napoleonic Wars were no exception. The Peninsular campaigns were launched on the mistaken idea that there were powerful Spanish armies with which the British could unite. Wellington went to the Low Countries to fight alongside Prussians, Austrians and Russians. In earlier times, the victories at Crécy and Agincourt were won during extensive raids rather than wars.

3 Wellington's army consisted of 24,000 British, plus 43,500 Dutch, Belgians and Germans from the Duchy of Nassau (present-day Hesse). The Prussian army under Field Marshal Blücher reduced the proportion of the British still more.

4 John Ellis, *Armies in Revolution* (Croom Helm, 1973).

5 *Proletariat, Culture and Lifestyle in the 19th Century,* ed. Dietrich Mühlberg.

6 'We Don't Want to Fight' was written in 1878 by G. W. Hunt, advocating British intervention against Russia in the Russo-Turkish war. People disposed to fight the Russians were called Jingoes, and so eventually were any super-patriots. See *Stevenson's Book of Quotations,* by Burton Stevenson, 9th edition (Cassell, 1958).

7 Morris, *Farewell the Trumpets.*

8 This theory is explored by John Ellis in *The Social History of the Machine Gun* (Croom Helm, 1975).

9 Barbara Tuchman, *The Proud Tower. A Portrait of the World Before the War 1890–1914* (Hamish Hamilton, 1966).

10 For this graphic description, and for many other stimulating ideas and facts, I am indebted to vol. 3 of Major-General J. F. C. Fuller's classic work, *The Decisive Battles of the Western World* (Eyre & Spottiswoode, 1956), as well as to his other writings.

11 There was a treaty of 1839, but it did not define Britain's exact obligations and certainly didn't make it necessary for Britain to send her troops overseas to defend Belgium's frontiers.

12 This quote from Eduard David is taken from *Rites of Spring* by Modris Eksteins (Bantam Press, 1989).

13 This was a development of the convoluted but simplistic ideas of General Langlois, who said: 'A battle lost is a battle one thinks one has lost; for a battle cannot be lost physically'.

14 Victor Wallace Germains, *The Kitchener Armies* (Peter Davies, 1930).

15 Colonel Clay was the chief recruiting officer for the London District. He said one doctor was examining 400 hundred men per day. See A. Babington, *For the Sake of Example—Capital Courts Martial 1914–18, the Truth* (Leo Cooper, 1983).

16 Churchill's words, see *The World Crisis* (Sandhurst Edition, Thornton Butterworth, 1933).

17 Of 2.4 million men examined in the 1917–18 period, over 1 million were either unfit for military service or suited only to non-combat duties. See J. M. Winter, *The Experience of World War I* (Macmillan, 1988).

18 John Keegan, *The Face of Battle* (Jonathan Cape, 1976).

19 Michael Howard, 'Haig-bashing', *London Review of Books,* 25 April 1991.

20 Musketier Karl Blenk, 169th Regiment, quoted by Martin Middlebrook in his remarkable account, *The First Day of the Somme* (Allen Lane, Penguin, 1971).

21 Ellis, *Social History of the Machine Gun.* The statement about the positioning of German machine-guns is quoted by Ellis and taken from Lt-Col. G. S. Hutchison's *Machine Guns: their History and Tactical Employment* (Macmillan, 1938).

22 A. J. P. Taylor, *The First World War* (Penguin, 1970). Some sources give a figure of 620,000. Taylor gives German casualties as 450,000 and says that many years later the British official history 'performed a conjuring trick on the German figures, and blew them up to 650,000' to make it seem that the Germans had suffered a defeat.

7 Passchendaele and After

1 B. H. Liddell Hart, *A History of the World War*

1914–1918 (Faber & Faber, 1936). Liddell Hart called it 'the last scene in the gloomiest drama in British military history'.

2 E. W. A. Hobart, *Pictorial History of the Sub-Machine Gun* (Ian Allan, 1973).

3 Martin Middlebrook, *The Kaiser's Battle* (Allen Lane, Penguin, 1978).

4 Trooper C. H. Somerset, 9th Machine Gun Squadron, quoted in Middlebrook, *The Kaiser's Battle*.

5 Col. H. C. B. Rogers, *Tanks in Battle* (Seeley Service, 1965).

6 Michael Howard, 'Haig-bashing'.

7 Denis Winter, *Haig's Command* (Viking, 1991).

8 Winter, *Haig's Command*.

9 My father was one of them.

10 Figures from Clive Ponting, *1940: Myth and Reality* (Hamish Hamilton, 1990).

11 These figures from Samuel Hynes, *A War Imagined—the First World War and English Culture* (Bodley Head, 1990). Hynes says that the Germans executed 48 soldiers, the French executed about the same number as the British, while the Italians executed twice as many as the British. Anthony Babington, *For the Sake of Example*, quotes the Service Historique at Vincennes as saying that up to the end of January 1918 the French executed 133 soldiers. The German archives at Freiburg im Breisgau say there are no figures available and blame a British air raid, a response I have had to many other queries. Babington says the Canadians executed 25 soldiers but only one of these was sentenced for cowardice.

The German armed forces in the Second World War had a quite different policy. Between 26 September 1939 and 31 January 1945 German courts martial pronounced death sentences upon 12,545 men. Of these about 6,000 were carried out.

12 Australians were exempted from the death penalty by the Australian Defence Act for all crimes except mutiny and desertion to the enemy.

The Australian government resisted very strong pressure by Haig and kept it their way. No Australians were executed. See Hugh McManners, *Scars of War* (HarperCollins, 1993). The American Expeditionary Force executed 11 of its soldiers. The Judge Advocate said that all of them were found guilty of murder or rape.

13 McManners gives a different total for the First World War British executions: 3,080 death sentences with 312 actually carried out. Of these he says 277 were British, of whom 3 were officers. Babington, *For the Sake of Example,* says 346 executions and gives details of soldiers subjected to brutal punishments such as the wearing of leg-irons. Babington gives details of the way questions were answered in Parliament.

14 Winter, *Haig's Command.*

15 Mussolini became dictator despite the monarchy being retained, but in the long term this ensured continuity as Italy changed sides and Mussolini was assassinated.

16 One of the few reliable histories of the Freikorps is *Vanguard of Nazism—the Free Corps Movement in Postwar Germany 1918–23,* by Robert G. L. Waite (Cambridge, Mass., Harvard University Press, 1952).

17 Paul Johnson, *A History of the Jews* (Weidenfeld & Nicolson, 1987).

18 Dreyfus was an Alsatian Jew. Falsely accused of spying, he was sentenced to life imprisonment by court martial. Subsequent developments revealed corruption and prejudice in the French army and deep-seated anti-Semitism throughout French society.

19 Albert Speer, *Spandau, the Secret Diaries,* translated R. & C. Winston (Collins, 1976).

20 Liddell Hart, *History of the World War 1914–1918.*

21 Antony Kemp, *The Maginot Line—Myth & Reality* (New York, Military Heritage Press and Stein & Day, 1988).

22 Kemp, *Maginot Line.*

23 Kemp's book is a clear and concise account that

also provides a good bibliography and details of which parts of the Line can still be visited.

8 France in the Prewar Years

1 Cabinet Papers. See Ian Colvin, *The Chamberlain Cabinet: how the meetings in 10 Downing Street, 1937–1939, led to the Second World War* (Gollancz, 1965).
2 Figures (except France aircraft) are taken from R. A. C. Parker, *Struggle for Survival* (OUP, 1989). The figure for French aircraft production—which was still in chaotic disorder—is hard to find. In September 1939 only 60 aircraft were manufactured. On the other hand, some American Curtiss planes were bought. To give a more realistic idea of French capability in other fields, I have calculated this total from the number of aircraft delivered in August 1939 according to evidence given at the Riom trial, a post-mortem on the French defeat instituted by Marshal Pétain in 1942. This public relations exercise was devised so that the politicians ruling defeated France could lay all the blame for their country's disaster upon their predecessors. Nevertheless, the trial does yield some useful insights into what took place, although the aircraft figure remains unreliable.
3 Colvin, *Chamberlain Cabinet*. Colvin used cabinet documents released by Act of 1967. See also *The Eden Memoirs: Facing the Dictators* (Cassell, 1962).
4 He told Sir Horace Wilson this. See Colvin, *Chamberlain Cabinet*.
5 Sumner Welles, *The Time for Decision* (Hamish Hamilton, 1944).
6 Lord Ironside, *The Ironside Diaries 1937–40* (Constable, 1962).
7 A. J. P. Taylor, *The First World War*.
8 At the time of writing 1991 the Czech government is once again desperate for hard currency and finding it hard to abandon the armaments market.
9 Richard Overy and A. Wheatcroft, *The Road to War* (Macmillan/BBC, 1989). They refer to H. Aulach, 'Britain and the

Sudeten Issue 1938',
*Journal of Contemporary
History,* 18 (1983).
10 Lord Swinton to Colvin.
See Colvin, *Chamberlain
Cabinet.*
11 Quoted in Leonard
Mosley, *On Borrowed Time*
(NY, Random House,
1969). Mosley was a
respected foreign
correspondent and his book
is a carefully researched
account of the years leading
up to the outbreak of war
in 1939.
12 William L. Shirer, *The
Nightmare Years* (Boston,
Mass., Little, Brown, 1984).
The Sir Lewis B. Namier
quote comes from Shirer's
In the Nazi Era (1952).
13 This opinion from a
Treasury statement
classified Most Secret,
attached to Cabinet
Minutes and uncirculated.
See Colvin, *Chamberlain
Cabinet.*

9 An Anti-Hitler Coalition?
1 Donald Cameron Watt—
in his *How War Came*
(Mandarin, 1990)—suggests
it was Halder and gives
German sources and
circumstantial reasoning.
2 Colvin, who knew his way
around Whitehall, took his
story to Sir Alexander
Cadogan who, as
permanent under-secretary,
was immediately in charge
of Britain's Secret
Intelligence Service.
3 General Sir Frederick
Pile, G. O. C. Anti-Aircraft
Command 1939–45, in his
book *Ack-Ack* (Panther,
1956).
4 Pile, *Ack-Ack.*
5 The Secretary of State for
War was the war minister.
Chief of the Imperial
General Staff (CIGS) was a
title given to the 'first
military member' of
Britain's Army Council. He
commanded the entire
British army in its outposts
throughout the world,
although orders were given
in the name of the Council.
Local British army forces
had their own commanders
including the commander-
in-chief Home Forces, who
had direct control of the
army in the United
Kingdom. A British infantry
division of this period had
17,500 men, an infantry
brigade about 3,000 men.
An infantry battalion—
more usually called a rifle
battalion—had about 800

men. A rifle company had about 120 men of which five would be officers.

6 In 1928 Germany took over 28 per cent of Soviet exports and sent them a similar percentage of their imports. In 1933 Germany supplied 46.5 per cent of Soviet imports. After that trade reduced and dried up.

7 There is considerable disparity about what this agreement should be called. I have followed the Stationery Office and Churchill in calling it a German-Soviet Pact.

8 Anthony Read & David Fisher, *The Deadly Embrace—Hitler, Stalin and the Nazi-Soviet Pact 1939–1941* (Michael Joseph, 1988).

9 These were the words of Gustav Hilger, a Russian expert with the German diplomatic corps. See Read & Fisher, *Deadly Embrace*.

10 W. S. Churchill, *The Second World War,* vol. 1, *The Gathering Storm* (Cassell, 1948).

11 Various dates have been given for this meeting. Donald Cameron Watt says 26 July. Read & Fisher give June, which may be a printer's error. Also some accounts give the restaurant's name as Ernest, but Ewest at 26a Behrenstrasse was a famous restaurant listed in *Grieben's Berlin Guide* (Berlin, 1936).

12 Donald Cameron Watt provides the Foreign Office references.

13 *Documents concerning German Polish Relations and the outbreak of hostilities between GB and Germany on September 3, 1939* (HMSO, 1939).

14 For Hitler and Goebbels' opinion noted in Goebbels' diary entry for 23 August, see diary extracts, *Sunday Times,* 12 July 1992.

15 Halder's position in the army command can be seen from this chart. The Wehrmacht meant the Armed Forces of Germany's Third Reich. In 1935 a small office— Oberkommando der Wehrmacht (OKW)—had been formed on the clear understanding that it was a bureau to coordinate matters of interest to all three services, and not to subordinate them. But Hitler used this OKW to control the High Command of the Army (OKH) and the other armed services.

```
┌─────────────────────────────┐
│  Führer & Chancellor:        │
│  Adolf Hitler                │
└─────────────────────────────┘
              │
┌─────────────────────────────┐
│  OBERKOMMANDO DER            │
│  WEHRMACHT—OKW               │
│  Chief: Wilhelm Keitel       │
│  Chief of Operations Staff:  │
│  Alfred Jodl                 │
│  Deputy: Walther Warlimont   │
└─────────────────────────────┘
              │
┌─────────────────────────────┐
│  OBERKOMMANDO DES            │
│  HEERES—OKH                  │
│  Commander-in-Chief:         │
│  Walter von Brauchitsch      │
│  Chief of Staff: Franz Halder│
└─────────────────────────────┘
```

16 Donald C. Watt, 'Before the Blitzkrieg', in *History of the Second World War* (Purnell, 1966).

17 Mr J. McLoughlin, the telephone operator, said: 'This human touch at the beginning of the world's greatest conflict will always remain vividly with me'. See *The Last Day of the Old World,* by Adrian Ball (New York, Doubleday, 1963).

18 E. S. Turner, *The Phoney War* (Michael Joseph, 1961). Turner takes his story from Vic Oliver's memoirs, *Mr Showbusiness.*

19 Flak (Flugabwehrkanone) is a gun used against aircraft. Some German guns were dual-purpose weapons designed for use against aircraft and against ground targets.

Panzerkampfwagen, abbreviated PzKw, is an armoured fighting vehicle.

Panzerabwehrkanone, Pak, is an anti-tank gun.

20 More exactly there were six armoured and four 'light' divisions fighting in Poland. (Guderian is in error in his memoirs when he includes only three light divisions in the units that fought there.) There were additional army and SS motorized units as part of 'Panzer Verband Kempf'. Light divisions were Panzer divisions with fewer tanks. See Len Deighton, *Blitzkrieg—From the Rise of Hitler to the Fall of Dunkirk* (Jonathan Cape, 1979).

21 Louis Ducloux, *From Blackmail to Treason—Political Crime and Corruption in France 1920–40* (André Deutsch, 1958).

Ducloux was director of the Criminal Investigation Department of the Sûreté Nationale.

22 Guy Chapman, *Why France Collapsed* (Cassell, 1969).

23 General André Beaufre, *1940 The Fall of France,* translated by Desmond Flower, with preface by Basil Liddell Hart (Cassell, 1967).

24 Martin Alexander, *The Republic in Danger: General Maurice Gamelin and the Politics of French Defence 1933–1940* (OUP, 1993).

25 Chapman, *Why France Collapsed.*

26 Ponting, *1940: Myth and Reality.* Reference CAB 66/1 WP (39) 15 (8.9.39).

27 Major Robert M. Kennedy, *The German Campaign in Poland,* Pamphlet 20-255 published by the US Department of the Army in April 1956 and based upon information from German commanders, says that a total of 55 divisions were arrayed against Poland on 31 August 1939. Major-General F. W. von Mellenthin in *Panzer Battles* (Cassell, 1945) says 44 divisions.

28 George Forty & John Duncan, *The Fall of France— Disaster in the West 1939–40* (Nutshell Publishing, Tunbridge Wells, 1990). A most interesting contribution to the writings on this subject.

29 Gamelin sent the orders through General A. L. Georges, although it would have been more logical to have sent them through his local commander.

30 Brigadier Sir John Smyth, *Before the Dawn* (Cassell, 1957). Quoted in *The War on Land,* edited by Ronald Lewin (Arrow, 1972).

31 Ralph Arnold, *A Very Quiet War* (Rupert Hart-Davis, 1962). Quoted in Lewin (ed.), *The War on Land.*

32 John Keegan, *The Second World War* (Hutchinson, 1989). Keegan's credentials as senior lecturer at Sandhurst for 26 years endorse these descriptions of the BEF.

33 Quoted in M. Hamilton, *Monty,* vol. 1 (Coronet, 1985).

34 R. A. C. Parker, *Struggle for Survival* (OUP, 1989).

35 Ponting, *1940: Myth and Reality.*

36 A. J. P. Taylor writing in